HARLEM NIGHTS

HARLEM NIGHTS

The Secret History of Australia's Jazz Age

DEIRDRE O'CONNELL

MELBOURNE UNIVERSITY PRESS

MELBOURNE UNIVERSITY PRESS
An imprint of Melbourne University Publishing Limited
Level 1, 715 Swanston Street, Carlton, Victoria 3053, Australia
mup-contact@unimelb.edu.au
www.mup.com.au

First published 2021

Aboriginal and Torres Strait Islander readers are warned that the following story may contain images of deceased persons.

Front cover image: Sonny Clay's Colored Idea arrive at Sydney Circular Quay, 19 January 1928. (Sam Hood Collection, State Library of NSW.) Back cover image: Sam Hood photographs the Sonny Clay's Colored Idea performance of the 'Australian Stomp', 20 January 1928. (Sam Hood Collection, State Library of NSW.)

Cover design by Design by Committee
Text design and typesetting by Cannon Typesetting
Printed in Australia by McPherson's Printing Group

A catalogue record for this book is available from the National Library of Australia

9780522877649 (paperback)
9780522877656 (ebook)

CONTENTS

Sonny Clay's Colored Idea arrive at Sydney Circular Quay, 19 January 1928.
(Sam Hood Collection, State Library of NSW)

PROLOGUE
THE FRAME-UP

THIS IS THE story of an Australian political conspiracy. Not the kind that faked the moon landing or concealed alien life, but a secret plan designed to limit individual freedom, consolidate power and engineer social change.

The year was 1928. It was a time of technological wonder and flux, when people sensed a world growing smaller and turning faster, and time speeding up. When efficiency was glorified and its lolling, time-wasting twin derided and scorned. In homes, factories and offices, American gadgetry was transforming Australian lives, saving minutes, even hours. The citizenry expended the surplus on a new category of time a Puritan once called 'idleness' and advertisers labelled 'leisure'.

In this new world, the single working girl made herself modern. Dance halls, moving picture houses, magazines, the wireless and gramophones opened gateways to the globe. Department stores stocked affordable copies of Paris fashions: fox stoles, Mary Jane shoes and skin-tight geometric knitwear. Hollywood vamps and ingenues narrated the pleasures and perils of Manhattan's glamour and sophistication. Eye-rolling flappers telegraphed the allure of mascara, kohl and shingled hair. The fetish of the age, the female leg, specifically the knock-kneed or kicking dancing leg, was of more uncertain origins—although persistent allusions to 'jungle rhythms' pointed to other, and othered, worlds.

To a generation of leisured Australians, this looked and felt like Progress. But to committees of concerned citizens, policymakers and advisors, it smacked of Degeneration.

The dizzying speed of the modern world portended spiritual exhaustion, warned moral reformers and gatekeepers. Modern debauchery empowered 'inferior' people who were 'weakening' the 'human stock'. Jazz violated the laws of harmony and tipped the world into chaos and confusion.

The 'rising tide' of Black and Brown people and 'Negrification' of American popular culture imperilled the supremacy of the 'British race'.

To these many anxieties, one disgruntled former prime minister offered a simple, catch-all solution: 'racial purity'.

'We are a white island in a vast coloured ocean,' proclaimed William Morris Hughes in the year of this particular political conspiracy. 'If we are not to be submerged, we must ... build dykes through which the merest trickle of the sea of colour cannot find its way.'[1]

When Billy Hughes wrote these words, Australia had never been so White, or so British, the result of a hard-line immigration policy that had deported thousands of Pacific Islanders and refused entry to all but a handful of Chinese migrants and other people of colour. Still, the former leader fumed: outraged that his party, the Nationalist Party, had gone soft on White Australia (and insulted that he was now a lowly backbencher, the victim of cold political expediency). The dykes he envisaged were all-encompassing in scale—and the rewards might even include his return from the political grave.

In so many nebulous ways, Billy Hughes was the spiritual godfather of the chain of events that was about to unfold, a master orator spinning a seductive vision of an all-White modern Australia.

Of course, he did not administer the conspiracy. That role fell to Major Longfield Lloyd, the New South Wales director of the domestic intelligence-gathering bureau, the Commonwealth Investigation Branch. Major Lloyd's experience in dyke-building dated back to Billy Hughes' internment policies of the Great War and purge of 'enemy aliens'. Indeed, Lloyd's swift progression through the ranks of military intelligence was hastened by the patronage of his friend and mentor.

In 1927, Major Lloyd had overseen the deportation of a knot of Black American boxers, one of whom was married with a child to a White Sydney woman. Yet the dyke continued to leak. From the pages of the daily press, the bold typeface of Tivoli Theatre advertisements announced the imminent arrival of a Black American jazz revue, Sonny Clay's Colored Idea, the first to reach Australia: '25 Negro stars. 100 wonder minutes. Something New in Entertainment: Real Syncopation and Real Symphony.'[2]

As bandleader Sonny Clay later told it, the 'frame-up' began with a sinister message tapped through to the SS *Sierra* the day the steamer came into radio contact with Sydney. On board were Harry Muller, the Tivoli Theatre's West Coast agent and seventeen members of the Colored Idea, the all-Black jazz revue pieced together by Muller.

They were a remarkable bunch of dancers, comedians, vocalists and musicians. 'Whirlwind stepper' Willie Covan first choreographed the Charleston on the Harlem stage. Nini Coycault was a Louisiana trumpet master of 'weavy patterns' and 'shivery stuff'.[3] Cabaret singer Ivy Anderson could bring an audience to tears then wow them with a mad shuffle. She would soon shoot to fame with the Duke Ellington Orchestra. And, of course, 28-year-old Sonny Clay, the lanky, baby-faced bandleader was on the upward curve of a meteoric career. Five years earlier, he was playing fill-in spots in Tijuana jive joints. The week before he left California for Australia, the marquee lights outside Hollywood's favourite 'Harlem nightclub', the Plantation Café, spelt his name. Inside, starlets waved to him from the dance floor. Big-name stars thanked him with hundred-dollar tips and bootleg liquor.

Sonny Clay projected himself as a man of the future, born of a disciplined devotion to the expansive sonic universe of rag, jazz and blues. An ally of the New Negro movement, he refused to conform to minstrel caricatures and the deferent 'shuffling darkey'. He was part of a push seeking to weave Black culture into the very fibre of modern life.

The message received on the steamer aimed to clip Sonny Clay's wings. The senders were cryptic in their words, but clear in their hostility.

'Something' undefined yet menacing 'was being saved up' for him, Clay later recalled.[4]

The threat confused Sonny Clay. He had met scores of Black comedians, jubilee singers and dancers who had toured Australia and returned with grand tales of triumph. Audiences 'lauded them up to the sun,' they boasted.[5] The press held them in high esteem. But this message suggested he, a jazz musician, was somehow unwelcome.

Only Harry Muller understood the code—although the Tivoli agent kept the messy details to himself. He knew that Black jazz musicians occupied a special place in Australian bureaucracy. In Sonny Clay's rhythms, gatekeepers heard strains of a contagion that would contaminate the 'pure' British racial imagination. To prevent the mongrelisation of the mind, they had already blocked several efforts to import Black dance bands—and had no intention of allowing one to slip through the door. They resented Harry Muller's clever workaround that circumvented the rules.

The message the ship's radio officer passed on to Sonny Clay signalled the cat and mouse game was far from over. Only in hindsight did the bandleader understand that when the SS *Sierra* steamed through Sydney Heads, his enemies were 'waiting' with 'scalping knife ready'.[6]

Certainly, Inspector Adams of the Commonwealth Investigation Branch stood on the gabled wharves of Circular Quay, waiting for the San Francisco steamer on the morning of 20 January. This in itself wasn't unusual. Adams inspected every passenger boat. His task was twofold: firstly, to keep tabs on all 'aliens', the migrants and travellers from beyond the British Isles. And secondly, to prevent the entry of 'prohibited and undesirable passengers' as defined by the Immigration Act.

In the nine years since the Great War, this definition had already changed three times. Originally Inspector Adams determined undesirability by race, ethnicity and health—a diseased Briton as unwanted as a healthy Asian. But unnerved by the whiff of rebellion, both Irish and Bolshevik, and a surge in Southern European immigration, legislators had added political ideology and occupation to the list. With the docking of the SS *Sierra*, Inspector Adams identified a new undesirable occupation to add to the list of usual suspects.

As the gangplank lowered, people on the dock sprang into action. The Tivoli Theatre's publicity team unfurled a placard on the pier, and another on the ship, spruiking the opening dates of the Colored Idea. On deck, technicians from Radio 2FC strung microphones and the Sonny Clay Orchestra hit the airwaves, banging out the freshly composed 'Australian Stomp'. The sound was hot yet restrained. A clarinet and trumpet wove ribbons of sound around the tight swinging beat, as if supplying two musical answers to a single question. To unfamiliar ears, it sounded like a jumble of brass with melody sacrificed to rhythm. It was faster, busier, rawer than the symphonic jazz of the White Californian bands known on Australian shores.[7]

A press photographer captured the moment. Hoofers Ivy Anderson and Dick Saunders jumped as if with joy. Beside them stood Sonny Clay, opened-armed and welcoming. Scattered around him were his musicians, unconstrained by regimentation, tooting the trumpet on an engine box or kicking back on the banjo. Their smiles were open but not wide enough to distort. Their gaze met the camera, warm and direct, without a glint of dewy-eyed gratitude or the comical roll of a minstrel. They were Black without blackface, fun without self-parody, high energy without Jim Crow buffoonery.[8]

At the docks to welcome this new type of jazz, Gayne Dexter, editor of a popular film magazine, was thrilled by what he heard. For years, he had watched high-society films where beautiful young things, from Manhattan or Montmartre, shimmied to a 'Negro jazz' orchestra. Finally, he too could experience the quintessence of modern cosmopolitan style. That week, his editorial congratulated Harry Muller for his tenacity and vision.

Harry Muller was less assured. A stocky customs officer, with neither the disposition or savvy to understand the currents of global culture, could exercise his discretionary powers and subject the visitors to the notorious White Australia dictation test, bringing the tour to an abrupt end. Only when the gatekeeper accepted their exemptions and stamped all seventeen passports could Muller breathe easy.

As Sonny Clay's troupe made their way to the street, a good-natured crowd clustered around them. Few, if any, Sydneysiders had seen a plum-coloured suit, as worn by one young horn player. Or the white jacket,

Sam Hood photographs the Sonny Clay's Colored Idea performance of the 'Australian Stomp', 20 January 1928. (Sam Hood Collection, State Library of NSW)

Sonny Clay and his bandsmen surrounded by Sydneysiders as they leave Circular Quay. (*Daily Telegraph*, 21 January 1928, State Library of NSW)

homburg hat and cane sported by the nineteen-year-old banjo player. A group of young women, keen jazz fans, rejoiced at their sight, a sign sure to hearten Harry Muller. As he well knew, the 'fairer sex' constituted two-thirds of cinema audiences, with the consumer power to make or break an act.

Another press photograph snapped the reception. Sonny Clay stood centre frame, flanked by his bandsmen, encircled by a crush of locals: a gaggle of boys to his left and three young women to the right, one of them gently tugging the hem of her dress and extending her leg.[9]

There was much for Inspector Adams to ponder. Firstly, the numbers: not since the Great War had so many Black American men landed in Sydney at one time. Secondly, clothing. Such elegance on the grandsons of enslaved Americans expressed a desire to renegotiate the social contract. Somewhere between the growl of the trombone, the sharply tailored suits and the casual presumption of equality, the Sonny Clay Orchestra projected an idea that, while hardly a coherent political manifesto, still felt like a threat.

Finally, and perhaps most troubling, was the enthusiasm of the young White women. All the officers at the Commonwealth Investigation Branch believed the success of the White Australia Policy hinged on female fidelity. White women were the mothers of the race—and some morally aberrant women were prone to breeding in the colour and needed to be saved from themselves.

Inspector Adams returned to the Investigation Branch office to report the threat to the nation. Major Lloyd thereupon instructed his agents to begin a surveillance operation on the Sonny Clay Orchestra.[10]

This was hardly the first time Sonny Clay had been the object of White suspicion. As recognised by fans and foes alike, the jazz troupe carried the styles, slang and sounds of an alternate future. One whose appeal unsettled the colour line. Whose angular intrusions disrupted the balance of neo-classicism. The Colored Idea's jazz revue projected a 'coloured idea' that loosened an individual's bond to a nation or empire and plugged audiences into a cosmopolitan modern push stretching from Shanghai to Paris.

Before Major Lloyd's investigation ended nine weeks later, a collection of lives would collide: musicians, theatre agents, modern dance lovers, intelligence officers, union bosses, policemen, reporters, magistrates, social reformers, politicians, bureaucrats, beauty queens and domestic servants.

Authorities would angst over White women 'consorting' with members of the jazz band and display indifference to White men preying on Aboriginal women. Police would arrest five female friends of the band. Tabloid newspapers would titillate readers with details of a 'nude' 'Negro orgy'. Eugenicists would fret about the unregulated sexuality of 'wayward' women. Major Lloyd would mobilise a secret army of disaffected war veterans. And Billy Hughes would deliver a rousing speech warning the federal government to end the 'menace' of Negro jazz—or else a group of patriots would.

The force of the disruption would expose the class, race and culture war at the heart of Australian Modernism.

PART I

Tijuana Nights in Phoenix and Los Angeles

1
THE EDUCATION OF SONNY CLAY

CRUEL IRONY RENT Sonny Clay's Australian tour. Major Lloyd's surveillance operation focused not on him, but his bandsmen. Even so, his name lay at the heart of a scandal that besmirched his good reputation back in the United States, and clung like a bad smell for years to come. The even crueller irony is that, if not for the incident in Australia, Sonny Clay would be little more than a footnote in jazz history.

The annals of Black jazz have been written as the triumphant tales of Big Men (leavened by occasional Big Women): The First, Greatest, Legendary, Most Famous. Beneath this pantheon of generals was an army of travelling performers, struggling year in, year out. Some attained fleeting success, others never realised their ambitions. Sonny Clay was something of a captain in this army. He led a band of working musicians at a time when 'the Negro' was in vogue and Jim Crow segregation was at its height. He negotiated business deals that opened up new markets for Black jazz bands and travelled across oceans and geopolitical borders to seed the Harlem sound.

He was the spokesperson, first ballyhooing his band, then defending it. The lone voice accusing the Australian government of a 'frame-up' and asserting the right of his bandsmen to associate with whomever they chose. He fought a battle not of his own making, but hardly at odds with the struggles faced by New Negroes back home in the States. His courage to speak truth to power was shaped by a life journey that owed as much to heavyweight boxer Jack Johnson as educator Booker T Washington, that looked as much to the Mexican Revolution as the Harlem Renaissance.

Before the clock struck eight on the morning of Friday, 22 September 1911, a hundred or so people gathered outside the Sante Fe depot in Phoenix, Arizona, waiting for their honoured guest, the great educator Dr Booker T Washington to arrive. Forty-eight years had passed since Abraham Lincoln's Emancipation Proclamation and the city's three hundred or so Black residents were staging a jubilee.[1]

Balancing a solid bass drum on his chest stood tall, skinny, eleven-year-old Sonny Clay in a military-style uniform. Close by was his father, William Henry Clay, and fourteen young men in identical attire, each carrying a selection of horns, cymbals and kettle drums. They were bearers of a tradition born in the wake of emancipation: the Colored Brass Band.[2]

In the Black sections of Washington County, Texas, where Sonny Clay's father was born forty years earlier, the free people's brass bands had trumpeted the path from American slave to American citizen. Whether opening a Black Republican convention, honouring a visit from a congressional nominee, or celebrating an election day victory, the jubilant marches of the hometown 'colored band' kept the community's eyes on the prize. They were the mortar in the bricks of the free people's democratic life—even as White supremacists waged a campaign of terror.[3]

When Sonny Clay's family moved west to the newly irrigated soils of Arizona's Salt River Valley in 1910, his father carried this flame, forming and bankrolling the Phoenix Famous Colored Young Men's Band.[4] The tunes they rehearsed for Dr Washington's visit had altered little since Reconstruction days, yet the march of 'Negro progress' no longer beat to the same political drum.[5]

Since the end of the Reconstruction in 1877, White supremacists had torn down the scaffolds of the nascent multi-racial democracy. Few in Washington County dared cast their vote after three Black Republican leaders were found hanging from a pecan tree. No brass band played outside the courthouse in 1897 when Sonny Clay's grandfather sued the railroad company for throwing him off a White only carriage.[6] Knowing one's place became a fact of Black daily life, enshrined in law and policed by vigilantes beyond law.

The Clay family hoped for a new beginning when they moved west to Arizona. Boosters promoted the territory as the last patch of frontier, a 'land of tomorrow where a man could forget his past and begin again'.[7] But the spirit of Texas also followed them. Arizona would enter the Union upholding a legal doctrine the Supreme Court called 'separate but equal' but most people knew as the anything but equal 'Jim Crow'. From housing to hospitals, a line separated people according to race.[8]

Yet as Booker T Washington insisted, racial segregation and political disenfranchisement did not impede race progress. 'In all things that are purely social, we can be as separate as the fingers, yet one as the hand in all things essential to mutual progress', ran the most quoted line from Washington's most famous speech.[9]

He measured advancement, not by political office, but in the trappings of respectability and restraint; in the school, church house, business and home; by the absence of violence and the protection of the law. This was the message the triumphant fugues of the Phoenix Famous Colored Young Men's Band would announce to the Emancipation Jubilee. The progressive Phoenix Negro was on the up and up.

It was close to half-past eight before Dr Washington's train pulled into the depot. William Clay's brass band serenaded the revered leader as he ambled to a waiting automobile. The vehicle then set off down an avenue festooned with stars and stripes, followed by a carefully ordered parade. Jubilee queens proclaimed the civilising waters of feminine virtue. The Indian School Band confirmed the complex nature of southwestern race relations. Brightly coloured floats advertised a pantheon of prosperity and enterprise, while the Phoenix Famous Colored Young Men's Band stretched their six-march repertoire all the way to Eastlake Park.[10]

Thus began the Phoenix Emancipation Jubilee, a three-day extravaganza of jollification and education. On Saturday night an ox was cooked up for the grand march and barbecue. Thousands filled the tabernacle tent to hear Dr Washington extoll the virtues of education, respectability and restraint; of Black men and women labouring with their hands.

Whatever the topic, Dr Washington's mantra of racial uplift did not change. Each lecture reiterated the value of a high moral standard. Stable employment. A bank account. Savings. Home ownership. Income tax. He warned them against the 'menace of the drifting class', rootless individuals, prone to superficial displays of wealth and profligate, unclean behaviour. 'A man without a home is an unsafe citizen,' he cautioned, while prosperity would reward the industrious, thrifty and patient. Just as the 'laws' of human progress had elevated the 'stronger' White race, so it would uplift the Black but never so far as to outstrip them. By being the servant of all, the Negro could be great.[11]

Phoenix's White newspapers proclaimed Dr Washington as 'the greatest Negro of the twentieth century', applauding a message free from demands for political representation and the vote.[12]

Sonny Clay made no mention of Booker T Washington's visit to Phoenix during his 1960 interview with John Bentley. Perhaps it's unsurprising. Jazz record collectors such as Bentley were mostly White, middle-class men invested in a history of jazz founded in brothels and lowdown juke joints, not regimental bands and Black enterprise. But for all its limitations, John Bentley's interview—a mix of taped recordings plus a sketchy handwritten transcript of the tapes that perished—remains the most comprehensive account of Sonny Clay's thoughts and career.[13]

In 1960, Sonny Clay was sixty-one years old and a postman, his health ruined by alcoholism. Regret seeped through the stories of his life—the bad decisions, the bootleg liquor, the 'scalping knives' in Australia, the phone calls he never made. Untouched by the bitter tears of self-reproach were two childhood memories, both centred on the romance of the travelling musician.

The first was the Circus Days in his childhood home of Houston, Texas. On those days, either Ringling Brothers or Sells Floto arrived by railroad, a procession of stock cars and coaches bearing a thousand people and creatures from every corner of the globe. Sonny Clay lived in the 'colored' section of town, directly opposite the tracks, and on Circus Days his front yard view of the railroad became a ringside seat to the greatest show on earth.[14]

A short scramble away at the rail yard, a boy smitten by the circus could count off the Barbary lions, Bengal tigers and Californian seals descending from the stock cars. Or help roustabouts cloak the elephants, ready for the downtown street parade.[15]

Few could resist the call. On Circus Days, city workers turned away from the cotton trade to behold gravity-defying acrobats and body-befuddling contortionists. It was a time of wonder and drift. A readiness to abide situations that, only the day before, would have been unthinkable.

As a rule, a Black man in a fine cut suit was not a sight tolerated in Houston, Texas. And if a travelling man in a plaid ensemble appeared at Union Station, likely an officer of the law would escort him to a locker room and insist he change into a porter's uniform, lest he start forgetting his place.[16] But on Circus Day, Sonny Clay had every reason to believe the people of his race could do more than serve. He founded his faith in one man: PG Lowery, the cornet player who led the circus sideshow band, first at Sells Floto and later at Ringling Brothers. Hands down, Lowery fronted the finest brass band and ragtime orchestra from the mid- to southwest.[17]

'It ain't but the one and that's P.G.,' Sonny Clay once told a newspaper columnist, remembering the thrill of Lowery's band marching through the business streets of Houston, looking sharp as a haircut in suits of blue wool and gold braid.[18] Clay fixed his attention on the three drummers—bass, snare and cymbal—who twirled and tossed their sticks, setting a beat that slid between the ragged and the regimented. He could see Black and White people cheering them on. Hear the wave of applause that followed them down the street.

If it were not PG Lowery's year in Texas, it would be another Black sideshow band. For Lowery had turned a generation of Whites onto the joys of syncopation—and unleashed a demand for more. By the time Sonny Clay was ten, there wasn't a circus in the southwest without a Black ragtime band.[19]

Sonny Clay's second memory was the 'Bugle Call Rag' played on a Phoenix street by three brothers from Pine Bluff, Arkansas. Several popular songs riffed off the army bugle call but something about this combination of trumpet, banjo and fiddle woke adolescent Sonny Clay to the promise of the future.[20] The horn slurred and cried, did all that blues stuff in amongst the rag, a sonic experiment in bending sound and rhythm. The trumpeter 'would have been a star today', recalled Clay.[21]

Pine Bluff lay in the Arkansas bayou on the western edge of the Mississippi Delta. A river connected it to New Orleans. As in slavery days, so in freedom, cotton made the town. Plantations were vast and White men were few. On Sundays, churches rang with a bluesy gospel choir. It was a world Sonny Clay never knew. Unlike blues guitarist Big Bill Broonzy who was raised in Pine Bluff in the early 1900s, Sonny Clay never cut the earth with a plough or picked cotton till his hands bled, nor watched his parents bury one infant after the next, nor subsisted on a diet of cornmeal and pork fat. He knew nothing of levee camps and prison farms, nor learned to play music to the rhythms of the sawmill and train.[22]

Sonny Clay, instead, was freedom's grandchild. He hailed from a prosperous family, anchored by steady employment and regular income. His father owned a barbershop on the Whiter, west side of town. His mother, her days as a domestic servant behind her, earned extra income from boarders. Sonny was on track to graduate high school, one of two Black seniors at Phoenix Union High, taught in the same classrooms as White students (although, under the school's segregation policy, separated by a small screen from the rest of the class).[23]

As pianist in his father's band, he played the Texan Circle Two Step and a selection of 'Paul Jones' dances at the White Phoenix Country Club. He knew the flavours of Mexico. Had watched the pageantry of the Saturday night street dances. Heard the Mexican migrant workers' serenades of strolling Mariachi bands: the cornet braying over violins and strumming guitars, the open-throated harmonies and yelps of laughter. He knew how to read 'every speck' on the sheet music page. Could list the principles of music, the tonic and diatonic, the contrapuntal and counterpoint. Was drilled in the progressive catechism that yoked a higher order of music to racial and spiritual uplift.[24]

He knew too, the hostility and suspicion heaped upon itinerant musicians wherever they roamed. For these were the 'drifting class' warned off by Dr Washington. Rootless men and women, without homes, bank accounts and income tax receipts who splurged on diamond pins when times were good—and hocked them when they were bad. They were men and women who muddied the distinction between work and leisure, industry and pleasure. Mothers warned their sons of the profligate life.[25] Washerwomen refused to handle their laundry. Black preachers denounced them from the pulpit. 'Show folk ain't nothing. You hear me? They ain't nothin',' was the gist of a sermon endured by one horn player.[26] Yet, these cautionary tales did not immune Sonny Clay from the draw of the bugle call and circus drum.

The precise circumstances of Sonny Clay's sidewalk encounter with the 'Bugle Call Rag' are unknown but he framed the episode as a conversion, a moment that realigned his musical direction and ushered in an intensely creative period.[27] He dedicated himself to mastering the trap drum and xylophone, and the performance art of acrobatics and juggling. He experimented with fancy embellishments on the piano. From sheet music stocked at the local Woolworth, he studied the blues of WC Handy and rags of Scott Joplin. He played alongside gramophones of old-time jubilees, and up-to-the-minute blues, foxtrots and rags, some performed by Chicago's and New York's finest Black musicians. He was part of a first generation whose access to shellac discs did to music what Gutenberg's printing press had done to the written word.[28]

In mid-1917, a new word appeared on gramophone labels: 'Dixie Jass Band One Step' by the Original Dixieland Jass Band, 'Everybody Loves a Jass Band' by vaudevillian Arthur Fields.[29] At its best, 'jass' was a spirited polyphonic duel of woodwind and brass, born of regimental brass, Missouri rag, Tennessee blues, Latin zest and the laconic drawl of New Orleans. More often than not, it was a commercial confection moulded by Tin Pan Alley's novelty machine. Even so, these songs invited experimentation. Sonny Clay played with the tempo and stripped back the melody to improvise on the harmony. With brash self-assurance, he dismissed complaints that his music was too noisy and confusing, that the public would never accept it. Looking back over these years, Sonny Clay congratulated his adolescent self for staying ahead of the game. 'Could see change coming,' he vaunted in his interview.[30]

In September 1918, Sonny Clay's four-piece jazz orchestra introduced the Phoenix Riverside Ballroom to a new modern sound, playing to the city's three racial groups on segregated nights. Admirers declared them 'the best jazzers that ever jazzed'.[31]

Sonny Clay recalled blowing his first pay cheque on a pair of baggy tailored trousers to hide his 'ludicrously skinny legs'. It was the first of many thousands of dollars spent on draping himself in fine cut cloth. Light-skinned, well-spoken, with high cheekbones and wide, vulnerable eyes, he was doomed to look far younger than his years—although one who carried responsibilities far heavier than his classmates. A year before he graduated high school, Sonny Clay married 22-year-old Verbena Graves and moved into her family's home. Six months later, the couple gave birth to a son (who would one day be a California superior court judge). Sonny Clay claimed he had the chance to pursue a career in law. But once he was a family man, he decided show business was a more lucrative bet.[32]

Destined to look far younger than his years, bandleader Sonny Clay in 1926. (*Jazzfinder Magazine*, September 1948)

Clay credited his high school bandmaster for helping him land his first professional job. Yet this same bandmaster also sidelined him in school performances. Sonny Clay and the other Black senior did not appear in the school concert nor attend the senior ball. Instead, they marked their graduation with the congregation of the AME Church. At a special banquet, the preacher invoked Black unity while paying tribute to the two fine young men who were uplifting the race.[33]

According to Dr Washington, this was progress. A logic embraced by Phoenix's Black leaders who affirmed their unequal place in the life of the city as they negotiated concessions. 'We do not oppose it for any desire for social equality,' stated a Black businessman as he begged Phoenix's city council not to remove Black students from local schools.[34] 'We do not ask for social equality,' prefaced the president of the Colored Women's Club, as she battled to stop a screening of the Ku Klux Klan homage, *Birth of a Nation*.[35]

But even in Arizona, Booker T Washington's model of racial uplift was beginning to fray. The insecurity created by the Mexican Revolution saw the deployment of tens of thousands of Black soldiers to the southwest. As on the battlefields of France, so on the borders of Mexico, Black troops expected their service to the nation to be rewarded with full citizenship rights under the US Constitution.

2
INDEPENDENCE DAY

BANISHMENT WAS THE fate of most Black battalions in the United States Army: a posting to a remote and lonely corner of the country or territory, far from White populations. The four Black regiments fighting the Germans in Europe had been separated from their White countrymen, serving on the frontline under the French Tricolour rather than the Stars and Stripes. The remaining three were deployed to the US/Mexico border, bringing Big Northern City ideas about rights, equality and justice to Sonny Clay's young ears.

Mostly, the Tenth (Colored) Cavalry guarded the 2000-mile border from Nogales to Yuma, Arizona, the monotony broken by the occasional incursions of warlord bandit Pancho Villa, and a cat-and-mouse game with gun-running rebel Yaqui Indians. Recreational diversions at Fort Huachuca included brothels, baseball and music. The mounted cavalry band were so skilful that White folk routinely enlisted them for public concerts and patriotic parades, finding them 'an unexpected source of oft-remarked excellence'.[1]

For Black Arizonans, the 48-piece Tenth Cavalry band signalled so much more. Twelve years earlier, President Roosevelt conceded to Booker T Washington's entreaties and, for the first time, appointed Black bandmasters in Black regiments. Amongst African Americans in the southwest, Tenth Cavalry bandleader Wade H Hammond was a revered name.[2]

On 27 June 1919, Wade Hammond and the Tenth Cavalry Colored Guard Band arrived in Phoenix to perform at an air tournament to honour the White Maricopa County men who had served in the Great War. The following day, they played at a Black community barbecue at Eastlake Park. It was inconceivable that Sonny Clay had passed up the chance to see them.[3]

The mood was upbeat although injustices, big and small, rankled the crowd. Black folk had agreed to billet the bandsmen, but the White memorial committee insisted they sleep on the floor of a local hall, with few sanitation facilities. More troubling was the fate of the White officer who, the previous year, shot dead a Black soldier for saluting him with a cigarette in his mouth. Despite sustained efforts by Black servicemen, local military authorities refused to prosecute the killer.[4] Most galling was the wave of racial violence rolling across the nation that summer. The Armistice of 1918 delivered neither peace nor democracy for Black veterans, instead discharging a deadly White backlash. A few weeks earlier in Charleston, South Carolina, a brawl between a Black and a White sailor in a downtown poolroom ended in the deaths of six Black men. Strikingly similar dramas unfolded in Putnam County, Georgia, Monticello, Mississippi, New London, Connecticut, Memphis, Tennessee, and Annapolis, Maryland—the death or maiming of a Black man at the hands of Whites. Police intransigence. Groups of young Black men defending themselves with sticks, knives and guns. Punishing White retribution.

'Bitter' was the word Black Americans recited over and again. 'Bitter' that the president refused to condemn racial violence. 'Bitter' that Southern Democrats filibustered an anti-lynching law. 'Bitter' that authorities interpreted Black demands for equality and justice as Bolshevik-inspired subversion.

Five days after the community barbeque, on 3 July 1919, the Tenth Cavalry trekked thirty dusty miles from Fort Huachuca to the copper mining town of Bisbee, ready to lead the Independence Day parade. When they arrived, several thirsty men headed to the Black-designated Silver Leaf Club in the tenderloin district. Consistent with military regulations, they carried loaded weapons. But the sight of armed Black men so rattled the sheriff that he and his freshly deputised townsmen fixed upon disarming them.

A gun battle raged for hours and before the sun rose on 4 July, six cavalrymen lay close to death. Yet still the Tenth Cavalry band led the Independence Day parade down Bisbee's main street as if they, and the heavily armed White spectators, were indivisible under one flag. 'God fashioned a Nation of Love and called it—America,' read the *Arizona Republican*'s front-page tribute, a column inch away from news of Bisbee's 'race riot', one of dozens of outrages scourging the country.[5]

The White Arizona press regretted the violence while affirming the White man's righteous 'sense of superiority'. They advised Whites to exercise moderation and urged Blacks to keep quiet and be patient. 'A good thing not to do is "start something",' ran one tip.[6]

The Black people of Phoenix ignored their counsel and instead formed a chapter of the NAACP, the National Association for the Advancement of Colored People. Breaking with the teachings of Booker T Washington, they demanded the right to vote, political representation and equal treatment under the law. In the absence of police protection, they formed self-defence units.[7]

In contrast to clearly defined racial tensions in southern and northern states, the southwestern leg of this 'race war' was fought on two fronts, with no clear consensus on who was fighting whom—or who qualified as 'colored' or White. Anti-miscegenation laws classified Mexicans as Whites, yet in daily life all but the wealthiest lived on the other side of the colour line. Poor Mexicans competed with poor Blacks for the same low-paid jobs, stoking divisions between 'native-' and 'foreign-' born workers. Whites fretted about the political solidarity between Hispanics and Blacks, pointing to the racial equality edicts of the Mexican Revolution.[8]

America's most famous exile, the Black heavyweight boxer Jack Johnson, was the poster boy of this alliance. Six years earlier he had fled the United States to avoid a prison sentence for a trumped-up charge of trafficking women for immoral purposes. By 1919, Johnson and his White wife, Lucille, lived a charmed segregation-free life in Mexico City, frequenting the finest clubs and rubbing shoulders with the revolution's movers and shakers. Anyone who read Black newspapers could follow their Mexican adventures.

In the weeks after the Bisbee shootout, the *Chicago Defender* recounted the fate of a White drug store owner who refused to serve

Johnson a drink: city authorities revoked his trading licence, forcing the White man to come cap-in-hand to Johnson's palatial home, pleading forgiveness. The store owner had learned the hard way that Mexico was no 'white man's country'.[9]

Johnson delivered a sponsored message. His glowing praise for the Mexican Revolution assured him the patronage of the Carranza government. And against a backdrop of racial violence in the United States, his adventures served as an indictment of President Woodrow Wilson's empty promise to make the world 'safe for democracy'.[10]

In 1919 Sonny Clay witnessed the national reach of White supremacy—a diffuse, interlocking system of control sanctioned by state institutions and policed by economically insecure men convinced of their racial superiority.

He also witnessed a defiant Black response, a paradigm shift away from accommodating White supremacy to a bold pledge to dismantle it. For an ambitious Black youngster insulted by the indignities of Jim Crow, disillusioned by racial atrocity and weighed down by the burdens of family life, Mexico offered a tantalising escape. Before 1919 was through, Sonny Clay and clarinettist Charlie Green left Phoenix to seek their musical fortunes south of the border. In joining the 'drifting class', Sonny Clay would stray from Dr Washington's path.

3

ACROSS THE RIVER STYX: SONNY CLAY'S TIJUANA

UNTIL 1919, MEXICO's border towns were little more than trading posts. Then the Anti-Saloon League persuaded Minnesota representative Andrew Volstead to sponsor the National Prohibition Bill. As the bill began its tumultuous journey through the US Congress that year, Baja California's economic desert sprang to life. Governor Estaban Cantu lowered taxes and built dams and highways, determined to woo the moneymen behind America's breweries, bottling plants, racetracks and casinos.[1]

By the time the Volstead Act came into effect in January 1920, the sagebrush plain was an oasis. Hundreds of thousands of American tourists flooded down the boulevards, eager to slake their thirst, free from the messing of do-gooders. Any virtue earned by a Protestant work ethic was expended by the luck of the draw. Governor Cantu reaped the tax revenues.[2]

Mr and Mrs Herman Koenekamp of Denison, Iowa, chronicled their Mexican adventure in a letter to their local paper. A clergyman's billboard had damned the drive from San Diego and Tijuana as 'the road to Hell', although the Koenekamps found the road hellish with bumps, ruts and general cussedness. Still they persisted, pushing on to a clump of government houses where an arbitrary line delineated the USA from Mexico. There, a customs officer issued them with a one-day pass to play hooky from Prohibition America—a single automobile in an endless wave of daytrippers.

Yes, the muddy dribble known as the Tijuana River did evoke the River Styx in Mr Koenekamp's mind. And the staccato of the automobile hammering the rickety bridge rattled a sense of imminent collapse. Of civilisation, they wondered. Or the moral fibre of one sorry soul. Though once through to the main drag, the couple were surprised to find a village that felt like 'home'. Not the tidy streets of Denison, Iowa, but the collective imaginings of a nation that once was the frontier.[3]

Tijuana 'strikes you first as a Wild West main street scene in the movies, with a dash of Coney Island', reported one stunned daytripper. No cobblestone Spanish piazza lay at its heart. Instead, cowpunchers in stetsons and tourists in sombreros strolled past wonky shopfronts signposted the Cafe Savoy or Hotel de Paris—although the plaster arches of the bordello, the Moulin Rouge, came closer to its Gallic promise.[4]

Dollars were welcome, English was spoken and the continuous jangle of jazz stretched the length of the main street. Not the lightly syncopated social jazz of hotel dance orchestras but a raw, raucous sound. In spaces no larger than dishpans, college kids and taxi dancers urged on players conjuring rags from overworked pianos. On the high-polished boards of well-appointed saloons, dancers swooned to ten-piece 'Negro' orchestras.[5] At the Monte Carlo casino, Mr and Mrs Koenekamp watched a Fancy Dan peel hundred-dollar notes from a fat roll of cash and pondered the irony that, far from quelling vice, the Volstead Act had fermented a heady brew. In a world where drinking a mug of beer made criminals of law-abiding citizens, a spirit of rebellion took root.[6]

As they headed back to Denison, Iowa, Mr and Mrs Koenekamp declared the wide-open freedom of Tijuana as 'fun, conservative fun'. But for Sonny Clay and a cluster of Black entertainers escaping overzealous sheriffs and murderous lynch mobs, the impact was electric.

Sonny Clay's route to Tijuana diverged from the Babbitts of the Midwest. As he later recalled, he and clarinettist Charlie Green first stopped at Los Algodones, a well-armed customs post on the Colorado River—and home to a strip of bars and brothels patronised by reservation Indians, Chinese road crews, American Buffalo soldiers, and Mexican revolutionary guards. But when a group of mutinous Mexican soldiers lynched ten Chinese labourers, they quickly moved on.[7]

Next port of call was the gated red-light district of Mexicali, a social experiment in state-regulated vice. Most famous was the Owl, an oversized cantina that sprawled like a scarlet city over an entire block. Around the clock, gamblers chanced on cards and dice, a fine whiskey never far from reach. Percentage girls worked the floor while an eight-piece jazz ensemble kept it loose at premium rates. Upstairs, slumming parties haunted the observation gallery, more interested in voyeurism than vice. The carousing in the back rooms never ceased.[8]

Sonny Clay kept on moving, shuttling back and forth across the border. North into Calexico, west to San Diego, then south to Tijuana where he discovered his El Dorado.

Never before had he played to such passionate crowds; dancers loved their jazz hot and rhythms raw. Never before had he seen Black and White people mix so freely. If a person had the green stuff, they could drink at the German beer hall, bathe in the hot springs, thrill at the bullfight, dabble in chance or seek the pleasures of just about every colour flesh. The charms of Tijuana held him in a spell. He kept returning 'for the sake of the atmosphere', even when the money was better north of the border.[9]

For Tijuana's African American residents were not doing time in hotel lobbies and kitchens but owned sumptuously appointed hotels, bars and Cadillacs.[10] Black millionaires were fixtures of the Monte Carlo racetrack and casino. By the paddock, professional betting men with names like 'the Owl' earned big bucks spotting the ringer.[11] In shining mahogany bars, diamond studded dandies celebrated their winnings. Horse breeder Bob Rowe, once the undisputed kingpin of New Orleans' tenderloin, always took home 'plenty of potatoes'. George and Mabel Ramsey juggled horse breeding, cabaret management, property development and a few vaguely defined pursuits—it was never clear how they made their riches.[12] Horse trainers Kid and Helen North were easy to spot: he in a tight-fitting salmon shirt and tartan tie, she in a sable coat with a five-figure price tag.[13]

When he first left Phoenix, Sonny Clay felt conflicted about the 'wandering existence' of an itinerant musician, conscious of his family and community's disapproval. In Tijuana, his inner torment eased. Detractors painted the village as a false Garden of Eden where sinners ate from the tree of ignorance, blind to good and evil. But for Sonny Clay it was a road to Damascus, the scales falling from his eyes. He saw an oasis of enterprise, watered by universal rights, free from the weeds of American wrongs. A place where style was a virtue and a class of bon vivants saluted their liberty, untouched by the binding passions of hearth and home. Tijuana presented a seductive alternative to Booker T Washington's Black America.[14]

Sonny Clay became a regular face at Sly Stewart's opulent bars, the Newport and Kansas City, forging connections with Black gamblers and entertainers from San Diego and Los Angeles.[15] He formed a musical partnership with 'Pops' Woodman, a nose-to-the-grindstone trombone player who had just moved west from Mississippi. He bonded, too, with 'Ragtime' Billy Tucker, a *Chicago Defender* columnist who knew every mover and shaker trawling the West Coast. The two men shared a love of the 'moist soils' of the desert town. They quoted Robert Burns as they toasted the sanctuary where 'a man's a man for a' that'.[16]

A fortuitous chain of events placed Sonny Clay under the tutelage of New Orleans pianist Ferdinand 'Jelly Roll' Morton. They first met in Bob Rowe's San Diego hotel on the eve of a Tijuana racing carnival. Of course, Sonny Clay knew 'Mr Jelly Lord' by reputation. As a composer, he was stunning, bristling with ideas. No one before him had notated the swinging, sophisticated language of New Orleans ragtime jazz. As a pianist, he was a virtuoso. In cutting contests from Biloxi to Chicago, Jelly Roll Morton's languorous strolls and finger-breaking rolls were unbeatable. Since arriving on the West Coast four years earlier, he had created a sensation. The Hollywood crowd adored him.

Ferd Morton took the veneration in his stride, spruiking his own magnificence and reciting the tale of his grandmother's cradle-side deal with the devil. Those who knew him did not discount the tale. He 'dressed like a mad prince', recalled a musician. 'A man with strong spiritual and magnetic forces,' said another. Gold teeth filled his mouth. A diamond decorated his front tooth.[17]

Sonny Clay hitched a ride with the musical legend in his spanking new twelve-cylinder roadster, a captive audience for Ferd Morton to relive his triumphs, denounce his competitors and air his many grudges. Tellingly, Morton's three bandsmen followed behind, squeezed into a Stutz Bearcat built for two.[18]

For as his musicians could attest, Ferd Morton was an ornery toad: a paranoid and jealous man riddled with grievances he just had to scratch. He strolled around with a Colt 45 pistol in his pocket, liable to bawl out a bandsman for the smallest quibble. Yet no one questioned his remarkable talent. His tunes shone so brightly that Sonny Clay joined a long line of musicians willing to risk Morton's gun-waving madness just to figure out how the hell he did it.[19]

By the time they had reached Tijuana, Sonny Clay was the xylophone player in Jelly Roll Morton's band. For the next three months at Sly Stewart's Kansas City Bar, he watched the nightly ritual unfold. The master sauntered in, regal but casual, removing his coat with a fancy flourish, carefully laid to reveal the silk lining. Sitting behind the piano to strike the first dramatic chord—Mr Jelly Lord had arrived.[20]

Each night, Sonny Clay studied the layers of textured arrangements. In these months, Jelly Roll Morton wrote the joyous 'Kansas City Stomps', a work feisty enough to propel a duel of brass and wind, yet delicate enough to savour the banjo's trill, the tuba's grunt and the piano's shimmer. In time, this masterful mess would become a template for Clay's own compositions.

Sometimes the master let the apprentice occupy his piano seat. Sonny Clay recalled Morton encouraging him to take musical risks. To experiment with chord structures, develop riffs and play with the breaks. Until then, Sonny Clay mostly played xylophone and drums. Now he approached the piano with the same rhythms in mind. He took on solos, slapping the keys and hitting the blue notes in ways that forever sealed his reputation as Jelly Roll's protégé.[21]

Unfortunately, Ferd Morton's golden touch did not extend to the racetrack. After a three-month losing streak in Tijuana, he returned penniless to his home in Los Angeles.[22]

Sonny Clay's visits home also failed to deliver a bounty. At first, he frequently returned to Phoenix, but the gaps grew longer until he barely showed up at all. In 1921, his wife Verbena gave birth to their second child, a girl, who died before she was three months old.[23] In his 1960 interview, Sonny Clay dodged the uncomfortable question of his family life, framing his decision to leave as essential to his career. His two-year stint in Tijuana opened up new ways of being.

For much of Sonny Clay's life, former heavyweight champion Jack Johnson was the most recognisable Black man on the planet. So naturally, when the boxer motored into Tijuana one April afternoon in 1920, with his wife and her Mexican maid, a wave of jubilation erupted in the streets. Black and Mexican doormen and waiters huddled around him, reaching to shake his hand. The fraternal order of Elks honoured him with a grand feast. For Jack Johnson was a force of nature, who had battered down the colour line to claim the heavyweight title in Sydney, Australia, in 1908 and retain it in Reno, Nevada, in 1910.

Less triumphant, though no less compelling, was his private life. He openly travelled with his White wife and made no efforts to hide his complicated relationships with other White women. In 1912 the FBI tried to bring him down, pinning him with a White slavery charge. But he dodged that bullet by fleeing the country, first to London, Paris and Madrid. Then, in early 1919, he moved to Mexico City, living what appeared to be the high life.

But Jack Johnson was on borrowed time. Even before the assassination of his patron President Carranza in May 1920, his Mexican fortunes had turned. Ordered to leave the country, he was in Tijuana to negotiate the terms of his surrender. As the countdown began, the press contingent grew.

A showman to the last, Jack Johnson showed no sign of distress, even as the thumbscrews tightened. By night he frequented gambling houses and, once his wife left for Chicago, danced with all types of women in late-night cafes. Each morning he jogged to the border, sometimes sticking his toe over the line to the delight of onlookers. By day he held court at George Ramsey's bar, the Main Event, flashing his golden smile at the stream of curious tourists (and enjoying a cut of the profits). He told admirers that

Former heavyweight champ Jack Johnson (centre) outside the Main Event in Tijuana, 4 July 1920. Ragtime Billy Tucker is on the right of frame, a line of admirers to the left. (www.doctorjazz.co.uk)

he would return to the United States as a free man. He would fight Jack Dempsey and reclaim his title. He would feast on pork chops and beans at his favourite San Diego restaurant.

On 4 July 1920, a photographer snapped Johnson outside the Main Event, alongside Sonny Clay's pal Ragtime Billy Tucker and several others. To the side of the frame, a line of Black men fixed their gaze on the boxer's physical majesty, as if his proximity might draw them into the legend.[24]

Thirteen days later Jack Johnson bid Tijuana goodbye. In a performance staged for the press, he began his last walk to the border, a knot of reporters following in his wake. The party stopped at the Main Event as Johnson shared a drink with several White women, shedding a tear of sadness as he walked away. It was hard to leave friends, he said.

Over the rickety wooden bridge and across the border, the former champ surrendered his passport to a federal agent, surrendering neither dignity nor optimism.

'I am on my way to home, sweet home,' read his official statement. 'Returning voluntarily to take whatever punishment that lies in store for me, seeking no higher reward than the privilege of spending the balance of my days in my native land and to die and be buried in her sacred soil.'[25]

A newspaper photograph memorialised the moment: the fugitive and federal agent, smiling and relaxed, like old friends out for a Sunday drive. And indeed, they shared a meal of pork chops and beans in San Diego before the agent escorted the prisoner to the jailhouse. Inmates welcomed him with a rousing 'Hail, Hail, the Gang's All Here', capping off a day filled with spontaneous cheers. 'Among white and black alike' there was 'the deepest sympathy for the great fighter', noted one report.[26]

Defiant, charming and good-humoured, Jack Johnson could not fail to impress. Sonny Clay had the rare privilege to study him at close range. To fathom the political subtext in the boxer's appeal to national unity. To ponder the patriotic flourishes that smoothed over racial ruptures, enabling the fugitive to claim his rightful place in his American home. Jack Johnson returned, in triumph, impervious to the hatred of his enemies, as if the forces that drove him into exile never existed. Little did Sonny Clay know, one day he would draw on these lessons to execute his deportation from Australia with a modicum of style.

More immediately, Sonny Clay felt the pull of new opportunities. His Tijuana connections had paved the way to a new destination. After six months of slapping the keys at Sly Stewart's Kansas City Bar, he joined his friend Ragtime Billy Tucker and headed to the City of Angels.[27]

4
SOUTH CENTRAL AVENUE, LOS ANGELES

Los Angeles sprawled: a coastal belt of gap-toothed development and automobiles, buckled by mountains, soothed by sea and watered by private utilities. At the turn of the twentieth century, Sunset Strip was little more than a cow path. Watts was a marshland good for crawfish and catfish, while Santa Monica was somewhere out in the country. But as each decade passed, the White population doubled and redoubled and the city sprawled even further. Single storey, free-standing bungalows radiated out into farmland and along the coastline. Hillsides sprouted the homes of the new Hollywood elite: white stucco mansions with horse stables, tennis courts and breathtaking views. Only the thirty blocks along the southern artery of Central Avenue grew tighter. The Black population was growing just as fast, but the so-called 'colored belt' had barely widened a notch.[1]

Sure, White Californians upheld the colour line with less fortitude than their Texan cousins.[2] The Black citizenry could vote without intimidation—a few Black representatives even sat in the California State Assembly. Nor did they live in constant fear of Judge Lynch, as they had back in Georgia and Texas.[3] But still, a system some called 'James Crow' governed Black lives. It was loose enough for a person to advance, even thrive, but tight enough for Whites to decide where Black folk could live, who they married, and how they moved through the city. Californian miscegenation laws, for instance, rendered 'void and illegal' any unions between Whites with 'Negroes, Mulattoes and Mongolians', while a system of residential covenants and deed restrictions created what one resident called 'invisible walls of steel'. Black folk could not 'lease, rent, purchase or occupy' a property south of Slauson Avenue or west of South Park and Avalon Boulevard—although by wile and persistence, some Black homeowners penetrated the northern barrier, moving across Jefferson Boulevard towards the downtown area.[4]

As Southern migrants crowded into South Central Avenue, a once orderly district of church-going, house-proud residents became a hothouse of contradictions: poverty vied with prosperity, hardship two-stepped with enterprise, high culture collided with folk tradition, social climbers crossed paths with flophouse bums, political protection rubbed up against progressive zeal.[5]

By the time Sonny Clay arrived in Los Angeles in early 1922, South Central Avenue was lined with Black-owned businesses and offices: dry goods stores, insurance companies, newspapers, tailors, barber shops, undertakers, fraternal associations, beauty parlours, hot dog hawkers, shoeshine stands, fortune tellers, cafes, theatres and pool halls. The strip bustled but, as a cultural phenomenon, was well shy of Harlem or South Side Chicago. Musically speaking, Los Angeles was a 'toddling town', home to church choirs, classical recitals, brass bands and 'ricky-tick' mom and pop ensembles.[6] It was the poor cousin of San Francisco's Barbary Coast, the electric strip where get-off men in Black clubs made people cry and scream, and push-me, pull-you couple dances like the Texas Tommy were born. As one Barbary Coast bandleader had scorned: those Los Angeles musicians might be playing the notes correctly, but they 'ain't playin' nothin''.[7]

Sonny Clay arrived in Los Angeles when the fortunes of the two towns had begun to turn. A few months earlier, social purity leaguers pressured San Francisco police to raid the Barbary Coast's clubs and dives, shutting the vibrant sporting district for what proved to be the very last time. San Francisco's loss was Los Angeles' gain as scores of Barbary Coast musicians headed south. Amongst the exodus was a coterie of young Oaklanders who had infused the rag jazz beat with the walking bass lines of boogie-woogie. And a core of seasoned New Orleans jazzmen, some students of the mythical trumpeter Billy Bolden.[8] A decade earlier, these New Orleans men headed west when social purity crusaders pressured city authorities to shut down the brothels and dives of Storyville for what proved to be the very last time.

For this network of musicians, the centre of Los Angeles sat at the corner of Twelfth Street and Central Avenue, the crossroads of the B and U streetcars. There, Reb Spikes of the Spikes Brothers Music Store ran the closest thing to Los Angeles' Black musicians' union—a de facto clubhouse where newcomers could establish their musical credentials, swap yarns about life on the road or maybe pick up work or, at least, the work available to them after the White union snared the lion's share. But even on this skewed playing field, Black bands had a rare market advantage.

'Every cafe in town is continuously crying out for us,' reported Ragtime Billy Tucker in his *Chicago Defender* column. Already, Dink Johnson and the Five Hounds of Jazz were peeling a wicked onion at the Harmony Inn. Curtis Mosby's Blues Blowers had sailors coughing up nickels and dimes at Solomon's Penny Dance Hall on Santa Monica Pier, while at Leakes Lake, in the marshy wilds of Watts, King Oliver's wails and thrills had people jumping out of their seats. Billy Tucker put out a call for a peppy jazz band, a combination unafraid to put some holy-roller grunt into their syncopation. He had 'plenty of sunshine, work, money' for them; 'everything any sane person desires'.[9]

Sonny Clay quickly picked up work, a mix of solo jobs and fill-in spots with the New Orleans masters: Kid Ory, King Oliver and, of course, his old mentor, Jelly Roll Morton. He and Billy Tucker wrote songs with catchy titles like 'Ain't but the One', their eyes on the million-dollar sales clocked up by blues divas Bessie Smith and Mamie Smith. He nabbed short contracts with talking machine companies, composing, arranging and accompanying White recording artists. He helped Sophie Tucker mix Yiddish burlesque with the Southern blues and kept Rudy Wiedoeft, the White bandleader at the Cinderella Roof Ballroom, in a fresh supply of tunes. He sometimes made guest appearances on the Cinderella Roof but mostly he worked behind the scenes, instructing White performers in the mysteries of Black syncopation.[10]

The role, he soon discovered, brought little prestige and even less money. Rudy Wiedoeft 'went east and presented these songs as his own ... grew famous ... released recordings without SC's knowledge', reads the handwritten summary of Clay's 1960 interview.[11] Newspaper reports confirmed his claim: by 1924, Sonny Clay's songs earned Wiedoeft a national reputation as the 'Sousa Band of Jazzdom' and 'Synco Harmonists Supreme!'[12] For Sonny Clay, 'records were nothing more than a pocket change idiocy contrived in the east for the benefit of no one in particular'.[13] As far as he could see, the real money was on the cabaret and theatre circuit.

Sometime in the early 1920s, White folk began appearing on Central Avenue at an hour when most working Black folk were tucked up in bed. And not just any old White folk but 'rich people, actors in silent movies and those who knew what was going on in show biz', as one musician recalled.[14] Most came for music, dance and cabaret entertainment, although some came in search of special kicks; the bizarre sexual predilections of rich Whites were the stuff of legend amongst sex workers and old-timers.[15]

A spate of Black and Tan clubs opened catering to a range of price points, from the White college students who filled the hastily formed 'dance academies' to the sumptuously appointed cabarets for 'the spending class of ofays'. The drinks were reliably 'wet', the band hot and bluesy while a multi-talented diva and her skimpily costumed, exuberantly hoofing chorus line headlined elaborate revues.[16] 'Red hot' eccentric dancer Carolynne Snowden headed the Creole Cutie chorus girls at the Apex Club, which was run and perhaps owned by Black businessman Curtis Mosby although, according to rumour, he fronted a White crime syndicate.[17] However, there was no doubt his band, the Blues Blowers, was the hottest dance orchestra on the strip. 'Those were hectic days, hectic days,' remembered saxophone player Leo Davis, recalling fights between rival gangs spilling onto the orchestra dais. 'You get the fists right and that would be the end of that.'[18] For Carolynne Snowden the Apex Club delivered a different professional bump. Her headline role translated into motion picture work—once she swapped her sequin gown for a maid's apron.

In the fall of 1922, eight months into his Los Angeles adventure, 23-year-old Sonny Clay recruited five musicians with an appreciation for hot rhythms, blues and stomp. He wished to capitalise on the White craze for slumming—as well as cater to Black dance audiences.[19] Several halls on Central Avenue were still in the 'service of the community' and promoters promised a 'shake that thing' 'jam up time' with Sonny Clay's Eccentric Harmony Six.[20]

The following year, Sonny Clay persuaded half of the much-celebrated Black and Tan Orchestra to jump ship and join his crew. In doing so, he secured Ernest 'Nini' Coycault (pronounced Cwah-co), a Louisiana trumpeter who had perfected his style in the bordellos of St Bernard Parish before pushing west to the Barbary Coast in 1908, 'shattering the air' with his 'a-tootin'' and 'scrapin'' and 'gumbo stuff'.[21] Nini Coycault was a 'sweet trumpeter, who sang out but didn't blast', Sonny Clay told John Bentley—and for the Arizona bandleader, an ongoing source of inspiration. Coycault's New Orleans licks inspired a raft of compositions that won Sonny Clay a deal with Vocalion Records.[22] As he keenly understood, Nini Coycault was a hard man to replace and Clay managed to keep hold of him for years—even as the rest of the line-up chopped and changed more often than the name: after the Eccentric Harmony Six came the Stomping Six, then the California Poppies, then the Rhythm Demons.[23]

Considerable prestige clung to the title 'bandleader' but the position called for a hard head, aggressive self-promotion and 'a lot of push'.[24] As many observed, Central Avenue's two leading frontmen, Reb Spikes and Curtis Mosby, were highly disciplined, even ruthless and uncompromising—and far better at business than music.[25]

To keep his band in work, Sonny Clay had to maintain existing networks and turn new connections into opportunities. He could make himself unpopular on Central Avenue if he tried to unseat a resident Black band. Or risk physical harm by pushing a White orchestra out of a job. And when he secured steady work, he paid for the smart tailor-made suits. And got heavy with club managers if they came up short on payday. And kept a musician in line if he turned up to the job half-drunk from the night before. 'I've seen them make some bad mistakes in that condition,' winced Reb Spikes.[26]

Somewhere between the Cinderella Roof and a Central Avenue dance academy, Sonny Clay came to the attention of a team of European-born film producers, directors and actors—Adolphe Menjou, Paul Bern and Jette Gould. The trio had carved out a reputation creating the 'Continental sex picture', although 'slumming picture' was also an apt generic title.[27] 'Jazz, jazz and still more jazz, wild social activities, bathing baths, heavy drinking and love-making', promised the publicity for their 1924 film *Sinners in Silk*.[28] The plots usually began with a bored bourgeois American couple whose mad pursuit of bacchanalian abandon collided with a glamorous but drunken vamp, and a slick though brutish sheik, most likely at a Montmartre club or Manhattan society party. As one film critic observed, no party scene was complete without a 'colored jazz band with a trick leader' who was 'going at the jazziest pace possible'.[29] That role was frequently filled by Sonny Clay.

At a time when Black screen roles were confined to chauffeurs, roustabouts and maids, Sonny Clay played the young, handsome 'colored jazz bandleader' in dozens of films and two-reelers. The producer, he recollected, was confused by Nini Coycault's bright complexion which did not conform to his primitivist fantasies of Darkest Africa—and, for the band, roused much laughter.[30] By 1960, Clay had forgotten the names of the films, although he recalled his band donning 'grass skirts' and assuming the identity of a 'Zulu band' for a scene in a French cafe.

Trade magazines indicated the scale of demand. The sultry Russian actress Alla Nazimova gave Alexandre Dumas' *Camille* a sophisticated art deco makeover with 'automobiles, feminine coiffures' and 'a negro jazz band'. *Dante's Inferno*, the journey of a slumlord millionaire through the nine circles of torment, involved 'full nudity' and a 'comical negro band', while *The Snob*, a cautionary tale about a once happily married man's obsession with status, featured a 'high powered negro jazz band' at a New York supper club.[31] Most audacious was *Circe the Enchantress*, where screen siren Mae Murray appeared in a 'feverish' party scene getting 'hot feet' and dancing 'with a colored jazz trumpeter'.[32] 'I stand for jazz and gaiety and a certain bizarre slant on life,' she explained to a film magazine.

'Whatever I may be like off the screen, that is what I am like on the screen and shall continue to be until the public taste changes.'[33] Like so many of Hollywood's jazz enthusiasts, Murray was the child of European migrants raised in the great urban melting pots, less attached to the Yankee racial hierarchies of the previous three hundred years.

On their many visits to Hollywood motion picture studios, Central Avenue entertainers noticed a pronounced shift in racial protocols. As one actor reported, at meal breaks the entire cast, from studio chief to extras, ate together in one big dining room. What 'a grand and glorious feeling' it was for a headline star to 'eat beside you regardless of color' or to accept 'the warm and unprejudiced handshake of the big officials', he wrote. Even on films that reproduced an antebellum South where devoted flunkeys deferred to chivalrous gents, a free and easy spirit still pervaded the set.[34]

'Filmland goes Harlem', despaired gossip columnist Rosalind Shaffer. 'The chic thing to do nowadays in Hollywood is to betake oneself and friends to the Apex Nite Club, down in the colored belt', and watch the 'eight fast stepping Apexettes' and hear Mosby's Dixieland Blue Blowers, 'so hot they burn holes in a concrete wall'.[35]

More alarming for Shaffer were the leading actors who entertained Black colleagues in their homes and the young starlets working on their suntan. Why, she fretted, Joan Crawford's complexion was so deep, one gin-soaked actor could hardly be persuaded she wasn't 'high yella'. Who knew what that made of the coloured-folks-can't-dance-with-Whites rule.

Herbert Howe from *Photoplay* magazine offered her little consolation, describing his night at the Apex Club as 'a most biggety affair'. Slickum, the 'colored boot-black' from the Metro Goldwyn lot, had introduced him to all the Black celebrities.[36] Howe, at least, paid lip service to 'the strict etiquette' that forbade him to dance with a glamorous cabaret performer. 'My complexion was off but what with my deepening coat of tan and a natural kink in my hair it won't be long, hey! hey!'[37]

Sonny Clay had felt these cultural headwinds since his days in Tijuana, but by 1925, Black observers gave the social phenomenon a name: the 'Negro vogue'—a White affection for 'all things Negro', or at least what 'chic' White people imagined was 'Negro'.[38]

This fantasy of Blackness found voice in the literary prose of a generation of White bohemians and cosmopolitans who experienced Black music as a psychodrama where primitive 'African' musicians rescued 'over-civilised' White dancers from generations of Victorian sexual repression. Black rhythm, in this formulation, was a brand of bodily and psychic liberation—a Freudian antidote for a generation of Whites crushed and constrained by the narrow rules of 'correct' behaviour.[39] But what felt and looked like 'the new' reprised old familiar themes, grounded in dubious theories of biologically inscribed racial difference.

Music critic Roger Pryor Dodge, for instance, believed that 'Negro' jazz players did 'not consciously' plot and compose, but derived their musical inventiveness from 'uncontrolled frantic moments' of '*subconscious* improvisation'. In other words, an ability independent of artistry and skill but contingent on the spontaneous outpourings of an inescapably primitive Black essence. These ideas underpinned White bandleader Paul Whiteman's contention that his White, and thereby conscious, brand of jazz was a 'lusty bawling infant whose mental development has hardly begun'.[40]

The same ideas informed Hollywood screenplays like *The Jazz Singer*, which followed the fortunes of a young White jazz musician played by Al Jolson, locked in an Oedipal struggle with his domineering father, who insisted he pursue a career in classical music. Jolson's character only resolved this dilemma by donning boot polish and becoming 'Black'. Only then could he cast off his parent's bourgeois expectations and truly be 'himself'—a paradox culture critics now call 'racial cross-dressing', although, at the time, White modernists were blind to the irony.[41]

Sonny Clay, of course, knew there was nothing 'natural' about his hard-won musical skills. Nini Coycault's trumpet solos did not flow unchecked from an unrepressed id or by virtue of African ancestry. Yet to realise his professional ambitions, Clay needed to understand the White fad of slumming was more than a midnight visit to a Black and Tan club. It was the foundation of an alternative White identity founded on jazz—a mode of expression that played with the boundaries of race to challenge progressive purity. Simply put, few gestures terrified the establishment more than White youth sloughing off their Whiteness.

Clay's challenge was, somehow, to mould his performative self to meet these expectations—while retaining the core of his true self. It was a predicament hardly unique to Sonny Clay but faced by generations of Black performers. Hollywood actor Clarence Muse described wrestling with the 'dilemma' of playing to two audiences: a Black one who expected depictions of 'real' life and a White one who expected 'buffoonery' and entertainment.[42] One resisted White supremacy, the other generated wealth—with a whole lot of grey in between. For Black sociologist WEB Du Bois, this state of 'two-ness' was a hallmark of American Blackness. In 1897, he described the 'peculiar sensation' of 'always looking at one's self through the eyes of others, of measuring one's soul by the tape of a world that looks on in amused contempt and pity'—a phenomenon he called 'double-consciousness'.[43]

Sonny Clay was equally aware that the so-called 'Negro Vogue' coincided with the Black intellectual and artistic fervour of the Harlem Renaissance and the New Negro movement. 'I'm the NEW NEGRO, of much sterner stuff/And not the "old darkey" so easy to bluff!', read the 1919 poem of a Harlem elevator operator who knew his destiny lay beyond the caged shaft.[44] By 1925, theorist and critic Alain Locke mapped out the path to the new mindset. In the preface to the *New Negro* anthology, he called for Black performers to transform unexamined cultural patterns into conscious choices by rejecting 'unjust stereotypes' and creating new ones.[45]

The clarion call rang in Central Avenue show business circles. Columnist Buddy Brown applauded the new generation of performers who refused to make themselves 'ridiculous for the edification of the ofay'.[46] Billy Tucker laid bare the collision of free market forces and regulated race restrictions that resulted in White money controlling Central Avenue's entertainment world. 'Could a Race Man ... open a cafe strictly for colored patronage ... in the heart of the white business district?' he asked. 'Wake Up ... fight for the right which is yours.'[47] He entreated readers to create places where 'our people' could enjoy themselves and 'our money' could come 'back into our OWN pocket'.[48] To accumulate institutional power, the musicians of Central Avenue unionised, founding Local 767, an affiliate of the Musicians Union of America that still denied full membership rights.[49] Around them, Black entrepreneurs built elegant hotels and cafes and explored the possibilities of new media.[50] As one radio promoter noted, a Radio Ball—as live transmissions from ballrooms were known—could turn an audience of several hundred into hundreds of thousands, even millions.[51] This new technology knew no colour line but drifted through the ether into the domestic living spaces of Black and White America.

5

THE LOST ANGELS

AT HALF PAST one in the morning, Radio KHJ Los Angeles broadcast the jazzy modern beats to the night owls of the nation, only stopping at dawn to give the transmitter tubes a chance to cool down. The stated ambition of the Lost Angels, as the crew of White jazz hounds liked to be known, was to transmit music so hot it kept listeners up all night—as if no one had a care for the regular hours of the workaday world.[1]

In April 1925, Radio KHJ was at the Rose Room, in the heart of downtown Los Angeles, sending the sounds of Sonny Clay's Rhythm Demons through the airwaves. The *Los Angeles Times* had billed them as the 'original sons of Satan' and compared to the White jazz band in the line-up, their New Orleans polyphony inflected a suite of popular songs with devilish glee.[2]

The Lost Angels pitched the Rose Room as a haven of city sophistication, although locals knew it as a 'nickel a dance' place, crowded with White sailor boys hot-stepping with young women who earned extra income as taxi dancers.[3] Sonny Clay entertained the Rose Room crowd 'more times than he could remember' but not until the Radio Ball did things begin to 'move fast'.[4] Suddenly every booker in town wanted him. Rival station Radio KNX won a piece of the midnight action, broadcasting the Rhythm Demons live from the Merry Widow Cafe, a Hollywood Boulevard rendezvous favoured by Charlie Chaplin, Fatty Arbuckle and a clutch of studio 'bathing girls'.[5]

By July, Sonny Clay secured a regular seven o'clock slot at Radio KFI, wedged between a 'radiotorial' and a pipe organ recital.[6] He wrote and recorded a batch of tunes with Sunset Records, then Vocalion: the sauntering 'Roamin' Around' and breezy 'Bogaloosa Blues', each an uplifting interplay of New Orleans licks, thrum-thrum banjo and Harlem stride piano. In Chicago, a town he had never even played, 'Bogaloosa Blues' sold eight thousand discs on its first day.[7]

On Central Avenue, his regular Monday night residence at Hiawatha Dancing Academy was full to overflowing. One local reporter noted the 'joys of the crowd' as they danced to the high-spirited strut of the music.[8] The local newspaper burst with pride: 'This wonderful musical organization ... has made history for our group along musical lines.' The radio broadcasts had reached 'millions', earning Sonny Clay's band a 'national reputation'.[9] Billy Tucker, too, basked in the glow of his friend's success: 'Sonny has made a fine reputation since coming out this way and is in demand all over the coast.'[10]

Before 1925 was through, an electric sign outside a Washington Boulevard cafe illuminated Sonny Clay's name.[11] The Plantation Café, as the name suggested, was a white-pillared mock plantation house

One of the many iterations of the Sonny Clay Orchestra in the mid-1920s. Louisiana trumpeter Ernest 'Nini' Coycault is fifth from the right. (polarityrecords.com)

plucked from a fairytale rendering of 'Ole Virginny', although the club's reputation as a 'Harlem nightclub' transformed the antebellum playground into a searingly modern experience, at least for the exclusively White clientele.[12]

The cafe traded on its Hollywood connections. Celebrity appearances littered the weekly roster, from middling stars to motion picture directors boasting an expert eye for undiscovered female talent.[13] The Hollywood pack tended to show up on Sundays—the most impressive arriving by plane, fresh from a 24-hour journey from New York. Bootleg liquor was Sonny Clay's abiding memory of these evenings. They 'would kill themselves drinking', he recalled in his 1960 interview. Often 'starlets' approached him, hoping for a guest spot on vocals. More often, a 'big actor' brokered their appearance; he would 'sponsor' each turn 'starlet by starlet'.[14]

Sonny Clay recalled striking up a friendship with two Hollywood heavyweights. Matinee idol John Gilbert grew up poor but had the bearing of an aristocrat, or the profligate son of one, with four ex-wives and a reputation for carousing (rapidly deteriorating to inebriation). He routinely fell in love with his leading actresses, and his latest film *Flesh and the Devil* had broken all box office records, thanks in part to the tabloid's fixation with his on-and-off screen affair with co-star Greta Garbo. According to the rumour mill, Garbo snubbed him at the altar, and Gilbert, in a drunken stupor punched studio kingpin Louis B Mayer. Sonny Clay, however, remembered a 'perfect gentleman' who nursed his broken heart with bathtub gin and the yen to hear over and again the lilting 'I'd Climb the Highest Mountain (If I Knew I'd Find You)' made famous by Al Jolson that year. In ten years' time, alcoholism would kill John Gilbert, but in 1926 he was a powerful connection for Clay to cultivate and a glorious entry point into a rarefied world.

The bandleader's other Hollywood pal was veteran director DW Griffith who Clay, surely, had known by reputation. In the late 1910s, Phoenix's Black community had petitioned the local sheriff to block the screening of Griffith's most famous—or infamous—film *Birth of a Nation*.[15] Griffith's depiction of the Post Civil War Reconstruction era most offended Black viewers. He conjured a world turned upside down by Black men drunk with power after winning the right to vote. They divided a union of White brothers and violated the honour of White maids. Enter the heroes: the Ku Klux Klan, White vigilante horsemen who rescue the captive maid, lynch the transgressors, disarm the Black soldiers and prevent Black men from casting their vote. Griffith's faithless revision of events matched a scrupulous attention to material detail: the guns and buggies were historically accurate. The sum total was a story so powerful that even Phoenix's sheriff agreed to ban its release, fearing it may spark a mutiny amongst the Black Buffalo soldiers stationed nearby.

Far from a champion of White supremacy, Sonny Clay encountered a 'very friendly' man, although one demoralised by a run of box office failures and tainted by sexual scandal—in 1920, Griffith's young protégé and lover, Clarine Seymour, had died from a botched abortion. After years in the professional wilderness, Griffith had returned to Hollywood in 1927 looking for the fresh start that would never materialise.[16] At the Plantation Café he handed over ten- or twenty-dollar tips for Sonny Clay to play, again and again, WC Handy's 'Beale Street Blues'.[17]

Sonny Clay, of course, knew the song well—every Black cabaret musician did—although, surely, Griffith's identification with the song posed a puzzle: the man whose movies inspired the rise of the second Ku Klux Klan and sanctioned an untold number of beatings and lynchings embraced a degree of cultural miscegenation his on-screen characters would have reviled. He had crafted a narrative to justify Jim Crow segregation, portraying Blacks as unworthy of full citizenship rights, yet in private embraced cosmopolitan culture, finding in African American music a balm for his inner pain.

According to *Birth of a Nation*'s leading actress, Lillian Gish, this was because Griffith bore the Black race no ill will. 'Mr Griffith loved black people,' she explained in her biography. 'We never thought there was anything against the blacks.'[18] The film critic Bryan Curtis, however, has advanced a more convincing explanation: Griffith did not have a 'coherent political idea in his head', but instead was pulled along by the currents and eddies of faddism. 'He had a sophisticated lifestyle, but he wasn't a sophisticated thinker.'[19]

In so many ways, the sight of DW Griffith slipping Sonny Clay a ten-dollar tip to hear his favourite tune captured the paradoxical White embrace of African American culture. 'Beale Street Blues' was a sporting man's Prohibition lament dressed up in the folk idiom of the Mississippi Delta. The song's closing couplet invoked the spiritual renewal of a baptism: 'I'm goin' to the river, maybe by and by.' Which then flipped into a delicious blasphemy: 'Because the river's wet, and Beale Street's done gone dry!'

The song affirmed the small acts of defiance that epitomised the Plantation Café: a sly winked nod to the bootleg liquor that splashed from dainty teacups and the high stakes gamblers buried away in back rooms. The right to consume alcohol was a 'most prized possession of American liberty', protested one cabaret owner bankrupted by Prohibition.[20] It was a battle cry uttered by a person who had never faced the tyranny of murderous lynch mobs. Instead, Black music and dance signalled White opposition to a tyrannical law that stymied personal freedom. Racial relativism became a proxy for moral relativism and DW Griffith buddying up to the 'colored' bandleader of the Plantation Café over a few shots of hooch was part of this too.[21]

Sonny Clay looked back on these years with a mixture of reproach and nostalgia, tickled by his outlaw status beyond the workaday world. During his next residency at the Vernon Country Club, Clay won the attentions of radio evangelist 'Fighting Bob' Shuler, who spared no outrage detailing the 'drunken carousal' of brazen women dancing to the 'whine' of 'Negro jazz'.[22] Clay, and indeed club-owner Baron Long, welcomed the notoriety. The roadhouse was strategically placed beyond Los Angeles city limits where dry laws were soft and clubs stayed open all night. Long considered himself a connoisseur of African American jazz and blues, and had personally selected the Sonny Clay Orchestra for his strictly White clientele. Sonny Clay, in turn, paid tribute to the sporting crowd, showcasing 'Ace in the Hole' which exalted 'the con men and the boosters, the card sharks and crap-shooters'—and, of course, the Hollywood A-, B- and C-listers and suburban mom and pop tipplers. The audience responded in kind, happily throwing money at the band. A drunken tip could, and did, double the band's weekly salary. The recklessness was contagious. It was nothing for Clay to fling around hundred-dollar bills or splash out on tuxedos for the band. Sonny Clay felt a rebel's pride clocking out at six in the morning, just as the factory workers at the neighbouring canning factory punched in for the day.[23]

As a celebrated bandleader, he enjoyed certain social privileges, moving in circles never imagined back in Phoenix, Arizona. He had won the affections of Ivy Anderson, one of Central Avenue's brightest upcoming stars. At the Apex Club, her beguiling charm brought audiences to tears before wowing them with four variations of the Charleston, danced 'long, short, deep and wide'. Her 'magic' was 'in her personality', remembered one colleague. 'The moods she projected were fantastic.'[24] Ivy Anderson's ever more frequent guest appearances with the Sonny Clay Orchestra further amplified his public success, as well as giving him a reason to go home.

Yet the musicians of Central Avenue never forgot the conditional and temporary nature of their privileges. Entertainers always left the club by the back door. Taxis rarely accepted Black rides and woe betide a Black musician caught walking around the Glendale, Inglewood and Pasadena streets at night. Soon as the gig was over, the band needed to jump into their buggy and get out of 'Little Texas'.[25]

Daily life was as precarious as an acrobat balancing a stack of chairs on their chin. The task required intuition and keen observation skills played out in a transgressive environment amplified by pleasure-seeking, heightened by testosterone and dulled by bootleg liquor. At any unspecified moment, goodwill could evaporate, and the situation turn violent and ugly. Many Central Avenue performers carried guns, doubtful the law would protect them.[26]

Sonny Clay had been reminded of this lesson when Tijuana authorities charged a Black military veteran with the murder of a local policeman. An armed mob of Mexicans gathered outside the jailhouse fixing on lynching the accused, prompting the overnight flight of the Black population to San Diego. In a blink, the 'wide open' freedoms of Tijuana had snapped shut.[27]

Black sociologist Max Bond's survey of 'Negro life' in Los Angeles taught Sonny Clay a different type of lesson. The study loudly celebrated the success of Black professionals and organisations but was silent on the achievements of musicians and entertainers. As Bond saw it, the jazz musician's nocturnal life was not a milestone on the path of racial uplift. Neither eye-watering salaries nor the accolades of wealthy Whites translated into status and respect amongst the Black establishment.[28]

Musicians shrugged off sniffy judgements and embraced their outlier status, swapping tales that mythologised the Flawed Hero. The alcohol-fuelled escapades of Apex Club drummer Baby Lewis were legend: the outrageous lies he told his wife after stumbling home after a three-day bender, the purity and exuberance of his drumming and his heartbreaking acts of self-sabotage.[29] Compared to their Central Avenue neighbours—the domestic servants, janitors, porters and schoolteachers—musicians led radically different lives, blurring the line between work and pleasure, production and consumption, effort and effortlessness. More than simply crossing race lines and breaking class barriers, they leapt into exotic, strange and dangerous worlds.

Sonny Clay, schooled in Booker T Washington's catechism of deferred gratification, felt conflicted. He watched colleagues like Rudy Wiedoeft drink themselves to death. He knew he should invest his salary in a house. He knew the music business was uncertain. The pace of change bewildered him. 'SC stayed drunk. He was scared stiff,' scribbled John Bentley as he listened back to the bandleader's 1960 interview.

Sonny Clay's life embodied the liminal slippages of Jazz Age America. By the mid-1920s, he had more money and influence than respectable Black citizens felt he deserved; wore sharper suits and mixed with more powerful people than White unions could stomach; and played music with more rhythm than melody, enticing a public to dance with more freedom than grace. This was not racial advancement in the steady, diligent, God-fearing sense of the word, but it was impressive, extravagant and spectacular.

PART II

In California with Harry Muller

6
THE BEST BOX OFFICE JUDGE IN AUSTRALIA

HARRY MULLER LOVED California. He loved the faux-Byzantine excess of his office at the Alcazar Theater in the heart of San Francisco. He loved the streams of Australian actors, musicians and vaudevillians who dropped by bearing tales of adventure on the road to stardom. He was tickled to hear he looked like wartime US president Woodrow Wilson. And he did: the same owlish, wire-framed glasses, same tidy symmetry and ash blond hair—although since arriving in the United States in 1925, too much of the good life had rounded his belly and face.[1]

Mostly, Harry Muller loved his job. As the West Coast theatre agent for the JC Williamson Company, he scoured California's vaudeville theatres and cafes in search of the finest acts to entice across the Pacific and consolidate the Tivoli Theatre's reputation as Australia's leading vaudeville chain. Or as he summed up his job: 'Reviewing shows, interviewing acts and talking Australia'—and he may have added, selling 'America' to cinema and vaudeville audiences back home.[2]

In the 1920s, terms like 'cultural diplomacy' and 'soft power' had no currency but from a contemporary perspective, these skills described much of Harry Muller's job. One entertaining conversation at a time, he dispensed wit and charm to explore common values and compare national quirks and differences to consolidate trade routes, create cultural experiences and acquire technology and know-how. His employer

Harry Muller, the Tivoli Theatre's talent scout based in San Francisco. (*Everyones* magazine, State Library of NSW)

Jack Musgrove was generous in his flattery: Harry Muller was 'one of the best buyers of talent that ever represented Australia abroad ... He's had less failures than any other man ever entrusted with such ticklish work. I don't think he ever picked a dud.'[3] Others called him 'the best box office judge in Australia'.[4]

The reason was simple: Harry Muller loved show business, smitten from the age of eight when a travelling tenor visited his childhood home of Palmerston, New Zealand, and employed him to run errands. As a young man, he was lured away from his respectable career in law by the local vaudeville theatre. He married an actress and flirted with many more.

An apprenticeship with Sydney sporting promoter HD 'Huge Deal' McIntosh taught Harry Muller the value of sheer audacity. In 1908, HD famously bankrolled the prize fight of the century, stumping up the largest purse in boxing history, and shaming Tommy Burns into breaking his 'White only' rule to give Jack Johnson a crack at the heavyweight title. From controversy, HD minted publicity, pitching the fight as a battle for racial supremacy, commanding the attention of the world while pocketing a small fortune.

Harry Muller was too good-natured to match HD's ruthlessness and bombast. After years managing theatres in hard-bitten industrial towns from Dunedin to Port Adelaide, his expertise lay in providing novel and affordable entertainment for working people—and managing notoriously prickly talent.[5] Years of experience instilled in him a faith that the latest happenings in the United States would soon play out on Australia's shores. Just as cigarettes, motorcars and labour-saving gadgets had reshaped Australian suburban life, so gramophones, moving pictures and dance crazes remoulded leisure time.

Once in California, talking American show business to Australian ticket buyers tripped off his tongue. As he wrote in a series of letters to Sydney film magazine *Everyones*, nothing came close to the US behemoth. Its 'vast scale' and 'professionalism' staggered him; its 'splendour and gorgeousness' took his breath away.[6] Think of the logistics of a Ringling Brothers Circus tour, he implored. Each night delivering a show with three rings, two hundred performers, five hundred animals, and thousands of costume changes and props. Then dismantling the big top and transporting it down the road to the next town for the following one-night stand come wildfire, earthquake or auto-crash. It was all dazzling evidence of the 'slick' way Americans stage-managed industrial-scale entertainment.[7]

Harry Muller's hunt for talent often took him and his wife to Los Angeles. The journey alone, in their spanking new Studebaker Six, inspired reverie: 'Concrete roads the whole way,' he thrilled.[8] In Los Angeles, he looked over talent at theatres big and small, before catching up on the latest thing, the market shifts and game-changing technology.

At the opening of Los Angeles' palatial new Orpheum Theatre, he struggled to square the scale of luxury, the ridiculously low admittance price, and the funniest, classiest performers on the planet. (Several were *en route* to the Tivoli, he assured readers.) He dwelled on the dressing-room facilities and state-of-the-art lighting system, delighting in the way a spotlight could direct the audience's attention. It was a 'wonderful demonstration of what brains, taste and money can do'.[9]

A smaller innovation also caught Harry Muller's attention. Fanchon and Marco Productions, a brother and sister dance team who had moved into management, were enjoying remarkable success, rolling out short, low-budget, high-energy stage shows at picture palaces—a format known as an 'idea'. Could this be a way the Tivoli could stave off competition from moving picture houses, he wondered?[10] Either way, 'Australian entrepreneurs will have to wake up and ... do a lot more overseas buying'.[11]

Occasionally, the Mullers pushed beyond Los Angeles for a weekend at the Tijuana racetrack and an overnight pit stop in the hotels and speakeasies of San Diego.[12] 'We had to have a drink, in fact several,' he joked, 'just to prove the country has not gone as dry as some people are led to believe.' But of all the delights of Southern California, nothing beat the motion picture industry. The manager and businessman in Muller was, of course, intrigued by the streamlined production process churning out eight hundred feature-length films a year, and countless two-reelers.[13] 'No description of mine could convey any idea of the magnitude of the operations,' he reported after inspecting several 'big time' studios. But a photograph of himself and Charlie Chaplin, still dressed as the Tramp, best summed up the industry's charms. That, and scores of chorus 'girls' in glittering headdresses and veils, fresh from film sets conjuring the decadence of an ancient and exotic land. 'The glamour in picture work would appeal to any woman with the requisite looks,' he observed, as if to rouse fantasies of celluloid fame in the minds of *Everyones*' young female readers. Muller himself was not immune to the pull, flattered when a producer insisted on screen-testing his wife.

Muller took particular pleasure in relaying the successes enjoyed by Australians in Hollywood and vaudeville. Most famous was the 'fearless mermaid' Annette Kellerman. Up-and-coming starlet Ena Gregory was also 'doing exceptionally well'. 'Miss Australia' had passed through Hollywood en route to the Miss America pageant in Atlantic City, while Sydney sirens the Henry Twins had just snared a 'big part' in Fred Niblo's *Ben-Hur*.[14] They, and a network of actors, comedy directors and orchestra conductors 'were enjoying life in the movie colony immensely'.[15] Muller talked up the close friendship between the United States and Australia. Twenty-five thousand US sailors were just back from a goodwill visit to Sydney and Melbourne, each filled with high praise about their 'wonderful welcome', some longing to return to 'the girls they left behind'.[16]

The highlight of Harry Muller's Hollywood adventures were the 'private entertainments' hosted in his honour, one in the 'beautiful' hill-side home of a studio chief. At this point, Muller's liberal name-dropping retreated to a tight-lipped coyness. 'The talent in that room would have made up a bill that no theatre in any part of the world could present,' he teased, careful not to reveal a single name. Still, he assured *Everyones* readers that several 'big name' actors loved receiving letters from their Australian movie fans. Many told him of their hopes to visit one day.[17]

Perhaps Harry Muller knew a cold logic underpinned the movie folk's attentions. Box office receipts confirmed that Australia was a small but highly lucrative market. Of the 721 moving pictures screened in 1925 in Australia, 676 were made in Hollywood.[18] Per capita attendances were amongst the highest in the world—about eighteen films per person. Statistical averages, however, masked demographic patterns.[19] Two-thirds of cinema audiences were young women hankering for a taste of metropolitan sophistication. Of all the films screened at Sydney's Union Theatre—the westerns, adventure tales and comedies—'jazz stories of the Mae Murray type' drew the 'top attendances'.[20] To maximise the appeal of society dramas, exhibitors targeted publicity campaigns at young women. 'Emphasise the jazz atmosphere. Stage a dance prologue,' advised one trade film exhibition magazine.[21]

Harry Muller's letters, however, did not name all the latest Hollywood trends. For instance, he made no mention whether the music at the elegant showbiz party was supplied by a local 'Negro orchestra'. Or whether the evening ended with a slumming trip to 'Darktown'—although he did muster a few mild digs at the press' fixation with the motion picture industry. 'All I can say about it is that Hollywood is the nearest approach to heaven I ever expect to get to, notwithstanding all the stories we hear about it to the contrary, most of them emanating from folk who know little or nothing about the place.'[22]

Muller was referring to the tabloid media circus whose rise mirrored Hollywood. The same technological advancements powering motion pictures also powered banner headlines and photographs. Covering Hollywood gossip was an industry in itself. Undercover reporters hid in hedges and spied into actors' homes hoping to capture a latter-day Sodom and Gomorrah on the brink of moral collapse. They claimed to witness a decadence that far exceeded the feverish jazz parties of the screen: the scantily clad starlet offering herself in lust, the gaunt 'Negro' peddling dope, the 'ultra-fast set' 'dancing hilariously', and, of course, the cabal of Jewish producers profiting from human degradation.[23] 'Are film stars as wicked in private as gossip would have them? Are the orgies of antiquity being renewed by them here in America today?' teased a magazine published by Hearst newspapers. 'Is Hollywood Babylon reincarnated?'[24]

Harry Muller knew stage folk tended to live in a 'topsy turvy land' complicated by travel and long separations.[25] As social columnists frequently observed, the 'rules' of an 'actor's marriage' already factored divorce.[26] Even so, as far as Muller could see, a person's private life was 'nobody's business but their own'—although he could not deny the political influence of celebrity moral crusaders.[27] Former Republican Postmaster-General William H Hays was pushing for production codes targeting nudity, drug use, sexual perversion, blasphemy, lustful kissing and, consistent with California's anti-miscegenation laws, any 'sex relationships between black and white races'.[28]

But really, Harry Muller had not known a time when someone wasn't fretting about the immorality of show business. As the record showed, he had been quick to slap down prudes and hypocrites—even if she was the wife of the Australian prime minister. When Dame Mary Hughes once took offense to a pantomime Fairy Queen's 'indecent' attire, Harry Muller let it be known the costume was as traditional as the dame's 'fondness for supper beer or a little drop of gin'.[29]

To his mind, the scandalmongers on the pulpit and in the press were cut from the same cloth as his mentor, 'Huge Deal' McIntosh. The American circus world had a word for it: 'ballyhoo'.[30] And a job title. The Ballyhoo Men. They barked outside circus tents peddling nightmares and dreams, projecting people's imagination to an unseen place—somewhere shocking, thrilling, apocalyptic, just beyond the screen, in the up-coming generation, in the not-too-distant future, a phantom almost in reach.

Harry Muller had analysed the process when he reverse-engineered the logistics of the Ringling Brothers Circus. The performance, he noted, began long before the spotlight singled out the ringmaster, when the citizen zeroed in on the newspaper advertisement or poster on a wall.

The ritual unfolded as they purchased the ticket, counted down the days, alighted from the streetcar and walked through a cityscape, into the carnival, down an avenue of ballyhoo men, towards the big top. 'All sorts of grafting lines are placed before you to relieve you of any change that you may happen to possess,' observed Muller. An extra dime to tour the animal menagerie. A quarter to 'peek' inside the sideshow and behold 'freaks, midgets, fat women, skeleton men' and other incomprehensible sights—a sum he gladly paid.[31]

That was what he desired to bring to the Tivoli stage: something rare, unexpected, even forbidden. Muller's job was much more than talking 'Australia' to Americans, it was talking ballyhoo to a leisure industry audience back home.

7

THE REAL CHARLESTON

Harry Muller was a link in a global supply chain, sourcing and supplying entertainment for Australian audiences. It was a peculiar game. At its coldest, entertainment was an exercise in parking people in seats, a diversion for them to fill empty leisure hours. At its most sentimental, show business put smiles on people's faces, brought tears to their eyes and put wonder in their hearts—an emotional intensity that minted fond memories, an episode in the story of their lives. At its most lofty, entertainment was a form of knowledge: about the world, about fashion, about social and symbolic meaning. Harry Muller's place in this game was constrained by more pedestrian concerns. He dealt with talent—human beings who boarded ships and had needs and foibles that demanded his attention.

When Harry Muller first arrived in San Francisco, he was confident he had a formula to land some of America's biggest names, but as the months, then years, wore on, Muller realised that this was not to be.

Each week, he surveyed an impressive sweep of vaudeville talent and every week he invited a selection to undertake the twenty-day boat trip across the Pacific and grace the Tivoli stage. To his mind, the advantages were overwhelming. US entertainers practically lived in the theatre playing three shows a day, seven days a week. But with only two shows a day, six days a week on 'Australia-time'—to use the showman's parlance—performers had time for recreation and friendships outside the theatre. Sure, he was unable to 'consider salaries on an American basis', but here was a chance to see the world. Why, wrapped up his spiel, it was almost a vacation.[1]

Every week, almost every act turned him down. American vaudevillians, accustomed to the Orpheum's dressing rooms, sniffed at the Tivoli's concept of luxury—and the substantial cut in salary. 'Getting down to the meat of things, let us assure you that it is no easy matter getting these fellows here to see what an attractive proposition Australia time really is,' he grumbled to *Everyones* magazine. 'I get real tired of having to explain what the trip really means. A really good second to closing act wants so much money that it is a heartbreaking job to talk to them.'[2]

Granted, Harry Muller had persuaded a few: monkey act Max and Moritz, frog contortionists The Darlings, cowboy crooner Oklahoma Bob Albright, and Chinese comedian Ben Nee One. He came close to snaring a dancing horse and 'Pawnee Indian girl' routine but walked away, unable to meet the ever-spiralling demands (the horse's specially built stall on the ship proved the deal-breaker). Still, Harry Muller dreamed of securing a dazzling headline act: a money-making novelty remembered for its fun, fashion and innovation. Much to his annoyance, the Tivoli agent based in Chicago beat him to the punch.

'The whole country appears to be worked up to the padded cell stage over the latest ballroom calisthenics known as the Charleston dance,' Bob Conkey informed his Tivoli employers in December 1925.[3] Unlike the Foxtrot craze of the 1910s, this dance made no pretensions to balance or grace. Angular, elbowed, pigeon-toed, dancers stomped and swivelled with such free-form intensity that experts predicted the decline of the White race. It was the fastest, wildest, most exhilarating dance ever to grip the nation.

Bob Conkey made no pretence about his dislike for jazz music and dance but he could not deny it was 'very much in the good graces of Mr and Mrs Vaudeville Audience'. Lines outside the Chicago Theatre were three abreast as Syncopation Week broke all records. Across the country, picture houses and vaudeville theatres held Charleston dance contests in their thousands. The three big vaudeville chains contracted the winners, shelling out eye-watering salaries.

As White Americans vaguely understood, the national 'affliction' was somehow 'Negro' in origin, possibly linked to a dance hall in Charleston, South Carolina.[4] Black entertainers knew it as 'a real old Southern dance', a modified cotillion step set to a distinct two-beat rhythm; different versions had been doing the rounds on the Black variety stage for decades.[5] But only in 1925 were these steps compared to madness, epidemics and medieval dance manias, blamed for murders, divorces and structural damage to buildings. 'Charleston mania' fell on towns 'like an insidious plague'. 'Symptoms' compared to 'epilepsy' or the 'delirium tremors'. 'Shaky' 'vibrations' disturbed bricks and mortar.[6] But behind the febrile metaphors was a commodity and a supply chain, developed by Black eccentric dancers, packaged by Broadway and Hollywood producers and disseminated by radio and cinema.

As Willie Covan later told it, in 1923 he was the choreographer of *Runnin' Wild*, one of the all-Black Broadway revues rewriting the rules of musical comedy. One day on the streets of Harlem, we stumbled upon three sparkling young performers dancing for nickels. To ward off competition, he snapped up the team and reworked their dance sequence for his female chorus line. 'The kids only had that first little step and a sort of Camel Walk, so we added an Airplane and a slide,' he recalled, naming the dance 'Charleston', the nickname of one of the 'kids'.[7] Stride piano master James P Johnson completed the routine composing a tune grounded in the syncopated two-note motif so beloved by the Gullah longshoremen he once entertained in the basement sweatboxes of Hell's Kitchen.[8] Cecil Mack's lyrics reconfigured an old routine as new:

> Buck dance, wing dance, will be a back number,
> But the Charleston, the new Charleston.
> That dance is surely a comer!

The moment the chorus dancers hot-stepped onto Broadway's New Colonial Theatre, the Charleston generated a 'wow'.[9] White choreographers seized on it, replicating every kick and twist. Vocalion Records plugged a recording of Johnson's showtune in the New York dailies—'If you Fox-Trot, Get This!'—while Tin Pan Alley tunesmiths milked every Charleston theme.[10] Picture houses delivered the most powerful jolt—and demonstrated the reach of the new medium. From Hollywood's film lots to the world came silent moving images of sassy Charleston-hoofing starlets. A cautionary tale about the dangers of abundant pleasure usually excited at least one Charleston scene, often a wild party in a grand Park Avenue residence, of course with a 'Negro orchestra'.

In early 1926 the celluloid Charleston debuted on Australia cinema screens.[11] Colleen Moore in *We Moderns* consolidated her standing as the quintessential flapper while *Sally, Irene and Mary* followed three aspiring chorus dancers hoofing and side-kicking through a pleasure-mad world.[12] For the factory girl and small-town initiate who yearned to follow in their footsteps, dance lessons were no further away than the instructional two-reeler, *Learn the Charleston in Six Lessons,* at their local picture house. It was the surprise earner of the year, reported exhibitors.[13] The Charleston craze also highlighted the limits of moving pictures. The images were silent, the soundtrack supplied by in-house musicians that ranged from a thirty-piece orchestra to a clapped-out pianola.

Tivoli agent Bob Conkey had found a vaudeville stage act to outmatch the cinematic allure: Joe Sheftell's Southern Revue, an all-Black show that featured the 'real Negro Charleston' as performed by 'the originators of the dance'. In a Charleston-saturated marketplace, Conkey had hit on a unique selling point, something never seen in Hollywood film. Implicitly, and likely unintentionally, he pitted the White face of the celluloid Charleston as a pale imitation to advance an alternate view of modernity and Blackness.

Certainly, Joe Sheftell understood the political implications of his revue—and wove these conditions into the contract. In Black American show business circles, Sheftell was known as an outspoken 'race man' who was 'not afraid to air his views before anyone, no matter what his creed or color'.[14] He and his wife, mezzo-soprano Minto Cato, had played cabarets from Tijuana to Paris and strongly identified with the Harlem Renaissance mission to cast off denigrating minstrel clichés and reframe the representational language that conveyed Black life.[15] The publicity campaign, they stipulated, was to state clearly the Southern Revue was 'not a minstrel show'. There would be no hammy routines about the Shuffling Darkey and Happy Slave but instead traditional songs, modern dances and 'genuine Negro stars'. Artwork presented sopranos in ballgowns and ballet

Joe Sheftell's Southern Revue brought the 'real' Charleston to Australia in July 1926. (*Sun*, State Library of NSW)

choruses in tutus.[16] For Sheftell and Cato, blackfaced minstrelsy was the counterfeit, an ersatz of Black culture: its true source lay elsewhere.

Joe Sheftell's mostly female troupe arrived in Australia in July of 1926 for a four-city tour. Whether it was the quality of their showmanship ('each and every performer is a top-notcher'), their assault on the senses ('a riot of whirling legs, clapping hands and syncopated rhythm') or the cultural insularity of the audience ('the whole thing is exotic and bizarre'), the show was a runaway success.[17] In Sydney, Melbourne, Brisbane and Adelaide, the chorus line's fancy footwork, the comedian's snappy wit, the cast's infectious enthusiasm, to say nothing of the showgirls' achingly modern costumes—a parade of feathered and sequined gowns, geometrically patterned soldier suits and plenty of female leg—were met with rapturous and tumultuous applause. 'These performers cram more genuine work into their thirty-minute tenure on stage than any other act within knowledge,' waxed one reviewer.[18] Another called them 'one of the most important acts that has ever come to this theatre'.[19]

Just how the Southern Revue was 'important', the reviewer never explained—possibly alluding to a transmission of cultural knowledge and symbolic meaning. Exposure to the troupe, for instance, enlarged the musical vocabulary of the Tivoli's Sydney orchestra.

As Minto Cato reported, she worked closely with Tivoli conductor Will Quintrell on the arrangements of the spiritual 'I Couldn't Hear Nobody Pray', orchestrating a response to represent the chorus. The effect, she wrote, was 'simply beautiful' and gave Quintrell 'a better idea of the real original rhythm' enabling him to convey the 'sorrow and sadness' of the traditional songs just 'as they were really meant by our forefathers, who created and originated them'.[20]

One dance routine plotting 'the evolution of modern ballroom dances' also offered a factually imperfect history lesson that shed light on contemporary culture.[21] In marked contrast to the minstrel show that situated Black folk in an eternal cotton plantation, this sequence followed an evolutionary progression from the African Jungle to the American Metropolis, a melange of buck and wing, cakewalks, foxtrots, shimmies and Charlestons. In doing so, they told the story of the 'Negro's progress' through a great 'chain of rhythm' linking African beats to George Gershwin's 'Rhapsody in Blue'.[22] By connecting the 'primitive' to the 'modern'—or even asserting the 'primitive' *as* 'modern'—they claimed Black America's rightful place in a decade defined by jazz.

The Southern Revue's political message, however, bypassed a group of Sydney reporters, who were more puzzled by the dancers' 'ivory' complexions. If Blackness was a mark of primitiveness and Whiteness was a badge of civilisation, why did these women not choose to pass? Why would anyone needlessly carry the curse of Blackness? Such questions gave Joe Sheftell the opportunity to educate the press. Firstly, on how 'proud' the entire troupe were 'to be classed as Negroes' before moving on to the 'achievements of Negroes in all professions'.[23] While some pressmen directed racist snipes at the revue, at no point did they receive Sheftell's lecture on Black progress as a threat to White Australia, the 'dusky beauty' of the dancers softening the force of their cultural diplomacy.[24]

Not to be outdone, in August 1926, Harry Muller matched Bob Conkey's triumph. For the princely sum of £1000 per week, he secured the Henry Santrey Syncopated Orchestra, a forty-piece all-White orchestra that, from a distance, resembled the Paul Whiteman Orchestra, the most celebrated jazz band in the world.[25] 'Believe me, it took some work,'

Harry Muller told *Everyones* magazine. The Tivoli went so far as to declare them 'second only to the great Paul Whiteman', while Santrey upped the hyperbole on his arrival by claiming to have 'originated the first jazz band in New York eight years ago'.[26] In fact, Santrey was no originator but an opera-trained tenor, although Australian pressmen never questioned his credentials, eagerly asking him about the 'meaning of jazz'.[27]

Henry Santrey's origin story refuted Minto Cato's claim of cultural authenticity. The 'Negro' originators, he explained, played a 'cheap', 'sugared', 'extremely common' sound in 'slum saloons and dance halls'. Whereas he preferred the label 'symphonic syncopation' emphasising melody over 'noise', the nutritional equivalent of 'musical roast beef'. To play the 'jazzed up' classics, he conceded to occasionally break the rules of harmony, garnishing the cascading strings with note-bending brassy wails, but this 'sacrilege' was done in the spirit of modernity.[28]

Santrey was citing an influential school of jazz criticism that attempted to reconcile working-class popular entertainment with a progressive mission to enlighten the masses. One sought relaxation, the other education. In this formulation, a homeopathic dose of 'primitive' vitality was enough to re-energise the 'sterile intellectual products' of European music and create a uniquely American idiom, without undermining the harmonic principles of the dominant culture. 'Negro' ragtime, blues and jazz were mere gestation periods, a prelude to an opening act dominated by White artists—an elastic category that on this occasion included Jewish composers.[29]

Certainly, Santrey's music swung well enough to satisfy Australian lovers of modern music. At the Cinderella Midnight Revel, dancers had a chance to Foxtrot, even Charleston, to his big band orchestra. Gayne Dexter of *Everyones* 'vastly' enjoyed the evening but was 'now like Oliver Twist—asking for more'.[30]

The Tivoli's professional reputation hinged on granting audiences their wishes. Harry Muller and Bob Conkey had supplied two jazzy hits that generated money, created personal memories and deepened cultural engagement. But the cold economic truth of the Tivoli's bottom line told a different story: shilling for shilling, the Southern Revue was just as popular but far more profitable than Henry Santrey's Syncopated Orchestra. A paying audience was hungry for jazz music and dance, no matter if it was 'sugared' or 'roast beef', if the performers were Black or White.

The revelation solved Harry Muller's American conundrum. The economic logic that made 'Australia-time' so unappealing to White vaudevillians did not apply to Black musicians and entertainers who worked longer hours for less money and enjoyed fewer opportunities. With a Black revue, Harry Muller could secure an up-to-the-minute, quality act, prepared to undertake the long journey across the Pacific. In mid-1927, he began to piece together a revue drawn from the best Black talent Los Angeles had to offer.

8
TESTING THE WATERS

On 5 January 1928, Harry Muller and seventeen of the twenty-one members of the revue known as Sonny Clay's Colored Idea boarded the steamer *Sierra* in San Francisco. A *Chicago Defender* columnist wondered if his friends were 'seasick by now', a less-than-subtle reference to their alcohol-fuelled farewell party the previous night.[1] It was the beginning of what was expected to be a pioneering show: the Sonny Clay Orchestra would be the first Black jazz band to tour Australia—and one with impeccable musical credentials, beloved by Hollywood luminaries, college students and sailors alike. The musicians bristled with modern heat, the quintessence of the 'Negro Vogue'. If Harry Muller was the box office judge he believed he was, Sydney and Melbourne vaudeville audiences were in for a spectacular treat.

Harry Muller had pieced together a revue of outstanding talent. Granted, it bore more than a passing resemblance to the Hi Brown Idea, a Fanchon and Marco production staged at Loew's lavish State Theater in April 1927, both in form and content.[2] The 'idea' format promised a short sharp burst of live entertainment, usually before the celluloid feature. It mostly featured young talent prepared to work cheap—although the Hi Brown Idea were hardly show business rookies but, as the *Los Angeles Times* noted, some of the 'hottest' 'names to conjure with in Darktown theatrical circles'.[3] In other words, Central Avenue veterans with limited access to mainstream audiences: multi-talented Ivy Anderson and eccentric dancer Angelus 'Babe' Henderson—who were both aboard the *Sierra* (although two days into the journey, an injury forced Henderson to leave the troupe).

The Colored Idea also bore traces of Joe Sheftell's High Brown Revue at the Plantation Café. The floorshow was essentially the same routine seen in Australia the previous year (plus a few hula and South Sea Island numbers), although in keeping with the times, comedian and dancer Dick Saunders, who had wowed Sydney and Melbourne audiences with his rapid-fire Charleston, now offered a rapid-fire Black Bottom, the latest dance craze. Driving the High Brown Revue's spirituals, shakes and shimmies was a band with a deep appreciation of the Black Southern vernacular: the Sonny Clay Orchestra. In June 1927, they had returned to the Plantation for another extended residency.[4]

Several figures in this line-up would travel with Harry Muller to Australia: Dick Saunders as the Master of Ceremonies, and most of the Sonny Clay Orchestra—although until the moment of departure,

The multi-talented Ivy Anderson (later known as Ivie Anderson), a headline act in the cabarets of Central Avenue. (Mills Artists Inc.)

the line-up was in play. Trumpeter Nini Coycault's place was assured, as were several members of Mosby's Blues Blowers.

For a week in July 1927, a whirlwind dance act known as The Four Covans headlined the vaudeville bill at Los Angeles' Pantages Theater.[5] Led by Broadway veteran Willie Covan (who choreographed the street dance act that sparked the Charleston craze) and supported by his wife Florence, brother Dewey and seventeen-year-old Elmer Turner (who for publicity reasons was presented as Dewey's wife), the dance team had perfected a 'breathtaking' style of tap dance that drew on Arabian acrobats, Russian kazatskys, classical ballet 'plus a double Around The World, no hands'. As one colleague recalled, The Four Covans were 'headliners in any league and Willie was the star', a leading interpreter of Black modern dance, taught by fabled masters of the buck and wing.[6] They too were aboard the *Sierra*.[7]

In Perth, on Australia's west coast, the four members of the Emperors of Harmony prepared for their long land journey across to Sydney to join the Colored Idea. Led by William Hann, a veteran of the Methodist Church's Chautauqua circuit and several Broadway shows, the quartet specialised in hymns, sentimental ballads, Appalachian yodels, and syncopated ditties that were popular before the Great War.[8] From Townsville to Perth, they had won praise for their 'meticulous harmonizing' and 'voices of gold'.[9] In a buoyant mood, second tenor Eddie Caldwell penned a letter to the *Chicago Defender*:

> Great things are expected of this revue and should it work out as expected it will mean a new field for all artists of the Race who have talent. We are all proud of the esteem in which the Race artists are held in Australia and all who have been here have evidently striven to maintain a high standard.[10]

Caldwell's experience was consistent with other Black visitors to Australia. Performers left for a 'shadowy continent' largely known for its boomerangs, kangaroos and White Australia policy that placed a 'bar' on 'all kinds of coloured folk'. Yet to the puzzlement of many, once inside the country, they 'found absolutely no such thing as prejudice'. Or 'if there is any we have not yet come into contact with it', as members of the

Royal Southern Singers reported in 1923.[11] On railroad carriages, and in hotels and eating establishments, local White folk happily shared spaces with Black Americans and West Indians—a privilege seldom extended to Chinese and Indigenous folk. Like most Australians, Harry Muller probably shrugged when asked to explain why one racial group was exempted, and others not. It had always been like that.

And it was. Though numerically tiny, Black Americans and West Indians had been part of the grand narrative of Australia's colonisation. At least eleven members of the African diaspora arrived as convicts on the First Fleet. John Moseley, for instance, had been enslaved in Virginia, until siding with the British during the American Revolutionary War. He then fled to London where he eked out an impoverished existence until transported to Botany Bay.[12] In 1854, New Yorker John Joseph, a veteran of the California goldfields, was one of thirteen diggers tried for high treason for leading the famed rebellion at the Eureka Stockade.[13] National mythmakers cast Black Americans as Westerners, in contra-distinction to Easterners, the differences measured less in skin colour and more in clothes, food, language and religion.

A few African Americans settled in Australia. Many more visited as athletes, entertainers and merchant seamen, and later, as soldiers. In 1877, twelve years after the Civil War, the brilliant theatrical entrepreneur Charles Hicks brought the Georgia Minstrels to Sydney. Expecting to face discrimination and scorn, they met critical acclaim and commercial success.[14] Several performers remained. Irving Sales and Charlie Pope were much-loved fixtures of the Tivoli, while the 'brilliant' Hosea Easton—'without exception, the best banjoist Australia has seen'—taught the locals a thing or two about finger picking, bedding a sound that percolated through to Australian folk and bush music.[15]

In the 1880s, an iteration of the Fisk Jubilee Singers travelled the length and breadth of the country, their choral arrangements of the sacred freedom songs stirring outpourings of White sympathy for enslaved Christians in faraway lands.[16] At an Aboriginal mission on the Murray River, the Fisk's songs induced 'ecstatic delight' in the listeners. 'They seem to recognize us as brethren from a far distant tribe,' reported the choirmaster.[17] For decades after, Maloga Mission's Aboriginal preachers sang these sacred hymns.[18]

One Fisk chorister remained in Australia. Orpheus McAdoo was born into slavery in North Carolina and, by sheer grit and tenacity, graduated from Hampton College. In Sydney he established a touring company that introduced a procession of cakewalkers, ragtimers, brass bands, humorists, eccentric dancers and physical comedians to Australian and New Zealand audiences.[19] 'Mr McAdoo has a great reputation in this country ... the people over here talk about him just as we do of Fred Douglass,' reported one trombone player.[20]

The number of Black entertainers in Sydney reached its zenith in 1899, when a rival company landed with an impressive array of talent from Chicago and Missouri, including ragtimer Ernest Hogan, comedian Billy McClain and soprano Flora Batson.[21] 'There is no color line to fight. You are known for what you are,' read the bandleader's letter to the Black press.[22]

The sum of these experiences led historian Richard Waterhouse to conclude that Australians accorded Black Americans a 'special place' that set them apart from other non-Whites.[23] Even with the implementation of the White Australia policy in 1901, once inside the country, no Jim Crow laws restricted their choice of residence. Nor did any anti-miscegenation laws limit their choice of spouse. Still, a complex set of caveats and social protocols set limits on their freedoms—particularly in their relations with White women. The experiences of boxer Peter Jackson in the 1880s and Jack Johnson two decades later are illustrative.[24]

In 1886, Caribbean-born Peter Jackson was the undefeated heavyweight champion of Australia. Despite fame, wealth and extraordinary athleticism, he elected not to marry, breaking with a White woman he loved, thereby maintaining his professional reputation as a 'gentleman'.[25] Jack Johnson, in contrast, sought no such approval, although his bid to shame heavyweight champion Tommy Burns into breaking his 'White only' rule won considerable popular support. As one sports paper declared, no athlete should draw the colour line because 'it wasn't an Australian's or Britisher's game to run away from a rival'.[26]

The mingling of interracial sweat in the ring did not extend to Johnson's personal life—or at least, the personal life of his sweetheart, a young White Sydney pianist named Lola Toy who became an object of abuse and public ridicule.[27] Johnson's reputation survived untarnished, especially when sporting promoter 'Huge Deal' McIntosh staged the greatest sporting event in Australian history. After a short-lived burst of hostility, crowds cheered him from Sydney to Kalgoorlie. Brass bands greeted him with 'See, the Conquering Hero Comes'.[28]

Twenty years later, Harmony King Eddie Caldwell noted the public continued to venerate Black sporting champs. Since 1926, at least five Black American boxers worked the local circuit. When 'Tiger' Payne trounced a South African prize fighter, the press hailed him the 'undisputed champion of Australia'.[29]

Over their three-week Pacific crossing, Harry Muller likely relived some of these fables with Sonny Clay. Certainly, the two could swap tales about their brushes and near-brushes with Jack Johnson: Clay in Tijuana, Muller in the shadow of HD McIntosh. Muller was an 'entertaining raconteur' with an 'innumerable store of anecdotes' about actors and performers and, as Honolulu slipped from view, Sonny Clay had every reason to be swayed by his optimism. The bandleader was a race pioneer on the high seas of adventure, delivering a new American idea to Australia.[30]

Harry Muller, however, surely knew they were merely testing the waters. As was his habit, he presented a selective precis of Australian trends, electing *not* to tell Sonny Clay how the accolades and adoration masked the wheels of bureaucracy. But as he well knew, the arrival of every Black American generated a flurry of memorandums, telegrams and letters that clarified their status and tracked their movements.[31]

Nor did Muller chronicle the ways the racial rhetoric had hardened under the leadership of Prime Minister William Morris Hughes, then broadened under his successor, Stanley Bruce, who welcomed small numbers of Southern and Eastern European migrants.

He did not concern Sonny Clay with administrative details: explain the care taken by the Tivoli management when filling out the jazz band's visa applications, alert to the jurisdictional implications of each term. To do so would unpick a tangle of factional alliances that bonded *some* politicians to *some* union leaders over *some* policy objectives. The consequences of these power games played out in the negative:

for every story of a successful Black American tour was another that didn't happen.

In 1923, for instance, Melbourne hotelier Tom Carlyon of St Kilda's Carlyon Hotel appointed his eldest son to travel to the United States and assemble a troupe of Black musicians, singers, dancers and comedians. Once arranged, Carlyon submitted the visa applications to Senator George Pearce, minister for home and territories. The official response can be found in the Immigration Branch's *Book of Precedents*: 'American Negroes—proposed introduction band for Carlyon's Dancing Palais—refused.'[32]

The same year, Sydney dance promoter JC Bendrodt of the Palais de Danse underwrote a production of similar scope and ambitions. He was confident that a Black floorshow and dance orchestra would introduce the 'latest American ideas' and enable Australian dance musicians to benefit from their 'excellence'.[33] Again, the department refused, citing the Carlyon precedent.[34]

Around this time, Sonny Clay's pal Ragtime Billy Tucker announced he was taking his stage show, The Strutters Drag, to Australia. He reached no further than Hawaii.[35] In 1926, the Black press reported a Central Avenue band, the Ferris Family Jazzland Revue, were about to tour Australia and New Zealand.[36] Again, these plans came to nothing.

A pattern was emerging. Comedians, jubilee singers and dance troupes toured Australia but not dance band musicians.

JC Bendrodt was a businessman with political connections and appealed the ruling, accusing the minister of unfair practices: Black entertainers routinely performed on the vaudeville circuit, so why prohibit them from dance halls, he asked.[37] 'Protests from local unions' was the departmental response.[38] And protest they would.

In the wake of Tom Carlyon's application, the Musicians' Union of Australia had ratified a rule to 'prohibit the admission of colored races as members'—a policy robustly defended by Senator Pearce. 'There is no need to worry about colored musicians. We will not admit them,' he announced in late 1924, amid rumours that yet another Melbourne *palais* planned to import a Black orchestra. Pearce, however, posed no objections to visiting White American orchestras. Music was 'international', he approved, and such visits would help 'raise the local standard'.[39]

In mid-1926, Senator George Pearce resigned from politics, replaced by Senator Sir Neville Howse, a patrician war hero ideologically undisposed to the union cause. His position on 'colored musicians' was unclear. Certainly, he supported a Southern European immigration program to populate Australia's 'empty' north and critics thought him soft on White Australia.[40]

In late 1927, Harry Muller again tested the precedents, seeking eighteen visas for the Colored Idea. On the face of it, the union ban on 'colored musicians' posed no problems to a variety theatre stage act who fell outside the jurisdiction of the Musicians' Union.[41] Nonetheless, the Tivoli management took no chances.[42] Nowhere did the paperwork mention 'musicians', preferring the term 'colored theatrical artists'. That December, Howse issued fifteen exemption certificates without comment. In early January, after a last-minute line-up change, he granted three additional certificates.[43]

Harry Muller chose not to share these messy details with Sonny Clay. As far as the bandleader knew, the White Australia policy had not hindered his colleagues, and should not hinder him. After all, he had no plans to immigrate, only to do business, 'play music and make a little money'.[44]

Three days out from landfall, Sonny Clay subsequently brushed off a ship officer who alerted him to a message tapped through to the wireless cabin. 'Something was being saved up' for the troupe. Clay laughed it off. What could possibly go wrong?[45]

The clues lay in Harry Muller's address to the press corps at Sydney docks. 'The real thing in jazz is peculiar to the Negro,' he announced.

> I waited until I thought the time had come to let Australians confirm my judgement in this respect. I had heard Sonny Clay's Plantation Band through the air, piano rolls and gramophone selections. Then I found myself dancing to his band at Rose Room Ballroom. Finally, I witnessed a performance at the Orpheum Theater in Los Angeles. Australia it was for them—from that moment![46]

Muller chose his words carefully, falsifying some points, emphasising others. Sonny Clay's orchestra had certainly created a 'sensation' at the

Rose Room in September 1927.[47] And in December, they played Los Angeles' plush New Orpheum Theater.[48] But according to an announcement in the *Chicago Defender*, Muller contracted the band five weeks before this show.[49]

For a man preoccupied with the latest American trends, there were several points of contact Harry Muller neglected to raise. He had known of Sonny Clay since their breakthrough Radio Balls in 1925 yet made no mention of Clay's weekly gigs in the clubs and dance academies of Central Avenue. He claimed to know the 'real thing in jazz' yet did not expound upon the vibrant music culture along the strip. He name-dropped the 'very fashionable' 'Plantation Days cabaret' which was 'extremely popular with movie stars' but remained silent on the 'very fashionable' midnight slumming adventures into 'the colored belt'.[50]

Instead, Muller distanced himself from the racially ambiguous world of Jazz Age Los Angeles. By neglecting to mention the 'Negro vogue', Muller conjured a disembodied troupe, wafting into the White entertainment world and vanishing again. This, he implied, would be Australia's experience of the 'real thing in jazz': a show that was Black enough to deliver an 'authentic' experience of 'real jazz' but brief enough to prevent a new wave of Black entertainers from reconfiguring the cultural landscape.

Harry Muller also drew another line, meaningful only to government bureaucrats and the Musicians' Union executive. He first heard Sonny Clay on phonograph, then danced to them at the Rose Room, but did not have his epiphany that 'Australia was for them' until he watched them while seated in a vaudeville theatre. In that moment he knew that the 'time had come': he had found a way to circumvent the union's prohibition on Black musicians.[51] In another time and place—a dance hall, for instance—the moment was not yet ripe.

PART III

Rattlin' Fine Sydney

9

MY BLUE HEAVEN

MODERNISM RENEGOTIATED TRADITIONAL relationships. Cubist cityscapes dispensed with foregrounds and backgrounds to relay a kaleidoscope of sensations. Electromagnetic radio waves dissolved matter into energy and back again. Unconscious forces remapped the mind. And jazz soloists charted new territory beyond the diatonic and chromatic scale. It was a proposition welcomed by a sizable= chunk of Sydneysiders, keen to see, taste and hear the shock of the new. The arrival of Sonny Clay's Colored Idea promised to break the bonds of tradition.

For weeks, the publicity department at Sydney's Tivoli Theatre had been ballyhooing the 'Idea' as a 'special kind' of stage format 'hitherto unknown in Australia'. It was compact and efficient and, of course, 'all the rage in America' and had taken 'London and Paris by storm'. Those who experienced it would be 'initiate[d]' into 'an entirely modern creation'.[1]

For Gayne Dexter, the Tivoli's emphasis on form over content seemed academic to the point of hair-splitting. He yearned to hear the slurs and shakes of what promised to be 'America's best negro jazz band' and as the editor of film industry magazine *Everyones*, was at Sydney Circular Quay on that January day, ready to greet the visitors. Based on the quarter page advertisements run by the Tivoli in all the daily newspapers, he expected Sonny Clay to be a stout middle-aged man with a genial, fatherly warmth, so was stunned to see a long, skinny, wide-eyed kid descend the gangway.[2]

Gayne Dexter, screenwriter, film producer and the outspoken editor of *Everyones* magazine. (*Table Talk*, State Library of NSW)

The Tivoli initially portrayed Sonny Clay as a mature, genial bandleader. (*Daily Telegraph*, State Library of NSW)

The bandleader was eight years younger than Gayne Dexter, but even in his sharp bespoke suit, he looked much younger. 'Sonny Clay strikes the observer by his youth,' noted Dexter, wondering if this man-child was all that was promised—although once they began chatting, he recognised a kindred spirit.[3]

Like Clay, Dexter was a busy man, editing a weekly magazine while promoting a film, *The Romance of Runnibede*—a story he had adapted for the screen and produced, securing American finance and landing a 'real' Hollywood star, Eva Novak. So Dexter appreciated the complexity of Clay's job; it was no small task for a bandleader to 'keep his orchestra together and manage his own business', he wrote. Clay, for his part, understood the intricacies of the film industry, plus had the inside scoop on intriguing Hollywood gossip. They were two ambitious young men, charged with the possibilities of the modern world and taxed by the challenges of leadership. Their mutual respect soon translated into friendship—and a run of happy days at the racetrack. As Clay quickly discovered, Dexter was the son of Sydney's number one tipster and knew all the jockeys and trainers.[4]

Of all Sydney's entertainment writers, Gayne Dexter was most alert to the cultural significance of Sonny Clay's Plantation Band. He understood the descriptor 'Plantation' spoke less to an idealised antebellum South and more to Los Angeles' premiere 'Harlem nightclub' so beloved by movie stars. His article that week about the Colored Idea's arrival imagined the SS *Sierra* as a 'Jazz Ship', electrified with rhythm, bearing the mysteries and exoticism of a new brand of jazz and blues. Hot beats, not cold formats, propelled modern culture.[5]

A devotee of Hollywood motion pictures, Dexter had seen scores of crackling good society dramas given the modern treatment with a 'Negro jazz band'.[6] Most recent was Ernst Lubitsch's *So This Is Paris,* which, he was delighted to report, had escaped the snip of New South Wales' film censor. 'One of the "birds" you did not get,' he chuffed.[7] Instead film-going audiences from Sydney to Broken Hill could behold a 'glittering panorama of Parisian life'. In the famed artist's ball scene, an eight-piece Black jazz orchestra presided over a Dada-inspired primitivist pageant, as five hundred White revellers (all winners of Californian Charleston contests) gyrated and thrummed to a silent beat. At one point, a wheeling kaleidoscopic camera trick captured the dancers' altered states of perception as their physical boundaries began to blur, a cubist entanglement of pulsing White limbs, strumming banjo and bleating saxophones. 'Grandpa would throw away his crutches, to see these quick-steppers doing the latest to Solomon's negro jazz orchestra,' read country town reviews.[8] The picture house orchestra or, more likely, the local pianist or piano roll struggled to match the jazz frenzy on screen. With the Sonny Clay Orchestra in town, Gayne Dexter could finally hear jazz music as 'interpreted by the originators' and perchance be moved to such heights.[9]

Dexter's curiosity about this avant-garde brand of European and American Modernism was shared by thousands of Sydneysiders.

In Rowe Street in downtown Wynyard, husband and wife team Duncan and Augusta MacDougall aspired to create a bohemian artist quarter like New York's Greenwich Village where they had lived in the 1910s, when 'Negro' ragtime had unleashed the Turkey Trot dance craze, and the 'new woman' advanced 'alternative views of marriage'. From an attic theatre, the MacDougalls staged experimental dramas that wove the politics of race into the crisis of existence. Eugene O'Neill's *The Emperor Jones* and *The Hairy Ape* were favourites. 'Strangers' were invited to readings held each Sunday night.[10]

In The Rocks, a circle of painters gathered at the Julian Ashton Art School to learn from teachers who had studied the hard lines, geometric shapes and dissecting planes of Vorticism and Cubism in London and Paris. The paintings of Sydney's Modernists rarely vanished into a jigsaw of abstractions, although the flat geometry of Margaret Preston's teacups and flapper portrait, and Grace Cossington Smith's meditations on the Sydney Harbour Bridge set them apart from the pastoral nostalgia of Australian landscape painters.[11]

One of these art students, 22-year-old Dore Hawthorne split her time between designing patterns in an embroidery factory and editing *Undergrowth*, a magazine of 'Youth and Ideals' as shaped by European avant-garde Modernism. She and co-editor Nancy Hall translated lectures by Paris Cubists about liberating art from beauty and literality to uncover a subjective 'primitive intensity' and see 'truth' as 'it really is'. They sensed 'a time poignant with possibility'. Their hearts were 'full of yearning'. They felt part of a 'global movement' that was 'creating the spirit of our own times'.[12]

If these artists were, somehow, unaware of European Modernism's debt to the unknown and unnamed sculptors and wood carvers from Dahomey and the Congo, they certainly attended, even organised, Sydney's annual artists' balls. These famed bacchanals took their primitivist cues from artist masquerade balls staged in Paris and London—and more recently Hollywood's film lots.[13]

Less easy to discern in historical records, although clearly visible on city streets and beach promenades, were the working-class lads who knew little about Cubism but much about the cut of their trousers and slick of their hair. Crime reports detailed their 'eccentric' fashion choices: blue pencil stripe jazz coats, padded around the shoulders and snug around the hips, matched with grey 'Oxford bag' trousers with 22-inch cuffs, the look often finished with a light tweed cap.[14]

Most weekends in Bondi, nineteen-year-old Jim Russell was amongst the crowd who took 'their dance seriously', ready to master the latest modern American steps and dazzle in competitions at the Palais Royale. After the 'frenzied flame' of the Charleston, Russell awaited the next 'new joy-dance'. He transcended the many facets of Modernist Sydney: a working-class kid from Coogee with a passion for boxing and dance and a flair for drawing, he worked as an illustrator alongside Gayne Dexter and organised the Black and White Arts Club's annual balls.[15]

On the afternoon of Saturday, 21 January 1928, and twice daily, bar Sunday, for the following four weeks, Gayne Dexter, Jim Russell and thousands of Sydneysiders travelled to the Tivoli's flagship theatre in the Haymarket district to hear the 'real thing' in jazz.[16] Some came to sample the cosmopolitan delights of 'slumming', albeit Tivoli style: a sober and seated version of the 'Harlem nightclubs' of Paris, New York and Los Angeles. Others came to study style and technique or fathom the relationship between modern art's departure from objective representation and modern music's departure from formal melody. Despite the 'sweltering' heat, the theatre was 'jammed', the 'enthusiastic crowd' ready for an experience that might match, even exceed, all fantasies and expectations.[17]

The curtain rose on a brightly coloured set with master of ceremonies Dick Saunders serving as 'major-domo, guide, philosopher, and friend', to quote one approving review, although some in the audience struggled to catch his rapid-fire American patter as he welcomed Sonny Clay's Plantation Orchestra onto the stage. For the next hour, the ten-piece band 'reigned supreme', interspersing each speciality act with two or three numbers. They played hot jazz pieces never heard before: the fun-loving

'Everything's Hotsy Totsy Now', the 'rattling fine' 'St Louis Blues' and the 'wonderful' full-blown 'Tin Roof Blues'. Dick Saunders enlivened Sonny Clay's composition 'The Ghost of the Black Bottom' with an eccentric rendition of the 'real Black Bottom'.[18]

They 'certainly put their heart and soul into their numbers', observed *Labor Daily.* Ripe with 'weird Jazz effects' and rich with 'well-chosen solos', added the *Sydney Morning Herald.* Although some, 'irked' by the 'blare of the saxophone trumpet and trombone', found the band too noisy. Yet not 'frenzied' enough for others who hankered for a hard finish, the piano, saxes, banjos and trombones 'hitting on all eight'.[19]

Less expected was the orchestra's skill in 'rendering classical airs' and popular Tin Pan Alley hits: 'Me and My Shadow' made famous by Al Jolson, the winsome, dreamy 'Rain', even 'The Rosary', a religious ballad sung by Irish tenor John McCormack although performed in 'a manner entirely new to Australian audiences'.[20]

So too, reviewers were divided over Ivy Anderson, whose comedy and hot-step routine ended on the coquettish love ditty 'Dinah' made famous by Ethel Waters in a Broadway cabaret. Lyrics matched 'Carolina' to 'finer' and 'China'. A clearly smitten writer at *Smith's Weekly* pronounced Anderson a 'lady of exceptional artistic ability'; she was 'best thing in the show' and deserved more stage time. A *Truth* reviewer, conversely, was unsettled by her 'scratchy' voice. Her delivery was too 'fast'; she overwhelmed an audience 'trying to keep track of her stepping with their eyes and sort out her accent and dialect with their ears'.[21]

A note of astonishment underpinned the praise lavished on The Four Covans. Critics did not expect to behold such 'amazingly quick dances', 'such rapidity and in such perfect time'. 'A Russian number was as surprising as it was finished. Watching four colored people do a difficult Cossack dance was most remarkable,' marvelled one review. The spirituals, yodels and comic songs of the Emperors of Harmony grounded audiences in more familiar territory. Several reviewers anointed them 'the best ever'. 'Had he been born white', basso William Hann would have been a singer at the Metropolitan Opera House, remarked the *Sunday Times.*[22]

To close the show, the entire cast assembled on stage for the Australian debut of 'My Blue Heaven'—the Tivoli had procured exclusive performance rights. The winsome croon met the approval of all; 'very attractively played, sung, danced and harmonised'.[23]

For the next two weeks, the Sonny Clay Orchestra had a regular evening spot on 2FC, the transmission reaching listeners in Newcastle one hundred miles away. The broadcast triggered complaints about the demise of quality music and a spike in sheet music sales of 'My Blue Heaven'. Most importantly, every Tivoli performance was a near sellout. To Harry Muller's great relief, the Colored Idea were a 'decided box office success'.[24]

10 THE JAZZING SPHERES

'SONNY CLAY'S IDEA burst like a ray of colored sunshine on the patrons of the Tivoli yesterday afternoon. The band is all your dreams of jazz come true,' lauded the entertainment writer at the *Truth*. Less flattering was the Tivoli advertisement sitting alongside the review: the distorted face of a three-toothed tar baby eating a watermelon.[1] On the page of a single newspaper, the reader faced two competing views of the Colored Idea: one celebrating modernity, the other minstrelsy. The bifurcated message spoke to a messy contest of ideas at play in Sydney over the contours of modernity in Australia.

Gayne Dexter advanced a fashionably cosmopolitan view of the Colored Idea. Until that time, he had never heard jazz played by the 'originators' of the form. And while listening to the Sonny Clay Orchestra, he 'realised that jazz as played by a European' and a 'real Negro' were 'entirely different'. 'It is all in the syncopation,' he explained. 'One, brought to America by the original African Negroes—is natural—the other, an acquirement, is artificial.'[2]

The realisation was, in fact, more a recitation of a primitivist tenet of faith. Dexter's comment indicated a familiarity with Greenwich Village critiques that drew on a Freudian unconscious to re-imagine racially inscribed difference about primitive and civilised states. Back in 1923, Gilbert Seldes had catalogued 'two strains' of jazz: 'the negro and the

Mr. McKinnel is a newcomer to this country, and a fine and sensitive worker.

Hugh Williams is pleasant as the youthful government officer, and Gwynne Whitby, capable as the Counsel's wife. Marjorie Playfair shows evidence of careful training by Boucicault for her part of the Chinese girl.

His own composition, "The Ghost of the Black Bottom," is followed by the real Black Bottom, accompanied by a dance by Dick Saunders, who appears to be majordomo, guide, philosopher, and friend to the rest of the company.

The Four Harmonisers sing Southern melodies the way they should be sung, and their yodelling is one of the best things ever heard on the Tivoli stage, and indeed on any stage.

The Covans do some very clever dancing, especially in their "Bolshevik" number. Ivy Anderson does not quite "get over," perhaps because of her decidedly scratchy voice. The last concerted number of the Colored Idea is "Blue Heavens," very attractively played, sung, danced and harmonised.

It is really a corrective for the false sentiment that has grown up around criminals, and attempts to give to the plain policemen some of the credit which generally goes to the detectives.

Another one of Mr. Gordon's plays is "Crime"—rather far-fetched, but distinctly amusing. The drama opens with criminals rehearsing a jewel robbery with all the accessories—even a dummy policeman with rings marked on the vital spots on his body. All the participants in the robbery go through their parts until they are action-perfect, and the second half of the play shows the crime being executed.

There is only one hitch. One of the men loses his head and kills a cop, instead of following instructions and only winging him.

The idea is original, and the "College for Crooks" scene is very clever.

The play is difficult to produce owing to the number of people required for street scenes.

WHY will they do it? Leo Franklyn suffered from sunburn so badly that he could not appear for a couple of nights last week, and Reginald Sharland could only just do his part. It's a hard world when a little surfing can't be indulged in without pain!

Ten of Sunny Clay's Coloured Ideas, all lined up for action. They opened at the Tivoli last night.

"GREATER THAN SANTREY."

SATURDAY'S TIVOLI AUDIENCES PROCLAIMED SONNY CLAY'S BAND THE GREATEST ATTRACTION OF YEARS.

TIVOLI

SONNY CLAY'S COLORED "IDEA"

24 NEGRO STARS

100 WONDER MINUTES

SOMETHING NEW IN ENTERTAINMENT

including

SONNY CLAY'S PLANTATION BAND

Real Syncopation and Real Symphony.

The Four Covans
Whirlwind steppers.
Ivy Anderson
Colored Comedienne.

Dick Saunders
How dat Boy can dance.
The Harmony Emperors
Singing what 'am.

...VERNMENT RAILWAYS

...CURSIONS

SAFE & SATISFACTORY

THE COMFORT

A bifurcated message: on one page the Colored Idea are presented as purveyors of modernity and minstrelsy. (*Truth*, State Library of NSW)

intellectual'. 'The shakes, thrills, vibrators, smears, and slides are natural to him, although they produce tones outside the scale, because he has never been tutored into a feeling for perfect tones, as white men have', read 'Toujours Jazz', Seldes' influential and misguided essay.[3]

Dexter's investment in primitivist fantasy reached beyond bohemian posturing to inform his view of Aboriginal Australia. In these same weeks, he was rolling out a publicity campaign for his film *The Romance of Runnibede.* The flagship advertisement depicted a young White woman tied to a tree trunk, surrounded by generically primitive Black men in grass skirts (not unlike the Zulu costume donned by Sonny Clay in a Hollywood lot). 'A white girl captured by blacks—torn from her home, her lover, and all she held dear—carried off into the depths of the bush—perhaps to a fate more terrible than death,' read the text.[4]

The campaign and film reprised a recurring motif in stories about the Australian and American frontier: the captive woman. The idea of a beautiful White maiden lost to civilisation, held at the mercy of savages, governed the conventions of a popular literary genre that usually ended in heroic rescue missions and punitive raids. They were narrative balms to soothe colonial violence, although in 1928, Gayne Dexter only saw romance and opportunity, hoping the Australian story would translate for American audiences.[5]

If Dexter was blind to his own primitivist reflexes, his review of the Colored Idea's debut performance displayed a keen awareness of the power held by Australia's gatekeepers. For Dexter, modernism was a 'style-condition' shaped by cosmopolitanism; an aesthetic born of intercultural exchange. To his frustration, officials compounded Australia's geographic isolation by obstructing the circulation of these ideas. Censors banned words and images. Immigration officers blocked the flow of people. Protectionism privileged imperial nostalgia over commercial demand. The result was a culture lag that placed Australia at least 'two years behind New York'. This deficit denied Dexter the opportunity to be truly modern and he welcomed anything plugging that gap, while agitating for more: 'The show is clean, well-dressed, fast and one of the best one-hour entertainments yet brought to Australia. Incidentally if Sonny's allowed to depart without affording us the chance to strut our stuff to his syncopation, every cabaret and dance hall management deserves bankruptcy.'[6]

Gayne Dexter was personally acquainted with Tom Carlyon and JC Bendrodt, the two dance promoters who had tried unsuccessfully to import Black dance orchestras, so surely knew his comment challenged the Musicians' Union's 'no colored bandsmen' rule. Certainly, in the coming weeks, Dexter continued to rouse the union's ire, celebrating the beneficial influence of a touring Italian opera company and quoting visiting tenors who lamented the low technical standards of Australian symphony orchestras.[7]

Indeed, Dexter battled any group attempting to control or limit his cosmopolitan world. When empire men called for a quota system that favoured British films because Hollywood 'propaganda' made Australians 'think that America is far greater than the British Empire', Dexter excoriated the 'loud-mouthed speakers at loyalty' who pushed second-rate British productions on film-goers 'under the guise of patriotism'.[8]

When nativists complained that Hollywood domination was 'stifling' nascent efforts to articulate a distinct Australian culture and identity, Dexter scorned their parochialism, extolling a spirit of internationalism over nationalism. 'Motion pictures have gathered the artistic genius of the world and centred it in Hollywood,' he countered. 'Every nationality' had contributed to its greatness; 'brother and sister Australians' were there. Dexter reserved a special sting for the Censorship Board who bowdlerised

American and European films, blasting their 'hypocrisy' and 'astigmatism', equating their 'petty, vindictive' brand of Christian morality with 'the viciousness of the Puritan'.[9]

Colleagues at *Everyones* suggested Dexter courted controversy, especially after he 'dropped a couple of sticks of dynamite' on the 1927 Royal Commission into the Motion Picture Industry, telling them that 'beauty' was the 'merchandise of the motion picture' and Australians were 'practically barren of beauty'.

'Nature made a wonderful job of this continent, but as human beings we are an ugly race,' lectured Dexter. That year he had judged a beauty contest and carefully evaluated a thousand young women, so could confidently assert 'the pure Anglo-Saxon' was 'developing a racehorse face'. To audible gasps, he warned the price of racial homogeny was physical unloveliness. The 'corrective' he proposed was an immigration program akin to the United States' melting pot, prioritising the 'good-looking races' such as the 'Latin and Slav'. 'American beauty', he emphasised, was 'the product of mixed bloods'.[10]

Dexter received hundreds of letters condemning him as a heretic for questioning the sacred assumption that 'untainted' British stock raised on Australian fresh air and sunshine would give rise to a physically superior race. Close to three decades had passed since the implementation of the White Australia policy. So, by the late 1920s, the mix of immigration restriction laws, mass deportations, soft eugenic programs, Indigenous segregation and family separation policies was, surely, delivering some kind of bounty.

Monitoring the signs of racial regeneration was a national preoccupation. Newspaper pictorial pages dwelled on the 'god-like' toned and sculpted limbs of summertime swimmers. Advocates of the physical culture movement likened Australian sporting prowess to the 'strength and beauty' of Ancient Athenians and Spartans.[11] Historians like Keith Hancock detected the hand of destiny, seeing the quest for racial homogeny as 'obedient' to divine law and science. Science, he believed, had 'warned' of the 'dire peril' of race mixing. God, he contended, had 'set aside' the continent 'exclusively' as Britain's 'Southern empire'.[12]

Dexter shrugged off such grand prophesies. He had spent too many days conducting his own research, evaluating beauty contestants, casting screen actors and reviewing motion pictures to be swayed by promises of racial renewal. 'Gentlemen,' wrapped up his address to the commissioners, 'we can't have everything.'[13]

Gayne Dexter's sensory, communal, consumption-based view of modernity was an anathema to the disciples of Friedrich Nietzsche at Australia's 'highbrow' arts and culture magazine, *New Triad*. Instead, they looked to Classical Greece and Rome for aesthetic inspiration, as well as national purpose.[14] 'Modernism in art' came in two guises—true and false—argued Jack Lindsay, son of artist Norman Lindsay. The first was an evolutionary pursuit of Classical Beauty and Truth. The second was 'a cosmopolitan confusion of white and n____r charlatans'. Unsurprisingly then, the *New Triad* dismissed Sonny Clay's Colored Idea as the 'riff-raff of the music halls'.[15]

Bernard Heinze, director of Melbourne's Conservatory of Music, concurred with Lindsay. In an open letter, he deplored the 'fiendish', 'Negroid spirit', the 'seductive yet diabolical force' that had violated the balance and harmony of European music and defiled all enlightened rules of artistic engagement. This 'evil' now seeped like a cancer through the healthy White race.[16]

The theme was taken up by the *Sun* newspaper which, over the course of the Colored Idea's Sydney season, concocted several stories, drawn from 'expert' opinions stated many years earlier, to signal their distaste for 'Negro jazz'. 'Twisted Legs, the Degradation of Jazz' alerted women to the moral, physical and matrimonial risks of jazz dancing: 'A man cannot respect a girl who indulges in such shamelessness amid the savage rhythms and the whinings of a jazz band.'[17] 'Jazz Swept Over World like Disease' lamented the 'giant step backwards' in the 'march of progress' while 'Young Folk Raise Hell in Modern Sodom' anticipated 'civilization' going 'down in ruins'. 'Our foundations are falling apart.'[18]

The articles mobilised several well-worn dystopian metaphors: a diseased body politic, a violation of Darwin's laws of evolution, a structurally compromised Greek temple, and the maddening effects of the 'jungle'. Each allusion funnelled into more comprehensive discourses about the problems with today's youth.

Most narratives began with the Great War, the earthquake that shook civilisation to its core. The younger generation, disorientated and set adrift, then rejected the shaky pillars that so grounded their parents and turned, if not to the decadence of Sodom, then the African jungle for inspiration. Hot propulsive rhythms explained everything from sexual abnormalities, bizarre crime and the mindless pursuit of sensory pleasure. As one commentator observed, 'jazz' was 'not so much a new idiom in music as a new habit of mind'.[19]

The week the Colored Idea arrived in Sydney, the *Bulletin* magazine published a wry poem that drew on Platonic cosmology and Pythagorean logic to make explicit the relationship between aesthetics, modernity and race—and poke fun at the worry warts. Written under the pseudonym Hasen, 'The Apotheosis of Jazz' recounted a dream—'a troubled sleep'—which took the dreamer 'past shoals of common sense and reefs of fact' to the outer heavens where they encountered the 'rhythmic harmony' of the Music of the Spheres, the diatonic scale that ordered the universe. This was the force that determined the orbit of planets, differentiated darkness from light, enlightened minds and illuminated the path of civilisation.[20]

The poet imagined a radio transmission shattering the reverie and an American radio announcer telling the 'wobbling world the jazzy news!'

> As in some limping Negro theme,
> The sharp, bright tones of shining suns were slurred.
> And here a star was seen to hesitate,
> And there, a steady planet swayed and dipped;
> Until whole systems seemed to syncopate ...
> And back to the chaos slipped the jazzing spheres![21]

With mock doom, the poet blamed the note-bending onslaught of 'Negro' jazz for creating a 'wobble' that threw the finely tuned celestial spheres off balance, auguring a collapse into primordial chaos. Even as satire, the poem still recognised the racial dynamics underpinning the competing aesthetics of modernity. Classicists equated tonal purity with racial purity, melodic harmony with social harmony. By implication, order and equilibrium—the 'unwobbling' of the music of the spheres—could only be restored by separating the forces of 'darkness' and 'lightness', the impulse propelling the White Australia ideal.

A week into the Colored Idea's run, *Smith's Weekly* posted a second review of the show, this one unfavourable, dwelling on the ruptured order. Sonny Clay's band had no business playing Irish ballads like 'The Rosary', sniped the reviewer, while The Four Covans' 'Cossack dancing' was 'really best left to the Russians'. Just as the hot rhythms of jazz were out of place, so a new generation of Black entertainers were out of their preordained place. The reviewer offered a simple remedy: the Colored Idea should give 'more of the stuff that's expected of them. A revised offering of genuine plantation melodies and Negro dances would go big.'[22]

11
A COMPARATIVE VACATION

To accommodate local tastes, Ivy Anderson sang a little slower and the Emperor of Harmony's William Hann assumed hosting duties alongside Dick Saunders and, once the kinks in the show had been ironed out, the Colored Idea settled into their four-week Sydney run. If not for the leggy photographs of Ivy Anderson and Elmer Turner appearing in every edition of the working men's weekly *Beckett's Budget*, the troupe barely attracted publicity.[1] No publication photographed Willie Covan, one of the greatest dancers to grace Australia's shores. Nor was Sonny Clay quizzed on 'the meaning of jazz', as bandleader Henry Santrey had been eighteen months earlier.

For the musicians, Australia lived up to Harry Muller's promise. With only two shows daily, six days a week, Tivoli-time was a 'comparative vacation'. Performers had ample opportunity for late nights and leisurely mornings; entire days devoted to recreation and friendships. To attract returned patronage, mid-way through the season, Sonny Clay and his troupe introduced several new numbers: Broadway favourite 'The Girl Friend' and the Paul Whiteman Orchestra's moody 'Moonlight on the Ganges'.[2]

In a 1977 oral history interview, alto sax player Leo Davis recalled the dynamics of the rehearsal room. He was a 'serious-minded' musician, 'aiming to reach the top'—if not an orchestra, then something (in the end, it was Los Angeles' Black musicians' union). Trained at Fisk, he expected bandleaders to prepare scrupulous arrangements then drill the band to perfection. Consequently, he was often 'outspoken' in rehearsal, sharing his considerable technical knowledge with his fellow bandsmen. 'I'd say, "man, you didn't play that right. This chord works here." Or "let's go over this again"'—often to his colleague's marked disinterest. By his own admission, he never excelled at improvising.[3]

To Davis' mind, Sonny Clay fell short on arrangements. So, beyond head pieces, 'there wasn't much co-ordination'. This 'every-man-for-himself' approach worked fine in a six-piece band but was 'hit and miss' in a ten-piece combination. To address these perceived shortcomings, Davis, in his spare time, devoted long hours to mapping out arrangements for three saxophones and three brass instruments, but when he arrived at rehearsal, Sonny Clay barely glanced at the sheets. 'He was satisfied with what he was doing. Thought it was great because he had been doing it for so long,' recalled Davis, the frustration of a perfectionist still evident after fifty years.[4]

Leo Davis was not the type of man to sit idle. Once, when he was an unemployed violinist, a bandleader told him, 'Leo if you had a saxophone, I could give you a job tomorrow night.' So, Davis hustled the loan of a saxophone and stayed up all night practising his scales. The next day, he assumed his place in the orchestra, 'playing more saxophone than anyone in the group'. Another time he was stranded in New Mexico, so taught himself Spanish. But he was no choir boy, drinking far too heavily in those days.[5]

Sydney was a city of myriad charms beckoning Leo Davis. The theatre management had secured the troupe several comfortable apartments in Kings Cross, the most cosmopolitan corner of a staunchly White city. If the tabloid newspapers could be believed, these streets were ruled by the Razor Gang, a bunch of street toughs who slashed the faces of their victims with blades but no one, except police reporters smitten with American wise guy gangsters, put them on a par with organised crime. Instead 'sly groggers' ran Sydney's illegal supply of liquor—alcohol was only legally available within tightly prescribed hours. On Sunday, the band's day off, the pubs and just about everything else were closed; only Kings Cross' 'sly-grog' shops stayed open.[6]

To African American eyes, Sydney felt like an amalgam of the United States. Letters to the Black newspapers compared Sydney's 'hustle and bustle' to Chicago or New York but without the skyscrapers—and Harlem, joked one writer. The 'marvellous' harbour conjured San Francisco, although the 'rare beauty' of the sculptural sandstone cliffs and 'rippling blue water' were 'beyond compare'. The humidity rivalled Florida, although some relief could be found a short walk away on the foreshores of Sydney Harbour. The electric storms and rolling thunder at day's end roused memories of Georgia.[7]

Sydney's population roughly matched Los Angeles—1.2 million and growing by 30 000 people per year. As in LA, migration powered a building bonanza. Over the previous decade, California bungalows had overrun orchards, market gardens, poultry runs and the last of the Indigenous bush camps. The demographic make-up of the two cities, of course, hardly compared. Sydney was overwhelmingly British and Irish, although as one letter boasted, for all the talk of 'English stock', 'truly America has set the pace'. Stores were filled with US imports.[8]

No laws prevented the bandsmen from roaming where they pleased and eating where they liked. The Emperors of Harmony had close links to the Methodist Church. For others, Sydney's 'most beautiful' racetrack held great appeal. 'Racing every day', a member of the Royal Southern Singers wrote in 1923. 'We go out and stay until after the third race and then catch a car and get into town, on time to go on our turn ... Man, I never saw so much money since the good old days in California.' Sonny Clay, who was introduced to Sydney's 'colourful' racing fraternity by his new pal Gayne Dexter, likened the scene to the good old days in Tijuana.[9]

Almost every Black entertainer who passed through Sydney in the 1920s reported being 'royally entertained' by the city's small 'colored' community. 'Some from America and some are natives and some from the British West Indies' read letters, a mix of show business veterans, boxers, waterside workers, labourers and street hawkers. Many were condemned to 'hard work'; no other fields were open to them. All were 'absolutely hungry for their own race'.[10]

The dockside district of Woolloomooloo, a short stroll from Kings Cross, was home to a cluster of Aboriginal families and a small, well-organised group of 'coloured Britishers', the families of Indian and

West Indian merchant seamen who had settled in Sydney before the White Australia policy.[11] Back in 1907, they had staged a grand farewell to boxer Jack Johnson, attended by a young Aboriginal waterside worker named Fred Maynard. As his great-grandson, historian John Maynard, has told, by 1928 Fred led the Australian Aboriginal Progressive Association (AAPA), spearheading a campaign to end family separations and stop the theft of gazetted Aboriginal land.[12]

Black Americans noted Marcus Garvey's message of Pan-African 'solidarity and universal brotherhood' resonated powerfully in the AAPA. Battered copies of *Negro World* clinched from merchant seamen presented a history of the New World that tied European imperialism to Indigenous dispossession and the African slave trade. The same system of exploitation that enslaved Alabama sharecroppers and Congolese rubber plantation workers also devastated Aboriginal populations. Garvey's ideas inspired AAPA secretary Tom Lacey to dedicate 'nearly all' his time to organising Aboriginal people into a political force, determined to break the missionary and reserve system. He wrote letters to Garvey's wife, Amy Jacques Garvey, describing his demands for economic justice, decent living conditions and a say in policymaking. He also wanted Amy Garvey to send him 'some of your American papers' to 'distribute among our people' and 'enlighten them a bit'.[13]

African American visitors detected in Black Sydneysiders the stirrings of a Black Pacific alliance, a sense they were part of a global majority instead of a national minority. 'His Majesty King George rules more blacks than whites,' pointed out one Sydney woman of colour. 'Out of every seventh person who call him king, six of them are black.' News of Mahatma Gandhi's campaign for self-government in India invited a particularly imperial critique of race: within the British Empire, degrees of liberty and independence were apportioned by Whiteness.[14]

Some gaps in local knowledge took American entertainers by surprise. Black Sydney knew 'nothing' about the advocacy work of the *Chicago Defender*, the most widely read Black publication in the United States, even the world. It was readily accessible in London, Paris, even Cairo, Manila and Shanghai, but was 'impossible' to get 'out here'.[15]

In the pages of the *Chicago Defender*, readers could discover what editor Robert S Abbott called the 'great battle for independence of Black people the world over'. Or follow ongoing commentary about the 'global color line' constructed by an alliance of White settler nations, many along the Pacific rim. The newspaper also offered a robust analysis of White Australia, teasing out the ways White supremacy underpinned immigration, Indigenous, defence and diplomatic policy.[16]

The paucity of literature in Sydney about Black internationalism left entertainers and athletes playing an outsized role transmitting ideas and relaying events. Minto Cato, for one, clearly understood her role in fostering feelings of connectedness between Black people separated by geography—and how her presence unsettled White colonial rule. When South African authorities refused to allow the Southern Revue to tour, she observed that the 'white man' did not want 'modern Negroes' because 'the natives would see just how far behind they are' and start to wonder why 'they weren't getting as much education as they should, and there might be a terrible uprising for the greatly outnumbered whites'.[17]

Visiting entertainers and athletes also relayed Indigenous Australia back to Black America. For the most part, Black and White America's knowledge of Aboriginal culture could be summed up in a single word: 'boomerang'—an ancient tool that, in the age of aviation, held a special place in the popular imagination, straddling the modern and primitive. Alongside updates on the non-stop solo flights of Charles Lindbergh and Amelia Earhart, a swathe of US magazines celebrated the boomerang as the perfect marriage of a propeller and wing. It soared through the air with the speed of an arrow, circling in double loops, figure eights and double figure eights, to return to the thrower's feet. A discovery 'the savage accidentally made in their experiments and developed by them without any scientific knowledge of the mechanical laws in operation', marvelled the *Washington Times*, reiterating the fantasy of the unconscious primitive.[18]

More than an exemplar of aviation principles, the boomerang launched an American verb that embodied the sacred and profane. Department stores staged 'Boomerang Weeks' to flag bargains so irresistible shoppers kept coming back. Economists spoke of a 'boomerang' when pondering 'the self-correcting mechanism of the industrial order' otherwise known as boom and bust. Playwrights chose the 'boomerang' over cupid's arrow to warn that a shameful past would one day come back to smack a girl right in the face. Preachers could not resist mentioning 'boomerangs' while pondering Galatians 6:7: 'whatsoever a man soweth, that shall he also reap'. Black commentators applied the boomerang to the riddle of Jim Crow: no matter how hard authorities tried to cast off the race question, it kept coming back.[19]

Smitten by the science and poetry of the boomerang, time and again, American tourists, Black and White, expressed a desire to meet a 'genuine' Aboriginal person and see their well-practised hand launch the boomerang on its elegant path of ellipses and twists—and always, always, fulfill its symbolic duty and return to the thrower's feet.[20]

Naturally, they headed to an Aboriginal mission on the northern headland of Botany Bay: La Perouse. The world came to this corner of Sydney: Japanese princes, Finnish diplomats, Methodist missionaries, Samoan pastors, cruise ship passengers, and sailors of all nationalities. When the American Pacific fleet docked in 1925, a stream of 'Yanks' wound their way there, some personally chaperoned by blackfellas they had met in the dockside streets and drinking houses. Demand for boomerangs kept local artisans busy. The Black boxer Jack Johnson was also a regular visitor during his 1907 and 1908 sojourn in Sydney. He trained at a hotel in Botany Bay and every day jogged along the shore to the settlement and, by the time he left Sydney, had a fine collection of boomerangs and weaponry. 'The Australian natives must have been geniuses to invent such weapons,' he told the press, before elaborating on his plans to build a flying machine.[21]

Did Leo Davis and his bandmates put their Sundays to good use and ride the tram to La Perouse to see the boomerang throwers and learn a little more about their Black brothers and sisters? Certainly, each Sunday, thousands of daytrippers descended on the headland to enjoy its seaside charms. In the parkland opposite the tram terminal, Sydney's Aboriginal community stood ready to do business. Warriors exhibited their hand-crafted weaponry, decorated with the blackened pokerwork designs. Other stalls showcased women's handicraft: hand-carved coolamon bowls and boxes tiled with shells.[22]

Always in earshot was a gum-leaf band. Four men each held two eucalyptus leaves between their lips, the force of the air through the gap liberating a sweetness that trilled like a harmonica, buzzed like a kazoo and slurred like a trumpet. Few horn players could fail to be mystified by its simplicity, humbled by its cleverness and uplifted by its song. US visitors reported hearing a gum-leaf quartet extemporising with the moan of the didgeridoo, the whirl of the bullroarer and an ancient chant of two wizened men. Yet La Perouse was not immune to modern popular culture. The gum-leaf band also played a selection of well-known American airs. In January 1928, newspapers told of a young lad with a fine soprano voice who went by the stage name 'Piccaninny Pete' and danced the Dixie Stomp.[23]

The portrait of Black Sydney captured by American entertainers focused, mostly, on male figures. However, several musicians in the Sonny Clay Orchestra befriended what some reporters only described as 'colored women'. Exactly which musicians is unclear. The details are sparse, filtered through the uninterested eyes of White reporters in late March, an incidental moment playing out on the periphery of a more important drama. But even at a glance, the newsmen could see an exchange of friendliness, even tenderness, between them.

'A couple of members of the troupe had colored women waiting for them when the train pulled in,' observed the Sydney *Sun*, noting the 'warmth of the welcome'.[24] 'There were one or two affectionate meetings between some of the Negroes and colored women,' confirmed the Melbourne *Herald*.[25] Clearly, they had met before. Likely, several times.

In the months to come, when the Sydneysiders withdrew their welcome to the band members, these 'colored women' would prove to be the musicians' most steadfast friends. But who were they?

12
AMERICAN BOOMERANG

THE SHARD OF evidence is slight: a single display of 'warmth' and 'affection' between the dance band musicians and a few 'colored women' in the midst of a tabloid-fuelled panic about Black musicians socialising with a few White women. The implications are considerable: a jazz-age connection between Black America and Black Australia, an exchange of ideas about experiences of Blackness and ways of seeing the world—and, perhaps, an insight into stories about intimacy along the colour line.

How I have tried to identify these 'colored women', wading through records, pinning down facts and figures, attempting to convert circumstances into some semblance of certainty. But robust empirical evidence is maddeningly hard to find. The archive leaves no trace. People relegated to the margins of society generate few historical records, while the White practice of un-naming or disregarding the presence of Black people has created silences in popular memory.

No amount of searching will uncover the identity of a person whose name has never been recorded. But like an archaeologist reconstructing an urn from a shard, or a camp dweller building a home from random scraps of material, the task is not insurmountable.

Without a name, there can be no biographical account. But there can be informed speculation and plausible narratives about possible candidates, people who *may* have been in the band's orbit. Likelihoods buoyed with solid statistics, oral histories, circumstantial evidence, cultural context and processes of deduction—supported by a substantial body of historical scholarship.

The fragment, alone, holds clues. If reporters wrote 'Negroes and Negresses', then the women likely hailed from the Black West Indian and American cluster in Woollomooloo. But the reporters wrote 'Negro' and 'colored' as if these women stood apart from the African diaspora. The 1933 census lists several possibilities: Hindu, Maori, Papuan, Polynesian and, by far the largest group, 'half-caste' Aboriginal. Census takers counted 200 'half-caste' Aboriginal women in Sydney, compared to 145 men—imperfect figures that do not capture the transient population, or the Indigenous people designated 'full-blood' or 'white'.[1]

A series of photographs and memoirs brings individual subjectivity to these cold statistics, each scenario placing the women in a wider community.

For instance in 1928, Jorma Pohjanpalo, a 23-year-old Finnish diplomat newly arrived in Australia, took a short walk from the La Perouse headland, across to the spinifex sand dunes of Frenchmans Bay where he photographed a barefoot adolescent girl with windblown hair, her hand clasping the tip of a boomerang, as if ready to raise her arm and throw it. Her steady gaze and composure signalled a confidence that the material privations of her circumstances did not outweigh the rich cultural knowledge she held in her palm.[2]

If members of the Sonny Clay Orchestra also forayed beyond the main tourist site, they likely would have met her, too. For the young woman, almost certainly, lived in one of the tin shacks nestled in the sand dunes, part of the six-acre reserve run by the Anglican Church's United Aboriginal Mission. Only a handful of White people lived in the area: a few storekeepers, a policeman who supervised their daily lives, and a missionary of unwavering faith. In the not-that-distant past, this settlement was one of several Aboriginal camps that dotted Sydney's waterways. By the mid-1920s, the survival of this community hinged on government policies that assumed they were the 'remnants' of a 'poor dying race' predicted to vanish within decades.

The residents told another story. Most of the 160 residents were one way or another kinfolk, Dharawal and Gundungurra people mostly, with links to the South Coast, Burragorang Valley and the Blue Mountains, bonded by their exclusion from the White community, and their proud ancestral links to their great warrior tribesmen. They harvested fish and oysters, intimately attuned to the sea's cycles and currents. In the shade of the Moreton Bay figs, older folk sat around a communal fire, swapping yarns and fashioning traditional artefacts into souvenirs for tourists.[3]

To Black American eyes, the mission system was a mix of big city Jim Crow segregation and slave plantation paternalism, a world founded on racial exclusion, yet not so separate as to escape a hierarchy of dependency shaped by race and gender: the Master, the Mistress, the Overseer, et cetera. A little bit of Prohibition America lived in Aboriginal Mission Australia: no liquor, no gambling and, after six in the evening, no visitors, especially the White men who preyed on young women. And certainly, no members of the Australian Aboriginal Progressive Association who bad-mouthed the missionaries and Protection Board with their talk of citizenship rights and the vote.[4]

A campaign waged by the local mayor was illustrative. At the time the Colored Idea were in Sydney, Randwick council announced plans to evict the La Perouse community to make way for a golf course and housing development. It was a shameless land grab wrapped in the language of progress, paternalism and morality. 'In keeping with the instincts of the race', the council had found a 'more natural' alternative: a boggy exposed beach nearby. But the residents refused to leave. 'This is our heritage bestowed upon us,' read their petition, alluding less to real estate and zoning laws than a physical, spiritual and custodial relationship to place, shaped by ancestry and maintained by customary practice. As the head missionary pointed out, the land was also their 'legal right' under British law.[5]

The local mayor hit back, accusing the mission of 'closing their eyes to the increased half-caste population'—only strictly enforced isolation and supervision could prevent the birth of even more half-caste babies. The mothers of these imagined babies were, plausibly, the same women who befriended the American musicians.[6]

Hundreds of photographs taken by the Aboriginal Welfare Board documented Sydney's largest group of young Aboriginal women: the domestic servants who lived in White households in the city's leafy suburbs. One in Drummoyne. Another in Hunters Hill. Five in Woollahra and four in Mosman. The portraits capture little of their 'heartbreaking loneliness' but instead picture them holding bouquets, or standing beside artful floral arrangements, or a table set for high tea. Some wore starched uniforms with matching scalloped apron, collar and cap. Others were costumed in cloche hats, drop-waisted dresses, long beaded necklaces and Mary Jane shoes (a publicity exercise aimed to depict them as 'integrated' and 'assimilated'). (Once the photo had been taken the girls would remove their dresses for the next sitter, indicated one note.) All were wards of the state who had been 'rescued' by the Aboriginal Protection Board from 'degradations' of Aboriginal missions and camps. In the name of protection, with the goal of absorption, the board since the early 1910s began separating—or abducting—'quadroon' and 'octoroon' children from their families.[7]

It was a day seared in the memory of each stolen child: the overwhelming sense of hopelessness, powerlessness and fear as agents of state power rolled up in shiny cars and plucked them from schoolhouses, hospital beds and their parents' arms, deaf to their tears and pleas. These children, now known as the Stolen Generation, were pawns in a policy designed to solve the 'half-caste problem'—a 'problem' policymakers framed as one of population rather than interracial sex.[8]

The children were sent to Cootamundra Girls' Home and Bomaderry Children's Home and taught to 'think white—look white—act white' before serving their 'apprenticeship' in White middle-class homes. The Protection Board deliberately kept wages low, at sixpence a week, to prevent them from going back to their homes. So too, their matrimonial prospects were few. 'Most of the luckless girls must dismiss all thoughts of marriage from their minds,' read a 1924 report in the *Sydney Morning Herald.* If these women married at all—and so many of them did not—it tended to be to White men. An APB official agreed that their outlook was not very bright. 'What do you propose instead,' he shrugged, 'in camps the girls will fall prey to dissolute whites ... The freedom of young people is conducive to immorality.' The reporter was unconvinced, wondering if the 'apprenticeship system' was 'accelerating the extinction of the Aboriginal race'.[9]

The far-reaching power of the Aboriginal Protection Board was not without its gaps. As Yorta Yorta woman Margaret Tucker recalled in her autobiography, *If Everybody Cared*, she and her sister, May, found ways to circumvent the board's soulless vision.[10] In the 1920s, Margaret and May served in Sydney homes fifteen miles apart, seemingly isolated, yet stubbornly connected to each other and Sydney Black's world. May had first summoned the courage to steal away at night, somehow befriending a West Indian family in Woolloomooloo who welcomed her like a daughter. May's stories of their love and kindness stirred a deep discontentment in her seventeen-year-old sister. Margaret's current employers treated her kindly (the previous ones had not), although she resented calling them 'master' and 'mistress'. The words called to mind *Uncle Tom's Cabin*, an American slavery tale her mother had read and re-read to her back on the mission.[11]

One night, Margaret climbed from her attic window to join her sister at the home of the West Indian family in Woolloomooloo. 'It was a night I shall never forget,' she wrote. At a neighbourhood house party, she watched twenty Samoan merchant seamen perform an impromptu *taualuga*, singing in the rich deep tones of their language. She also met a Maori sailor, the two flirting and sharing stories about each other's countries and customs.[12]

Since childhood, music had been central to Margaret Tucker's world; she loved harmonising with her mother and sisters and was active in the mission and school choir. She sang a mix of old-time standards, Negro spirituals (introduced by the Fisk Jubilee Singers when performed at Maloga mission in 1886), and Yorta Yorta adaptations of these sacred African American songs. 'Bura Fera' was based on 'Turn Back Pharoah's Army'. Margaret's love of singing made her popular at dances and parties, like the wedding feasts on the mission where a three-piece Aboriginal band, on gum-leaf, violin and concertina, led the dance. Sometimes, she recalled, folk broke from their European polkas and jigs to form a corroboree circle.

The party in Woolloomooloo recalled the freedom, joy and togetherness of Margaret's stolen childhood—although the following night's absconsion did not end with such cheer. Her employers, discovering her escape, notified police. With the help of her new friends, she accessed an underground network, and eluded their grasp, finding refuge with a Syrian family in Redfern.[13]

By 1928, Margaret Tucker had left Sydney, although the hundreds of domestic servants who remained continued their small moments of defiance. Did any of these women connect with the Woolloomooloo network or slip away to the Tivoli to discover a previously unknown world?

'Steamy weather' was the forecast for Sydney in February 1928, a familiar cycle of hot, humid mornings with the hope of an evening thunderstorm. Although sometimes the Southerly Buster unleashed a deluge of deafening crashes and blinding lightning. Too often, the cool change didn't arrive and meteorologists lamented 'another oppressive night'.[14]

A short walk away from the musicians' King Cross flat, the sea breezes of Sydney Harbour offered a welcome respite. A little to the east was Rushcutters Bay. A little to the west, on the cliffs above Woolloomooloo Bay, was a rocky peninsula known as Mrs Macquarie's Point, both places where Aboriginal people camped a few decades earlier. They were beautiful, if not romantic, spots to while away a few hours, even set up a makeshift camp for the night, decipher the constellations of the southern hemisphere's night sky and, perchance, spot forks of lightning zigzagging across the horizon. The visitors may have learned *murawin*, the Dunghutti word for lightning. Or *munarra*, the Yorta Yorta word for thunder. Or *dhalba*, the Wiradjuri word for a sudden cloud burst of rain.[15]

Any of the women pressed into domestic service could explain to the American musicians the Aboriginal Protection Board policy of absorption, or 'breeding out the color'. Essentially it was an exercise in selective, state-sanctioned miscegenation, mostly structured around the reproductive practices of Aboriginal women. According to American race logic, the idea of absorbing the Black race into the White was simply not possible; one drop of Blackness was enough to disqualify Whiteness. But in Australia, miscegenation was a path whereby the Aboriginal race would 'vanish'. The logic hinged on the flawed and convenient assumption that Indigenous Australians predated the 'Caucasian, yellow and negro races' and appeared to be 'more closely allied to the white race'—to quote anthropologist William Lloyd Warner.[16] But much to the alarm of White policy administrators, contrary to predictions, the Aboriginal population was increasing—a situation echoing the American reading of the boomerang.

Of course, a core of rebellious domestic servants may *not* have been the 'colored women' at the train station in late March 1928. There were other candidates as well.

A studio portrait of Sophie Williams and her father Tom Williams, taken in 1916, just after he enlisted into the 33rd Battalion of the Australian Army, opens up another facet of Aboriginal Sydney. In 1928, Sophie was eighteen and Tom Williams, his wife Dolly and their extended family lived near a bushy tributary of the Georges River in a sturdy weather-board cottage, the nucleus of the Aboriginal camp known as Salt Pan Creek. Nearby a core of twenty-five people—the husbands, wives and children of eight families—lived on a sandstone escarpment in huts made of galvanised iron, hessian bags and packing cases. Another male circle lived close by.[17]

Oral histories capture a refuge for Aboriginal people who had escaped the harassment and paternalism of the Protection Board. They were a political lot, part of a vocal network of malcontents. Children grew up knowing it was better to live in a bag hut than on a mission station with a manager standing over them all the time. Sophie's father was a masterful crafter of boomerangs and woomeras and each week sold his wares at La Perouse. Was it possible she accompanied her father to La Perouse one Sunday and there accepted the Black American musicians' invitation to come see the show?[18]

Then there was the 'shingled girl of nineteen' a *Daily Guardian* reporter spotted at the Australian Aboriginal Progressive Association's inaugural conference in 1925, one of two hundred people demanding Indigenous self-determination. Over the next few years, women who knew the injustice and violence of family removals and domestic service had a champion in AAPA president Fred Maynard, a figure influenced by the vision of Marcus Garvey, the audacity of Jack Johnson and the freedom songs of the Fisk Jubilee Singers. 'We accept no condition of inferiority,' Maynard told politicians, calling for 'the complete emancipation of our people'. The 'rightful owners of the soil' demanded they 'be accorded, the same full right, and privileges of citizenship as are enjoyed by all'.[19]

While the names of the 'colored women' who befriended the Black American musicians have been lost to history, the stories of Black Sydney women carving out their place in a White nation that cast them as 'problems' highlighted their capacity to leverage even the smallest cracks in the system. Decades of targeted policy programs had not defeated them.

In another part of Sydney, the Commonwealth Investigation Branch was fixing its attentions on the visiting jazzmen, although the focus of their inquiries did not include the welfare and safety of the 'colored women'. Instead, they surveilled and documented moments when the Americans 'consorted' with White women. In these social interactions, the gatekeeper detected a policy infraction worthy of a national scandal.

PART IV

Views of Commonwealth Policy

13

MAJOR LLOYD'S INVESTIGATION BRANCH

MAJOR LONGFIELD LLOYD liked to be helpful, so much so that his working day often stretched long into the night. As the head of the New South Wales division of the Commonwealth Investigation Branch, he knew he wasted too much time fielding public inquiries about immigration policy and procedure. But, as he explained in an annual report, he believed the citizenry looked to him for an authoritative answer. His secretary, Miss Hayes, would not do. As an eminent figure in Australia's internal security force, he had helped build the machinery that raised and lowered the nation's gates.

Major Lloyd professed the public's 'absolute satisfaction' was his overriding priority. Although, by 'public' he meant the British public. By his own admission, he felt less kindly to the Southern European 'aliens' who appeared in his office wishing to begin the naturalisation process. It irked him that they could become members of 'the British community' with such 'ease'. To his mind, 'aliens' were interlopers who had carried 'none of our responsibilities' in the trenches and frontier while enjoying 'all the benefits'.[1]

Major Lloyd believed it was his patriotic duty to plot a circuitous and tardy path in their transition from alien to British subject—and prevent certain undesirables from becoming citizens at all. The legislative reforms of 1925 had expanded his powers, enabling him to formulate new categories of 'undesirability' and pinpoint new kinds of threats. These powers were imperfect (he was always pleading for more resources and manpower) but since taking charge of the bureau, he and his band of peace officers had successfully handled 'many difficult and delicate matters'.[2]

His friend and mentor, former prime minster Billy Hughes, hinted that Lloyd's devotion to public service sometimes tipped over into anxiety, pedantry and insecurity. 'Don't work too hard; don't undervalue yourself,' Hughes cautioned him in a private letter. 'Don't get so deeply immersed in details that you can't see the wood for the trees.'[3] But Longfield Lloyd did not believe he had lost sight of the big picture. His long working day underscored his pledge to cleanse the nation of enemies, both foreign and domestic, and populate it with good British stock. Purity was a tricky taskmaster.

The public mostly knew Major Lloyd as a loyal servant of the Crown, who ministered as *aide-de-camp* to the King's representative, NSW Governor Sir Dudley de Chair. Cloaked in the trappings of imperial pomp, Lloyd attended 'His Excellency' at scout hall dedications, society balls, and the Duke and Duchess of York's royal tour. 'His quiet efficiency and reserve acted as an admirable foil to the boisterous exuberance of the Lord High Chamberlain,' observed one insider at an official royal banquet.[4]

Photographs of Major Lloyd captured a thin upright man, with a centre part over a high prominent brow. His face angled down to a cleft at the point of his chin; a triangular symmetry broken by a beaky nose, softened by a tidy moustache and complicated by an occasional haunted fear in his eyes. Compared to the casual stance of the colleagues beside him, he stands almost at attention, forever moulded in the martial virtues of British imperial manhood.

Lloyd's internal letters, memos and reports—at least the ones that have survived—reveal a man with a pedantic concern for the budgetary constraints of his department, always seeking the most efficient route by the most rational means of transport. So too, he displayed a courtesy and deference towards his superiors that frequently spilled over into verbosity. 'I beg to express my acknowledgement of your concurrence in

Major Longfield Lloyd, director of the Commonwealth Investigation Branch's Sydney bureau. (EE Longfield Lloyd Papers, National Library of Australia)

the remarks I then made, and I'm gratified that you saw fit to accede to the whole of the matters brought under your notice' could, surely, be boiled down to 'thank you for incorporating my recommendations'.[5]

In this spirit, Major Lloyd's annual reports depicted a 'fully taxed' Investigation Branch, humming with efficiency. He had, at least, four agents in the field serving the myriad needs of an evolving federal bureaucracy, from monitoring subversion to catching pension fraud. At five o'clock each morning, his inspector-in-chief was at the docks, scanning the faces of passengers as they descended the gangway, on the lookout for individuals deemed prohibited and undesirable under the Immigration Act.[6]

The aliens who satisfied entry conditions continued to be tracked by other peace officers who juggled up to a dozen cases, each taking weeks to complete. 'There is always a flow exceeding the powers of absorption, even though the whole office staff, myself included take part in investigating work,' Lloyd noted.[7] Some cases were routine, others secretive. 'Special' operations monitoring the 'rag and bobtail of the revolutionary movement' were 'by far' the bureau's 'heaviest responsibilities'—although, as officers could attest, the 'least spectacular'.[8]

For Major Lloyd, the battle for the soul of the nation played out on the waterfront. Sydney was the busiest port in the country, the portal through which coal, wool, wheat and timber left Australia, and new technology, products, people, ideas and social problems arrived. Whoever controlled Sydney's docklands controlled national life—and by Lloyd's measure, the Communists were winning. They were 'a definite part of the labour movement' and 'within measurable reach of the state and federal parliaments', he warned.[9]

To detail Major Lloyd's ongoing wars on the waterfront is to bamboozle the reader with a procession of strikes and Investigation Branch operations to break these strikes—a web of shenanigans aided by intra-union strife and complicated by unabashed hostility between state and federal levels of law enforcement. After several brutal battles on the waterfront, the main lesson for Major Lloyd was glaringly simple: the Investigation Branch failed when pursuing legal channels and came out on top when deploying irregular methods.

The Jacob Johnson saga was a case in point, showcasing the range of official and unofficial powers wielded by the Investigation Branch. In a nutshell, in 1925 Prime Minister Bruce ordered Major Lloyd to deport Jacob Johnson, the Dutch-born leader of the Seamen's Union and alleged 'foreign agitator'. The PM even rushed through two laws to bolster the bureau's arsenal. The first, an amendment to the Immigration Act, gave the minister of home and territories discretionary deportation powers. Another clause made a person's 'occupation' grounds for removal.[10] The second, the *Peace Officers Act 1925* (passed when Labor premier Jack Lang prevented NSW police serving Johnson's deportation orders) created a statutory body to police Commonwealth law, an agency akin to the FBI but with far less authority. A freshly deputised peace officer promptly arrested Johnson.

For the first time Major Lloyd had at his disposal a team dedicated to the nation's internal security. How he interpreted these new powers would play a central role in shaping the contours of desirable citizenship. Yet, in the short term, he was unable to effect Johnson's removal. A High Court challenge, ripe with stirring speeches about democracy, liberty and the limits of executive authority, ruled in Johnson's favour—and translated into heroic headlines about the champion of the working man.[11]

Perhaps, Major Lloyd's most useful lesson from the Johnson case was tactical. No peace officer ever again attempted to deport the union leader, yet before 1928 was through, Lloyd's peace officers had sent him to prison, without the Investigation Branch ever being mentioned in the courtroom or newspapers. Major Lloyd would apply these strategies to a range of operations.

In February 1928, Major Lloyd penned a confidential report detailing the Commonwealth Investigation Branch's 'special' investigation into a 'Negro Orchestra' under contract to the Tivoli Theatre. The operation marked a new frontier in the interpretation and policing of Commonwealth law. The performers had arrived, not as aliens seeking naturalisation, but as visitors, commercial entities responding to market demand. As such, the case called for a close reading of the Immigration Act, particularly the reference to 'occupation'.

As Lloyd explained, he opened the inquiry on the strength of a single 'complaint' about the musicians' 'personal behaviour', lodged by an unidentified member of the public. This in itself was unusual. In the past, investigations arose in response to official requests. At no time did the public initiate inquiries—except, it appeared, in this case.[12]

The duty of collecting intelligence fell to at least four peace officers, all personally selected and sworn in by Major Lloyd. The lives of two, Robert Yates and George Longmore, offer a glimpse into the bitter internecine feud that lay behind Major Lloyd's shiny veneer.

Superintendent Robert Yates' career in law enforcement began in the NSW police in the 1890s, rising from a beat cop to a sanitary inspector, court bailiff and pension fraud caseworker in the attorney-general's department where he first met Major Lloyd. With the creation of the Investigation Branch after the Great War, Yates moved into internal security. He, for instance, arrested Jacob Johnson in 1925, the act thrusting him into unwelcome limelight. Johnson personally sued Yates for unlawful imprisonment and the case dragged on for years.[13]

By 1927 Yates was sixty-two, and 'feeling the effects' of 'very arduous and lengthy periods of continuous outside duty'. Since his divorce in 1913, he lived in hotels and moved often. He planned to retire soon, supplementing his police pension with the profits of a dubious gold-mining claim in Papua New Guinea. He and his syndicate partners—two of whom were 'Sydney's best known illegal bookmakers'—frequently met at the Investigation Branch office. According to a muckraking exposé by the *Truth* newspaper, one partner was so 'crook' he 'couldn't lie straight in bed'.[14]

The source of the exposé was likely Yates' colleague Captain George McFarland Beaconsfield Longmore who had joined the branch in 1926. To Yates' immense irritation, Major Lloyd was smitten by Captain Longmore, dazzled by his career in the British colonial service that read like a *Boy's Own* adventure story: an officer in the Royal Irish Constabulary, a police inspector in the Malay State Guards, a district commissioner with the Ugandan government, and a second lieutenant with the East African Rifles (the unit had a reputation for attracting rogues and chancers, while commanding a vast 'native' rank and file). Longmore could recount tales about quelling uprisings and riots. It was either 'kill or be killed', he once said about a sticky incident with the Chinese in Kuala Lumpur.[15]

Without question, Captain Longmore brought a fresh go-getter zeal to the Investigation Branch. At the same time the Negro Orchestra operation was underway, he was working the cracks in the Marine Cooks' Union strike still trying to land Jacob Johnson in prison. In recognition of his services, Major Lloyd awarded Longmore a special badge.

Whether driven by jealousy or revenge, Superintendent Yates carefully documented Longmore's methods, compiling evidence to prove the dashing captain shelled out hundreds of pounds in exchange for false testimony and secured statements at 'the point of a revolver'. Major Lloyd, Yates noted, sanctioned Longmore's 'dishonesty'—although by 1928, as Yates surely knew, this was far from a lapse in procedure.[16] Few, if any, picked Lloyd as the type to embrace the shadows of moral relativism and sanction expedience over principle, but such tactics were a hallmark of his military intelligence career.[17]

According to his official record, Longfield Lloyd was a military hero. Amongst the first to volunteer in 1914. Amongst the first to land on the beaches of Gallipoli in April 1915. As second lieutenant of the 1st Battalion's Company A, Platoon 1, he led a successful raid on the enemy's trench, personally shooting dead two Turkish soldiers. Like many of his brothers-in-arms, he would 'not have missed this for the world', a chance to defend King and Empire and fulfil boyhood fantasies of pluck and derring-do. By August, however, his combat career was over, ended not by gunfire but chronic diarrhea and typhoid. For close to a year, he lay listless in a hospital bed.[18]

In 1916, the newly promoted Captain Lloyd returned to Sydney to guard the home front. His new job in military intelligence called for more doggedness than courage; he was tasked with identifying and detaining 'enemy aliens' suspected of disloyalty—an ever-expanding criterion that, by 1918, included German-born residents and their Australian-born children and grandchildren.[19]

Numerous historians of interwar Australia have cited Longfield Lloyd's name when demonstrating the arbitrary and piecemeal administration of the War Precautions Act or illustrating the way the internment policies bled into agendas that were personal, ideological and overtly political. Few historians, however, have pondered the irony of a patrician young man pledging his political loyalties to two former stalwarts of the Labor Party and trade union movement: Prime Minister William Morris Hughes and Minister of Defence Senator George Pearce.[20]

Captain Lloyd's role in the arrest and detention of an Australian-born Riverina politician named Harry Paech illustrates what would become his trademark style. It was bold, even cavalier. Firstly, in his timing: weeks before the second of two bitterly divisive referendums over conscription, and secondly, in his disregard for evidence and civil rights.

In October 1917, Billy Hughes' government narrowly lost the first referendum and, determined to fill the dwindling military ranks with conscripts, set a second referendum for 20 December. On 7 December, Captain Lloyd travelled to a region populated by German settlers, ready to uncover instances of disloyalty. One measure, he determined, was support for the 'No' vote. In that regard, he deemed sixty-year-old Harry Paech to be the 'life and soul of the anti-conscriptionist party' and a 'highly dangerous' man—'mostly on general grounds' that were 'difficult to prove', although the local bank manager was certain Paech had 'prevented a great many possible enlistments'. As such Captain Lloyd was in 'no doubt' that Paech's internment 'would have a cleansing effect on the district'. Six weeks later Paech was arrested and held without charge for almost two years, never learning the precise nature of his offence.[21]

Captain Lloyd spent the remainder of that week in December inspecting the homes, farms, churches and schools of German settlers, demanding to see naturalisation papers, noting the 'fright' in the eyes of men easily twice his age. The search produced a few faded pictures of the Kaiser, and official judgements tagging people as 'unscrupulous', 'not trustworthy' and 'needs watching', although his most consistent observation was 'no corroborative evidence'—'nothing of a direct nature can be produced against him'. Still, Captain Lloyd suspected the district's 'German and Sinn Fein elements' were working 'hand-in-hand', and so called for a door-to-door search to flush out firearms and subversion.[22]

The historian David Dutton has argued that, under Billy Hughes' leadership, Australia emerged from the Great War 'notably more anxious, authoritarian and illiberal than the one that entered it, obsessed by the dangers of subversion, and determined to employ the full extent of its powers to observe, quantify, marginalise and deport those deemed disloyal'. The result was a less cosmopolitan, more British, White Australia with a 'sharp new emphasis on the racial difference of European races'.[23]

Lloyd's intelligence work helped navigate this turn. After the war, he played a pivotal role in the deportation of nearly seven hundred German 'enemy aliens', measuring their 'disloyalty' according to their faith or involvement with the labour movement.[24]

One of Lloyd's internees and deportees was Father Charles Jerger, a German-born Catholic priest publicly accused of disloyalty. Jerger, in turn, singled out Lloyd's name when accusing intelligence officers of soliciting 'bribes' and 'unnecessarily brutal' 'savagery'. 'Those in authority are neither Australian in person nor spirit,' read Jerger's statement. 'They are usurpers, violators of the rights of people, and as such should be hurled from the positions they debase.'[25]

By contrast, Prime Minister Billy Hughes congratulated Lloyd. In a personal letter, he contrasted Lloyd's 'seclusion' from the public eye with the valuable role he played 'from the wing ... prompting the actors [as they] pompously strut the stage in the glare of the limelight'.[26]

In turn, Major Lloyd rewarded Captain Longmore for finding the most efficient route to national security and racial purity—assuming he separated the two goals—even if the tactics were not 'all together cricket'.[27]

14
THE 'BLACK MENACE'

In the days leading up to his deportation from Australia, Sonny Clay told Gayne Dexter: 'We were hounded ever since we landed. While in Sydney we were harassed. Men broke into our flats at all hours of the night. Somebody was trying to get evidence against us.'[1]

Five weeks earlier, Major Lloyd told a different story. According to his report into the Negro Orchestra, Investigation Branch officers began monitoring a Darlinghurst Road flat occupied by the band's two trumpeters—the older Nini Coycault and younger Archie Lancaster—as well as tuba player Herman Hoy and dancer Dewey Covan. Officers quizzed neighbours, learning from the caretaker the 'negroes were always well behaved'. The landlady concurred; she had no reason for complaint. Although in the adjoining premises, a second landlady had seen 'several white girls in the flat', the party singing and playing gramophones 'until 1 a.m. or 2 a.m. in the morning'. The incident, however, neither shocked nor offended her.

Still, a peace officer managed to find a tenant in the same block who claimed to see inside the musicians' rooms. They witnessed something—the details were not made clear—and were so scandalised by the 'Disgraceful' behaviour, they lodged a complaint with the NSW police.

This evidence was enough to persuade Longfield Lloyd of the menace posed by the Negro Orchestra. As he wrote in his report: 'As far as this Office enquiry goes, it seems clear that the negroes in question consorted with white women and that this is highly objectionable, especially in view of the Commonwealth policy in such matters.'[2]

And what 'Commonwealth policy' was that?

Of course, Major Lloyd was referring to the White Australia policy—an idea much philosophised by advocates. 'We are guarding the last part of the world in which the higher race can live and increase freely, for the high civilization,' postulated intellectual Charles Pearson in 1894.[3] 'A united race' where 'members can intermix, intermarry and associate without degradation on either side', promised the nation's first prime minister, Alfred Deakin, in 1901.[4]

But beyond the Immigration Act, how was this philosophy realised as policy? The musicians had visas and exemption certificates, so were not prohibited immigrants. Federal law posed no restrictions on 'consorting'. Nor had legislators passed anti-miscegenation laws.[5]

The only federal ruling regarding Black dance band musicians was a ten-word, handwritten entry buried in the Immigration Branch's *Book of Precedents*: 'American Negroes—proposed introduction band for Carlyon's Dancing Palais—refused.'[6] But neither vetted in cabinet nor debated in parliament, these words hardly qualified as 'Commonwealth policy'.

There was, however, one comparable reading of Commonwealth policy—although not articulated by lawmakers. Instead, it was litigated by Ezra Norton, a browbeating newspaperman with a longstanding animosity to Jews, Africans, Mediterraneans, Asians, Aboriginal people and certain types of women—although his many hatreds did not disqualify him from a love of Chinese porcelain and Italian terraces.[7]

Ezra Norton owned the *Truth*, a national network of scandal-mongering tabloids he had not quite inherited from his brilliant but terrifying father, John Norton. (Ezra's personal story was riven with scandal: his alcoholic father disinherited him after Ezra testified in support of his mother during his parents' bitter and messy divorce. Ezra eventually secured the newspaper after a bitter and messy legal challenge.) A man plagued with agonising personal insecurities and doubts, Ezra Norton obsessed on the ills of society and the administrative loopholes compromising White Australia.

In 1926, Norton launched a new crusade against the 'Black Menace'. His fury centred on four Black American boxers brought to Sydney in

1925 by the promoters who ran the Stadium, a corrugated iron pantheon in Rushcutters Bay. Since arriving, middleweights Sunny Jim Williams, Frisco McGale and Tiger Payne, and lightweight Joe Hall had earned reputations as 'outstanding performers', their 'sensational' fistic bouts drawing 'packed houses' and delighting fans—although Ezra Norton, an avid boxing fan regularly seen at the Stadium, was clearly not among them.[8]

Over a series of full-page articles, his pressmen flagged two 'devastating dangers': firstly, the 'very humiliating' sight of Black boxers pummelling White opponents. And secondly, the admiration, even infatuation, their victories roused in a suite of White female fans. Young women expressed their 'devotion' in letters and approached the boxers on the street.

The absence of laws keeping 'the negro' in 'his place' galled Norton. As his paper railed, transgressions punishable by lynching in the United States played out daily on the streets of King Cross. 'Scotch it now,' pleaded his reporters. 'We have built up as a young, healthy, isolated race' and the 'intermingling of races' will 'curse' this country.[9]

Ezra Norton matched his high dudgeon about the 'Black Menace' with a nuanced understanding of immigration procedure and law. The boxers resided in Australia courtesy of an exemption certificate valid for six months, articles explained. Extensions were 'not hard to obtain', so long as the boxers' behaviour met the satisfaction of the NSW police force, which to *Truth*'s mind was compromised and corrupt. 'Strings' had been 'tugged at', wheels had 'been revolved', turning a six-month sojourn into years—an outcome 'distinctly contrary to the statutes of the land' or, at least, Commonwealth policy.[10]

Each tirade ended on a plea for action: 'Such direct flouting of the country's laws and ideals must not be tolerated.' When will 'immigration authorities protect our Australian ideas'? When would these loopholes be plugged? At times, the *Truth*'s call-to-arms hinted at extra-legal measures. 'Unless we White Australians take some action, this botched boxing business will go on unchecked.' 'How long before some force is brought to bear.' 'Let such action be taken immediately ... The land that tells the world it is purely, simply, wholly and solely a WHITE MAN'S LAND.'[11]

Three decades earlier, John Norton had also noisily championed White Australia, although the father and son's arguments were no longer the same. Gone were the doomsday predictions of 'cheap' 'coolie' labour undermining the wages of White working men (a 'problem' that largely existed because most non-White labour was excluded from union ranks).[12] Instead Ezra fretted about the high fertility rates of small numbers of non-White Australians, the wayward behaviour of young White women and the threat of racial degeneration—even if his own family history of generational violence, alcoholism and adultery defied every presumption of the biological exceptionalism he attributed to the British 'race'.[13]

Beyond Ezra Norton's passion for boxing and horseracing, little is known about his private life. He was a 'lone wolf', although over the decades, his editorial decisions displayed a marked fealty to Captain George Longmore of the Commonwealth Investigation Branch. In the 1920s, Norton exposed the improprieties of Longmore's rival, Superintendent Yates. In the 1930s, the *Truth* simply ignored a juicy corruption investigation into Longmore's tactics. So close did Norton's and Major Lloyd's views align, he appeared like a mouthpiece.[14]

To counter the *Truth*'s slanderous attacks, Sunny Jim Williams and Tiger Payne penned open letters defying 'anyone to impugn' their 'conduct'.[15] As Black Americans they, of course, keenly understood the precarious protocols at play. 'So far as my speaking to any young ladies, that is something I do not do,' insisted Williams, although he was unable to prevent women approaching him on the street. 'But I never had anything to do with them.'

'It would ruin me professionally and I take care I do not fall for it,' added Frisco McGale.[16]

The boxers highlighted a more complicated problem. Young White women's reproductive choices lay at the cornerstone of the White Australia policy, but many seemed unaware of these rules. The *Truth* could not deny the pattern. 'Young girls' were 'ignorant of the danger to the community which their crazy actions generate', admonished reporters. 'They must be taught. They must be protected against their own lack of knowledge and individual depravity of outlook.'[17]

Almost miraculously, the threat of the 'Black Menace' vanished. When Sunny Jim Williams renewed his extension in May 1927, a run of bad luck plagued him. A thief ransacked his flat and stole his diamond jewellery. Newspapers implicated him in an assault charge. A referee disqualified him for 'illegal tactics'. Crowds who once lauded him began to hoot and jeer. So too, other newspapers began decrying the sight of a 'colored fighter' skittling the 'more sensitive and delicately formed descendants of the Aryans'. 'Ethnology definitely proves that the Negroid races are on a different evolutionary plane than the Aryans,' ran the polygenist reasoning.[18]

In August 1927, the Stadium's general manager suddenly resigned. The following day, the *Truth* ran an exposé about the boxers' pampered life 'behind locked doors'. 'The imported n______s like Australia, Australian money, and Australian women. They manage to get a share of each, but they don't boast about it.' Innuendo ran wild: from NSW policemen 'courteously' apologising to the boxer as if somehow beholden to them, to a White woman washing the boxer's dishes. Most likely, she was Joe Hall's Australian wife. Another White woman was a neighbour. As she explained, she and her husband often visited the flat.[19]

Williams sued the *Truth* for libel. But three weeks later, in September 1927, he and Joe Hall were steaming back to the United States. A 'boxing fan' lamented the extreme measures. 'Why should we draw the color line?' he protested. 'Sporting contests between all the races' can sweep away 'misunderstandings and prejudices'. Williams 'will be missed', agreed a sportswriter, wondering how the Stadium would draw crowds. A contest between two leading White Australians had pulled the 'smallest' 'attendance in years'.[20]

The departure for Joe Hall was most wrenching. Forced to leave behind his wife and child, he 'raised all sorts of barriers', forgetting 'one thing and another until the taxi was so delayed', and was 'dumped unceremoniously aboard as the steamer's lines were dropped'.[21] Two weeks later, Joe Hall returned to Sydney, desperate to be reunited with his family. But he reached no further than a customs officer who, in accordance with the Immigration Act, tested his literacy in Dutch—which, of course, he failed. A magistrate then sentenced him to six months in prison as a prohibited immigrant.[22]

Smith's Weekly, in their fanciful and jocular way, celebrated 'the black-out' with a piece titled 'Rise of the White Gladiator'. It opened in a Roman stadium. A 'blond giant' who had neglected his training and grown careless and over-confident found himself cornered by 'the biggest and blackest panther'. If the story thus far was improbable, it ratcheted up a notch, as the White gladiator turned his 'steady compelling gaze' on the 'black demon of the jungle' who 'wilted' and slouched sullenly away. With that, the gladiator strolled to his cowering 'enemy' and 'slew him'. 'The Menace has lifted and the white gladiators are free to rise once more,' concluded the heroic, if implausible, tale.[23]

Beyond the written record lay the tales of other White gladiators who, vigilant and alert to their training, used more than their gaze to fulfil Charles Pearson's vision quest. They, at least, believed they were 'guarding the last part of the world in which the higher race can live and increase freely, for the high civilization'.[24]

15
SYNCHRONISING OPERATIONS

It was the type of weather that tested a tour manager's ingenuity. A near Biblical deluge had washed away the main southern track between Cootamundra and Wagga Wagga. A bridge collapsed under the weight of a freight train, dumping the locomotive into the flood waters. And a theatre schedule required the twenty-one members of the Colored Idea to travel from Sydney to Melbourne.

On the morning of Friday, 17 February, the troupe left Sydney promising to be back for a return season. Their journey stopped at Cootamundra, a town perhaps meaningful to the bandsmen who had befriended the 'colored women' as the site of the Aboriginal Girls' Home. Twenty-four hours later, they were still three hundred miles short of their destination. Clearly, the company would miss the opening show that afternoon at Melbourne's Tivoli Theatre.[1]

The Colored Idea opened on Monday afternoon, drawing a capacity house, the audience demanding encore after encore. An orchestral arrangement of 'Tin Roof Blues', first recorded by the New Orleans Rhythm Kings in 1923, was a 'wonderful hit'. 'The rhythm was faultless,' reported one aficionado of modern music. 'No shoulder or shoe could resist shuffling to its compelling movement.' Word of mouth guaranteed a run of 'large' houses.[2]

The troupe's relocation was a development overlooked by the Sydney bureau of the Investigation Branch. A new battle on the waterfront and an old feud between warring agents had distracted the peace officers pursuing the Negro Orchestra case, causing them to blunder the operation.

Captain Longmore was busy cooking up evidence to prosecute union boss Jacob Johnson. Superintendent Yates was busy cataloguing Longmore's policing methods, a litany including conspiracy, collusion and false evidence. The 'general unsavoury atmosphere' contravened 'every sentiment of decency and the principle of justice', read Yates' final accusation. One of the stool pigeons was blunter: 'The whole thing was a "frame-up" from beginning to end.'[3]

Captain Longmore struck back. Or at least the *Truth* did, running a second exposé about Yates' gold-mining syndicate, detailing a foiled raid: NSW police were poised to bust a shareholder's illegal gambling operation but federal police got there first, destroying the incriminating evidence.[4]

Major Lloyd's confidential report into the Negro Orchestra side-stepped all these messy details. Instead, a sheen of efficiency buffed his account of the peace officers staking out the musicians' flat, identifying a night of gramophones and song with White women. A ponderous gravity raised the alarm to the breach of 'Commonwealth policy'. A steadfast confidence underpinned his faith in the operation's successful conclusion, while a bureaucratic circumlocution conceded he had failed to accomplish the mission.[5]

Yes, the peace officers had somehow found a tenant who witnessed a 'disgraceful' but unspecified act. But no, this incriminating evidence did not translate into a police raid and deportation order. As he explained, the Investigation Branch lacked the authority to stage a raid, so he relied on the NSW police's co-operation. Police liaison had long been Superintendent Yates' job so likely he co-ordinated the response, assuring Lloyd the police raid was imminent—'proposed for the latter portion of this present week'. Confident matters would proceed, Lloyd turned to other tasks.[6]

But no raid came.

Indeed, the NSW police did nothing to assist the Investigation Branch. A week after Sonny Clay's Colored Idea had wrapped up their Sydney season and left for Melbourne, NSW police claimed to be 'unaware' of their departure. Frankly, the Investigation Branch had not noticed it either.[7]

It was an embarrassing gaffe, although one Major Lloyd shrouded in procedural verbosity. 'Here this office's enquiry was hampered by the necessity of awaiting the proposed police coup which would have been spoiled by any prior scouting of a detailed nature.'

Of course, Major Lloyd made no mention of the extracurricular activities hampering the investigation. Behind the spit and polish of official reports lay a murky world of graft and corruption that determined who would be raided, or not.

Still, Lloyd desired the satisfactory resolution of the Negro Orchestra case, so recommended a decisive course of action founded on what his officers had failed to do.

With the Colored Idea in Melbourne, Lloyd urged his Victorian counterpart to continue investigations, only this time 'synchronise' operations with police 'from the outset' to ensure that the results would be 'conclusive upon all points'. Do not rely on the evidence of 'outside persons', he cautioned. Those people likely held 'divergent views' and did not censor such 'questions of behaviour'. Only a 'thorough' investigation and a 'coordinated' police raid would guarantee enough 'detailed evidence' to affect the desired result.[8]

From 'the wing', Major Lloyd was 'prompting the actors', setting in motion a chain of events that, if all went to plan, would formulate a new category of 'undesirability' within the Immigration Act and cleanse White Australian popular entertainment of 'colored musicians'.

On 24 February, Major Lloyd sent his report in triplicate to Major Harold E Jones, the federal director of the Investigation Branch in Canberra. Jones, in turn, forwarded two copies to Victoria. One to Inspector Roland Browne, Lloyd's counterpart in Melbourne. The other went to General Thomas Blamey, a former military commander and Victoria's current commissioner of police. 'If you consider that local investigation is necessary', read Jones' letter, he could assign a federal officer to 'work in conjunction' with Victoria police.[9]

Major Jones sensed correctly General Blamey concluded an investigation to be necessary. The police chief was an outspoken advocate of White Australia, who saw the 'right type' of population growth as a defence strategy to ward off 'irrepressible' 'race increase' in China and Japan. To his mind, national barriers were 'race barriers'—a battle plan that mobilised British immigration and the reproductive power of White women.[10] 'For Australia, the final triumph would be the complete unity of the Anglo-Saxon race,' he declared in 1921.[11]

Blamey was also a tough and uncompromising champion of law and order, with an impressive track record in crushing the forces that threatened chaos. He, like many other members of the Melbourne Establishment, openly admired the 'orderly condition of life maintained by Fascism'.[12] Since taking command of Victoria police in 1923, he had purged suspected radicals from the ranks and promoted men trusted for their loyalty. Blamey's opponents wondered if he understood the difference between the police force's role of maintaining the peace and the military's mission to annihilate the enemy. Even his supporters conceded his 'autocratic' style sometimes erred towards the 'heavy-handed'.[13]

General Blamey immediately swung into action, appointing his most trusted officers—Senior Constable Harry Dunn and Constable Leslie Saker—to carry out Major Lloyd's recommendations.[14]

That same week, the *Truth* newspaper underwent a perceptible shift.[15] In January 1928, the Sydney edition had celebrated the Colored Idea as a 'burst of colored sunshine' and 'all your jazz dreams come true'.[16] A week after the troupe opened in Melbourne, the local edition pronounced them 'a huge disappointment'. 'It is palpable that they are a dance and not a stage band,' read a snipe designed to cast aspersions on their capacity for fine art.[17]

Reviews in other newspapers were perfunctory.[18] *Table Talk* magazine dismissed the orchestra's 'Sambo jazz' and 'asthmatic trombones'. Ivy Anderson's rendition of the 'Alabama Stomp' was 'bearable' but hardly 'wonderful'. The *Argus* and *Age* did not review them at all.[19] Those that did agreed the support act, a 'perky' English fiddler, was the highlight of the show.[20]

The following week an editor at the Melbourne *Truth* juxtaposed a quarter-page photograph of Dick Saunders and Ivy Anderson dancing the Black Bottom alongside a skit about an African American seaman. Written in a faux Black Southern dialect, the seaman boasted about hoodwinking the two 'pow'ful big' White gatekeepers at the dock. At first, he pretended to 'capitulate' and pay the entry fee, but then broke into a Black Bottom and danced all over the officials.

'Yes suh, ah steps emphatically on that white man's foot, an' when he stoop, ah step some more.'[21]

The anecdote may have defied reason but as a comment on the band's arrival, it took little associative logic to read the troupe's confidence as arrogance, commercial success as theft and racial pride as White subordination. The 'Black Menace' had arrived.

PART V

The Making of Modern Melbourne

16
THE CARLYON TOUCH

THE CONVICT 'STAIN' weighed on the White Australian imagination. Champions of racial purity prophesied the evolution of a superior race but scholars of the day, swayed by eugenic studies that followed families over generations, convinced that hereditary traits extended to national and racial characteristics, portended doom. Eugenic logic dictated that the convicts transported to the penal colony would pass their criminal nature on to their progeny, giving rise to 'poor quality' 'stock' and condemning the young nation to degeneracy. Such an orthodoxy made a nonsense of the White Australian promise to breed better populations.

Still, historian Keith Hancock was upbeat. He was a Melbourne-born Rhodes scholar who, in 1928, was in the midst of tracing 'six generations of British enterprise in Australia' from penal colony to progressive liberal democracy. At first, torn between his Anglo-Saxonist loyalties and faith in the science of eugenics, Hancock was relieved, then thrilled to detect a generational pattern he considered exceptional.

Hancock hypothesised that the colony's criminal stain—what he called 'original sin'—had *not* been transmitted to subsequent generations but washed away by the enterprising gold-diggers of the 1850s. The free settlers had injected a vigorous strain of self-respect, industry and vitality into the national character, enabling 'the health and vigor of the stock' to reassert itself. 'Forget the wicked prolific Jukeses and remember only the prolific virtuous Bowdlers,' wrote Hancock, referring to two influential

US studies in eugenic heredity. This 'is one of the best and most hopeful facts in all of human history ... a brilliant argument for the optimist'.[1] To his mind, the gold-diggers were the 'first authentic Australians', the country's true founders and keepers of a sacred flame. The Anzacs were known as 'Diggers' for more than digging trenches.

When recounting their rise through Melbourne society, members of the Carlyon family proudly recalled their noble gold-digging forefathers: Thomas, the Welsh fortune seeker who staked out a claim on Ballarat's goldfields; and his strapping son, Tom, who rose from being a 'grease monkey' on a Murray River steamboat to own a string of Melbourne hotels. 'A man of progressive ideas' with a 'tenacity of purpose', Tom Carlyon had turned ideas into businesses and buildings, applauded *Table Talk* magazine. 'It was characteristic of the Carlyons to do everything well. Thoroughness is tattooed into their souls.'[2]

Although an unwavering allegiance and eternal gratitude to the British 'race' was not. Indeed, the Carlyon family's bohemian tendencies upended Hancock's tidy eugenic narrative about self-evident cultural and racial hierarchies. Tom's brother, Francis, for instance, bucked convention, working as a boxer and living with a trapeze artist in a travelling circus.[3] Tom's sons—Dean, Tom Jr and Norman—nursed a passion for Black American rag, jazz and blues, creating a home environment conducive to modern music and dance.

The three brothers had grown up dividing their time between the rarefied world of Geelong Grammar and the cosmopolitan bubble of the Carlyon Hotel. Tivoli acts routinely stayed there. At home, the boys mixed with visiting divas and troupers who built international careers on bizarre eccentricities. They spied vaudeville stars stumbling into executive suites, often with a complicated mess of sexual partners.[4]

At school, they bore witness to the 'patriotic fervour' and 'dark significance' of the Great War. Norman recalled waving 'farewell to school pals' as they reached enlistment age then attending 'memorial services in the school chapel to those who had already been killed in action'.[5] The fragility of life shaped the Carlyon brothers' commitment to joyous enterprises. Together they sought to fray Melbourne's reputation for strait-laced respectability and marked distaste for the 'incoherency, crudity and chaos' of Modern art. Or, as one admirer noted, the Carlyon brothers made a

Puritan town like Melbourne 'a little more bearable after the gong has gone for the last drink'.[6]

In 1919, Tom Snr acquired the Esplanade Hotel on the boardwalk of St Kilda, and his three sons began their apprenticeship in the hotel trade. All types of people passed through the Esplanade's doors. At dawn, the wharf labourers clocked off their night shift and headed to Carlyon's bar. At midday, socialites played bridge in a dining room framed by ocean views. In the evening, Dean adjudicated modern dance competitions in the newly built ballroom.[7]

A regular page in the *Bulletin* named 'Poverty Point, Carlyon's Hotel, St Kilda Melbourne' relayed the behind-the-scenes gossip in Melbourne art and the stage.[8] One evening, Russian ballerina Anna Pavlova and her troupe 'wound up its Melbourne sojourn with jazz at Carlyon's'.[9]

The Carlyons were best known for hosting exotically themed balls that conjured Parisian cafes, Spanish cantinas, Ancient Egyptian mishmash and Oriental hotchpotch. Photographs of gleeful Sunday night soirees hinted at breaches in licensing laws—and one night, police raided the ballroom, overturning tables and chairs, slapping guests, even drawing revolvers, their heavy-handed tactics raising accusations of brutality.[10]

Eldest son Dean took particular pride in managing the ballroom's orchestra. In 1922, he introduced Sydney band the Syncopated Six promising a 'special flair for jazz'—although most Australian dance band musicians, trained in military-style marching bands, tended to be heavy on the beat.[11] The displaced rhythms of jazz eluded them.

On a quest to find *that* sound, Dean and younger brother Tom left for San Francisco in 1923, intending to land a 'real' jazz band—specifically a 'real' Black jazz band, the first to reach Australia. The venture, as already recounted, reached no further than the minister for home and territories, Senator George Pearce. 'American Negroes—proposed introduction band for Carlyon's Dancing Palais—refused,' read the bureaucrat's entry in the Immigration Branch's *Book of Precedents*. As the minister explained, 'representatives of orchestral bodies', namely the Musicians' Union of Australia, had prohibited such bandsmen. Dean returned to Melbourne with a White bandleader, while Tom remained in the United States.[12]

As Norman later told it, Leon and Herman Phillips, the two brothers from Spokane, Washington, who ran St Kilda's Palais de Danse, ultimately shook up Melbourne's dance scene. In early 1924 they forked out £300 a week to secure Frank Ellis and his Californians, a White ensemble who had created a stir in Sydney. The swinging American beat landed like a 'big surprise' and 'revolutionized entertainment' in Melbourne. The sound was so startling that even an Arbitration Court judge agreed local musicians could not 'get the rhythm'. The Carlyon brothers soon got to know Frank Ellis: he stayed at their hotel and, much to their alarm, mixed with the girlfriend of Squizzy Taylor, a notorious gang leader and alleged murderer.[13]

In early 1925 Dean Carlyon, wise to Senator Pearce's commitment to at least some Musicians' Union bylaws, again travelled to Los Angeles. This time, he secured James Backelder and his Californian University Collegians, certain they would set new standards in Melbourne's dance world. Opening night drew a large group of 'dancing enthusiasts' and several industry guests, among them Musicians' Union Federal Secretary Cecil Trevelyan. But a shonky agent had switched the personnel, and the Californians were an unqualified 'failure', so inept and out of tune it was impossible to dance. Embarrassed by the 'derogatory remarks', Old Man Carlyon subleased Bert Ralton and his Savoy Havana Band from the Tivoli Theatre, an outfit stamped with the 'London and Paris' seal of approval. The Collegians were 'continuing their "studies" elsewhere' drolled a dance columnist—although it would be a long time before Dean lived down the blunder.[14]

In these months, the younger Tom Carlyon was studying 'the science of American hotel management' at the luxurious Bellevue Stratford Hotel in Philadelphia. Like his father, he was convinced Australia's economic development lay in 'its adoption of American know how'. As the adage ran in the Carlyon household: high American standards were a 'consistent reminder that Australia was really "down under"'. But when his father died suddenly in 1925, Tom Jnr's American sojourn came to an abrupt end. He came home to Melbourne to take over the family business.[15]

Tom Carlyon returned to a city bristling with possibility. After much anticipation, the Charleston craze hit in the autumn of 1926, arriving on movie screens and in dance *palais*, as demonstrated by specially imported exhibition dancers. Or more precisely, two Charlestons arrived—one English, the other American—a new frontline in an old battle for cultural and economic supremacy.[16]

In motion picture houses, the American Charleston reigned resplendent. 'Watch 'em flash that Charleston! Charleston!' read intertitles as three chorus dancers—Sally, Irene and Mary—in chiffon party dresses kicked and stomped from one wild party to the next. An instructional two-reeler, *Learn the Charleston in Six Lessons*, explained every American step. Meanwhile over at the Tivoli, crowds flocked to see the 'Real Negro Charleston' danced by Joe Sheftell's Southern Revue.[17]

A clutch of Melbourne dance columnists, each a self-appointed arbiter of correct and incorrect dance steps, watched in alarm. The American Charleston 'should have never been brought into this country' protested the *Truth*'s 'Dancing Expert'. The raised foot 'will never be allowed'.[18] Miss Foxtrotter, the dance columnist at *Table Talk* magazine, agreed: the 'Negro' 'grotesqueries' of the 'ugly bent leg action' violated the 'basic principle of poise and balance', she seethed.[19] Others offered a sociological explanation: the Charleston was a 'Negro' step from Harlem and satisfied a perverse White American 'urge' for 'primitive songs and music'.[20]

Miss Foxtrotter urged dance hall promoters to promote the 'correct' steps as determined by 'English dance masters'. Namely, 'the swinging hip movement of the London style' which had been 'stripped' of 'unsightly positions' and stamped with 'refinement and beauty'. To her mind, the standardised steps of Britain's ballroom dance academies served as an imperial quarantine where dances, 'contaminated' by 'miscegenated' American popular culture, could be cleansed and 'perfected' before being exported to the dominions. They arrived in Australia with no more than 'a negro touch'.[21]

Despite Miss Foxtrotter's 'laudable attempts' to persuade Melbourne dancers to remain loyal to their British roots, the American version gained ground. The city's dancing public had voted with their feet. Bruised shins and torn silk stockings were testament to nights of unrestrained side-kicks.

Within six months, the number of palladiums doubled, each staging dance competitions with ever-spiralling cash prizes and attracting 'phenomenal' crowds. The Wattle Path Palais' semi-final commanded more interest than the referendum over expanding federal government power, chuffed one commentator. Five thousand people crammed into St Kilda's Palais de Danse to watch a showdown between the 'real' American Charleston and the 'revised' English stomp. When the American style came in second, the English Charleston became an unlikely trophy of British superiority. If the city's dance experts could be believed, the way a person swung their hip or lifted their leg could make or break an empire.[22]

Tom Carlyon observed the lucrative leisure time industry with interest. A visit to the Green Mill in Los Angeles several years earlier had given him an 'idea'. Now with an inheritance at his disposal, he spent over £30 000 transforming a disused circus space at the southern end of Princes Bridge—essentially a galvanised iron barn lined with fibro cement sheets—into a modern dance resort.[23]

From the rotating sails of a giant windmill to canal houses, tulips and rainbow waterfalls, Melbourne's Green Mill attempted to replicate its Los Angeles namesake (which by 1926 had morphed into the Plantation

Tom Carlyon, the precocious 26-year-old entrepreneur who applied American know-how to create Melbourne's most popular dance resort, the Green Mill. (*Table Talk*, State Library of NSW)

Café). Three tiers of mezzanine seating overlooked a cavernous dance hall with a newly sprung floor. A lighting rig illuminated the ceiling with 'futuristic stars'. So great was the anticipation, on opening night the crowd smashed through a plate glass door and swept through the entrance 'like a tidal wave into the mouth of an estuary'. It was an 'instantaneous success'.[24]

Every night since, dancers congregated in their thousands. Martin Kett's peppy orchestra kept the dance floor humming (at least until Kett was sacked for drunkenness and domestic violence, replaced by American-born Joe Aronson). A chorus line of ballerinas and an assortment of novelty acts, many on loan from the Tivoli, presented cabaret entertainment. Curiosities like Oliver the Cave Man added offbeat fun, carolling sing-a-longs from the hole in the Green Mill Mountain.[25]

To draw audiences, Carlyon applied the American science of marketing or 'exploitation' to stage stunts and novelties, a procession of marathon dances, beauty pageants and roller derbies. To cultivate a sense of fealty amongst regular patrons, he mailed out a free weekly magazine, even sent them cake to mark the Mill's first birthday. 'The "Carlyon" touch is a hallmark of excellence in dancing fare,' approved Miss Foxtrotter, who *may* have been Tom's new bride, Addie Scott, a member of vaudeville dance team the Exquisite Eight. Certainly Miss Foxtrotter, if a harsh critic of the American Charleston, was a reliable champion of Carlyon's ventures, with a detailed knowledge of his thoughts.[26]

Unlike his friend Gayne Dexter, Tom Carlyon never appeared at a Royal Commission to lambast the White Australia policy or denounce quota systems that favoured British trade. Nor did he reflect on show business as a balance of art and commerce, a global enterprise, unsuited to protectionist economic policy. Diplomacy mattered to the hotelier-cum-dance hall promoter. Confrontation was not his style, trained instead in soothing ruffled feathers and disarming by charm. Reporters noted his 'natural fund of affability'. 'He is, in every sense, a nice boy', read a compliment encased with the lingering perception the 26-year-old was still a kid who 'gambled recklessly' in an 'uncertain' field.[27] One of those gambles was pushing the confines of Sunday entertainments. Another was testing the limits of the Musicians' Union's rulebook.

17

A STERLING ADVERTISEMENT FOR AUSTRALIAN GIRLHOOD

THE BUSH INDUCED a 'deep mystery of joy' in the English novelist DH Lawrence during his 1922 sojourn in Australia. But the 'little fences', 'forlorn bungalows' and rusty corrugated iron of the built environment baffled him. It was as though the townships had 'tumbled haphazard off the pantechnicon of civilisation ... and there lay, busy but not rooted in. As if none of the houses had any foundations.' Lawrence may have been describing Broken Hill, a settlement five hundred miles northwest of Melbourne that was more 'agglomeration of fag ends' than city.[1] A flat, treeless, dusty grid of a town bounded by open-cut mines and marked by streets named Gypsum and Oxide, it offered young men a lifetime of work in the mines and young women even fewer options.[2]

These horizons expanded when the Adelaide Express steamed into Sulphide Street station on 6 September 1927. On board was Beryl Mills, otherwise known as Miss Australia. The largely female crowd broke into applause the moment she stepped onto the platform and, over the next five days, kept patient vigil outside her hotel, before mobbing her car.[3]

For five nights, the 21-year-old beauty queen appeared at the local Union Theatre, speaking about the transformative power of the Miss Australia Quest. With the aid of newsreel films, she traced her journey from ordinary country girl to one of the most admired women in the nation, reliving her prize-winning trip across the Pacific: first to Hollywood where she appeared in a film, then Atlantic City for the Miss America beauty pageant.[4]

Beryl Mills' popular appeal ran deeper than her wholesome, radiant beauty. A farm-raised, university-educated woman, she aspired to marriage, motherhood and a career in journalism. Asked to name her favourite living writer, she nominated Louise Jordan Miln, a bohemian American novelist whose stories about Western encounters in China 'threw a vastly different light on the colored question'. Modernity, technological sophistication and cultural innovation, Mills learned, was not the exclusive preserve of the West.[5] As for her favourite composers, she named Edvard Grieg, the Norwegian romantic of 'Peer Gynt' fame, and Samuel Coleridge-Taylor, the British–Sierra Leone symphonist known for his cantata of Longfellow's poetry. Her answers impressed. A 'brilliant speaker' of 'rare intellect', Beryl Mills was 'a sterling advertisement for Australian girlhood', lauded *Everyones* magazine.[6]

More than swelling national pride in her throngs of female admirers, Beryl Mills inspired hope. Beauty, brains and cultural savvy were the currency by which a girl from the back country could rise above her circumstance and lead a life less ordinary.[7] In glorifying Miss Australia, they glorified themselves.

The dressmaking and millinery students at Broken Hill's technical college thrilled at Beryl Mills' visit to their classroom, vowing to handcraft a veil for her upcoming wedding. And they did. Five months later, photographs captured the new bride wearing a silken tulle train scalloped with lace, embroidered with flowers, banded with satin and capped with pearls. Through an act of artistic expression, the young women of Broken Hill won a place in what was then Australia's most absorbing fairy tale. For them, popular culture was more than passive consumption but a way to express their lives, dreams and aspirations.[8]

In 1927 a report published by the Travellers' Aid Society noted a surge in country girls leaving their hometowns for Melbourne. Many were runaways bored by the monotony of country life, resentful of the 'hard rule' of their parents and stifled by the purgatory of factory work and domestic service. Some fled family 'difficulties'. Others craved excitement or were 'stage struck'. They dreamed of winning a beauty contest, even

Hollywood fame. 'Most of them think they are bettering themselves,' noted the report.[9]

Edna Langdon of Railway Town, Broken Hill, was one such modern girl. Unlike the many who turned to the Travellers' Aid Society for assistance, her luck in the big city of Melbourne had not yet run out. By February 1928, the eighteen-year-old was a finalist in the Green Mill's beauty pageant. Already her image had been captured on film and mass produced in newspapers and newsreels. If she shone brightly enough to win the quest, she might be the next local girl to 'make good' in Hollywood.

Born Edna Ewart in Coventry, England, in 1910, she was raised in a compact terrace, one of 130 identical new homes built for the upper ranks of the working class. Her father was a coach trimmer, producing bicycles and buses for a global market. Her mother, Flo, was a dressmaker and homemaker. Her sister, Kathleen, would forever be her closest friend. But the sudden death of Edna's father in 1918 exposed the Ewart family to the fragile prosperity of those relying on a single male breadwinner. Widows in such circumstances often faced destitution. Perhaps for this reason Flo married an Australian soldier named Les Langdon, whose inscrutable, solitary ways belied a complicated past. In 1920, Flo and her two daughters migrated to Australia and, for the next six or seven years, lived in Les Langdon's flimsy, iron-roofed bungalow on the dusty outskirts of Broken Hill.[10]

Like his father before him, Les worked in the mines. Flo made dresses, while Edna and Kathleen took ballet lessons. An undated photograph portrayed the girls in French clown outfits, belted at the waist with an intricate white neck ruffle. Most arresting was the unflinching gaze Edna fixed on the camera, her eyes framed by a heavy fringe and smooth, straight bob—an up-to-the-minute Egyptian bob, as debuted by Hollywood flapper Colleen Moore in *Flaming Youth*. 'The picture that made Australia sit up and take notice', ran a 1924 advertisement in the Broken Hill press.[11]

Beyond the story of Edna Langdon's brief and tumultuous encounter with members of the Sonny Clay Orchestra, little is known of her life. In the 1940s and 1950s she worked as a dressmaker, tailoring quality clothes for a well-heeled clientele. Perhaps she acquired these skills from her mother. She also may have learned her trade at the local technical college,

Edna Langdon (left) with her sister in Broken Hill, circa 1924, both sporting a modern bob. (Jeffrey Fitzsimmons)

placing her in the same classroom as the devotees who so lovingly stitched Miss Australia's wedding veil. In the late 1920s, however, Edna described herself as a dancer—although dancing in Broken Hill was a hard-won pleasure.[12] In late 1926 through to mid-1927, the Palais de Danse remained shut after the manager crossed horns with the Musicians' Union when an out-of-town banjo player neglected to follow a minor procedure. The union's draconian response to a trivial offense raised questions of a hidden agenda at play.[13] For an aspiring dancer, the strike presented a compelling reason to leave.

Edna Langdon arrived in Melbourne to discover a world a little closer to the chimera witnessed on movie screens. She basked in the 'free and easy' atmosphere of Coffee Dans on Swanston Street, where a person could dine, dance and sing if they felt so inclined. 'The place is rigged out like the original Coffee Dans in San Francisco', approved *Everyones* magazine, including a set of wooden spoons on each table for customers to bang along to the music—and, incidentally, replicate moments from the artist's ball in *So This Is Paris*. Customers were welcome to 'make as much noise as they like'.[14]

On the banks of the Yarra River at the southern end of Princes Bridge, Edna Langdon also discovered the Green Mill, Melbourne's most ambitious American Jazz Age transplantation. By day, the venue doubled as a roller-skating rink and velodrome. By night, it drew a rowdy crowd, committed to uproarious fun—and a few legal violations. The two policemen who regularly patrolled the resort had charged revellers with all types of misdemeanours: a waitress for wearing stolen jewellery; a twenty-year-old tinsmith for sneaking in a flask of alcohol; a 22-year-old carpenter for obstruction; a confectionery worker for hawking stolen fur coats.[15]

The exacting dance columnist Miss Foxtrotter distanced herself from the dance floor. Despite her close ties to Tom Carlyon, she bemoaned the 'awful' and 'slovenly' dancers who stumped around on flat feet, the men's 'grimy and dirty' hands staining the 'dainty fabrics of ladies dresses'. Arms flung about like semaphores, limbs pumped like handles, bodies crouched as if shrinking from an impending catastrophe.[16] For people like Edna Langdon, such liberation from correctness, freedom from accuracy, deliverance from a narrowly prescribed etiquette felt like democracy.

In 1927, the Green Mill staged the country's first dance marathon—their biggest promotion yet. Radio 3LO transmitted updates, a cameraman shot newsreel footage and a newspaper photographed exhausted marathon dancers being fed and shaved. The three-day event attracted fifty thousand curious onlookers and widespread condemnation. An 'unedifying spectacle', decried the *Argus* newspaper.[17] A 'silly business' that did nothing to benefit the 'vitality of the race', weighed in the Victorian minister of health.[18] But the naysayers missed the point: mocking the progressive gospel of efficiency was part of the fun.

The same year the Green Mill partnered with film exhibitors First National to launch the Film Star Quest, a beauty pageant and nationwide search for a 'girl' with 'motion picture possibilities'. 'All girls anxious to gain fame on the screen' were invited to send their photograph to the Green Mill's 'casting office', read an announcement. The 'lucky' winner would appear in a Hollywood picture. Eleven thousand hopefuls applied in Victoria alone.[19]

The Film Star Quest organisers entrusted none other than screenwriter and magazine editor Gayne Dexter to find that 'girl'. Every Tuesday night, before a capacity crowd, Dexter dispensed lessons in 'screen technique' to a batch of entrants, before filming a very public screen test. Each week, he devised different scenarios: the homespun country girl in the farmyard, the comedienne throwing mud packs in the beauty parlour, a scorned woman toying with a revolver in a gambling den. 'Most of the contestants wish to play "vamp" parts,' he noted. As he well knew, the trend directly reflected ticket sales. 'Jazz stories of the Mae Murray type' drew 'top attendances'.[20]

In April 1927, the nine finalists from across Australia and New Zealand gathered at the Green Mill. Miss Foxtrotter likened the crowd's yelp to a 'high powered explosive' when Sydney hairdresser Phyllis Gibbs was crowned the winner. Several women fainted and others were crushed in the crowd.[21]

By May, Phyllis Gibbs was on her way to Hollywood. In San Francisco, a cavalcade of police motorcycles escorted her through the streets to an official welcome by the mayor. In Hollywood, she sat a screen test and appeared in a Cecil B DeMille studio film. Back in Australia, the press lauded her as 'unspoiled, unaffected and sincere', 'a perfect specimen of Australian girlhood'.[22]

A consummate self-promoter, Gayne Dexter managed to direct some of the limelight back on himself. It was this experience that led him to warn that Anglo-Saxon Australians were developing a 'racehorse face' and lobby for an immigration policy welcoming 'good-looking' Latins and Slavs. His 'scandalous' words inspired the theme of the Green Mill's 1928 beauty pageant: The Artist's Model.

To prove 'Mr Dexter's sight needs immediate attention', Tom Carlyon would commission 'a famous artist to paint the winner of his new Model Girl contest'. The painting would be entrusted to a visiting English actress, who would then take it home with her and, presumably, show it to all her theatrical friends—or so ran the publicity.[23]

The competition invoked a nostalgia for the impoverished studio artist, a figure who had been widely replaced by commercial artists cranking out advertising and print promotions to meet the boom in mass marketing. There ended any pretensions to bohemian romance as quest organisers notified pageant entrants that a bathing costume parade was a part of the deal. Two decades earlier, it was unthinkable for a respectable young lady to conspicuously display the flesh of her limbs and form of her body—and even in 1928, it affronted notions of modesty. Several Christian women's organisations lobbied to ban beauty competitions. The Green Mill pageant organisers pushed back, drawing on the rhetoric of the modern physical culture movement. There was nothing immoral or vulgar about the sight of a healthy White Australian body, they ventured. Indeed, it would refute the slanders uttered by Gayne Dexter and restore national pride.[24]

Sometime in January 1928 Edna Langdon responded to the Green Mill's entreaties and submitted her photograph for consideration. Of the thousands of applicants, she was one of sixty chosen to appear in the heats.[25]

Every Tuesday night in January and February, the dance hall did 'huge business' as a panel of judges evaluated the facial beauty, figure, deportment and 'artistic manner' of twelve young entrants. The evening climaxed with the Fountain of Life, a two-tiered 'living chandelier' ornamented with the contestants in their bathing suits. Carlyon professed a Louis XVI design but, as *Variety* magazine confirmed, 'living chandeliers and undressed ladies' had been the 'usual revue adjuncts' in Broadway cabarets since the early 1920s, an opportunity to showcase beauty contest winners, all plucked from obscurity. More recently, *Sally, Irene and Mary,* the flapper film about three chorus girls, featured an Egyptian-themed 'living chandelier'. As any film fan knew, one of the stars, Joan Crawford, began her career in a dance hall competition.[26]

Strapped to the Fountain of Life, bathed in a golden light, cascaded by tumbling water, Edna Langdon and her fellow contestants drew on a palette of expressions that affirmed their playfulness and innocence while masking the force of their ambitions. They were objects of intense public scrutiny and judgement; decorative feminine consumables fixed by the male gaze. 'Spectators craned their necks and strained their eyes at the wonderful Fountain of Life as it made its triumphal way around the dance floor,' reported Miss Foxtrotter. 'Some of our best-known folk stood amongst the throng.'[27] One week, the special guest was Police Commissioner General Blamey, a man known to appreciate feminine beauty—although he, of course, watched from the balcony.[28]

As Edna knew from previous heats, judges followed a familiar script to spin out the drama. They professed to be deadlocked, unable to choose a winner, so deferred to the crowd. One by one, each contestant struck their final pose, as the judges calibrated the audience's shouts and cheers. Edna did not draw the loudest holler, but as second runner-up, she was through to the semi-final.[29] She was one more step on a path that would cross with Sonny Clay's touring party and the forces arrayed against it.

18
MISS 1928

THE ARTISTS' MODEL QUEST dangled cash prizes worth £250 but when broken down into ten heats, three semi-finals and a grand final, Edna Langdon likely walked away with less than a pound. Still, even a small sum could bolster her weekly salary as an office clerk; the basic wage for a single woman hovered around £1 6s. The real trophy was the promise of celluloid celebrity and fame. And on 27 February, the eight contestants in the first semi-final tasted a nibble, their portraits appearing in a *Herald* advertisement, a few short column inches away from the faces of major Hollywood stars.[1]

The stamp-sized image of Edna Langdon captured her pretty, neatly proportioned face. A soft shingled bob distinguished by a not-quite-artful snail curl on her forehead suggested a home mirror style. But her studied sideways glance, alluring and coy, signalled a savviness with the screen techniques of the cinematic close-up. In motion pictures, the dart of the celluloid flapper's eyes often kicked off an eyeball ballet to relay their restless mind, intense emotions and striking beauty. 'Some part of her was always in motion in all her waking moments—if only her great rolling eyes,' wrote a studio executive of Clara Bow. 'An animal vitality ... made her the center of attraction.'[2]

A Tivoli advertisement sitting on the other side of the fold opened up other frames of reference. It was the promotion for the Colored Idea's

Melbourne season and featured a sketch of a tuxedoed saxophonist tooting his horn and tapping his foot. 'Here we are' read the by-line. The figure was likely Leo Davis, although the realism the graphic artist invested in the clothing and body language did not extend to the musician's face,

Edna Langdon appears in a Green Mill advertisement (third from bottom on right) a few column inches away from a Tivoli advertisement promoting the Colored Idea. (Melbourne *Herald*, State Library Victoria)

any idiosyncratic features obliterated by a generic cartoonish Blackness. A strip of text, however, mirrored the information on the Green Mill's advertisement: the following week, 6 March, Sonny Clay's Midnight Dance Revel would appear at the Green Mill's Australian Cup Midnight Ball.[3]

A more nuanced connection linked the photographic image of Edna Langdon and sketch of saxophonist, maybe Leo Davis. He, too, had his eyes cast to the side, emphasising the whites of his eyeballs. The shared visual language spoke to the same iconographic trope. Along with a wide gaping smile, the eye roll was a hallmark of blackface minstrelsy, the gesture signifying the Southern fool's stupidity. The tic was explicitly rejected by followers of the New Negro movement, although it remained deeply embedded in White perceptions of Black people. Likewise, the flapper's eye roll also conveyed their disassociation from rational thought. Films of the 'jazz type' oscillated between the heroine's rejection of domesticity and precocious independence—and spells of giddiness, faints and swoons, mostly in her lover's rescuing arms.[4] The celluloid flapper hovered on the cusp of unconsciousness and worldly power.

The Australian media portrayed such modern working girls with a jaundiced pen. Most weeks, the *Bulletin*'s David Henry Souter ran cartoons of heavily made-up young women with cropped hair, fox stoles and skin-tight geometric knitwear. They wrapped their long angular limbs around a chair or sofa as they slouched, smoked, drank and schmoozed with a man in search of sexual favours. But consumption-based sophistication could not obliterate working-class naivety. 'Will you love me when we're married?' ran one caption.[5] They were too bird-brained and fidgety for their decisions to be taken seriously. 'The modern flapper is so synthetic,' read a Sunday newspaper puff piece: synthetic from her shoe leather to the sheen on her bobbed hair.[6]

Marketing men knew otherwise. The globalised economy that powered the rise of mass production and explosion of commodity goods and services had given rise to a new managerial class, lampooned in popular culture as the 'Tired Business Man'. The administrative work they generated was largely met by young, educated women equipped with telephones, dictation transcribing machines, front strike typewriters and carbon paper for duplicates and triplicates. Materially and morally independent, keenly aware of their capacity to remake the modern world, young working women assumed their place in the streets of the modern city. Each day, newspapers photographed Melbourne's best-dressed 'girls': a procession of White women in ready-to-wear outfits purchased in department stores. Their consumption patterns had the power to make or break a product or an industry.[7]

'Have you booked Miss 1928?' read Paramount Picture's double-page advertisement in *Everyones* magazine. The angular, geometric artwork centred on a stylish, self-contained female blissfully unaware of two smart gents seeking her attention. 'Miss 1928! Bobbed hair, knee high skirts. Smart, sophisticated, up to the second. Every business must please her or perish ... Eager for entertainment but mighty shrewd in choosing it ... She dictates motion picture styles today just as she does clothes or cars ... What are you doing to win Miss 1928?'[8]

The male management teams at the Tivoli and Green Mill believed they were doing their utmost to meet the 'craves' of Miss 1928, re-creating the sophisticated worlds movie-goers witnessed on the screen and tempting them with the promise of artistic recognition, social and professional advancement, celebrity, wealth and matrimony.

When the first semi-final of the Artist Model Quest rolled out on 28 February 1928, the pageant drew a 'sprinkling of Melbourne artists' and vaudeville stars, the Emperors of Harmony from the Colored Idea. Bandleader Joe Aronson, 'the Rajah of Jazz', infused his orchestra with faux-Indian exoticism, sitting turbaned and cross-legged on the floor (a routine 'borrowed' from a Los Angeles bandleader). Edna Langdon and nine other semi-finalists once again paraded across the stage in their bathing costumes and strapped their bodies to the 'Living Chandelier'.[9]

As the second runner-up in her heat, Edna was something of an underdog—a few rivals also exuded an ethereal Hollywood glamour. Her moments in the limelight were brief but, whether by flashing a few dance steps or striking an elegant, even vampish, pose, she somehow projected the qualities of an artist model to emerge victorious, the winner of the semi-final. Next stop was the grand final and, just maybe, the pageant trophy. A year earlier, Phyllis Gibbs had won the Film Star Quest on the same stage.

While Edna was absorbed in the publicity for the grand final—her image filmed and packaged into a newsreel to be screened in picture houses across the country—Sonny Clay's Colored Idea were building a momentum of their own.[10]

The company's cold reception in the Melbourne press contrasted with the heat generated at the Tivoli Theatre each day. The grapevine had proved stronger than the critic's judgement, and what began as a reliable attraction grew into a remarkably popular show. One dance columnist, detecting new rhythms in local dance bands, swiftly corrected their misconceptions. '"Hot" Means Nothing' she admonished, urging dancers not to show 'appreciation' for the 'screeching clarinet obligato' which 'America calls "hot"'. Local jazz hounds, who styled themselves in opposition to the conservative taste-makers, ignored such directives to embrace the most significant moment in Melbourne Modernism to date.[11]

If jazz was 'the Cubism of motion', as a snooty critic once scorned, then a night at the Melbourne Tivoli approximated the fashionable happenings in Paris: the plastic poetry of Jean Cocteau, the globular film experiments of Man Ray, the 'syncopated abandon' of Josephine Baker's cabaret show. A piano teacher named Percy Prout, who mixed with people curious about the audacity of the black notes and the logic of the blue ones, honoured Sonny Clay at a Masonic banquet. An ink sketch artist responsible for the Tivoli advertising dispensed with the minstrel clichés, emphasising each performer's sophistication and style. Audiences returned to hear the new symphonic arrangements Sonny Clay added to the programme.[12]

In this spirit, Tom Carlyon invited Sonny Clay and his troupe to perform at the Green Mill's Australian Cup Midnight Ball on 6 March. It would be their first dance hall appearance—a test of union tolerance and measure of consumer demand.

The Australian Cup was the oldest and richest long-distance horserace in the country, a day when Melbourne's social diarists noted imperial posturing from the viceroy's wife through to the lord mayor.[13] The Green Mill's Australian Cup Midnight Ball attracted none of these dignitaries or diarists, catering to a more rambunctious crowd ready for 'a feast of Fun Fast and Furious'. 'It is recognised the World over what WONDERFUL DANCE TIME colored folk can play,' urged the Green Mill's advertisement that day. 'LET'S MAKE A NIGHT OF IT TONIGHT.' 'Dance to the strains of the Demons of Rhythm, Sonny Clay's Colored Syncopators.'[14]

Edna Langdon and other finalists, of course, attended the midnight ball—and likely made a stage appearance. The second semi-final had been held earlier in the evening and the Green Mill's management rarely passed up a cross-promotional marketing opportunity.

Watching The Four Covans defy gravity, Ivy Anderson moan a shivery blues and the Sonny Clay Orchestra 'burn holes in a concrete wall', Edna Langdon too could report 'a most biggety affair' in her adopted home of Melbourne—or something akin to reports penned by social diarists in Hollywood.[15]

Circumstances suggest the Artist Model finalists were introduced to the special guest performers. Edna, it appears, conversed mostly with drummer extraordinaire David 'Baby' Lewis. In Los Angeles he was a fixture at Central Avenue's Apex Club, with legions of young admirers and a penchant for good times. Without stretching the truth too far, he could regale her with first-hand accounts of Hollywood celebrity. Lewis was personally acquainted with cabaret dancer Carolynne Snowden and comedy actor Stepin Fetchit, who played the love-struck servants in the MGM feature *In Old Kentucky*, screening at Melbourne's Hoyts picture palace that week. Also in the film was Dorothy Cummings, an Australian country girl who had 'made good' in Hollywood.[16]

Consumption may not be a conscious political act, but for Edna Langdon and hundreds of other modern working girls crowded in the Green Mill that Tuesday night, consumption was a cultural choice—an act of discernment based on aesthetics and personal taste. By moving through a simulated space construed as the preserve of the rich, rebellious and daring; by listening to the note-bending wails of the saxophone and cornet; by dancing with knock-knees and flapping elbows; by shingling their hair, and wearing dresses of bold colours and geometric prints, their stockings rolled down, their hemlines above the knee, their arms stacked with heavy bracelets, the working girl of Melbourne 'made' herself modern.[17]

New forms of mass media were compressing international time and space, complicating a person's allegiance to a geographically defined nation or empire. The mechanical reproduction of image and music transmitted a lexicon of styles, slang and sounds to a global audience, enabling those savvy enough to cultivate an alternative cosmopolitan subjectivity founded on jazz. By dancing to the Sonny Clay Orchestra in the Green Mill that night, Edna Langdon was part of a modern push that stretched from Montmartre to Melbourne.

19
JAZZ NIGHT

THE GREEN MILL was many things: a business where entrepreneurs sold commodities for profit; a dream factory where modern working girls escaped mundane reality; a forum where specific types of music, dance steps and hairstyles mattered, where young people created their own subcultural codes of identification. But the corrugated barn was also a regulated space, subject to the constraints of the Musicians' Union of Australia and their commitment to a national culture founded on 'racial unity'.

Tom Carlyon was keenly aware that the Musicians' Union's federal secretary Cecil Trevelyan tolerated the Midnight Ball's violation of the no 'colored musicians' rule, likely through gritted teeth. But when Carlyon pressed on, nutting out a deal with Sonny Clay, securing the Colored Idea for one week at the end of the Tivoli run, Cecil Trevelyan staged an intervention. Hard on the heels of the Green Mill announcement, he dashed off a telegram to Carlyon which read: 'Will you undertake that the public will not dance to blacks?' A second cablegram read: 'Union objects most strongly to Sonny Clay's band playing Green Mill or any other dance hall.'[1]

The Musicians' Union had a small membership base but wielded considerable clout. In 1926, they shut down Broken Hill's Palais de Danse when the manager ignored a union directive. In March 1928, when Trevelyan telegrammed Carlyon, the union was in the midst of a two-pronged war against Italian musicians. The Sydney office was battling Hoyts over an imported thirty-piece orchestra at its flagship picture house, while the Melbourne office fumed over the 42-piece orchestra touring with Signor Auturo Gonzales' Grand Opera Company. 'None of us'—as in the Australian public—'want the Italians', insisted one state secretary, ignoring numerous signs to the contrary. In January, eager crowds had burst through the wharf barriers to greet Hoyts' Italian orchestra, while the Melbourne establishment and other lovers of 'good music' lionised Signor Gonzales. Ticket sales were robust.[2]

The Musicians' Union executive ought to 'realize the futility of trying to apply unionism, patriotism or jingoism to the populace where entertainment is concerned', advised *Everyones*' Gayne Dexter. 'Music is labour to the man who sits and fiddles, but it is art to the listening public' and union campaigns against imported musicians lacked the 'first essential ingredient of success: public sympathy'.[3]

Trevelyan's telegram to Carlyon presented the dance hall promoter with a dilemma more complicated than Dexter's 'labour' versus 'art' argument. 'Art' was a fluid conceit, the value of a work determined by arbiters of 'good taste' and challenged by consumer demand. Those who welcomed the refined and uplifting influence of Italian opera did not necessarily extend their sympathies to a Black American jazz orchestra.[4]

Tom Carlyon weighed up his options. His powerful social connections offered him a certain unspecified protection. His business partner, Fred Matear, was also a business partner of Police Commissioner General Blamey, who in January had attended the Artist Model Quest.[5] But Carlyon's family still flirted on the fringes of insider respectability. They were unconventional, barely a generation away from their egalitarian working-class roots and used to challenging the dictates of moralists and sticklers for the law. For years, Carlyon's family flouted wowser statutes at the Sunday soirees at their St Kilda hotel. More recently, Tom battled church groups over Sunday trading. 'Clerical gentlemen would take us back to the dark ages,' argued one advocate.[6]

Understanding popular taste and the modern entertainment marketplace was Tom Carlyon's most potent weapon. He knew dancers were thirsting for Sonny Clay's 'potent, overproof, brand of syncopation' and could see no sense in a rule that allowed Black musicians in vaudeville theatres but banned them in dance halls.[7] With a confidence born of powerful connections, bohemian contempt and an elite education, Tom Carlyon shrugged off Cecil Trevelyan's telegram, ready to take the naysayers on.

In her column, Miss Foxtrotter dismissed the union's threats of industrial action as 'Much Ado'. 'No one can tell' why Sonny Clay's engagement had stirred so much 'heart-burn among musicians', she wrote. 'Had it not been for the enterprise of some of our dance hall managers in importing American bands, it is likely we should be still dancing to the old-time music ... Musicians admit that they have learned a lot and still have much to learn from the musicians from overseas.'[8] Even this disciple of the 'correct' ballroom dancing was unable to fathom why dancing to a White jazz band was acceptable and a Black one was not.

A clunky twelve-line poem about a Melbourne man's experience of the Colored Idea's Tivoli show offered one explanation. Written by the otherwise unknown John Wilson, 'Jazz Night' persistently used racial slurs to describe his experience of the Sonny Clay Orchestra. How he, a White individual seated in the stalls, saw and heard the Black performers on stage: the 'yowl' of Leo Davis' saxophone, the puff-cheeked blast of Nini Coycault's trumpet, the chatter of Sonny Graven's talking trombone and intensity of Baby Lewis' 'howl'. Wilson's poem ended, not with a sense of racial satisfaction, but a longing to be his racial other:

> Ain't they all a happy crew, madly, gladly gay?
> Don't you feel like you'd like to go giddy same as they?
> Drain the cup of Mumbo-Jumbo to its blackest bottom
> Shake and shimmy on the floor just as if you'd 'got 'em'.[9]

Wilson's poetic allusions were hardly original. Three years after Josephine Baker's 'Danse Sauvage' launched *le tumult noir* in Paris, the idea that jazz was the music of the African jungle was a well-worn primitivist cliché. For at least a century White explorers, missionaries and novelists had portrayed Africa as a land steeped in magic, where the supernatural forces had strangled scientific reason and religious restraint.[10]

Nor was it particularly imaginative to extend this logic to a jazz concert and perceive the performance as a ritual, the hot rhythms as an elixir, and the drummers as latter-day witchdoctors. 'Mumbo-jumbo will hoo-doo you' read the signature line of Vachel Lindsay's 1912 'cymbalist' jazz poem 'The Congo (A Study of the Negro Race)'—or, more accurately, a study of White fantasies of Black essentialism. Lindsay's poem was often critiqued in Australian literary columns, and performed at poetry recitals and modern ballets.[11]

Anthropologist JG Frazer's 'Law of Contact or Contagion' lent academic weight to the idea: 'Whatever [the magician] does to a material object will affect equally the person with whom the object was once in contact, whether it formed part of his body or not,' read his definition of sympathetic magic.[12] New York ethnomusicologist Natalie Curtis applied this 'law' to African ritual music and dance to explain how rhythm opened a psychic crack enabling unseen forces to enter 'men's bodies and control their thoughts and actions'.[13] To be touched by 'primitive' rhythms was to be voodooed or bewitched. The rise of Freudian psychology brought a new twist to this belief. Since at least the 1910s, Greenwich Village Bohemians had cast the Jazz Jungle as a deeply Freudian landscape, a chance to unlock repressed memories and allow subconscious creativity to flow.[14]

Likewise, John Wilson was hardly the first White person to wrestle with the dilemma posed by 'Negro jazz': if he drank from 'the cup of Mumbo-Jumbo', and engaged in a night of unchecked primitivism, would he return a less anxious, more refreshed version of his White self? Or, by some magic, would the rite destroy his individuality and free will? Would a night of racial cross-dressing liberate or obliterate?[15]

The significance of Wilson's poem lay in the unoriginality of his ideas, revealing the extent to which racial thinking had permeated his musical imagination. He explicitly understood that while seated in the stalls, he was protected from the jazz 'contagion', for the 'Mumbo-Jumbo' was the 'shake and shimmy', the dance. Hot rhythms were powerful stimulants that physically affected the people who danced to it, quickening the pulse, relieving tension and altering feelings and minds.

According to 1920s public discourses, no group fell under this spell more readily than young women. The ecstatic female dancer was the period's defining motif. Jazz Age writers and artists fixed on the image to express the delights of instinct over reason, freedom over restraint and boundless pleasure over steady toil.[16] In a surprising number of jazz-themed motion pictures and stageplays, young women, both White and light-skinned Black, entered a fiery jungle glade only to be seduced by the 'throbbing' tom-toms, which compelled them to dance in a wild orgiastic frenzy, until they finally collapsed into unconsciousness. The malleable nature of a woman's body rendered her helplessly receptive to the rhythms of Black music. Ideas about sympathetic magic and trance possession transformed their musical reverie into an act of miscegenation.[17]

Scientific research of the time confirmed the perception. Psychological studies presented hypnotism and autosuggestion as a malevolent state of dissociation and an untapped form of power enhancement. Leading eugenicists linked unrestrained female sexuality to feebleminded suggestibility.[18] One influential report into the causes of prostitution concluded:

> The feeble minded girl, not able to take results into consideration, not keen enough to foresee the consequences of immoral acts, and too ignorant of her own body to understand the meaning of her feelings and the result which attend relaxation from a normal standard, falls an easy prey in the hands of a seducer.[19]

Philosophers and political scientists voiced their mistrust of crowds, viewing mass spectacles as a dehumanised herd, diminished in reason, governed by emotions and easily swayed by charismatic figures proffering unscientific solutions. 'The sinking of individuality in the purposes of the larger unit carries with it a suggestion of potentially irresistible power,' wrote Sydney educationalist Meredith Atkinson.[20]

If 'Negro Jazz' was the conduit for liminal jungle magic, then the public dance hall facilitated the enactment of this rite. Unlike the theatre, no curtains or stage physically separated the audience from performers. Instead, dance hall managers harnessed technology, rhythm and group identification to cultivate dream-like spaces free from social distinctions.

People of all classes mingled in an escapist environment celebrating freedom, joy and the transgressive subcultural values.[21]

Such were the anxieties shaping the agenda of Melbourne's social purity associations and vigilance leagues. But nowhere in the Musicians' Union's campaign to prevent White people dancing to Black musicians did they verbalise this complex set of fears about primitivism, mind control, racial purity, female emancipation, youthful leisure and cheap urban entertainments. Nor did they refer to Clause (q) of Section 4 of their rule-book, which clearly stated their opposition to 'colored musicians'. Instead, the federal secretary, Cecil Trevelyan, repeated the same terse argument, citing high rates of unemployment amongst its members at the hands of imported Americans.[22]

Tom Carlyon understood Cecil Trevelyan's bluff. He too could play the national pride card. 'Sonny Clay's Band will be an added attraction at the Green Mill and will not displace one Australian musician,' reported his proxy, Miss Foxtrotter. 'The policy of giving jobs to local players has always been one of the principles of the Green Mill management, and if any voice is raised against this new departure it will certainly be an unwarranted expression of base ingratitude.'[23]

Carlyon's gesture, however, did nothing to placate the federal secretary. Each day ticked closer to Sonny Clay's opening show at the Green Mill and a much anticipated showdown.

But the squabble was a red herring. Unbeknownst to the dance hall manager, though not the union boss, the real battlefront was elsewhere. As a reporter from the *Truth* later quipped: 'Fate stepped in and settled it her own way.'[24]

PART VI

Keeping Orchestras British

20

CECIL TREVELYAN'S QUESTIONS OF PRINCIPLE

SHORTLY BEFORE NOON on 11 July 1900, George Sanderson, the amiable manager of Belfast's Empire Theatre, left his office, stopping to inform an attendant of his plans to cycle the fifteen-mile road to Whitehead for a swim. He would be back by 6 o'clock, ready for the evening show.

But George Sanderson never returned. He was last spotted cycling through Whitehead village. At Blackhead lighthouse, a few miles to the east, a man noticed a bundle of clothes neatly folded on the rocks and when no bather appeared, grew suspicious and notified police. From the suit pocket, an officer pulled out a card reading 'George Sanderson, Empire Theatre, Belfast'.[1]

A call to the theatre confirmed the policeman's suspicions: Sanderson had drowned, although dragging operations never recovered the body. Nonetheless, by the end of the day, his wife Janie learned her husband of eight years and father of her two young children had died. The next day, an obituary paid tribute to a Derby man who had arrived at the Empire Theatre six years earlier, a flautist who moved into management, turning a business burdened with debt into one of profit.[2]

It bothered Janie Sanderson that neither George's bicycle nor body were found—and four years later she discovered her instincts were sharper than the policemen. Her husband, she learned, had faked his own death.

As he confessed in a letter to his father: 'I fell in love more like a madman than any sane person and I gave up all for the girl I loved.'[3]

On that fateful day, Sanderson had cycled to Blackhead with two sets of clothing. He left one on the rocks then, likely, pedalled to a seaport ten miles north where he and a young Antrim woman crossed the English Channel to Scotland. On 21 July 1900, the couple were in Liverpool and under the names Mr and Mrs Cecil George Patrick Trevelyan boarded a steamship for Sydney.[4]

The scale of the deception astounded Janie Sanderson. Until learning of her husband's duplicity, she thought they were 'perfectly happy', unaware of his infatuation or his capacity to leave his children destitute and never see them again.

Cecil Trevelyan's elaborate deception spared him the shame of a scandalous divorce, although a 1903 letter suggested that, ten thousand miles away in Sydney, he was unable to escape what felt like divine retribution. 'I have been out of employment nearly the whole time since and a good deal of the time I've been half-starving' without a 'sixpence in the world'. His new bride, already in 'delicate' health gave birth to a stillborn daughter. 'I think you will say we have been sufficiently punished,' the 'erring son' confessed to his father.[5]

'Trevvy's' Australian colleagues would never know this sordid history. His obituary in 1935 detailed a mostly invented past. 'Of Cornish stock, Mr. Trevelyan was born in Dublin sixty-four years ago, and came to Australia in 1901 (aged 31)' to become a 'valiant and untiring champion' of the musician, read one tribute to the long-reigning federal secretary of the Musicians' Union of Australia. Colleagues told of a 'picturesque' figure whose breezy style added 'sparkle' to the sobriety of the Arbitration Court. 'Judges did not reprove him when he leaned his elbows on the bench, and score in hand, explained the difficulties ... They smiled tolerantly when he hummed a bar or two.'[6]

Trevelyan's surviving correspondence with dance palladium and theatre managers captured neither charm nor wit. Instead, his letters conjured a guarded man, suspicious of other people's hidden agendas, preoccupied with questions of 'principle'.

Unlike, say the waterside unions, the Musicians' Union was *not* a grassroots organisation but was created in response to the formation of

A studio portrait of George Sanderson before he assumed the identity Cecil Trevelyan. (Ancestry.com)

the Conciliation and Arbitration Court, a federal tribunal that adjudicated wages, conditions and disputes. Within this system, only officially registered trade unions could represent workers' interests.

When Cecil Trevelyan registered the South Australian branch of the Musicians' Union in 1911, members numbered less than one hundred. Still, he was authorised to impose rules and regulations on a fluid and freewheeling sector, calling out 'unfair' competition posed by non-union rivals. He even administered competence tests determining who could and could not join professional orchestras.[7]

Sometimes Trevelyan spoke of a dialectical struggle between capital and labour. But, in contrast to the nativist instincts of his comrades at Trades Hall who denounced British imperialism (while upholding Anglo-Saxonism), Trevelyan saw the Australian nation and British Empire as indivisible. The two patriotic songs he composed during the Great War captured his worldview. 'Fighting at the Dardanelles' celebrated the 'gallant deeds of Australia's Stalwart Sons' fighting for King and Empire, even if 'one or two' of these brave sons had 'disgraced our name'—a reference to the thousands of Anzacs who rampaged through Cairo's Wassir red light district in April 1915, ransacking brothels and burning buildings, some gleefully inflicting racial terror. Trevelyan, of course, knew about disgracing 'our name' and perhaps because of these failings, saw the promise of redemption as all the sweeter: 'When it came to fight, we held up our end.'[8]

'Won't You Take a Gun?', a recruitment song published midway between the defeat of Prime Minister Hughes' first conscription referendum and the announcement of the second, framed war as the ultimate test of masculinity. As if deaf to news of spiralling death rates, Trevelyan presented potential recruits with a stark choice: would they 'shirk or play the man?' 'Go where manly feeling leads you: Show the world that you have grit,' his lyrics urged. By following the path of high principle, a man could fulfil his 'duty' to 'King and Empire', prove virility and 'when all the fighting's over', reap honour and self-esteem.[9]

The lyrics matched the soaring rhetoric of Prime Minster Billy Hughes who routinely eulogised battle as an opportunity for the 'British race' to find 'its soul' and emerge 'purged of dross', 'purified by the spirit of self-sacrifice' and restored with the full 'valour of our ancient race'.[10] Notably, the Musicians' Union remained loyal to Hughes when the Labor Party expelled him and Trades Hall denounced him over conscription. Indeed, the NSW and Victorian branches embraced his hard-line policies, purging hundreds of German 'enemy alien' musicians. Trades Hall retaliated by de-affiliating the union.[11]

Trevelyan's South Australian branch elected *not* to expel their many German-born members although the debate over 'enemy aliens' sparked 'considerable heartburn' and talk of a breakaway 'All-British Union'.[12] Trevelyan's position remained unclear, at least until his appointment as federal secretary in 1923. Then, his commitment to a narrowly British White Australia was undeniable.

Under Trevelyan's command, the union worked to create a sector manned, firstly, by British Australians and, secondly, by British. The rule-book tracked the implementation of his ideals. Prior to his appointment, 'enemy aliens' constituted the only reference to nationality, ethnicity or race. In 1923, the union added a new objective, committing to 'uphold and maintain the White Australia and prohibit the admission of colored races as members'. By 1927, more barriers sprinkled the union rulebook. Clause (r) of Section 4 vowed to 'oppose' the admission of overseas contract musicians. Clause (v) vouched to 'keep orchestras British', capping the number of 'foreigners' to 10 per cent. Subsequently, scores of naturalised Italian-born Australians were denied membership. The few allowed to join were barred from executive positions.[13] 'We always preferred the British to the foreigner; we prefer the foreigner to stay at home,' read official statements.[14] Arbitration Court judges upheld these rules, sanctioning the union's wide discretionary powers.

White American musicians benefited from the rulebook's elastic definitions. Foreigners were 'overseas musicians *other* than natives of BRITISH (ENGLISH SPEAKING) countries', approved the executive.[15] So while Cecil Trevelyan grumbled about imported White American dance bands, according to the rulebook, Americans were English speakers, so met membership qualifications.

The Musicians' Union were hardly the only union to draw the colour line. The Arbitration Court, in league with the trade union movement, created a legal and bureaucratic framework that protected White labour—a system of entitlement commonly known as 'white man's work'. Unlike a shearer or dockworker, though, musicians were also artists, transmitting sounds that had a cultural value beyond the workplace. Old arguments about cheap 'foreign' labour undercutting White men's wages did not apply to Italian violinists and African American trumpeters and drummers who, often, commanded considerably larger salaries. Instead, Trevelyan deferred to a question of 'principle', insisting the 'skill and ability' of White Australian musicians was 'equal' to any in the world.[16]

Many in the music world challenged Trevelyan's tenet of faith. As the Palais Royal's manager JC Bendrodt carefully explained, he would gladly forgo the 'prohibitive expense' of importing an American band if locals could 'deliver the goods'.[17] A conductor at the Melba Opera Company described standards as 'extremely bad'.[18] So too, a Scottish tenor and veteran of the European operatic stage encountered orchestras wanting in versatility and skill, unable to 'accompany big musical works'. 'Australia should import foreign musicians to build up the nucleus of orchestras rivalling in technique and brilliance the best in Europe,' he advised.[19]

Bendrodt echoed this conclusion: Black American jazz players would give Australian dance musicians a 'valuable education'.[20]

Such arguments struck at the heart of Cecil Trevelyan's worldview: if inherited traits made the British 'race' superior and exceptional, how could an Italian or Black American be more skilful and accomplished?

Trevelyan fought back, attacking the 'qualifications' of the Scottish tenor, denying the 'superior skill' of American dance musicians. The 'imported jazz band' was 'the least artistic, the least musical' dispenser of 'noise', he decreed. The only thing an Italian could teach the British was working for 'pauper's wages', he sniped. When Hoyts Theatre requested an additional Italian bassist, Trevelyan suspected 'a ruse'. As he told a colleague: 'We have adopted an attitude ... based on a definite principle. Not for any race on earth should our members be asked to make room by stepping down.'[21]

Trevelyan frequently described union rules as 'principles'. In doing so, he invested systems and processes with a moral essence. Principles spoke to fixed virtues, an eternal creed, a cherished tradition to be violated or honoured. His opponents, by implication, were unprincipled, ideologically tainted, ill-equipped to advance a 'genuine' argument.

'The employer is chiefly out to make money ... We are chiefly concerned in a *principle*,' read his letter to a Sydney dance hall promoter.[22]

The 'pre-entry close shop' arrangement 'was one not of numbers but of *principle*'. It also ensured the union's complete control of the labour supply.[23]

Cecil Trevelyan's principles affirmed what he believed was the moral intelligence at the heart of the social order. First and foremost, White Australia was an ideal that went beyond immigration and labour laws to advance a blueprint for cultivating and maintaining a culture of 'Britishness'. He privileged British people, ideas, repertoires, idioms and cultural practices to reinforce the bonds of empire. He restricted membership to stop 'foreign' idioms from infiltrating the public imagination.

Still, Trevelyan's allegiance to principle did not mean he was unable to indulge in pragmatic backflipping and verbal gymnastics. On the face of it, he exercised power and control through what labour historian Kay Dreyfus has called 'the legalism of the minutiae of the rules'. Above all, the union prioritised 'the enforcement of the rules as set out in the

Constitution'.[24] Yet, the story of Trevelyan's opposition to the Sonny Clay Orchestra's appearance at the Green Mill can only be understood when factoring secret and irregular practices shared by a shadowy alliance who upheld an unwritten, but implicitly understood, constitution. The Musicians' Union's emphasis on processes and procedure were a distraction, a shiny patina of efficiency, transparency and order.

21
WAR ON AMERICAN PLAYERS

LATE IN OCTOBER 1927, the same week the Tivoli Theatre announced Harry Muller had 'signed up a colored combination', Cecil Trevelyan declared 'war on American players' irrespective of whether they were Black or White. Until that point, the federal secretary had begrudgingly accepted White American members. Now he lobbied politicians to introduce laws to restrict almost *all* overseas musicians.[1]

As Trevelyan knew from previous battles, persuading the Australian public to curb their zeal for foreign artists was more complicated in practice than in principle. This time, to win public sympathy, he had a heart-stirring tale about America's shoddy treatment of Australia's most celebrated brass band.

The saga centred on the Newcastle Steel Works Band, an ordinary factory brass band drilled in a repertoire of marches and popular classics. They were indistinguishable from hundreds of brass bands across the country who, for decades, did what the phonograph and wireless would later do: circulate and popularise music. Across the country, brass bands brought distinction to a day at the racecourse, education to an afternoon in the park, solemnity to an official ceremony, and a sense of oneness to a street parade, locking thousands of feet into a unified step. It was a deeply British tradition: the sound characterised by tonal uniformity and strictly controlled dynamics, the spirit sonically linking nationalism, militarism and working-class masculinity.[2]

In the early 1920s, Albert Baile, the leader of the Newcastle Steel Works Band, fixed his eye on the British Empire Championship and began recruiting the stars of the brass band competition circuit, the most decorated players in the nation. In so doing, he created an ensemble with musicians from every state in the federated nation, the first true Commonwealth band. In 1924, the Steel Works Band travelled to London and swept the board at the imperial championships, the victories launching them on the international touring circuit. Performing under their new name, the Australian Commonwealth Band, Baile and his boys played to 'millions' in Britain and the dominions, before accepting a lucrative run of engagements in the United States.[3]

As a Musicians' Union pamphlet told it, at this point the Commonwealth Band became the victims of American unfair play. The US deal hinged on the American Musician Union's co-operation and, naturally, Baile expected reciprocal rights. Alas, it was not to be. An intractable US union forced the Australian band to relinquish their contract 'at great financial loss'. 'The greatest band in the world', the boys who had 'out-Sousaed Sousa' and 'outplayed the Coldstream Guard's Band' had been boycotted by 'jealous' Americans, reported the Australian press. The band returned home to cities where US dance bands elbowed and crowded out local players.[4]

But there was more: the snub struck at the heart of the Anzac tradition. The Commonwealth Band blurred the lines between show business and military service, styling their uniforms—jodhpurs, knee-high boots and slouch hat with feathered spray—on the Australian Light Horse Brigade, whose mounted clashes were the stuff of Anzac legend. On their arrival in Melbourne in January 1928, for instance, the Commonwealth Band marched up Collins Street in full regalia alongside Will Kent Hughes, president of the Light Horsemen Association. At civic receptions, mayors compared the bandsmen's virtuosity to the Diggers' tenacity at Flanders.[5]

To Trevelyan's mind, the Commonwealth Band had proven the thesis that Australians equalled the 'superior skill' of any musician—and yet 'America' had treated them with disdain. For the federal secretary, this was a true measure of the power imbalance between the two nations. The US union guaranteed their members 'absolute protection' while an impotent Australian union was powerless to 'retaliate' and prevent waves of interlopers taking local jobs.[6]

Trevelyan drew on a colonial argument to relay his members' plight, positing the outsiders as invaders who encroached on another's sovereign land and dispossessed its inhabitants. On one occasion, the union likened their members to the 'Vanishing Australian', a term used to describe the false idea of a 'dying Aboriginal race'.[7]

Trevelyan offered a highly selective reading of events. According to his own rulebook, only *White* Americans could join the Australian union. The US union only represented *White* musicians. Moreover, hundreds of Australians worked in American motion pictures and vaudeville. Yet these distinctions were lost, even in a sober broadsheet like the *Sydney Morning Herald:* 'White American musicians and coloured bands may enter the Commonwealth without restriction' while 'Australians are debarred from earning a living in the United States', they protested in February 1928. The arrangement was patently 'unfair'—a word that lay at the heart of the Australian ethos.[8]

After months of campaigning, Trevelyan secured a meeting with Prime Minister Stanley Bruce, the Minister for Home and Territories Sir Neville Howse, the leader of the opposition Labor Party Matthew Charlton, and others.[9]

The day was 16 March 1928. A week earlier, Cecil Trevelyan sent Tom Carlyon a cablegram threatening consequences if he allowed the public to 'dance to blacks'.[10]

Three days earlier, a Commonwealth Investigation Branch official in Melbourne informed his Canberra chief that a planned raid had collapsed when members of the Sonny Clay Orchestra suddenly switched hotels.[11]

On 15 March, Cecil Trevelyan had arrived in Canberra and met with former prime minister and disgruntled backbencher Billy Hughes, who agreed to petition the leaders on the union's behalf.

The parallels between Trevelyan and Hughes were personal as well as political. Both were British-born men of 'low' birth who acquired political power and influence through the trade union movement. Neither had seen combat yet both saw war as the ultimate test of masculinity and race. Both tied Australia's fortunes to the British Empire, championing a post-war social order founded on racial purity. Yet even Trevelyan could not match Hughes' impending sense of doom.

Close to thirty years of overwhelming British immigration had not eased Hughes' fear that 'hundreds of millions' of 'backward' Black, Brown and not-quite-White people had fixed their eye on the 'empty' Australian continent. In a speech to Sydney's Constitution Club a few months earlier, Hughes said he suspected the League of Nations' talk of 'world peace' was a ruse to batten down the White Australia fortress. But he was ready to 'fight for our ideals ... by force ... if necessary'. 'Everything that mattered in the world—civil liberty, religious liberty—had been won after a long conflict of blood and sacrifice.'[12]

On 16 March, at Canberra's Parliament House, Hughes, alongside Trevelyan, presented the battle against 'foreign' musicians as another front in this perpetual war. It was a form of theft, he argued: tens of thousands of pounds were going into the pockets of 'foreigners' at the expense of Australians of 'at least equal efficiency'. Without protective legislation, locals were at the mercy of 'the latest foreign novelties'. Of course, he assured, the ban would not apply to highbrow European virtuosos or leading American brass bands. Such ensembles were 'educational' and 'beneficial' to the 'artistic life of the community'.[13]

Records of the 16 March meeting captured the political leaders' unease about the union's proposition. Was it a government minister's job to 'determine the skill of a particular' musician, wondered the prime minister? Surely, the commercial marketplace mediated public taste, and the dynamics of supply and demand.[14]

Trevelyan dismissed the prime minister's logic as not 'genuine'. The 'craze for novelty' was not market driven but 'created' by a morally and racially questionable entertainment machine which manipulated working-class audiences into choosing a 'foreign' band over a local one. 'The Australian's failing point is that he is Australian,' he argued. Only a ban would end this national humiliation that reinforced a sense of inferiority.[15]

According to official records, general discussion covered the untapped powers of the Immigration Act, although *not* the Investigation Branch's probe into the Colored Idea. But later, Howse let slip that Trevelyan had voiced concerns about 'colored musicians'.[16] Was that to remind them of

Senator Pearce's system of keeping 'American Negroes' out of dance halls? And how Melbourne's Green Mill had found a loophole?

The report Trevelyan lodged in the union magazine offered no clues. He was a man whose discretion could be relied upon, accomplished in secrecy and concealment. As a colleague once noted, the federal secretary was a masterful strategist, a chess player 'of some enviable repute'.[17]

The meeting complete, Cecil Trevelyan wound down his 'spirited campaign' to ban 'foreign' musicians.

Four days later—20 March 1928—the Green Mill held the grand final of the Artist Model Quest. Edna Langdon was one of the nine finalists but did not win a place.[18]

Elsewhere in Melbourne, Victoria police fixed their attentions on premises occupied by a group of Sonny Clay's bandsmen: Leo Davis, Baby Lewis, Sonny Graven, Louis Dodd and John Black.[19]

PART VII

Petty Sessions

22

CONSTABLE SAKER TELLS THE TRUTH

LESLIE SAKER AWOKE alone as he did most days in his California bungalow in Elsternwick. His wife slept in a separate bedroom. They lived as strangers, communicating through their children. The house was decent enough—leafy, modern, a short stroll to the sea yet not too far from the hustle and bustle—but it was not good enough for his wife who felt she should be breathing the rarefied air of Toorak, or so Les Saker claimed in a petition to divorce his wife after fifteen years of unhappy marriage. She made no effort to counter his accusation, simply noting 'we were never suited to each other and we have nothing in common with each other'.[1]

In January 1928, Les Saker was still a year away from filing for divorce and stumbling through the hollow motions of family life. As he complained, his wife made her own money teaching music and showed no interest in keeping house. Unable to compel her to launder his shirt and prepare his meals, most mornings he made his own breakfast before heading off to Russell Street's police headquarters.[2]

The rank of constable was a respectable job for a 38-year-old: secure, with the prospect of advancement, and was a significant step up from the railway signalman he once had been—although, again, not good enough for his wife who called him a 'common policeman'. She said he was 'beneath her'. She humiliated him in front of friends. She would leave their two children with her mother and disappear for weeks without warning or explanation. Saker's colleagues sometimes spotted her at the racecourse in Williamstown, smoking and drinking with other women, or on familiar terms with another man.[3]

As the bearer of a Victoria police badge, however, Constable Saker commanded a level of respect unknown in family life. He was a member of the plainclothes unit, a squad handpicked by Police Commissioner General Thomas Blamey—or his chief of staff, Superintendent Tom Dunn. The plainclothes unit stood apart from the rest of the force, operating in the shadows, prying into private spaces, uncovering breaches in the law while undetected by the citizenry and sometimes their own colleagues.[4]

Uniformed officers deeply resented the plainclothes detective's 'spook' operations into the police force itself. In 1923, over six hundred Russell Street officers went on strike to protest their excessive powers. The conservative state premier responded, appointing General Blamey as police chief to restore order. Blamey sacked the strikers, crushed the police union, overturned the promotion system and fast-tracked his favourites much to the bitterness, 'suspicion' and 'disgust' of uniformed beat cops. Above all, he elevated the plainclothes unit, assembling around himself what one reporter described as a coterie of 'hangers-on'.[5]

Such press criticism was rare. Crime was the main fodder of Melbourne's newspapers and the seven or so reporters based at Russell Street headquarters depended on police stories to fill the daily press. An intricate symbiosis bonded pressman to constable. A police spokesman made daily statements about arrests and convictions, but the fresher, juicier leads came from patrol crews at the end of a shift or leaks from an off-duty detective over a beer at the City Court Hotel. Late night drinking and gambling sessions in the press room oiled the wheels of the media machine. In return for hot scoops, reporters cast low-paid, low-ranking constables as champions of law and order.[6]

In the pages of the press, Constable Leslie Saker emerged as a tireless fighter of crime. At racetracks and street carnivals, he broke up games of chance and illegal betting operations. He raided sly grog shops, 'disorderly' houses and clubs who contravened liquor laws. For a time, he moved into burglary operations and armed robberies and, during a siege situation, heroically wrested a rifle from a violent man.[7]

Plainclothes Constable Les Saker, a familiar face in the *Truth* and reliable source for stories. (Melbourne *Truth*, State Library Victoria)

Of Melbourne's many news publications, the *Truth* newspaper showered Les Saker with a special type of glory. Few months passed without one or two photographs of Saker appearing in its pages: a three-quarter angle close-up, the camera almost imperceptibly tilted upwards to capture Saker's furrowed brow and hawk-like stare, the frame of his fedora's brim evoking a private detective of Hollywood and pulp fiction fame. A second full-length photograph revealed a hand-in-pocket man in a three-piece suit and hat, the un-regimented informality of his pose suggesting that moral relativism, as opposed to standard operating procedure, was part of the undercover game. Saker moved in a world of blurred lines and hazy distinctions, where the borderlines of the personal and public were not always clear.

When Saker paced the 'slums' of Melbourne, a *Truth* reporter was often by his side, taking a suburban reader on a tour of the city's netherworld. 'Let us pass quickly up Little Lonsdale Street and down Latrobe Street, passed its many brothels, gaudy "lollie shops", gaming houses and opium dens,' guided the reporter. At various points, Saker stopped to point out 'fetid' hovels where gaslight shed 'a dim flicker over the dissipated figures of degenerates' and 'painted and powdered' 'jezebels' lurking in doorways. On the corner of Exhibition and Collins, Saker drew attention to the 'Queen of the Boulevard', a 'fat beefy' 'harpie' who inflicted 'razor wounds and vitriol burns' on unauthorised newcomers. They walked past the joint where Cornbeef Maud sold little paper packets of cocaine cut with phenacetin for two shillings a piece. And down Heffernan Lane, where an 'inscrutable old Chinese' man peddled the 'blue-wraith sylph of forgetfulness' to 'the flotsam and jetsam of the slums'.[8]

On other nights, Constable Saker and the *Truth* reporter walked Melbourne's 'cancerous vein' where the 'Pathetic Half-Caste Population of the Submerged Tenth' formed 'a race apart', the 'depraved poor'. The reporter dwelled on the 'disastrous consequences' when 'black, white, brown, mixed and cross mixed into every possible color' and were 'preyed upon by every vice'. According to the reporter, few figures matched the degradations of the 'faded and soulless' White women who lived with Chinese men and bred 'half caste children' that lived 'like animals'. Within this calculus, racial inter-mixing begat moral degeneracy. The social malaise, the thriving 'vice' economy was a direct consequence of breaches in the White Australian fortress. More than poverty voyeurism, the reporter sketched a nation that might have been—an inverted world glimpsed through windows, a mushroom growth that fed off the night, where the private pleasures of marginal individuals posed the greatest public danger.[9]

A suburban reader might wonder why Constable Saker did not arrest these moral deviants. And, with much indignation, the *Truth* reporter blasted gutless politicians and their toothless legislation.[10] 'Observant plainclothes men' might witness a 'jazzy saturnalia' unfolding in a brothel but were powerless to stop the 'human vultures' feeding on the 'innocents'. The law demanded search warrants and by the time police completed their tiresome paperwork, every trace of evidence had vanished and with it any hope of conviction. 'Wider Powers Needed to Combat Big Evil' crusaded the *Truth* in May 1927. Law enforcers needed 'new powers' to address the 'fungus growth' that menaced the 'morals and safety of the public'.[11]

But as the pressmen well knew, police inaction had little to do with public statutes and much to do with a sticky web of entanglements. Commissioner Blamey had what an *Argus* reporter called 'a very unsavoury reputation' for 'boozing and womanizing', and was a familiar face in the brothels of Little Lon. Newspaper proprietor Keith Murdoch considered him 'amoral'.[12] In 1925, when licensing squad detectives raided 'Mabel Tracy's Elocution School', they stumbled upon a naked customer who flashed them Commissioner Blamey's police badge. Debate over the man's identity raged for decades. At best, Blamey had 'lent' his badge to an old army chum who wielded it like a free pass. Evidently, a Victoria police badge conferred a range of entitlements—exactly what remained unclear. During the official inquiry, Mabel Tracy upheld a 'policy of silence'.[13]

The press, too, covered the 'Badge 80' affair with discretion. Unlike the *Argus*, the *Truth* placed no 'Blame on Blamey', instead faulting the inexperienced young constables who had 'no right' to intrude into the privacy of a bedroom.[14] The editorial line echoed Blamey's views. He resented public scrutiny of his personal activities. 'I don't think anybody has any right to say anything about my private life,' he told his chief of staff.[15]

The incident illustrated the interlocking systems of mutual interest. If the police stopped feeding the pressmen—as they momentarily did in 1936, unhappy with the coverage of a police corruption inquiry—news copy would wither and sales plummet. The deal hinged on newspapermen papering over police irregularities and reassuring the public their civic institutions were in good order. The system worked.[16]

Les Saker frequently walked the Melbourne streets alongside Senior Constable Harry Dunn, although the latter explicitly shunned media attention, despite an impressive official record well suited for tabloid heroism. 'Dunn has one peculiarity,' read a rare snippet. 'He won't be photographed under any circumstances.'[17]

A less noble counter-narrative suggested why. In 1923, Harry Dunn had certainly won meritorious praise for breaking a street betting syndicate, yet by 1924, a Sydney scandal rag accused him of accepting a 'weekly contribution' from a suite of gambling dens, bookmakers, two-up schools and lottery syndicates. In 1926, he was awarded the Valor Badge for apprehending a gunman—or did he 'violently' assault a hunter as he drank a cup of tea? Dunn's promotion to senior constable in 1927 raised the matter of his assault conviction—he had beaten a solicitor who had visited a magistrate at his home.[18]

Commissioner Blamey valued Dunn's work 'very highly'. He was a man the 'criminal element was afraid of', vouched the police chief at an inquiry into Dunn's habit of extorting money from insurance companies to ensure the return of stolen cars. Convicted car thieves remained silent, 'afraid to give evidence for fear of reprisals'.[19] And Dunn's revenge could be swift and severe. He slapped a libel suit on the reporter who wrote the 1924 exposés about the Victoria police's 'vice of hypocrisy', corruption and graft. The reporter's mother, a Bourke Street tearoom psychic, was then subjected to ongoing 'police harassment' and 'vilification' in the *Truth*.[20]

The two sides of Senior Constable Harry Dunn were not mutually exclusive. Dunn was a beneficiary of Blamey's system of 'accelerated promotion by merit'—a subjective quality measured mostly by loyalty. More specifically, his brother was Commissioner Blamey's chief of staff and 'close friend', Tom Dunn. 'Blamey took more heed of Dunn's opinion on police matters in general than of any other man's,' wrote Blamey's biographer.[21] By the early 1930s, Tom Dunn's son, Ray, was Blamey's solicitor.[22] In other words, Harry Dunn was hard to touch, safeguarded by his brother's clout. Saker, by extension, fell under this protective shield.

Constable Saker's privileged position in the police force offered a range of opportunities to assert his masculinity, flex his authority, even vent his frustrations; he was one of the few Victoria police officers to carry a firearm. One defendant, charged with obscene language, told how Saker had arrested him at the point of a revolver, and once handcuffed, punched him in the face 'in a most cowardly fashion'. A war veteran accused Saker of twisting his damaged arm, flinging him to the floor and planting a boot on the accused's head. Another told how Saker planted evidence, arrested him for cocaine possession, then slapped his face when the man protested. Saker was among the four police officers who raided Carlyon's ballroom in 1926, one of whom pulled out a revolver and slapped a woman across the face.[23]

Such tales hardly surprised Melbourne's crime reporters. Blamey's 'promotion by merit' system spawned such abuses. Police were 'capable' of 'doing violence to the rights of able and conscientious men', one later recalled. Around town, people knew Blamey's plainclothes unit to be 'nothing but a licenced basher squad', henchmen carrying out the police chief's orders plus some for themselves on the side.[24]

Saker's sidelines suggest a man whose personal grievances bled into public policing. The Victoria police's Petty Sessions Register shows that, with remarkable frequency, he raided the homes of Chinese men, often in partnership with Dunn. Press reports had him smashing down doors, chasing suspects across rooftops, turning down bribes and uncovering tins of opium. He claimed to come upon opiated men who, shaken from a narcotic slumber, 'viciously' and 'violently' 'struggled' with police. Yet these arrests rarely, if ever, dinted the opium trade. At best, Saker secured a few convictions for opium possession and many more for being 'privy to the offense of opium smoking'. These were not the homes of drug kingpins but market gardeners and laundry workers, some of them long-time drug users.[25]

Saker also directed his energies at young women, arresting them for receiving stolen goods or vagrancy, although these too rarely translated into convictions. The Petty Sessions Register showed that on 9 February 1928, Saker charged one Ruby Singer with vagrancy, but after holding her five days, withdrew the proceedings. On 17 February, he apprehended Eileen Squires as a 'vagrant, rogue and vagabond'. After a week in remand, a magistrate sentenced her to one month's imprisonment. On 23 February, he arrested another two women, suspecting their perfume, umbrella and handbag were stolen property. Both were held on remand for five days, then discharged. Then on 25 February, Saker's steady drumbeat of arrests came to an abrupt end.[26]

Commissioner Blamey had received Major Lloyd's confidential report into the Negro Orchestra—and a letter from the Investigation Branch's federal chief hoping Blamey might 'consider' a 'local investigation' to be 'necessary'.

Perhaps on Tom Dunn's recommendation, General Blamey appointed Constables Saker and Dunn to carry out the investigation. As Major Lloyd meandered: 'A Police raid seems desirable as otherwise the evidence of outside persons must be relied upon with somewhat divergent views held by persons upon questions of behaviour in districts which perhaps are not by any means censorious in respect of such matters.'[27]

The words were garbled but the message was clear. Immediately, Saker and Dunn got to work, peering through windows into a new set of private worlds.

23
WOMEN WHO BITE POLICEMEN

In his later life, Ezra Norton, the notoriously secretive man who published the *Truth,* recounted a life lesson learned from his father, John Norton, when he ran the newspaper. It was a Sunday morning and John Norton was sitting on a balcony overlooking Sydney's Pitt Street. In a rare moment of tenderness, he called over his young son and, placing an affectionate arm around his shoulder, nodded to the people returning from church service.

'Look at them,' he said. 'Look at them and all this Sunday finery, the bloody hypocrites. Never forget this, my son. When you carry on my work in *Truth,* keeping up its traditions without fear or favour, you will be in the same position of trust as me, always able to pour a bucket of — over the lot of them.'[1]

In truth, Ezra Norton continued his father's legacy by trading *in* fear and favour.

Ezra grew up 'terrified' of his father's violent alcoholic rages. A lifetime of 'shocks and threats' made him 'nervous and excitable', according to a medical specialist testifying at his parent's very public and scandalous divorce.[2]

In turn, Ezra terrorized his staff. Norton's former employees recalled a 'cantankerous', 'rude' and 'ruthless' man, a 'tortured soul' with a permanently sulky expression. 'Once you had joined him it was all fear and you became his body-servant,' confessed a former editor. Norton summarily sacked reporters who failed to dig up enough scandals—even fired staff without cause, reserving special ferocity for the ones who showed fear. The daily anxieties and humiliations caused one cadet to grow 'nervous and twitchy'.[3] 'There was always a breath of relief when he had left the premises,' another recalled.[4]

The *Truth* reporter who documented the heroics of Constable Saker endured Norton's sadistic regime. His identity is unknown (certainly he was male); like all *Truth* reporters, he remained anonymous. No by-line accompanied his exposés, credited only as the '*Truth*'s Melbourne Representative'. Still, the word 'representative' over 'correspondent' or 'investigator' was revealing. *Truth* reporters fashioned a representation of the world that mirrored their daily lives: a threatening and hostile place, where danger and uncertainty lurked around every step, and the smallest miscalculation augured wrack and ruin. In its pages, Melbourne life unfolded like a melodrama, each bold headline crafted to deliver an instantaneous jolt that propelled the reader beyond their mundane lives to the climax of a crisis. In sum, the *Truth* was a twice weekly dose of torrid escapism with a comprehensive racing guide.[5]

At the same time, *Truth*'s representatives understood their work within a long tradition of activist journalism. They upheld John Norton's faith in the biological exceptionalism of Anglo-Saxon 'stock', the dignity of White working men's labour, and the millenarian promise of the White Australian ideal. The unnamed *Truth* reporter balanced utopic and dystopic worlds, one redeemed by two decades of racial purification policies, the other forfeited by 'coloured' ideas and practices—a combination that perchance might briefly win the patriarch's favour and affections.[6]

As he pursued the members of the Sonny Clay Orchestra, the Melbourne Representative showed no fear or hesitation, casting himself as a gumshoe detective in the case of the 'noisome and noxious' racial slur. He knew all about the Sydney operation: the bandsmen's rumoured 'conduct with white girls', the complexities preventing Lloyd's team taking 'action'. In other words, Saker and Dunn had shown him the Investigation Branch's confidential report.

As if conducting his own operation, the Melbourne Representative trained his gaze on the four performers identified in Major Lloyd's report, trailing them from theatre to dwelling. A fiendish villainy infused his description of the musicians 'laughing uproariously' as they headed off to the Tivoli Theatre. A sinister chill clung to his impression of 'flappers in their early 'teens, girls and mature women' hanging around the Tivoli's stage door, attempting to 'get notes' to them. 'Night after night' he saw women join the Americans for 'supper at Coffee and Jazz eating-house in Swanston Street'. Sometimes they danced. Such scenes convinced him the troupe 'required watching'.[7]

Nini Coycault, Archie Lancaster, Herman Hoy and Dewey Covan soon came to recognise the men who had them 'under observation day and night'. Their landlord told them how a policeman demanded a key, entered the flats and searched their belongings. A musician awoke one night to find a detective in his bedroom. Sonny Clay was in no doubt that the 'same party' who 'harassed' them in Sydney also 'dogged' them in Melbourne. As a precaution, the Tivoli's manager Percy Crawford moved the four men to a hotel—rumours of a planned raid had been trickling through from the Sydney office.[8]

The move frustrated the policemen's 'undercover' operation. As suspected, Saker and Dunn had been poised to pounce. Now with a concierge and lobby between the spies and their prey, 'it was not easy to surprise them', as the Melbourne Representative explained.[9]

Saker, Dunn and the Melbourne Representative turned their attentions to Rowena Mansions, a three-storey apartment block on the corner of Nicholson Street and Evelyn Place in East Melbourne. Until then its occupants, John Black, Sonny Graven, Louis Dodd, Leo Davis and Baby Lewis had only 'come under slight suspicion'. The *Truth* Representative took credit for the switch. 'Having charted their movements with accuracy and having ascertained exactly the nature of the revelries going on upstairs and downstairs in the flat, *Truth* placed this information in the hands of the police.'[10]

Stationed in a schoolyard opposite the mansion block, Constable Saker and the newsman monitored movements in and out of the building—although, for days, nothing of interest happened. Then, on Thursday, 22 March 1928, the *Truth* Representative observed activity he believed qualified as 'gross conduct'.

'All day long' White 'girls' 'slipped in and out of the flats' or 'sneak[ed] down the steps' then departed in a taxi. Likely, he referred to Dorothy Davis, a 22-year-old waitress from a remote Riverina town who had flitted from job to job since arriving in Melbourne several months earlier. In March 1928, the musicians hired her to buy food and cook their meals in exchange for one pound a week. Her companion was probably her flatmate, Dorothy McGowan.

Between 7 p.m. and 8.15 p.m. that evening, Saker claimed to see three Black men 'pulling' about two different White women. Or at least, given the size and angle of the first-floor window, that's what it looked like. As he later admitted, his line of sight was hindered by a tree.[11]

Inside the apartment were Edna Langdon and an unidentified friend. Two days earlier, Edna had appeared in the grand final of the Green Mill's Artist Model Quest, her third spin in the 'Gorgeous Fountain of Life', although this time she did not win a place.[12]

The night she visited Rowena Mansions, Australian aviator Bert Hinkler was at the Green Mill awarding a cash prize to the three place-holders. Edna did not join them but instead spent part of the evening dancing to gramophone records with her new American friends. The Texas Tommy, a forerunner of the Lindy Hop and Jitterbug, perfected in the cafes of San Francisco's Barbary Coast, called for a lot of push and pull.[13]

At eleven o'clock the following night, Friday, Saker and the *Truth* Representative were again in the schoolyard staring up at the window. Again, they claimed to see three musicians sitting and talking with Edna Langdon, and her 22-year-old flatmate, Nola Mackay. Shortly after midnight, the two women left the apartment and returned to their homes nearby.[14]

By now, it was too late for Saker and the *Truth* Representative to stop by the City Court Hotel for a beer, although sly grog and other 'vices' were never in short supply. At some point, Constable Saker returned to his unhappy Elsternwick home, to a wife who humiliated and shunned him.[15]

If the paper boy delivered a copy of the *Truth* the following morning, Saker may have noticed a small but significant break with standard typesetting practices. On page twelve, the entertainment page, two pun-based jokes were sandwiched between two advertisements. One read: 'Many a jazz party begins on the stairs and ends under the stares of the neighbours.' The other read: 'Women who bite policemen believe in going for authority tooth and law!'[16]

The gag lines appeared random and nonsensical, although broadly in keeping with the tabloid's sense of humour. But as Saker knew, these were clues planted by the *Truth* Representative to signal events about to unfold.

If all went to plan, a 'jazz party' steeped in jungle-frenzied mumbo-jumbo would be exposed to the public. And once again Constable Saker's three-quarter angle close-up would appear in the Melbourne paper, captioned as the man who 'spearheaded' the raid 'organised' by the *Truth*.[17]

24

SILK PETTICOATS AND MAUVE PYJAMAS

HEAVY RAIN SET in on Saturday evening and for four 'dismal' hours Constable Saker and the *Truth* Representative kept watch from the schoolyard opposite Rowena Mansions.

The events of the night would become the focus of extraordinary attention—and much contestation. By rights, the account of who-was-where and who-said-what should be told by all the participants; however, the surviving record privileges one party. Les Saker and the *Truth* Representative emerged as the primary witnesses, followed by Harry Dunn. Other versions of events survive only as fragments.

Shortly after eight o'clock, two women carrying parcels walked through the front door of the building—Dorothy Davis and Nola Mackay supplying food. Just before nine o'clock, the five musicians left for the Tivoli Theatre.

For the next two hours, the pressman and policeman stood watch in the rain, catching occasional glimpses of the women. At eleven o'clock, a taxicab appeared, and two musicians hopped out to collect Davis and Mackay.[1]

Saker and the *Truth* reporter followed close behind, trailing them to Coffee Dans where a party had gathered for supper. They counted several members of the troupe, as well as Edna Langdon and at least three other local women, maybe more. Saker's police report read: 'some [bandsmen] were dancing with white girls and others were seated at tables with white girls ... saw Negroes kissing girls and behaving offensively.'[2]

Edna Langdon recalled at closing time, about half past one, she and her friends Nola Mackay, Dorothy Davis and Dorothy McGowan accepted the musicians' invitation back to the flat. Just who made the proposition is unclear, but likely it was Baby Lewis—his capacity for good times was boundless. They were joined by two other women Edna recognised from the Green Mill but barely knew: Ivy Day, a live-in domestic, and Irene McCulloch, a probationary nurse. As Ivy Day later told it, she had met the banjo player, John Black, earlier that evening when he stopped by the Green Mill.[3]

The party travelled from Coffee Dans to Rowena Mansions in two taxicabs. Constable Saker and the *Truth* Representative, again, followed behind. Back in the schoolyard, they were joined by Senior Constable Harry Dunn and another plainclothes constable, Albert Hackwill. For the next hour, the four men stood in the cold slanting rain watching the windows.[4]

The two musicians who resided in the downstairs flat—Sonny Graven and Louis Dodd—showed no interest in socialising and readied for bed, perhaps alert to the Tivoli's warnings about detectives on their tail. Nonetheless, Irene McCulloch hovered in the sitting room. Dorothy Davis and Dorothy McGowan tidied up the kitchen—or at least, according to Constable Dunn's version of events. As Constable Saker told it, Dorothy McGowan was in the upstairs flat, along with Edna Langdon, Nola Mackay and Ivy Day and musicians Baby Lewis, Leo Davis and John Black.

Through sheets of rain and open curtainless windows, Saker claimed once again to see the men 'pulling' the women around—or more precisely, given the angle, 'the top of their bodies from the shoulders upwards'.[5]

The *Truth* Representative saw so much more. At Coffee Dans he had seen the owner welcome the troupe with 'gush and servility'. From his kerbside view outside Rowena Mansions, he saw the musicians 'brazenly make love' to drunken staggering girls. 'The n_____s and girls partly discarded their clothes and glistening black arms wound round white shoulders, the couples swaying crazily,' he wrote. 'The saxophonist came to the window of the upstairs flat ... Two white girls had their arms about him ... The big n____r who rattles the drums for Sonny Clay had Little Edna Langdon, a finalist in the Green Mill Artists' Model Competition clasped in his embrace ... the party was a veritable orgy.'[6]

Yet an hour passed before the police and pressman made their move: Dunn to the ground-floor flat, Saker with the reporter to the first floor. 'Police,' announced Saker as he knocked on the door. 'There was a wild scramble inside and I promptly forced the door.'[7]

The *Truth* Representative conjured the scene of a 'veritable orgy': the air 'poisonous with cigarette smoke'. The 'dregs' of beer and wine in bottles and glasses 'littered the table'. Cocaine flew 'around freely'. Unchivalrous Black men, flush with entitlement, offered bribes: 'Can we fix it so that we each have a l'll white pal to ourselves while we are here?'[8]

Saker also made much of the 'dregs' and 'disorder', but instead drew a picture of a lone officer single-handedly confronting a 'decidedly hostile atmosphere'.[9]

'How did these girls get here?' asked Saker, referring to Langdon and Mackay.

'To tell you the truth, they chased us here. We can't keep them out. These are not the only ones who have been chasing us,' Davis allegedly replied.

'I have tried to keep them out, but they won't go,' added Lewis.[10]

These were not the answers of gentlemen. As Saker told it, the Americans happily impugned the dignity of White women to save themselves—although he begrudgingly accepted 'they had not interfered with the girls'.[11]

Edna Langdon and Nola Mackay's version of events, based on a few surviving shards, suggested a pleasant Saturday night that was fun but hardly wild. And certainly not a jungle frenzy steeped in mumbo-jumbo where lascivious, hyper-sexual Black musicians seduced misguided young

White women. After a quiet drink, the two friends 'were all practically ready to go' when the police walked through, not smashed down, the door.[12] Edna was fully dressed, clear-eyed and sober—she did not smoke or drink. Nor did she see anyone else in a state of undress. Nor did she or Nola Mackay feel the musicians had besmirched their moral character to gain advantage. They did recall one of the musicians flatly stating to Saker, 'nothing wrong has taken place here'.[13]

For Leo Davis and Baby Lewis, the intrusion of White policemen into the private worlds of Black people was hardly new. They were no strangers to White supremacy or excessive police enforcement. Miscegenation was a state crime in California and the Los Angeles police department closely patrolled intimacy across the colour line. Beatings, fabricated evidence and infractions of civil liberties were routine procedure. Several senior LAPD police had been outed as Ku Klux Klan members, and most Black Los Angelenos assumed all White police officers were Klan sympathisers. Moreover, the LAPD had interests in bootlegging, prostitution and gambling rackets on Central Avenue. Curtis Mosby at the Apex Club paid his tribute, lest a standover man would 'come and kick the door', or even shoot the defaulter dead.[14]

Leo Davis was, at once, an outspoken and cautious man, speaking his mind while calculating the risks. In years to come, as president of Central Avenue's Black musicians' union, he would become known as a skilled negotiator, able to mediate disputes, muster rank-and-file support, and win re-election for years on end. Even his opponents conceded he was 'a nice man'.[15] Whatever verbal challenge he posed to Constable Saker, he established their right to freedom of association, while making clear no White supremacist unwritten law had been violated. He knew his legal rights as well as his music theory. 'Nothing wrong has taken place here,' he told Saker.[16]

Baby Lewis was a much more complicated man. His exuberance, though electric on stage, was tinged with danger, and his penchant for excess led him to do 'a whole lot of wrong things'. A sense of righteousness matched his recklessness. He was, as associates recalled, an intelligent and 'very well-educated man'. Raised in the Mexican district of San Antonio, Texas, the egalitarian spirit of the Mexican Revolution shaped his world-view until the political rise of the Texan Ku Klux Klan pushed his family's migration west. He was unbowed by the terror. A bandleader recalled an incident in Shanghai when Baby Lewis and two bandmates 'ran into some Southern prejudice' in the form of six White marines. Far from fleeing, the three won the fist fight.[17]

On this night in March 1928, Lewis was not so drunk and confrontational as to provoke the policemen. For all Saker's claims that 'an ugly situation seemed likely to develop', he did not arrest either musician for obscene language or disorderly conduct, as he had done dozens of times in his career.[18]

Constable Saker did not dally in the sitting room. Three doors led to bedrooms and Saker walked directly to one. He entered the room to find Ivy Day, 'a buxom type of girl' dressed only in a 'silk petticoat' and banjo player John Black 'in mauve pyjamas'—the details documented by the *Truth*. 'The girl burst into tears and weeping, pleaded to be allowed to go home,' continued the reporter. In a panic, John Black insisted he 'was not keeping her, that he did not know her, and that she had followed him to the flat'.

Satisfied he had conclusive evidence, Saker arrested all three women for vagrancy, a well-known euphemism for prostitution.

Constable Dunn had a less dramatic tale to tell. He 'raided' the downstairs flat, to find one musician asleep in bed, another preparing to retire and Irene McCulloch in the sitting room—until she suddenly escaped through the window. Somehow the seasoned policeman, a veteran of countless raids, had allowed the suspect to flee. He elected not to pursue her, instead arresting the other two for vagrancy.

Dunn brought Dorothy Davis and maybe Dorothy McGowan upstairs to join the others. Possibly for the first time, the five women sat together waiting for the Black Maria to take them to the Russell Street watch house. In that time, the *Truth* Representative observed an extraordinary range of behaviour. The women were, at once, bursting into 'drunken tears', 'listless and numbed' with cocaine, and vocal in their disrespect for authority. 'The girls smoked cigarettes and joked as though the whole business was an elaborate joke prepared for their entertainment.

They speculated how cold it would be "in the peter" and wondered whether they would go down to the gaol in a taxicab or Rolls Royce.'

One of the constables 'cautioned' them 'to have less to say'.

Still Dorothy McGowan piped up, 'If I don't say something I'm going to scream!'[19]

Whatever Dorothy McGowan had to say, neither the reporter nor policemen recorded it. But by now, the occupants of the flats sensed powerful forces at play.

The 1971 memoir of New Orleans slap bass man Pops Foster suggested what that 'play' might have been. Foster was a colleague and friend of Leo Davis and, in time, heard the messy details: 'The white musicians hired some white girls to get friendly with Sonny Clay's boys and get into their rooms. When the party got going good, one of the girls pulled a window shade down and that was the sign for the cops to come in.'[20]

In that formulation, Ivy Day was a stool pigeon, planted to entrap the musicians.

Certainly, Ivy Day was not her real name. She was Dorothy Anderson, a fact known to police by dawn the next morning—if Saker and Dunn did not already know. Yet police allowed the false name to stand uncorrected in the Petty Sessions Register. Ten months earlier, plainclothes constables had arrested one Dorothy Meredith Anderson for possessing stolen goods.[21]

And if Ivy Day was a stool pigeon, Irene McCulloch may have been one too. Plausibly, Dunn had allowed her to escape as she had no incriminating evidence to offer. More certain was that police never attempted to arrest her, despite assurances of 'a criminal summons' against her.[22]

Pops Foster was hardly the first person to accuse Constable Saker of entrapment. In December 1928, for instance, Saker arrested a woman called Trixie Ross for vagrancy, discharging her before the matter went to court. Ten days later, a woman named Trixie played a pivotal role in Saker's arrest of Charles Le Marchant, a chronic addict in poor health. In court, Saker presented Marchant as the 'mastermind behind the cocaine business', selling drugs to vulnerable young women. Marchant, unable to afford a lawyer, cross-examined Saker. 'You know in your own heart and conscience and before God, constable, that this is a faked story,' he began.[23]

Marchant's words echoed Leo Davis' measured response to a jazz historian's question about the ill-fated tour many years later: 'Trumped up is the correct term. The correct term.'[24]

25
TOOTH AND LAW

IN THE EARLY hours of Sunday morning, the five women slumped on benches at the city watch house as Constable Saker started the administrative wheels of law enforcement. For the first time in several weeks, his name appeared in the Petty Sessions Register: a rubber-stamped entry detailing his charge against Edna Langdon and Dorothy McGowan: 'Defendant at Melbourne of 25th March 1928 was an idle and disorderly person within the meaning of Part III of the Police Offenses Act 1915, for that she is a person having insufficient lawful means of support.' Constable Hackwill signed the other three. Harry Dunn's name was nowhere to be seen.[1]

Before leaving, Constable Saker also found time to recount the 'raid' to several news reporters. As Saker knew, it took more than a midnight arrest for a jazz party to end 'under the stares of the neighbours'. He needed to spin a tale where deviant women defied 'authority tooth and law', though by that time the Sunday newspapers had gone to press. There would be no newspaper coverage for at least another day.[2]

The Rowena Mansions Five were transferred to Melbourne Goal and passed the remainder of the night in a cell. Mid-morning, an unidentified bondsman paid the £10 bail money, securing their release until their court appearance on Tuesday. Likely, Sonny Clay had been woken to learn his bandsmen had openly associated with White female fans despite knowing they were under surveillance. The women were under arrest—and Clay's name would be soon drawn into unfavourable, potentially damaging, press coverage. He in turn likely contacted the Tivoli Theatre manager, Percy Crawford, who began the clean-up operation. This was not the first time stage performers had fallen foul of the law.[3]

Melbourne came to a virtual close on Sundays. Even trams did not run and unless the young women had money for a taxicab, they walked the streets with the churchgoers to their respective homes: Edna Langdon and Nola Mackay to East Melbourne, Dorothy Davis and Dorothy McGowan to Fitzroy, and Ivy Day to St Kilda. All were in their late teens or early twenties and lived independently of their families. None were affiliated with unions, political parties, church groups or women's leagues. Only their patronage of Coffee Dans and the Green Mill bound them together. Until this incident, all but 'Ivy Day' were unknown to police, novices in the criminal justice system.[4]

Not knowing where to turn, Nola Mackay and Edna Langdon returned to Rowena Mansions that evening, to weigh up their options with their American friends. It would not be a stretch to assume they disassembled the chain of events that led to their arrest, and perhaps chewed over the likelihood that Ivy Day and Irene McCulloch were stool pigeons. But the women's most pressing problem was financial: they faced a custodial sentence and needed money for a defence attorney. Leo Davis and Baby Lewis stumped up the legal fee—or at least, that was what they told Constable Saker when he once again intruded into their living space.

'You have brought enough trouble on these girls. Why are they here again?' he claimed to say, evidently not understanding that, to the musicians' minds, he was the source of the 'trouble'. Instead, Saker interpreted the moment as further proof the Black men 'kept' these patently incorrigible women. Nola Mackay and Edna Langdon didn't know what was about to hit them, but a system of justice able to plant stool pigeons could engineer much more.[5]

Constable Saker returned to Russell Street police headquarters, updating crime reporters on the women's lack of remorse, persisting in what the press would soon call 'disgraceful conduct'.[6]

Other interested parties, too, expected updates. If not Police Commissioner Blamey, then Chief of Staff Tom Dunn required a briefing, to evaluate any operational hiccups or extend congratulations. Blamey or Dunn happily could inform the Commonwealth Investigation Branch's Melbourne bureau of a job well done, yet again confirming the police chief's standing as a man who could quell the forces of chaos.

In turn, the Melbourne bureau told the head office of the Investigation Branch in Canberra that the federal and state wings of law enforcement had worked in 'concert' to effect encouraging early results—the musical metaphor alluding to the performance required to orchestrate a moral panic.[7]

The theatre of operations played out on several fronts. Constables Saker and Dunn had delivered the component parts of a scandal but the grand finale relied on rousing a potentially indifferent public to the threat of the 'Black Menace'. Such displays were essential to official claims they were responding to the will of the public, rather than dictating the terms.

PART VIII

Idle and Disorderly

26

THE EIGHT HOUR DAY

By the morning of Monday, 26 March, the torrential rain had cleared, and three and a half thousand union men and women assembled at Trades Hall, ready for the annual Eight Hour Day parade—a battle first waged and won in Melbourne seven decades earlier. It was a public holiday, a chance to remember the 'wild dream' that had become a global standard. According to the history lesson in the *Labor Call*, before the eight-hour day, the toil of workers maintained a leisured class. After the introduction of the eight-hour day, workers had time to cultivate their own cultural sensibilities—and enjoy days of rest and recreation as distinct from days of prayer.[1]

At eleven o'clock, the forty members of the Musicians' Union Gift Band led the procession down Victoria Street and into the heart of Melbourne. Twelve divisions followed, each headed by its own brass and pipe band. Smartly uniformed women from the Tobacco Worker Union marched in lockstep with unemployed workers, the red-shirted anti-Facisti Italians and the 'police strikers'—the officers sacked after the 1923 strike. Commissioner Blamey was a deeply unpopular figure in the labour movement, vilified for his inability to distinguish social reform from Bolshevism. Floats lampooned his brand of justice, contrasting a handcuffed worker beside two silk-hatted men sipping champagne: 'The employer who robs the worker lives in style,' read the banner. At the tail of the parade, members of the Theatrical Employees' Union formed a ghoulish squad in oversized Punch and Judy masks.[2]

Missing from the sweep of artisans and industrial laborers were the domestic and clerical workers, each dominated by women who worked in spaces too atomised to form unions. Chinese food producers and laundry workers were also denied admission to the ranks of unionism. Both groups worked outside the protections of the Arbitration Court and, for many, the luxury of an eight-hour day. An untold number of Indigenous workers inevitably paraded alongside their White comrades, although the sea of banners and crests gestured to a British or Irish heritage. The unstated assumption behind the term 'Australian worker' was 'White' and mostly 'male'. Anyone wishing to mobilise the sympathies of this group on this day had a ready-made crowd.[3]

Since early morning, the first news reports of the Rowena Mansions 'raid' had reached the public. A bare bones outline in the *Age* buried at the bottom of page ten described how Saker found five 'colored men in company with five young women' and 'single-handed in a decidedly hostile atmosphere' arrested the women for vagrancy.[4] The Adelaide *Advertiser* ran an identical article with one significant difference: 'all' the 'five young white girls' were 'alleged to be nude'. A later edition added that the bandsmen's 'conduct' had 'perturbed' 'authorities'. 'The Negroes have been repeatedly seen in the company of white women.'[5] The factual errors, omissions and distortions pointed to a police source intent on baiting the public, rousing them to indignation, even anger.

By the time the last of the Eight Hour Day procession had crossed Princes Bridge and passed the Green Mill, Tom Carlyon had capitulated. The Sonny Clay Orchestra's upcoming season at the Green Mill was cancelled, he announced. With a beauty contestant finalist implicated in the raid, he was powerless to counter accusations he was facilitating the ruin of young women. To deflect any suggestions of disloyalty, he renamed his house band 'Joe Aronson and his Australian Band'. Carlyon, perhaps, had some understanding of the forces at play, given his business partner Fred Matear's close links to Commissioner Blamey.[6]

Percy Crawford, the manager of the Melbourne Tivoli, soldiered on, suspecting the farcical raid was somehow linked to the Musicians' Union's opposition to the Green Mill shows. Ticket sales for the two Tivoli performances that day pointed to a strong house. Five days remained in the season and he was determined to see it through. He knew Sonny Clay and his bandsmen to be 'very decent fellows' and saw no cause for alarm.[7]

Neither, evidently, did the thousands of trade unionists in and around Bourke Street. As an afternoon of English folk dancing and choruses of 'Solidarity Forever' unfolded at a riverside picnic space, the members of the Colored Idea arrived at the Tivoli for the matinee. Thirty or forty people gathered outside the theatre to watch them but they neither protested nor hurled abuse and hovered simply as curious onlookers. Meanwhile, an upbeat audience thoroughly enjoyed the revue.[8]

By the time the Colored Idea wrapped up the afternoon show, Melbourne's biggest-selling afternoon daily, the *Herald*, was being sold on street corners. The Eight Hour Day parade dominated the first page. A horserace at Moonee Valley captured the second. The third page updated an evolving story: 'Negro Theatre Artists and White Girls in Flat: Federal Action Expected'.[9]

With an impressive knowledge of immigration law and procedure, the newspaper detailed the 'guarantees' demanded by the Department of Home and Territories 'when issuing permits to colored aliens'—and anticipated an intervention at the highest level of government. The reporter's writing style switched between passive and active voice: the source of the 'complaints' about musicians' 'disgraceful conduct' were vague, indeed non-existent, while the 'raid' was accorded the drama of a rescue mission: 'police burst in the door' to find 'scantily clad' 'girls'.[10]

Other grammatical quirks mired the 'facts' in ambiguity. The absence of closing quotation marks made it impossible for a reader to know where the landlady's comment ended. Did she just say: the musicians 'rarely brought anyone home after the theatre and were always quiet themselves'? Or did she also make the next statements: 'Two girls used to come to the flat every day to do the cleaning. One of them was a dancer and had been placed in a beauty competition.' Whether a typographical error or a conscious omission, the landlady's words blurred into the editorial, leaving the impression that Black men had employed a sterling example of Australian girlhood as their servant.[11]

Around six o'clock that evening, Percy Crawford received a telephone call from Inspector Hall, head of the plainclothes unit, who instructed him to cancel the evening show. According to police intelligence, Hall 'feared' the performers would meet with 'trouble'. To preserve order, he had despatched six uniformed and plainclothes police to guard the theatre.

Something about the exchange roused Crawford's suspicion and, at the close of their conversation, he immediately called police headquarters to learn that Inspector Hall was out of the city and had neither contacted him nor assigned any officers. It was clearly a bogus call, yet as promised, the plainclothes police duly arrived. Only the 'hostile reception' failed to materialise. Despite the 'strong police' presence, 'there were no overt signs of hostility from the crowded holiday house', reported the *Age*. The public's indifference surprised an Adelaide *Chronicle* reporter who chastised local newspapers for not giving the Rowena Mansions 'raid' 'much prominence'. The Americans, however, understood the performance that was underway. More than a display of police authority, this was White authority.[12]

The evening show proved to be the Sonny Clay Orchestra's last hurrah. Before the night was through, Percy Crawford announced, for the sake of 'public interest', 'the safest policy' was to terminate the contract. The Four Covans and Emperors of Harmony would remain, but the ten members of the jazz band would return to the United States on the first available steamer. As Percy Crawford recounted the fake telephone conversation with the police, his frustration was palpable. 'Such intimidation was not fair,' he told the press.[13]

Oddly, Crawford made no mention of his telephone conversation with a Home and Territories official. But according to Minister Howse, a staff member had informed Crawford the musicians were now prohibited immigrants. Under Section 4 of the Immigration Act, the minister had applied his discretionary power and cancelled their exemption certificates. If the Tivoli did not instigate the band's immediate removal, the government would do it for him. 'They must leave by the next boat,' ordered Howse.[14]

The staffer only told Crawford half the story. Minister Howe's instructions came from Roland Browne, head of the Victorian wing of the Investigation Branch. 'May Ministerial direction be given for [the] cancellation [of] Permits issued [to the] Negro Orchestra to ensure departure from Australia,' began his cablegram. 'Police opinion is that further presence [of] Negro [is] undesirable.'[15]

At first, Crawford prevaricated. The Tivoli management had planned to bring the Colored Idea to Adelaide—plus a return run in Sydney. But what choice did he have? Imported acts were the lifeblood of the Tivoli and relied on the Department for Home and Territories to issue visas. And thus, before a single charge had been proven in court, with barely a peep of public protest, the bureaucrat forced Crawford to pull the plug on a 'remarkably successful season'.[16]

The Eight Hour Day celebrated the triptych of modern industrial life: eight hours labour, eight hours rest and eight hours for what we will. Although, by the end of this Eight Hour Day, events made plain the layers of paternalism constraining the way working people enjoyed their free time. Bureaucrats filtered what young women and men could see and hear, censors limited their exposure to ideas. In a leisure time world fashioned by African American ideas and practices, consumer demand for modern entertainment and the White Australian ideal were on collision course.

27

A YOUNG WOMAN IN TROUBLE

In May 1925, Dorothy Anderson was a cook on a sheep station outside Ararat, a pastoral town one hundred miles west of Melbourne. It was big sky country bounded by dusky purple mountains, although the majesty of the landscape could not save the seventeen-year-old from the drudgery of the stove. Nor supplant memories of Melbourne where she had lived the previous year with her husband and child. The circumstances leading to her separation from both are unknown although two weeks into her new job, she was plotting her escape.

A farm labourer by the name of Charlie Sanders was sweet on Dorothy Anderson. Or at least, he trusted her enough to hand her his monthly cheque, believing she was doing him a favour. Dorothy also convinced her employer to pay her monthly salary two weeks in advance—and wrangled a day off work so she could cash both cheques at the bank in Ararat.

Dorothy Anderson did just that, then made a long-distance call, bought a train ticket and caught the next service to Melbourne where she was reunited with her child. Some weeks later, a plainclothes constable tracked her down at her Carlton home and charged her with larceny. Dorothy again used her powers of persuasion, this time convincing a magistrate and several justices of the peace there had been a mistake. She had not robbed Charlie Sanders of his hard-earned wages, explaining how she had written him a letter, promising to repay every penny. The fault lay with the messenger, a mutual acquaintance, who failed to deliver the note. Against police advice, the judicial bench unanimously agreed Dorothy Anderson had shown no 'felonious intent' and discharged her.[1]

Two years later, in May 1927, Dorothy was again a 'young woman in trouble'—and a face well known to South Melbourne police. No longer caring for her child, she worked as a domestic servant and lived in an Albert Park boarding house. One day she disappeared from the residence with her landlady's pearl necklace and earrings. Desirous to show off her treasures, careless to legal definitions of property, Dorothy wore them in full view in a cafe on St Kilda's Esplanade. There, a plainclothes constable spotted her and followed her to a rooming house where she confessed to the crime.[2]

Back before the magistrate, Dorothy Anderson acknowledged her guilt and pleaded for another chance to rise above her desperate circumstances. This time, the magistrate applied a custodial sentence routinely passed down on 'wayward' and 'uncontrollable' girls. Neither dismissing nor convicting her, he adjourned her case for six months, lodging her at a YWCA hostel for friendless girls. At the next court appearance, the matron's report would determine Dorothy's fate. If released, any infraction would condemn her to another indefinite custodial arrangement.[3]

Ten months later, in March 1928, Dorothy, if not entirely free, was no longer in YWCA care. Her path back to lawful behaviour was helped by an Ararat grazier, or more precisely his wife and adult daughters who lived in a grand home in St Kilda. Dorothy Anderson was their maid, living in the shadow of wealth and the trappings of privilege—a world of dainty lunches, charity balls, automobile rallies and society weddings. She heard the gossip, even hushed secrets, about the names dotting Melbourne's social pages. She could admire Mrs Kilpatrick's photograph in the Victorian edition of *Who's Who in the World of Women* and follow the elder Miss Kilpatrick's passion for fast motor cars and distant travel. Perhaps she helped Miss Kilpatrick shine and arrange her fine collection of goggles.[4]

It is not clear whether Mrs or Miss Kilpatrick appreciated the fragile state of Dorothy's liberty and vulnerability to the demands of plainclothes detectives. Almost certainly, they had no clue that their maid was among the 'five girls' arrested under scandalous circumstances. Nor did they know that on Tuesday, 27 March, Dorothy was to appear at Melbourne's City Court. And when she left the house in an off-the-rack skirt and blazer, fox stole and white cloche hat, Dorothy had a pair of goggles stowed away in a handbag, presumably pilfered from Miss Kilpatrick's collection.[5]

Dorothy had chosen an oversized goggle with a tinted eye shield. The design simultaneously protected her anonymity while making a fashion statement inspired by popular culture and aspirational style. Motoring and aviation gave rise to countless images of adventurous modern women in leather caps and goggles perched on their forehead. At least two flapper comedies screening in Melbourne that month cashed in on 'today's aviation craze' sparked by Australian aviators Bert Hinkler and Jessie Miller. On this day, Dorothy would embark on her own madcap adventure.[6]

She travelled likely by tram to the city centre—a four-mile journey that offered time to scrutinise the morning papers and learn of events since her release from the watch house. Under the banner 'The Color Line', the *Age* told of the band's cancelled contract and the follow-up inquiries conducted by Constable Saker: on Sunday night he again discovered Edna Langdon and Nola Mackay at Rowena Mansions.[7]

Such news was unsettling to a stool pigeon: the women Dorothy might soon incriminate had shared information with the man she framed. Unknown to her, headlines like 'flat orgy' were plastered over morning papers across Australia. 'Girls and Their Negro Friends in the Nude', read Darwin's *Northern Territory Times.*[8] 'All the girls were naked when the raid was made,' echoed Sydney's *Daily Guardian*. 'Further details supplied by police' confirmed a procession of 'different white girls' visited the flat. The prime minister was 'deeply concerned about the matter'.[9]

Whether Dorothy Anderson approached the city courthouse by foot, taxi or tram, while still a block away, she could see a crowd of men spilling off the pavement and into the street. At some point she positioned the tinted goggles over her eyes and shielded the lower part of her face behind her fur collar, ready to navigate what newspapers later described as a 'tremendous' 'jostling' mob in a 'hostile mood'.[10]

Newspaper estimates of the crowd ranged between eight hundred and fifteen hundred. Beyond their maleness, Whiteness and anger, their identity was unclear but 'long before the court opened', they packed its corridors, courtyard and doorways. According to one report, a 'well known' Black entertainer also showed up, possibly the elderly Charlie Pope, but the police sent him home, fearing for his safety. 'If the Negroes had appeared, there certainly would have been trouble,' contended one paper.[11]

What compelled hundreds of men to skip a day's work and stage the type of display police officers had anticipated the previous night? Did they gather spontaneously, a collection of aggrieved individuals? Or were they part of an organised protest, members of a network with lines of communication and chain of command? It would be one of several unasked questions dangling in the air that day.

A photographer from the *Truth* was also outside the court—no other publication had thought to bring one along—and captured four of the five defendants enduring the throng. 'The searching eye of the *Truth*'s camera' had a 'terrifying effect' on Edna Langdon who 'dived for a hole in the wall', they noted. Nola Mackay pulled her cloche hat low, her hand shielding her face as she deflected the wagging of someone's self-righteous finger. Dorothy McGowan and Dorothy Davis buried their faces in their fur collars, hunched and cowering. Davis, too, wore the tinted goggles.[12]

The *Truth* photographer, at this point, did not snap the woman known in police reports as 'Ivy Day'. Her goggles, however, 'created a stir' among the press corps. Indeed, the appearance of all the women drew much comment, if only to contrast the fashionable order of their bodies with their flagrant disregard for social norms.[13]

'Each of the girls wore fashionably cut dresses,' noted newsmen. Their 'pretty' faces and 'neat appearance' distinguished them from the 'class usually found among low associates'. They could have been drawn from 'an average gathering of shop-girls and clerks'. Such incongruities were the stuff of sensationalism: 'smartly dressed' bodies, pleasing Anglo-Saxon faces, 'disgraceful behaviour' and the inexplicable 'why'?[14]

The five accused waited in a court chamber, likely consulting with the defence lawyer appointed by Edna Langdon and Nola Mackay.

A *Truth* photographer captures four of the Rowena Mansions Five as they navigate the hostile crowd outside Melbourne City Court. Dorothy McGowan and Dorothy Davis, top left. Edna Langdon and Nola Mackay, top right. Man confronts Nola Mackay, bottom. (*Truth*, State Library Victoria and State Library of NSW)

Nathaniel Sonenburg was a veteran of the magistrate's court: a working-class Carlton lad, the son of London Jewish migrants who had built his career defending working-class people for their petty crimes. As such, he was wise to the quirks of the courtroom. He knew, for instance, the magistrate had a keen interest in the science of criminology, and frequently applied the latest welfare ideas to prevent first-time offenders drifting into careers of crime. Such sympathies boded well for the five young women.[15]

Nate Sonenburg had also defended scores of people arrested by Constables Saker and Dunn, so knew of their loose adherence to the truth, their penchant for inventing evidence and committing perjury. The solicitor had seen, first-hand, the seamless complicity that bonded judiciary to police: to protect the authority of the justice system, the magistrate never questioned the veracity of police testimony.

Sonenburg's suspicions about police methods did not outweigh his personal distaste for the women's modern lives. Even after Nola Mackay and Edna Langdon told him their version of the night's events, emphasising 'nothing wrong' had taken place, Sonenburg still considered them 'lax and careless'.[16]

Also unclear was whether the five defendants would stick together. 'Ivy Day' knew her debt to the police was not yet settled. Much would hinge on her testimony—and her powers of persuasion. By now Edna and Nola may have had some idea that the 'raid' was a frame-up, that 'Ivy Day' was a plant. But who was listening?

Did Sonenburg know at this point that 'Ivy Day' was not his client's real name? Did he understand why she had adopted a pseudonym? Did he have any insight into the intense government interest in what was effectively the trial of a misdemeanour, and a minor one at that.

If his understanding of events was incomplete, his legal strategy was clear—he would address the letter of the vagrancy statute. The women only needed to demonstrate they lawfully earned money. As such, questions of police procedure and the women's conduct were immaterial to the case. As he well knew, rousing the ire of the magistrate could lead to a guilty conviction and custodial sentence.

28
JUDICIAL THEATRE

AT TEN O'CLOCK, Police Magistrate AA Kelley and four justices of the peace—a middle-aged woman named Angela Booth, and three elderly men, Thomas Latham, Thomas O'Callaghan and WH Curtis—took their seats at the bench. The chairman of the bench had already cleared out the crowds elbowing for space in the public gallery, and the hundreds more clustered in the corridors and out in the quadrangle. Only those directly involved in the day's case were allowed to remain. Nonetheless, even in the half-filled courtroom, one reporter felt 'a buzz of excitement' when the name 'Ivy Day' was called. The woman approached the dock, her eyes still shielded by the oversized tinted goggles. To the charge of vagrancy, she entered a plea of 'not guilty'.[1]

So many aspects of the day are unclear. By now, police knew Ivy Day's real name was Dorothy Anderson. So why did the court allow her to proceed under an alias? An oath to tell the truth surely began with her identity. And why did the magistrate allow her to stand in the dock with her goggles on? The other four women lodged pleas of 'not guilty' with their faces exposed.[2]

As all knew, law enforcers used the 'insufficient lawful means of support' clause in the vagrancy charge to convict prostitutes—and, more vaguely, women in domestic arrangement with criminals and other undefined 'undesirables'. They were 'idle and disorderly' by virtue of keeping house for the wrong type of breadwinner.[3]

Constable Saker was the first to take the stand. His task was to prove the five women had been 'kept' by the American musicians. As both arresting officer and star witness, a policeman's testimony carried an authority no citizen could match. Reporters sanctioned it as the official narrative. As several *Truth* articles could attest, Saker's particular skill lay in embroidering salacious details into procedure-driven, faux-objective 'facts'. 'When a search of his room was made, I found a tin containing a drug wrapped in a pair of socks. A metal box and some celluloid sticks were found,' was typical of his style.[4] On one occasion, Saker's description of a brothel was of 'such a colourful nature that several members of the Bench bent their heads and became deeply absorbed in their papers', even as a *Truth* reporter recorded every tawdry detail.[5]

On this day, Constable Saker stuck to the formula. 'The raid had occurred in consequence of the many complaints received that white women were frequenting the flats occupied by negroes,' he began. The depravity he observed unfolding over three nights had one recurring theme: Edna Langdon being pulled about by 'the negroes'.[6]

At several points, defence attorney Nathaniel Sonenburg objected to the 'purely atmospheric' testimony. 'I thought the question of conduct had nothing to do with this case. I thought they were charged with having insufficient means of support,' he protested. Each time Magistrate Kelley waved him away: such 'circumstances' may be 'evidence' of Edna Langdon's 'means of support'. Once Saker had entered the flat and found 'dregs of wine' and a room in a 'state of disorder', he offered no further insights into Langdon's 'improper behaviour'. His most compelling evidence lay in the actions of 'Ivy Day'.[7]

Saker described opening the door to a bedroom to find 'Ivy Day' standing in her underclothes and John Black in bed in his pyjamas. At some point his testimony shifted, claiming to find 'Day *in bed* with a blackfellow', or at least that was how a *Sun* reporter heard it.[8]

Saker recounted their conversation. He asked Day: 'You have met this man before?'

'Yes,' she replied. 'I met him at a dance at the Green Mill.'

'I haven't been doing any work for some time,' she continued, 'but I'm going to do some for a Negro.'[9]

Saker had minted a readymade quote for the prosecutor that was both legally incriminating and factually incorrect. When cross-examined, 'Ivy Day' only had to confirm or deny Saker's statement.

The goggles still shielded Dorothy Anderson's eyes, the pseudonym still concealed her identity. Yet these protections could not immunise her body to the cut of Saker's words or the disapproving murmur through the court. A wave of anxiety and fear caused her chest to constrict and blood pressure to drop. Likely, a wave of nausea, light-headedness and blurred vision overwhelmed her. Certainly, her physical composure unravelled. She fainted, slumping to the floor.

Magistrate Kelley halted Saker's testimony and an official carried Ivy Day's limp body into an antechamber. Minutes later, her hysterical sobs echoed through the hush of the courtroom. 'When Day returned to the court, she had discarded her sun goggles, revealing her handsome features,' wrote one reporter. Not just unmasked, Saker's words had undressed and laid her bare. Descriptions of her underwear were now the stuff of the tabloids. Her behaviour would shock a nation. As she was weakened, the magistrate allowed her to sit.[10]

Saker continued with his testimony. He had successfully established the likelihood Ivy Day was a 'kept' woman, so he turned his attentions back to Edna Langdon and Nola Mackay. His evidence concentrated not on the raid but on the women's actions the following day when he found them procuring money from the Americans. Saker then introduced something new: on the night of their arrest, he had found a phial containing twenty cocaine tablets stashed under the chairs at the city watch house where the women sat while police processed their charge.[11]

No reporter chronicled Langdon's and Mackay's responses to Saker's damning evidence but incredulity, surely, counted among them. Did they turn to each other in disbelief and confusion? Wonder when their lawyer would object?

But Sonenburg said nothing. At one point in his career, he had attempted to expose Saker's perjury, placing defendants on the witness stand who described the force of Saker's fist on their face or the stamp of his heel on their heads. But Sonenburg had learned the approach did not advantage his clients. 'I have no reason to disbelieve police evidence,' Magistrate Kelley once said, as he judged some unfortunate guilty.[12]

Two years later, in 1930, Neil Gibson, an investigative reporter with a catalogue of personal grievances against Senior Constable Harry Dunn, self-published a pamphlet accusing plainclothes officers of routine perjury in the Court of Petty Sessions. Magistrates accepted police testimony as 'disinterested' and objective, while dismissing defendants' claims of police violence, blackmail and fabrications as tainted by personal interest. 'When police evidence is challenge[d],' railed Gibson, 'the Bench raise their eyebrow in surprise and ask, "Why would a constable tell a lie?"'[13] By the mid-1930s, Neil Gibson's exposé culminated in an inquiry into police corruption headed by Magistrate AA Kelley. In those weeks, Kelley would be forced to confront the plainclothes unit's involvement in the illegal cocaine trade. But in 1928, the plainclothes unit were untouchable.[14]

All Sonenburg could do was prod Constable Saker during his cross examination:

> Sonenburg: Did the negroes deny that anything improper had been going on in the place?
> Saker: No. They all put the blame on the girls.
> Sonenburg: Did each one of the colored boys say, 'Nothing wrong has taken place here?'
> Saker: They all said they had not interfered with the girls.
> Sonenburg: Supposing these had been white men, would you have gone into the place at all?
> Saker: We would not have got the complaints.
> Sonenburg: Why did you not go in on Thursday or Friday night?
> Saker: We knew Saturday night would be the big night.
> Sonenburg: You were waiting for the big things?
> Saker: Yes, and we got them [laughter].
> Sonenburg: You would be able to identify from Nicholson Street the negroes who were pulling the girls about?
> Saker: Only that they were black. A tree obscured the window a little.
> Sonenburg: Then people passing could not see it?
> Saker: People had seen it and complained.[15]

Sonenburg was not out to expose Saker's mendacity. Or the tendrils of police corruption. He merely had to demonstrate the women's source of income. As he told the court: 'These women lead their own lives and while we may disapprove of it and condemn it very strongly, the question here is what is their means of support. None of these women has ever been before a court before.'[16]

In electing not to challenge the allegations of immoral conduct, or irregularities in police procedure, Sonenburg ultimately affirmed what the Victorian police and Investigation Branch believed to be the greater crime: the violation to the White Australia ideal.

Ivy Day was the first of the accused to take the witness stand. Under oath, she claimed to be a 23-year-old 'nurse girl' employed by Mr and Mrs Riley of St Kilda Road, earning thirty shillings a week. Little in this statement beyond her age and street was correct.[17]

The prosecutor, Inspector Scales, cross-examined her at length. Or more accurately, he mostly asked her to confirm a series of statements about jazz culture as a gateway to moral debauchery. She agreed with the interrogator that 'she had met the men at the Green Mill'. Later in the evening, the 'girls at Coffee Dan's' induced her to attend the house party. They said, 'You are expected to come.' One of the 'coloured boys' had 'introduced' her to wine and she had become intoxicated. 'She was not accustomed to drink.'[18]

She confessed to giving police a false name.

'Is Day your proper name?' asked Scales.

'No,' she replied. 'I was advised not to give my correct name.'[19]

'By whom?' was the next logical question but it hung in the air, unasked. Neither the defence nor the prosecution were willing to explore her role in events.

Instead, Sonenburg asked Ivy Day to make an 'undertaking to the court you will not go back there again'. She obliged, her pledge winning sympathy. Reporters interpreted her collapse as a measure of guilt and her co-operation, a gesture of remorse.[20]

Edna Langdon and Nola Mackay, in contrast, appeared unrepentant and incorrigible. As the prosecution established, they were frequent visitors to the musicians' residence and had lured Ivy Day to the party. They contradicted Saker's testimony. Langdon denied she engaged in 'improper behaviour', and objected to the suggestion she was intoxicated. 'I do not drink or smoke,' she protested. 'We were all practically ready to go when the police came in,' explained Nola Mackay. Reporters saw two women who were blind to their moral turpitude. Why else would they have 'repeated their debauch' and returned to the flat on Sunday?[21]

Within the tabloid imagination, 'this most sordid story' unfolded like a continental sex film. At one point, Edna Langdon described herself as a 'dancer'—although also told the court she was a clerk at a Balaclava Road garage. Nola Mackay confirmed that, in addition to her salary as a dress-maker, she received a small allowance from her deceased father's estate. In a verbal flourish, a tabloid hack could fashion two Hollywood stock characters: the socialite and the showgirl.[22]

That week, a selection of cautionary and titillating tales about the Manhattan Socialite's and Hollywood Hopeful's pursuit of hedonistic pleasures screened at Melbourne picture houses. 'I drink from the cup of bliss and yet I find the dregs,' bemoaned one celluloid vamp.[23] Eugenic echoes surrounded the word 'dregs': the 'dregs of society' were the 'submerged tenth', the slum hovels of opium-addled Chinese men, degraded White women and their 'half-caste' spawn. And, as Saker and reporters repeatedly noted, the 'dregs' were the remnants of the wine bottle 'strewn' across the Rowena Mansions flat—the external environment mirrored a more intimate disorder.

Under cross-examination, the prosecutor cast Dorothy McGowan's and Dorothy Davis' moral degeneracy as a consequence of their ongoing contact with non-White men. McGowan worked for a well-respected Chinese herbalist, Tye Kee, but in this context her lawful means of support fed into miscegenation dramas about fallen women. Stories such as 'How Florrie Fell' were a staple among tabloid reporters: the 'scarlet sinner' on the 'primrose path' from the 'finely dressed flapper' to 'heavy-eyed party girl' to 'opium addict' lurking in 'filth and squalor'.[24]

As the musicians' cook, Dorothy Davis was on this 'road to ruin'. The prosecuting attorney greeted with derision her claims the men 'behaved like gentlemen' and 'treated me like a lady'. With a slip of the pen, tabloid reporters heard her say she '*lived* like a lady', a working-class woman of leisure, an idle girl dissatisfied with her lot who, wanting smart clothes and a life of gaiety, chose moral turpitude over industry and thrift.[25]

'Did you take breakfast to them in bed?' the prosecutor asked Davis.[26] If not outright prostitution, he implied something similar was taking place. The gendered wage differential gave rise to a culture of treating. According to the popular truism, men footed the bill for dates on the understanding that women would settle the account with sexual favours. Now in the face of 'flash-living "coons" with money to spend'—as every report made clear, the women earned a paltry sum compared to the men's weekly salary of £18—newspapers recast these patriarchal privileges as a menace. The musicians and the music they played were a vector of racial contamination and degeneration.[27]

As a piece of judicial theatre, the day's proceedings were riveting. Constable Saker and Inspector Scales had all but handed the newspapers their front-page story. But as a legal case, the evidence lacked substance; even Saker conceded that no acts of 'indecency' were committed. After a brief discussion with the four justices on the bench, Magistrate Kelley passed a ruling. 'You are all discharged,' was the sum of his judgement.[28]

The women were free to leave the court—and the few press snippets capturing these moments did not distinguish one woman from the other. An 'eager crowd' of men still hovered outside the courthouse and, learning of the judgement, clustered around the 'door'. The police moved them on, although they did not disperse. 'One courageous young lady' left the courthouse through the front door, protected by 'a score of excited female friends' who 'surrounded' her, showering her with kisses and congratulations. The others waited in the courthouse then 'got away ... singly or in pairs'. At least two, maybe three, 'hurried away in a taxi'. One woman left alone on foot and was 'followed by a section of the crowd'. Whether they hurled abuse or followed in silence, it made for a sinister ending to a gruelling day.[29]

Was it 'Ivy Day'? A *Truth* photographer captured her leaving the court with her face bare: lips pressed, eyes fixed straight ahead, refusing to meet the aperture. Her facial expression aspired to dignity but seemed

Dorothy Anderson aka 'Ivy Day' leaving the Melbourne City Court, no longer attempting to conceal her identity with aviation goggles. (Sydney *Truth*, State Library of NSW)

to burn with humiliation. Certainly, it did not match the heroic caption: 'DID NOT FEAR THE CAMERA or the publicity.'[30] Instead, she endured the moment, calculating the permutations of her fate: her job, her child, her liberty, her appearance, her self-respect, her complicity, her guilt.

The trial was over but, as the afternoon papers left the printing press, the wave of moral indignation had only just begun.

29
A CAPTIVE AUDIENCE

INTERRACIAL SEX OBSESSED White Australia. The fixation could be counted in novels, newsprint, films, science and statistics, each tale of racial commingling cloaked in emotions ranging from visceral disgust to melodramatic horror, spicy titillation, sordid tragedy and hand-wringing despair. At best, interracial love was a social and moral taboo, a doomed exercise. At worst, the mixing of the races was a violation of natural law, an agent of degeneration and decline. The consequences for those who crossed this line varied depending, firstly, on the combination of race and gender, and secondly on the environment: whether the interracial relationship played out within the bounds of the 'civilized world', or beyond it. One told the ruin of a virtuous White girl. The other gave free rein to White male fantasies about highly sexualised women of colour in far-flung corners of the empire.[1]

The 1926 Australian film *The Jungle Woman* explicitly spelled out these 'rules': 'Love knows no barrier of caste or color beyond the outposts of civilization, where no man-made law could reach out to say "Thou Shalt Not"', read publicity. Set in the 'wilds' of Papua New Guinea, the drama followed the adventures of a young White Australian prospector who fell madly in love with the chief's daughter. Could love in the highlands also flourish in Sydney or Melbourne? The young prospector would never know. Moments before their boat landed, his beloved perished in a tragic accident. He, in contrast, resumed his place in 'civilised' society without a blemish on his racial virtue.[2]

White Cargo, easily the most popular and controversial theatrical production of 1920s Australia, was less forgiving. The plot followed Longford, a 'spotless' young Englishman who arrived at a West African rubber plantation determined not to fall prey to the alcoholism and promiscuity of the White colonial men around him. But seduced by Tondelayo, a beautiful but wanton 'half-caste' woman, the 'damp rot of civilisation' set in. At his insistence, they marry—but his decency is undone, first by her 'sex-hunger' for other men, then by her lust for murder. Barely surviving her poison, he returns to England as 'White Cargo', an inversion of the transatlantic slave trade, his spirit broken by the fetid jungle.[3]

The play's message was unambiguous: White virtue was not biologically inherent but geographically contingent. No matter how noble the character, a primitive, amoral environment would break the strongest will. The play's conclusions resonated with Australian reviewers who likened the moral 'rot' to a back-country sheep station.[4] The difference was, in the White settler state of Australia, 'outer civilisation' lay within the nation's boundaries.

The short story 'The Black Madame Butterfly', published in *Smith's Weekly* in January 1928, told one such outback tale. It centred on an Aboriginal woman anxiously awaiting the return of the man she loved, a White bushman and father of her children, only to realise he had settled into a respectable marriage with a White townswoman. The storyteller wallowed in her pain before dismissing her as 'confectionary', a 'body servant' and 'joke'—ridiculous and disposable. Her plight was unfortunate but inevitable, shrugged the narrator; that's just how things play out in the bush.[5]

Disturbing reports from Central Australia fractured any feigned ignorance about the realities of back country concubinage. Letters to mission societies described physical abuse, starvation, sickness and sexual violence—and a surge in the number of light-skinned children born to Aboriginal women. In 1928, one missionary told how police arrived at a segregated reserve outside Alice Springs and ordered a group of young women to a cattle station twenty miles away. 'In fear and trembling', the women left, certain they would meet with a 'big gun or poison'. Instead, they were directed to 'strip off and paint up' and perform a 'corroboree' in a 'nude state' for the entertainment of eighty 'government men'. It was a 'shocking sight', relayed the missionary, although far from condemning the 'government men' at a prayer meeting the following day, the missionaries invited survivors to beg Jesus' forgiveness for being led into evil.[6]

Meanwhile, the cycle of frontier violence continued. Women's League campaigned to place buffer zones between Aboriginal women and the railway labourers' camps.[7] Seasoned missionaries sought even greater controls. 'Segregation under religious influence' was the Aboriginal people's 'only hope', implored Reverend Ernest Gribble at a 1927 Royal Commission into the massacre of twenty-nine Indigenous people—thirteen women and sixteen men—at Forrest River, Western Australia, at the hands of two policemen. (The policemen were tried for murder and found not guilty.)[8]

The scale of violence outpaced the paternalism of benevolent institutions. In August 1928, at a remote outpost known as Coniston, at least seventeen Warlpiri tribesmen died in a punitive police raid to avenge the deaths of two White settlers who had mistreated Aboriginal women and girls.[9]

Within the 'bounds of civilisation', sexual violence against domestic servants ran rife. Since the mid-1920s, Australian Aboriginal Progressive Association president Fred Maynard had been lobbying politicians, writing to newspapers and staging interventions to expose the national scandal that began when authorities invaded the sanctity of people's homes and departed with their daughters. Girls as young as fifteen had been raped and impregnated by their employers, then forced to return to their tormenter, held captive by their 'fear of the police'. Aboriginal Protection Board policies condemned Indigenous women to a life of 'slavery, misery and despair', exposing them to sexual predation and violence, with little recourse to justice, petitioned Maynard in the same weeks Major Lloyd wrote his report on the 'Negro Orchestra'.[10] The same authorities that fretted over White girls dancing with Black men were indifferent to the plight of Indigenous women.

Statistics suggest (however imperfectly) the scale of interracial sex between White men and Aboriginal women across the country. A comparative chart in the 1933 Census showed that, despite three decades of racial purification policies, overall numbers of non-Whites had barely changed. Between 1911 and 1933, the British population increased by two million while non-European numbers had significantly decreased. However, the mostly rural Indigenous 'half-caste' population had doubled in twenty years. Contrary to predictions of a vanishing race, Aboriginal numbers were increasing.[11]

For Indigenous people, these numbers told the story of their resilience and determination to be part of modern Australia. Those invested in 'racial unity' saw a 'racial tragedy', more reasons to create segregated self-supporting homelands to constrain the freedoms of Aboriginal people.[12] The *Truth* called for a 'thorough clean up' to reduce the 'startling numbers' of 'half caste' 'progeny' in Central Australia, urging authorities to recruit the 'right' type of policemen, who could withstand the lure of the 'primitive'. At no point did they or any other newspapers stigmatise White bushmen for derailing the White Australia mission. Quite the opposite: across the arts and popular culture, the stockman, drover and digger were deified as an idealised racial type.[13]

Tales of White women and non-White men *within* the bounds of 'civilisation' cast docklands and inner-city streets as a contest of inferior and superior power differentials. The narratives hewed to remarkably predictable scripts.

Jean Bruce Monckton's 1928 novel *The Shuttle of Life*, for instance, unspooled the tale of a virtuous White Sydney girl forced to marry a vindictive Chinese herbalist to save her brother from the gallows. Betrayed by a neglectful mother, duped by the promise of wealth and entrapped by opium addiction, she was powerless to resist the defilement of her body and the natural order. 'Women are the guardians of racial purity,' declared a minor character, 'and all normal, healthy-minded women recoil instinctively from doing anything that might pollute it.'[14]

Such narratives called for a hero to rise and protect White femininity. The January edition of *Smith's Weekly* obliged. A few pages on from 'The Black Madame Butterfly', another short story, 'Migrant Girl Saved from White Slavers', told the tale of a hapless British 'girl' en route to Australia. At a stop-over in a Far Eastern port, she was in the midst of being lured away by two Asian pimps when an Anzac veteran detected the deception and mounted a 'timely intervention'. 'In a trice, the Australian picked her up in his arms and ... told her to behave herself.' The clueless 'girl' foolishly resisted, only to later realise, if not for her hero's clear thinking, she would be a 'plaything for the scum of the Orient'.[15] The story brought together the frontier 'captive woman' of the past with the Black, Brown and 'Yellow' peril of the future to create a new genre, the White Slavery miscegenation drama.

The term 'White slavery' at first referred to the 'compulsory emigration' of convicts and indentured labourers in the nineteenth century. By the early 1910s, undercover reporters invoked the phrase to describe White women in big cities 'entrapped' by 'pimps' who were 'nearly all foreigners'—although any non-White would do. By the 1920s, White Slave Traffic was a League of Nations department at once tasked with suppressing international prostitution rings and, by its very wording, ignoring the plight of Black women.

Within popular culture, the phrase took on a life of its own. 'White slavery' was a highly charged proxy for *any* intimacy between White women and non-White men. According to the tabloid press, White Australian women married to Afghan camel-drivers were 'doomed to a life of close imprisonment under most barbarous conditions', little more than 'a household slave'.[16] 'Are the white slaves fallen women? No. Are they harlots? No,' sermonised a letter to the editor. 'They are the pure girlhood of the land; the young womanhood of the country lured to their doom ... by systematic bands of atrocious scoundrels.'[17]

On 27 March 1928, however, the White Slavery captivity narrative was not running to script. Commentators, to their disgust, noted that the Rowena Mansions Five were not lured, duped, blackmailed or coerced but acted of their own free will. Nor were they helpless women entrapped by predatory men but agents of their own destiny. Nor did Sonny Clay's musicians fit the role of 'pimp'. They did not profit from the women's labour—as any slave master would do—but were skilled professionals, earning a salary that was the envy of most White working men.[18]

'They are Americans and they interest me,' Dorothy Davis allegedly told Constable Dunn, who may have invented her answer.[19] Even so, within the tabloid narrative she emerged as a precocious figure, curious about other cultures and ideas. Exposure to the jazz musicians' undeniable 'American-ness'—their accents, style, ingenuity and swagger—had elevated her modern credentials, at least in certain fashionable circles. Like Eve biting into the apple from the Tree of Knowledge, the encounter opened her eyes to new ways of thinking and being.

The moment called for White Australia's mythmakers to recast the genre conventions and spin a new White Slavery tale. As with any modern adaptation, the task called for some nimble inversions and reformulations without altering the core rescue-from-captivity theme.

The five White women were unfit to play the virtuous but hapless Migrant Girl—each had been contaminated by miscegenated culture. Their role was more akin to *White Cargo*'s wily 'half-caste' Tondelayo or the wretched Madame Butterfly.

The role of the captive maid fell to the idealised White woman of the future, the White Australian Muse, a figure routinely imagined by ink illustrators as a demure and tender beauty in classical robes admiring the young nation's noble deeds or collapsed by the ocean's shores weeping in sorrow that she had been forsaken. Her distress begged for a chivalrous knight to protect her.

The Musicians' Union's woeful tale of the Commonwealth Band pointed to the predatory enslaver: the ruthless and expansionary American economic juggernaut that was swamping the fragile nation, feeding off its young. The Sonny Clay Orchestra readily fit the role of cultural coloniser. They were interlopers thwarting the emergence of an 'authentic' British Australian spirit, while unleashing a deviant sexuality in White women that turned them into willing concubines.

Within this mythological revision, an inversion of the colonial norm took place: White Australia was not a consequence of British conquest and Indigenous dispossession but a 'white Southern empire' handpicked by God, to quote Keith Hancock.[20] Or a 'temperate zone' uniquely fitted for the White race, to quote Charles Pearson.[21] In short, sovereignty sanctioned by natural and divine right. By this measure, the White Australian maiden was held captive by a predatory nation that had long compromised its racial probity. The rescue of national virtue and pride was as yet unwritten: its denouement still under negotiation.

PART IX

Unwritten Law

30
THE SYDNEY EXPRESS

DOUBLE, EVEN TRIPLE, standards came as no surprise to members of the Sonny Clay Orchestra. Life in the United States had taught them how Black and White people played to different rules. By 1952, as head of a racially segregated musicians' union, Leo Davis could name these rules by clause and bylaw. And as he did, younger colleagues noted Davis' marked distrust of Whites. He didn't want 'anything to do with no white man', recalled one musician, attributing the union leader's wariness to his age and Southern upbringing. Such patience turned to frustration when Leo Davis blocked efforts to amalgamate the Black and White unions. Far from seeing more opportunities and equal wages, Davis foresaw empty promises. 'You go to that big organization, and you'll get lost ... you'll be swallowed up,' he warned. To his mind, a hidden racial agenda lay behind the noble gestures of White people, whereas a Black-run union, at least, represented minority interests.[1]

Tuesday, 27 March 1928 was the type of day that affirmed Leo Davis' suspicion of Whites. The previous night, Percy Crawford had pulled the plug on the Colored Idea revue, and immigration authorities had cancelled their visas. That morning, Edna Langdon and Nola Mackay had protested their innocence at the City Court and Constable Saker's lurid version of events dominated the afternoon papers. The Melbourne *Herald*'s front-page headlines cast the bandsmen as 'Negro Undesirables', a threat to national 'security'—although, beyond the word 'consorting', the nature of this threat was vague. Still, the minister of Homes and Territories had plans afoot to prevent more 'Negro Undesirables' entering the country again, pledging to 'personally investigate all applications by colored people'.[2]

Perhaps Leo Davis was most vexed by the article's reassuring tone. It summoned a well-oiled administrative machine processing carefully crafted policy instead of a boorish, ham-fisted operation conducted by cultural philistines who knew nothing of Black arts and literature. Unfolding events bore the 'strong smell of cracker breath', as Harlem Renaissance novelist Claude McKay once quipped.[3]

The *Herald* also detailed the musicians' plans to leave Melbourne on the Sydney Express that evening—although, curiously, none of the protesters outside the courthouse earlier in the day thought to show their displeasure at Spencer Street Station. Nor did any news-hungry press photographers turn up. The pattern—photographers present to capture displays of public protest—would continue.

The overnight journey offered Leo Davis and his bandmates many hours to scrutinise the press coverage.

The Musicians' Union, relayed the *Herald*, were celebrating. In a rare public reference to their prohibition on 'colored musicians', a spokesman linked their campaign to 'prevent' the Green Mill's patrons from 'dancing to the Negroes' music' to their commitment to the White Australia policy—somewhat cryptically adding that 'proceedings elsewhere' had made it 'unnecessary' for them to pursue industrial action.[4]

Such comments roused Percy Crawford's suspicions the Musicians' Union had, somehow, orchestrated the deportation to avenge the Americans for heaping insults on the Commonwealth Band. These rumours were incomplete, although alerted the bandsmen to unseen forces at play.

If the bandsmen did not recognise Constable Saker prior to this date, his name would soon sear their memories. The policeman testified the musicians had said: 'We were trying to get the girls out of the flat. They won't go. The girls won't stay away. They are not the only girls who come here.'[5] Such statements were ludicrous; no man from Central Avenue would be so naive or careless as to besmirch a White woman when addressing a White police officer. Saker was deliberately attempting to inflame, even mobilise, cracker passions.

The *Herald*'s sub-heading suggested the report's narrative themes: 'Would work for a Negro'; 'Employed by Chinese'; 'Lived like a Lady'. Newspapers attributed the women's misplaced trust to a girlish dizziness and a racially and morally compromised environment. The wily musicians were hell-bent on debauching the flower of Australian womanhood before cruelly casting her aside.[6]

In 1947, a radio interviewer asked vocalist Ivy Anderson about the Australian tour. 'Very fine, very good,' she smoothly replied, recalling not the tour's ignoble end but the public's enthusiasm for her two 'Ethel Waters tunes'.[7] Anderson's professional diplomacy masked a sharper edge. Off stage, she could shock. By her own admission, she could '"blow up" easily'. Colleagues told how she 'bossed and cussed', expressing her grievances in a 'remarkably inventive, salty language'. This, combined with a low tolerance for racist jibes, could make for a 'very dangerous' situation. A colleague who toured with her in the thirties and forties recalled that she would 'tell a redneck off in a minute, especially if he used that word ... She'd fight any form of discrimination.'[8] Tellingly, Australian authorities did not compel Ivy Anderson to leave the country. It was her own decision. She, too, was on the overnight express to Sydney.

On that day in 1928, the machinations of White privilege and power were spelt out in print before them. During the Sydney season, a group of White male admirers had showered Ivy Anderson with compliments; for weeks on end, readers of *Beckett's Budget* ogled over her leggy photographs—none of which had raised a peep.[9] In contrast, the latest events offered an object lesson in moral panic. Those drawn into the scandal, on that long train trip north, could ponder the corrupt, masked and ambiguous nature of law enforcement and justice administration at work. Indeed, trace the legal alchemy that spun fabricated evidence into a media-sanctioned narrative, transforming a magistrate's judgement of innocence into a tabloid headline of guilt.

Another concern needled Sonny Clay. Of course, he understood the White supremacist game being played, but still he blamed Leo Davis and Baby Lewis for their weakness, carelessness and selfishness. They 'knew they were being watched' yet invited White women back to their rooms. And ultimately, as bandleader, Sonny Clay would carry the blame, although on the night of the raid, he was in his lodgings in another part of town with Ivy Anderson. In all their investigations, authorities never uncovered any evidence of him 'consorting' with fans, yet his name was at the centre of the fray. 'Everything is Sonny Clay,' the bandleader later complained.[10] And it was.

'A sensational raid on a flat occupied by members of Sonny Clay's colored company' was a typical opening line. More worrying, Constable Dunn had depicted Sonny Clay as a pimp: the 'boss' of a well-funded 'operation' whereby the musicians kept 'the girls'. Dunn 'asked the negro who was boss of the place and he said "Sonny Clay"', read newspaper copy.[11] Alongside questions of justice, fairness and the dignity of his race, the bandleader worried the brand name 'Sonny Clay' would bear, what one sympathiser later called, the 'stigma of disgrace'.[12]

Already William Hann of the Emperors of Harmony publicly distanced himself from the jazz band. As he impressed in a Methodist newspaper, the vocal quartet were not associated with the 'unfortunate incident' but conducted themselves as 'Christians and gentlemen' as witnessed by their impeccable behaviour over the previous six months.[13] Hann hewed to a path of racial advancement that believed exceptional and upright behaviour would dispel White prejudice. Had Sonny Clay's jazz musicians employed greater self-restraint, had Clay better disciplined his bandsmen, they would not be in this mess. Sonny Clay's band, by this litany, fulfilled every White assumption of Black immorality. As a result, all Black performers would be punished. 'The good has to suffer with the bad,' read one columnist's condemnation. 'Race actors ... enjoyed the hospitality of the natives for years' until Sonny Clay's band members brought 'scandal' to Australia, squandering commercial opportunities for others.[14] 'The Sonny Clay incident had reduced the chances of securing further contracts in Australia,' Hann rued.[15]

As a figure well accustomed to the limelight, Ivy Anderson could offer Sonny Clay useful tips: 'Knowing your audience is practically a course in mass psychology,' she once advised. Adapt yourself to the 'audience type the moment you walk out on a stage'. A 'negative stage personality' can offset a positive message. Timing is everything. Stay calm. Even if the roof were to fall down, don't let it bother you.[16]

Her counsel was invaluable. As the overnight express pulled into Sydney Central Station on the morning of 28 March, Sonny Clay knew he was fighting for his race, his reputation and his professional career.

31
BRITISH JUSTICE

SONNY CLAY STEPPED onto the platform of Sydney Central Station and a knot of reporters encircled him. Back in Los Angeles, he had a reputation for self-promotion, oiled by an unblinking self-confidence and the odd shot of bootleg whiskey. Even on this day, that bravado still sustained him. He, too, was versed in the politics of racial advancement and, like an avatar of Black exceptionalism, presented his case to the press, determined to defy their expectations. His vocabulary flagged a high level of education, his argument showed a perceptive grasp of Australian culture, his orderly conclusions demonstrated a sophisticated arrangement of ideas.

The band had not received a 'fair deal in Australia', he began, fixing on a term that struck at the heart of national pride. Australia was the land of 'fair wage', 'fair go', 'fair play' and 'fair dinkum'—and as some people might point out 'fair' skin. 'Fair as a Black man's bum' was a well-worn working-class axiom mocking the conditional and ambiguous nature of the word.[1]

Sonny Clay continued: describing how detectives had shadowed his bandsmen from the moment they landed. They tailed them from lodgings to theatre, broke into their flats and searched their belongings. Unable to find any incriminating evidence, police 'tried to get us on a moral charge—and failed'. The raid on the flat was 'a frame-up from start to finish', he bluntly stated. Reports of an 'orgy' were 'substantially untrue', stories about 'nude or semi-dressed girls' were 'all lies'. Despite the salacious allegations, police were unable to prove misconduct in a court of law. The magistrate had dismissed all charges, clearing the musicians of any wrongdoing.[2]

The analysis of policing practices concluded, Sonny Clay moved on to the musicians' legal rights. 'He could see nothing wrong with the boys going round with white girls so long as they treated them as gentlemen should,' scribbled a newspaperman.[3] In the coming days, Clay elaborated:

> I think that it is contrary to the principles of British justice that a man—even though he be black—has to travel thousands of miles across the sea to have his character dragged in the mire ... Now even if my bandsmen were guilty of what they were accused ... why should they be nailed for something that goes on nightly in Darlinghurst and St Kilda?[4]

Sonny Clay had lived in three American states—Texas, Arizona and California—where anti-miscegenation laws voided interracial marriage and police threw a raft of misdemeanours at casual liaisons. As he knew well, the whiff of sexual contact between a Black man and White woman had mobilised untold numbers of beatings and lynch mobs.

He also knew that in the ongoing battle for Black justice and equality, interracial intimacy was *not* a pressing issue. Indeed, for many African American leaders, it posed a thorny question. None publicly defended the issue and most avoided the topic, not wishing to sanction the exploitation of Black women at the hands of White men. As investigative reporter Ida B Wells had uncovered, the same White men who 'had created a race of mulattos by raping and consorting with Negro women' were the 'same white men who lynched, burned, and tortured Negro men for doing the same thing with white women'.[5]

It was a contention deeply personal to Sonny Clay. In his lightly complected family, sex across the colour line was an issue as plain as the noses on their faces—even if official record keepers had skilfully avoided documenting these entangled bloodlines. Only the word 'mulatto' peppered the lists of the 1860 Slave Schedule of Washington County, Texas. Tacitus Clay, for instance, owned twenty-nine humans. Eight were bi-racial; five of them children, including Sonny Clay's paternal grandmother, Ellen Ginyard. Tacitus' son and namesake owned four enslaved workers: two 'black' adult men, a fourteen-year-old 'black' female and a 'mulatto' baby.[6] So, it was not too much of a stretch for Sonny Clay to assume that Tacitus Clay was his family's kin as well as their captor. And if not Tacitus, then it was some White man in the district. Just as some prominent White man, long after emancipation, 'kept' his great-aunt in a state of concubinage, fathering at least one child.[7]

In 1928, the most prominent Black figure to advocate interracial intimacy was Jack Johnson. Years after his boxing career had ended, he was as famous for his marriages and relationships with White women as his fistic triumphs. To avenge him, fifteen years previously, US authorities conspired to nail him on a 'white slavery' charge, but in the drama that followed—his flight from the country and exile to Europe and Mexico—Johnson's defiance prevailed. If Sonny Clay had not witnessed the closing scene of this saga in Tijuana, his friends had, following Johnson's stylish last stand as he sauntered across the border and surrendered to US authorities, a moment of defeat enacted as a moment of triumph. In the same spirit, Sonny Clay refused to kowtow to this most sacred tenet of White supremacy.

As incarnation and legend, Jack Johnson loomed as large in Australian sporting folklore as in Clay's personal history. The boxer, with his White Australian trainer, Sam Fitzpatrick, had visited the country on two occasions: for four months in early 1907, and again in late 1908 when he famously claimed the world heavyweight crown. In that time, Johnson's private life became as closely observed as his physicality in the ring. After his first trip, Johnson's romance with a 21-year-old Sydney pianist named Lola Toy attracted considerable newspaper gossip—and subjected Toy to a barrage of verbal abuse and public ridicule. Toy sued but her attempt to salvage her reputation ended in public humiliation—and, at least, appeared to set the threshold of public tolerance for such relationships. Yet Lola Toy's shaming did little to regulate White female desire. When Johnson returned to Sydney in 1908, White women flocked to his training sessions at the Botany Hotel to admire his extraordinary athleticism.[8] After Johnson won the title, he began travelling openly with Nellie O'Brien, his White common law wife, leading to a permanent rift with his trainer. Jack Johnson was 'a different man before the fight', Fitzpatrick told the press. 'He would feed out of my hand then, but he is a hard man to handle now.'[9]

If Clay evoked the spirit of Jack Johnson while asserting the right to intimacy across the colour line, the Australian press recognised the parallels, too. Two weeks earlier, the *Bulletin* ran a cartoon depicting a boxing match between an unmistakably Johnson-like figure: bald, stripped to the waist and powerful yet, in this representation, apish and dull-minded, ready to overwhelm his alert but physically smaller White opponent. 'A Black Outlook' read the caption.[10]

Two decades after Johnson trounced Tommy Burns at Sydney Stadium, instigating a worldwide search for the Great White Hope, his physicality still symbolised a White dystopic future. More than White male subjugation, the fruits of this victory were the sexual favours of White women. For many commentators, the lesson of the 'Negro Orgy' was that an obstinate group of heretical women, undeterred by the big stick of public opinion, would continue to seek out Black American men

A BLACK OUTLOOK.

The *Bulletin* magazine conjures the image of Jack Johnson to signal a complex set of White anxieties. (*Bulletin*, National Library of Australia)

in 'flashy suits', ready to shun the creed of White Australia and shirk their national duty as 'mothers of the race'.

Sonny Clay's statement to the press pierced the illusion of inherent White virtue. His contention that unregulated sex went on 'nightly in Darlinghurst and St Kilda' deflated Anglo-Saxon exceptionalism. White Australian society, he contended, was just as lascivious and libidinous as any. As he told it, the 'frame-up' was a masquerade; a ritual re-enactment of White power designed to punish the sexual transgressor and reassert the illusion of biological and moral superiority. Inevitably, White women would breach the White Australian fortress and again social reality would make a mockery of the racial fantasy.

As Sonny Clay presented his case to reporters, the other bandsmen milled about the platform, some gathering their baggage. The press did not note the presence of any Tivoli Theatre representatives.

The musicians' only public support came from the two or three unidentified 'colored women' they had befriended several weeks earlier. 'A couple of members of the troupe had colored women waiting for them when the train pulled in and the recent occurrence had no effect on the warmth of the welcome they received,' observed the *Sun*. 'There were one or two affectionate meetings between some of the Negroes and colored women' was the sum of the Melbourne *Herald*'s interest in their relationship. Any suggestion of previous intimacy between these individuals roused no alarm; instead the pressmen read in the women's embrace a tacit acceptance of the musicians' 'immoral' behaviour.[11]

The White reporters never considered the women were expressing their solidarity. The warmth of their reception spoke to a shared understanding of the scandal's lopsided absurdity, the flagrant hypocrisy of a moral panic about a few White girls 'consorting' with African American men. The political calamity over a few Whites swinging to Black beats only exposed the nation's insecurities.

In March 1928, few if any Black Sydney women had been untouched by the double standards of interracial sex. Feigned and real White anxieties about the 'half-caste problem' threatened to uproot Aboriginal communities and destroy their family life. Protection Board absorption policies held women captive, forcing them to work for a pittance, curtailing their freedom of movement, and increasing their exposure to physical and sexual violence. State authorities sought to direct their reproductive practices to ensure the 'vanishing race' would vanish. Perhaps this moment offered the women a chance to disassemble the inner workings of White male privilege and White Australian nationhood, articulate the links between the personal and political, and expose, in their own small way, Australia's true interracial sex scandal.[12]

'We have been called names by men in the street, then followed a safe distance to a dark place and asked to go for a walk,' read a 1926 letter to the editor from an Indigenous woman.

> Most of us girls were torn from our homes and from all those that cared for us and put out in the world to make our way. Where the dirty lustful low swines of white men wait to rob a black girl of all she's got ... Yet white people are supposed to be the greatest race. In what way we would like to know? ... No, the white man won't play fair.[13]

By inserting themselves into the public drama at Central Station, the 'colored women' made themselves visible. By linking arms with the jazz musicians, they staked their claim in the modern world. For the White panic they were witnessing was not the dominant story, but merely a backlash to a longer, bigger story about the ideas powering twentieth-century culture. African American musical forms had minted the United States' distinct national sound. As any overseas tourist would tell, Australia's cultural uniqueness lay in Aboriginal customs, language and knowledge.[14] By casting White Australia as intrinsically unfair, these 'colored women' began the task of rewriting the national story.

The anonymity of these women in the eyes of White reporters contrasted with the newsmen's fascination with the bandsmen's 'flamboyantly hued ties and overcoats'. The musicians betrayed no signs of spending an uncomfortable night in a hard-back chair but emerged from the carriage impeccably groomed. 'One of them *strode* down the platform resplendent in a plum-colored suit and mauve spats. He wore a gold chain bracelet on his right wrist.'[15]

The reporter chose his verb well. 'Strolling' was a subcultural art form for urban African Americans and a tool of the trade for most jazzmen. They moseyed through public spaces, flaunting their differences with a studied amble and shoulder roll. Larger than life, exaggerated, even Cubist in inspiration, their style signified a refusal to bow to the racial order.[16]

Such sights had been known to stir violence from White Southerners in the United States, keenly aware that their own hayseed attire—boots and overalls—was the joke of the North.[17] The same amalgam of outsized bluster and cultural self-doubt informed aspects of the Australian psychology; the cultural cringe that vied with a sense of racial superiority. A Musicians' Union executive might insist that Black American and Italian musicians had nothing to teach White Australians, yet when the chips were down, the union struggled to assemble an orchestra to match the visitors' skill and versatility. In the same sense, the confident stroll of the sharp-suited jazzmen reminded White Australians of a sorry truth: no matter how hard Australians tried to out-British the British, the imperial hierarchy would *always* deem them inferior to English gentlemen. As Dame Margaret Greville reported after touring the country with the Duke and Duchess of York, Australians were 'uncouth', devoid of 'art' and intellectual curiosity.[18] The logic of Anglo-Saxon exceptionalism kept alive social gradations no plain-spoken White Australian could ever climb.

Sonny Clay ended his impromptu press conference with a final accusation. The 'raid' had been orchestrated by the Musicians' Union. Just as the American Musicians' Union forced Australia's leading brass band to abandon their lucrative stateside tour in October 1927, so the Musicians' Union of Australia conspired to punish the Colored Idea in March 1928. 'We are the victims of national revenge. The whole amounts to the greenest jealousy and most vindictive spite,' he protested.[19] It was an easy-to-digest tit-for-tat revenge tale—although one that vastly underestimated the combined power of Clay's enemies.

Scores of internal documents confirm a 'frame-up' contrived by the Investigation Branch in concert with the Victoria police.[20] But to suggest that a small union of three thousand members dictated terms to the national intelligence agency invested them with a political muscle they simply did not possess. But let's not dismiss Clay's claims as misinformed; the documentary evidence may be incomplete. Something gave Sonny Clay the impression that the Musicians' Union ran the show. Something more than ideology seemed to bond the Musicians' Union executive to the Victoria police and Commonwealth Investigation Branch. But what?[21]

Sonny Clay would soon glimpse this power. At the top of the platform, Sydney's Central Station opened out into a grand concourse. There, standing in wait for Ivy Anderson and the ten flamboyantly dressed musicians, stood several hundred White men ready to restore the racial hierarchy—and one or two press photographers ready capture it.

32
CITIZEN SOLDIER

Two hundred White men stood at the end of the platform, bringing the strolling bandsmen to an abrupt stop. Camera shutters clicked. Photographs, syndicated in newspapers across the country, captured the fear on Sonny Clay's face: his eyes wide, his eyebrows raised, nostrils flared, mouth clenched, all physical indicators of a tight throat and pounding heart. A profile shot of another snapped him with mouth agape, as if taking a sharp intake of breath. Another framed Clay gripping Leo Davis' arm and muttering in his ear. Others still showed the bandsmen bewildered and confused. Some peered coldly at the camera, their eyes watchful, their mouths firm, their movements clipped and defensive. They appeared isolated, vulnerable, 'ill at ease', as a reporter noted with barely concealed satisfaction. For all their bespoke tailoring, the men seem diminished, finally in no doubt that their personal safety was contingent on the restraint of these faceless White men.[1]

Leo Davis had lived through some 'hectic days'. At the Apex Club, he had seen gangsters beat rivals to a pulp. In his early show business days, he had toured the Black vaudeville circuit, working in a notoriously rough-house chain of theatres, and living, sleeping and eating in Pullman cars that passed through 'sundown towns' where Black travellers risked death if seen after nightfall. As a student at Fisk College in Nashville, Tennessee, a procession of gruesome lynchings rocked the state: Somerville 1915,

Sydney photographers capture the uneasy faces of the Sonny Clay Orchestra at Central Station as they encounter a gathering of two hundred White men. (*Sun*, *Daily Guardian* and *Daily Telegraph*, State Library of NSW)

Lebanon 1916, Memphis 1917, Estill Springs 1918, Knoxville 1919.[2] The advent of domestic cameras like the Kodak brownie camera had given rise to a grisly tradition of lynching photography. Printing technology had fostered a macabre cottage industry in lynching postcards, each image in circulation reminding a young Black man that the charred swinging body may one day be his fate.[3] Would this be that day? In an age when US culture was beginning to reconfigure Australian life, was the Ku Klux Klan among the American imports?

The newsworthiness of a photograph showing a phalanx of stern White men outnumbering fearful Black travellers was undeniable, offering a study of contrasts, the collision of two worlds, the frontline of a wider battle. Such an image was never published. Instead, newspapers concealed the identity of all but one demonstrator—a ruddy and dishevelled man, his grin revealing rotten and missing teeth. 'Why did he smile? Because ... the band has been shown the way to go home,' read the caption.[4]

News reports insisted that the White men made 'no demonstration' but silently followed the bandsmen to the taxicabs. Their menace was in their presence, the spectre of vigilante justice and the uncertainty as to whether NSW police—to quote one paper—upheld the view 'that the Negroes had put themselves outside the law'.[5]

The sole public face of a 200-strong gathering of White men at Sydney Central Station on 28 March 1928. (*Daily Telegraph*, State Library of NSW)

This was a shocking statement of admission. Then as now, vigilante justice pivoted on the idea there were two sets of crimes and two sets of punishments: one lay within legal statutes, the other fell beyond written law. Proponents of the dual system cited an unwritten constitution, a fealty to a higher God-given creed. Victims, their families and communities recognised a system of institutional power maintained through violence and fear. In Australia, audacious US-style carnival lynchings were largely unknown. Instead, punitive raids and massacres tended to play out in secret, recalled in hushed tones, circulating as hearsay and rumour, protected by a code of silence.[6]

The faceless White men at Central Station may have spontaneously gathered. But given the similarities with the mob outside Melbourne's courthouse the previous day and the marked absence of protesters at the Tivoli Theatre and Spencer Street Station, the displays bore the hallmarks of an organised protest. The disciplined silence of the men at Central Station did not tally with the actions of an impromptu mob united in rage. Indeed, their unwillingness to be photographed, quoted or named was consistent with the conduct of a clandestine militia dedicated to policing transgressions.

Without a doubt, both Investigation Branch bureau chief Major Longfield Lloyd and Police Commissioner General Thomas Blamey had the resources to 'assemble a formidable protective force in the twinkling of an eye'—as one official report described it.[7] Both were senior figures in two state-based irregular militias.

General Blamey was the 'supreme commander' of Victoria's White Army—also known as the League of National Security, the LNS or Ellen—a secret army that stood ready to preserve 'law, order and domestic peace' in the face of anarchy, revolution and disorder. As a former regional commander later told historian Michael Cathcart, 'Blamey was the boss, there was no question about that.' A foot soldier recruited at the University of Melbourne agreed: 'It was Blamey's show.'[8]

Historian Andrew Moore has named Longfield Lloyd as a founding member of a 'secret brotherhood' of military veterans mustered into service sometime in 1919, interchangeably known as the Garage, Guard, Movement, Association, Country, Citizen Reserve Corp and Western and Metropolitan Division. One constant was the small circle of officers at its helm: Major General Sir Charles Rosenthal, Major Jack Scott, Major Longfield Lloyd, Brigadier-General George Onslow and others.[9]

The federal chief of the Investigation Branch, Major HE Jones, saw both secret armies as unofficial wings of national security, essential to 'safeguard[ing] constitutional Government' from 'civil commotion'. The Victoria police strike of 1923 was one instance: the militia's aggressive use of wooden batons far outpaced the looting and mayhem on the streets. The last, intrigued-filled days of NSW Premier Jack Lang's government in 1933 was another. 'Officially' the Investigation Branch could not be 'directly or indirectly' 'associated' with the 'movement', 'unless instructed by our Minister'.[10] Unofficially, the bonds ran deep and tight—irregular methods ran second nature to Lloyd's bureau and Blamey's force.

Longfield Lloyd had a particularly close and enduring relationship with the Guard's field commander Jack Scott. From their first meeting in 1919 well into the 1940s, the two veterans of military intelligence looked after each other—a special brand of male fellowship Scott happily called 'mateship', although such terms rested less easily on Lloyd's patrician lips. However, when Lloyd needed a henchman, albeit one with an elite grammar school education, he turned to Jack Scott.[11]

Photographs of Jack Scott are hard to come by, although DH Lawrence based the literary character Jack Callcott on Scott in *Kangaroo*—a novel so close to an autobiography Lawrence described it as a 'letter-diary', the connections painstakingly pieced together by scholars Robert Darroch and Sandra Jobson.[12] Several times, Lawrence dwelt on the disjunction between Scott's 'strongly animal body' and 'long lean, rather pallid face', 'close-shut lips' and 'slow, dark, lingering eyes'. Others noted Scott's 'ladies man' charisma, although Lawrence, too, felt a 'thrill of desire' when Scott whispered 'politics and red hot treason' in his ear, spilling the inner workings of the secret army in stunning operational and ideological detail, unaware that each conversation was Lawrence's literary fodder.[13]

Jack Scott's manliness masked a complicated history. In 1917, he received the coveted Distinguished Service Order for 'conspicuous gallantry' leading a squad of machine-gunners at Flanders. In 1919, he served as Major-General Charles Rosenthal's deputy organising the repatriation of the Australian troops. Less recalled was his dose of venereal disease and hospitalisation for shell shock in July 1916. 'Headache. Insomnia. Had bad dreams. Pain in back. Tremor. Reflexes X. Depressed,' read his medical report—and as Lawrence hinted, impotence. Scott 'couldn't get his pecker up' but he could inspire loyalty and obedience in his platoon.[14]

By 1920, Lloyd and Scott had crossed paths, perhaps at the Imperial Service Club, or perhaps in military intelligence efforts to deport German-born Catholic priest Charles Jerger. Lloyd, as previously mentioned, was 'in the wings' overseeing the 'unnecessarily brutal' team administering Jerger's removal. Scott, in contrast, stood on a soapbox in a city park urging a contingent of 'loyal' veterans not to 'stand idly by' and accept 'rank disloyalty'. As the *Catholic Press* told it, a 'large, rowdy' mob of 'hooligans' then disrupted a rally of Jerger's supporters, fixed on invading the stage and hoisting a Union Jack. It became a signature move. The following year, Scott and his squad of 'Diggers'—the term designating a political faction rather than all war veterans—stormed a May Day rally organised by International Workers of the World supporters, determined to plant the Union Jack.[15]

Both events were followed by 'great patriotic' meetings where speakers representing the King and Empire Association and Returned Soldiers' League pledged to 'wipe away' the 'disloyal fringe' and protect the 'true spirit of Australia'. Others spoke in sectarian dog whistles and the carefully coded language of vigilantism. 'An aggressive loyalty' to Empire and King was at once 'the privilege of every free citizen' and the only acceptable political position, preached Major-General Rosenthal. Anything else—such as the struggle for independence in India and Ireland—was treason.[16]

By the time Jack Scott attempted to recruit DH Lawrence in the winter of 1922, he could boast of a national network of lodges. Scott commanded scores of 'little squads' of five—numbered to fit into a car for swift mobilisation.[17]

Behind the scenes, Longfield Lloyd endorsed the efforts of 'people, who, fired by the exploits of the Facisti in Italy' were 'clearing out the poisonous elements in our midst'.[18] A 1922 memorandum singled out the services of officer 'S', the organiser of a citizens' defence league.[19] In 1925, Lloyd asked Scott to mobilise '500 stalwart ex-AIF men' to fight protesters who were expected to block the deportation of union leader Jacob Johnson. As fellow militiaman Colonel Eric Campbell recalled, 'my friend Jack Scott' assembled the force 'in a matter of days'—although, as mentioned earlier, a high court ruling ultimately saved Johnson from deportation.[20]

Historians have tended to appraise both the Guard and White Army in terms of the anxieties about Communism and the labour movement. But as DH Lawrence suggested in *Kangaroo*, the primary focus of Jack Scott's literary alter-ego, Jack Callcott, was defending White Australia. As Callcott told it, socialism hinged on international working-class solidarity, and ultimately allegiance to all 'workers of the world' would trump loyalty to nation, empire and race. Hence the need for vigilance.

'As sure as guns is guns, if we let in coloured labour, they'll swallow us. They hate us,' Callcott told Lawrence's avatar. 'And they're only waiting till we haven't got the pull over them.' Then, 'we'll all be wiped out, wiped out'. 'It isn't one side only that can keep slaves,' he fretted. 'The real sense of liberty only goes with white blood.'[21]

Callcott's concept of 'liberty' was distinct from the 'vote-catching system' known as democracy. He dismissed the 'will of the people' as a ruse, instead advocating a system akin to the chain of command in the trenches. As he confided to Lawrence, he commanded a 'set of chaps with some guts in them' 'sworn to obey the leaders, no matter what the command, when the time is ready'.[22]

Jack Callcott's views were autocratic even by the measure of the day—yet still broadly consistent with sentiments in Returned Soldiers' League newsletters, which also likened peacetime to a state of perpetual war. Articles called on the nation to mobilise, as if for combat and fill the 'empty continent' with British settlers. 'Keeping Australia White' was a 'duty'. Any opposition was seen 'as bare treachery to those who made sacrifices in time of war'.[23]

At the same time, the league railed against 'colored immigration', which, by the late 1920s, referred to Italians, Greeks and Maltese. At the 1928 national conference, the league executive pledged to 'engender a better *feeling* for the British immigrant as against the Southern European'.[24] This 'feeling' translated into policy proposals that assigned civic privileges according to military service and ethnicity. Government contracts, for instance, should be awarded only to British companies that employed British people. Government-subsidised copra plantations in New Guinea should be the exclusive preserve of the Digger. Commentaries projected a vision of a racially segregated empire where colonised non-Whites served an elite breed of chivalrous White men.[25]

In league clubrooms in March 1928, fears about racial 'contamination' loomed large. The Melbourne sub-branch unanimously passed a motion stating that even though 'the women concerned were not such as might be desired', the fact of their Whiteness was enough to make 'the blood of every member of the AIF boil'. But thanks to the swift actions of the government, these 'weak-minded and frivolous women' could be saved from themselves.[26]

Was the company of men assembled at Central Station another display of Digger rage? Did Sonny Clay meet the gaze of a tall 'pallid' man with 'close-shut lips' and 'dark, lingering eyes'? Did the bandleader feel the same terror as DH Lawrence when Rosenthal, suspecting disloyalty, turned on the novelist and, growing 'hideous' and 'monstrous', roared 'I could have killed you'?[27] Two days later, Lawrence received a visit from a 'very malevolent' Jack Scott who instructed him to leave the country immediately. The next day, Lawrence arranged travel. Eleven days later he and his wife were gone, the writer never confirming the fictional and factual elements of the novel.

By the late 1920s, Scott was a prominent member of the Rose Bay branch of the Returned Soldiers' League in Sydney's eastern suburbs. If not a front for the Guard, the club's executive was frequently in Rosenthal's orbit.[28]

In 1927, the Rose Bay Diggers steamed with indignation about *The Big Parade*, a Hollywood war film and huge box office hit (by chance starring Sonny Clay's pal John Gilbert) that inferred 'America won the war': the doughboys arrived in Europe in 1917, swiftly broke the stalemate and overwhelmed the enemy.[29] The plot line unsettled claims that Anzac sacrifice delivered victory for the British Empire, giving weight to anti-imperialist jibes they were just 'cannon-fodder for British militarists and capitalists'.[30]

The Diggers' antipathy to *The Big Parade* was a lightning rod for a deeper discontent. In 1914, recruitment campaigns had promised self-esteem and elevated manhood, even racial renewal. As the fleeting post-war prosperity began to slip away and unemployment spiralled to 10 per cent in 1928, Rose Bay League men agreed that 'none of the diggers got any good out of the war, except a fine spirit of comradeship'.[31] Far from emerging 'purged of dross', 'purified by the spirit of self-sacrifice'—as Billy Hughes once divined—they bore physical, emotional and psychological scars, and endured them in stoic silence.[32] As their animus grew, the promise of reclaimed glory shone even brighter.

Jack Scott's commemorative address to these men on the dawn of the twelfth anniversary of the Anzac landing captured his gift for rallying weary, disillusioned men. His sometimes tender, sometimes quixotic homage balanced the veterans' 'grim' memories of fetid trenches with an elusive quality only known to warriors of 'character'—the 'Anzac spirit'—the distillation of all that was good and noble in the nation, yea, the world. By preserving this spirit in 'ordinary everyday relations', the fallen 'heroes' could become 'immortal' for they had given birth to 'Australia's nation hood'.[33] A rhetorical sleight of hand lay at the heart of Scott's mythmaking. More than making dead men eternal and broken men whole, it fulfilled an Anglo-Saxon and eugenic prophecy that White Australia would beget a morally and physically better Briton.

'It has been said' that Australians soldiers 'are a reincarnation of the ancient Greeks in Athenian pilgrimages to Parnassus', wrote one advocate of the body culture movement.[34] Journalist EC Buley dubbed them the 'new Argonauts'.[35] Essayist Compton Mackenzie likened them to 'Ajax or Diomed, Hector or Achilles', while war historian Charles Bean marvelled at the 'reservoir of lively energy' that enabled these 'huge men' to exact 'unbelievable efforts' as they faced the 'ancient test'.[36] Others noted how the 'classical cast' of the 'majority' of Australian soldiers proved wrong the 'lugubrious prophecies of racial degeneration' uttered by British critics who 'disbelieve[d] in the possibility of a White Australia'.[37] Allusions to the Ancient Greeks were not accidental: the beauty, strength, proportion and harmony of classicism offered a commemorative language to advance ideas of purity, immortality and an essential national spirit.[38]

Quite purposefully, the columns of Melbourne's Shrine of Remembrance evoked the Parthenon in the Athenian acropolis. Charles Bean imagined the Australian War Memorial as a hilltop monument of 'brilliant white stone' in the 'pure Greek style'.[39] More broadly, the Athenian citizen soldier of the fifth century BC was a model of White Australian manhood. John McKellar's 1928 poem 'Marathon', for instance, drew on the physical experience of a male runner to conflate the eternalism of classicism ('sun and shade weave symmetry around his ungirt grace'), with Progressive idealism ('his strength/setting each stride against distant goal') and the athleticism of 'the Athens way'.[40]

Without the slightest hint of irony, the architects of Australia's post-war social order appropriated the regular geometry and proportional uniformity of a Greek and Roman tradition to construct the White Australian masculine ideal while justifying the exclusion of Southern European migrants.

For Jack Scott, the paradoxes continued. The birth of a nation took place in a world of death and destruction in a distant land in the absence of women. A figure bristling with manliness had been rendered sexually impotent by the trauma of war. Liberty was an obligatory loyalty to a single idea. Freedom was surrendering independent thought and obediently following orders.

A 'classical cast' may seem a world away from the toothless and shabby man policing the racial order at Sydney's Central Station. Yet if, as circumstances suggest, Major Lloyd enlisted his friend Major Scott to mobilise his militia and show the musicians the 'way home', the moment encapsulated the cultural dynamic underpinning the politics of race.

More than a skirmish between Black and White, two aesthetic sensibilities were in play: the singular purity of the White Australian citizen soldier, cleansed by blood sacrifice, bonded by the steady measure of the brass band and elevated by the mythology of eternalism pitted against the sharp angular silhouettes of the jazzmen, bearers of a polyphonic sound that demanded two answers to every musical question. In that moment, the race war and the culture war were one.

33
THE CHARACTER TEST

As the newspapers told it, the Sonny Clay Orchestra's 'frigid' reception did not end with the two hundred faceless White men at Central Station but continued throughout the day as they struggled to find lodgings. 'All doors were closed against them today,' reported the *Age*, conjuring bandsmen 'trudg[ing] the city' weighed down with bags and overcoats shunned by city folk, eventually at nightfall securing less-than-comfortable rooms in a rundown corner of the city. Outside the door, two 'special officers' stood guard. The drama unfolded like a comeuppance scene in the theatre of ostracism. The president of the Nationalist Party's Women's League led a chorus of voices calling for permanent removal. 'The sooner such people are out of the country, the better ... send the Negroes back to where they belong,' berated Mrs AV Roberts.[1]

This narrative, while compelling, was largely a fiction. The bandsmen left Central Station in taxicabs, probably heading to the offices of the Tivoli Theatre who almost certainly sorted out their accommodation. Right to the end, JC Williamson and Company were a 'fine firm' who 'treated us well' confirmed Sonny Clay—if only behind closed doors. Gayne Dexter, who met with Clay in these days, recalled the bandsmen attracting 'public curiosity' but 'not antagonism'.[2]

This version of events, however, did not tally with the banishment playing out at official level.

As if responding to public demand, a federal cabinet meeting was underway in Canberra's Parliament House the morning Sonny Clay arrived in Sydney. Outside a door at the rear of the building, a small contingent of pressmen waited for a politician to leak an update—that's how they usually found out what was going on.

By the afternoon deadline, Melbourne's *Herald* had learned 'on the best authority' that the federal government planned to implement a 'total prohibition of colored bands from entering the Commonwealth'. The *Sun* demurred on this point, claiming the ban was not 'hard and fast, as there some time may be occasion to allow some special person to enter'. Either way, no new legislation was required. 'It is a question of tightening up the working of the regulations already in force'—namely, extending the obscure handwritten precedent set by Senator George Pearce five years earlier. Although Prime Minister Bruce made 'no official announcement', the 'veto' was 'practically assured'.[3]

Prime Minister Bruce would never make an official statement—perhaps feeling a tad uneasy about the government's role in mediating public taste. Certainly, a few weeks earlier he did not believe it was a politician's job to 'determine the skill of a particular' musician.[4] But consistent with press reports, the following week entertainment and sporting promoters received a letter from the Department of Home and Territories outlining new procedures concerning the entry of 'coloured theatrical performers or vaudeville artists'. Applications now needed to be made in advance, furnished with 'credentials' to the performer's 'general good character', supported with evidence showing how they would 'raise the local standard'. By design, no 'colored musicians' could pass the test: the 'character' of these players was inherently deficient while 'Negro jazz', by its very nature, did nothing to 'raise the local standard'. Like the dictation test, which used literacy in European languages to keep out 'undesirable' immigrants and visitors, so 'good character' became a proxy for racial and cultural screening.[5]

The individualised nature of the test enabled Sir Neville Howse to insist the ban had 'nothing whatever to do with the White Australia Policy' but was purely a question of moral character. Still, the *Herald* was clear about the government's intentions: 'Entrepreneurs ... need not apply for permission for the introduction of colored musicians as applications will not be considered.'[6] In other words, market demand would no longer determine the transmission and circulation of popular music. Instead, a vague administrative process would direct popular experiences of the modern. A policy known more by rumour than proclamation would check the ways the public could map their universe, bodies and minds.

When word of the new entry procedures reached Harry Muller, he was in San Francisco in the midst of contracting Wilbur's Blackbirds—an outfit headlined by veteran dancer Morgan Prince, best remembered for his association with the legendary Original Creole Band, and Georgia trumpeter Buddy DeLoach. They had hoped to include Australia on their Asia-Pacific tour but with the government ban on 'colored musicians' these plans came to nothing. The winning business model Muller had hit upon with the Colored Idea, delivering high quality up-to-the-minute American entertainment at affordable prices, had been rendered void.[7]

Musicians' Union Federal Secretary Cecil Trevelyan claimed the outcome as a victory for the White Australia policy. He was confident that 'all Australians' would agree music was 'much better done by Australian citizens' who were 'equal, if not superior, to the other musicians'. By claiming to speak for everyone, Trevelyan papered over the paradox at the heart of the federated nation. Adherence to his White Australian ideal was not a personal decision but a civic requirement. National unity founded on blood overrode individual choice, democratic liberalism and free market principles. As Trevelyan attested 'to all, IT WAS AN AUSTRALIAN QUESTION'. Conformity was mandatory.[8]

'All Australians' did not agree with Cecil Trevelyan. Behind closed doors, show business and sporting promoters condemned the character test. Speaking to the press on condition of anonymity, they denounced the ban as 'unfair to theatrical men' and an 'injustice ... against Negroes'.[9] They knew they could fill dance *palais* and vaudeville theatres with audiences hungry for African American music and dance. Union anxieties about White Australia were nonsensical to them. There was 'no question of the Negroes settling in Australia', protested one anonymous figure.[10]

Within industry circles, most agreed there was 'more behind the case than meets the eye'. Many fingered the Musicians' Union as the 'real cause' of the ban. The Sonny Clay Orchestra had been 'a decided hit with the better element of the citizens' and sub-par local players resented their popularity, read one explanation. The Musicians' Union's solution was to 'light the fires of prejudice' and so stymie excellence and promote mediocrity.[11]

Others accused the *Truth of* engineering the 'frame-up'. In a private letter, Bill Maloney, the publicity man at the Tivoli and Green Mill, noted the scandal sheet had a long history of hatred towards 'the Negro' and seized on the story 'until they reached the borders of persecution and victimization'. Sonny Clay had had a 'very raw deal' but 'one which we have no power to offset or rectify however willing we may be'.[12]

Their private expressions of sympathy brought some comfort to Sonny Clay—but still fell well short of a public display of support. To this end, Clay secured a meeting with US Consul Ezra Lawton, likely bringing along tuba player Herman Hoy, who knew Lawton from the army. In 1917, both had been stationed in the Arizona town of Nogales, defending the border towns against incursions by Mexican warlords. Clay impressed on Lawton that the raid was 'a deliberate frame-up', the band 'dogged' by dubious detectives from day one.[13] Surely the Australian government's ban on African American musicians undermined the spirit of co-operation and friendship between the two countries?

Lawton more or less shrugged. He agreed the bandsmen were 'not bad fellows' but, beyond vouching for Hoy's integrity, refused to denounce the ban or advocate the orchestra's cause. So too, in Washington, officials 'decline[d] to comment'. 'Unofficially', they believed it was 'Australia's business whether they permit foreigners to enter', reported the Associated Press.[14]

The US government's lack of interest and the theatre promoter's fear of speaking out left Sonny Clay unprotected, exposed and angry. The favour White folk once showered on him had evaporated. Only Gayne Dexter, the editor of *Everyones* who loudly criticised cultural insularity, agreed to give Clay an airing.

They met at the Tivoli Theatre, sitting beneath the stage on a big wardrobe trunk as stagehands around them heaved baggage onto a lorry bound for the San Francisco steamer. Gayne Dexter once thought Clay looked too young to carry the responsibilities of a touring orchestra but now saw him as a man burdened by the sins of others. He noticed a mistiness clouding the bandleader's eyes, a sadness mixed with exhaustion, frustration, disappointment and over-reliance on alcohol.

Clay 'hurled' his grievances at Dexter. 'It is dreadful to think that a man's reputation is smirched in a foreign country where he does not know the laws and can find no redress,' he began. 'Everything has been done to make innocent men seem like sewer rats in the public mind.' And yet 'I was not implicated in the charge'.

His irritation extended to Harry Muller. He 'should not have brought us out here knowing that there had been a bitter controversy concerning the Commonwealth Band'. Muller's promise of abundant free time and a 'comparative vacation' had proved to be the bandleader's undoing. 'I came out here to play music and to make a little money, not to fight a national grievance.'

He blasted his bandsmen: 'Was it possible to wet nurse them everywhere and herd them around like sheep.' He even excoriated the female fans: 'From the time the boys and I landed we were chased by women who popped up no matter where we hid. It was impossible to avoid them.'

Sonny Clay promised to retaliate, he would place the 'full facts' before the American Musicians' Union. Then 'the chickens will come home to roost'. Australian musicians would 'find it harder to get in than before'.[15]

Perhaps, even then, Clay knew the emptiness of his threat. No White union executive would spring to his defence; Black musicians were barely admitted as members.

In the coming weeks, Clay's relationship with Ivy Anderson would break down. His band would implode. His bountiful creative partnership with Nini Coycault would come to an end. In the 1977 interview, a coldness inflected Leo Davis' memory of Sonny Clay. They did not part as friends.

Sonny Clay's story was not one of ostracism but precarity: the turning point when his life, career and personal relationships began to fall apart. When networks that once supported him splintered and fragmented—and social systems founded on exclusion and fear took the form of a personal moral failing. Gayne Dexter, who had a nuanced, if incomplete, understanding of the complexities behind Sonny Clay's destructive rage, was more generous. Months later, when Clay sent Dexter a postcard recalling a golden sporting day at a Sydney racecourse, Dexter admired his 'forgiving spirit'.[16]

PART X

Purification Rites

34 STORM CENTRE

BEHIND THE CLOSED doors at the Tivoli Theatre, one name did not arise in the speculative frenzy about the hidden hand behind the 'frame-up'. One person remained out of view as Bill Maloney pondered the forces 'behind the case'. Unseen was a figure hiding in plain sight, who emerged as a pivotal force in every facet of the campaign to rid the country of Black American jazzmen: the federal member for North Sydney, the Right Honourable William Morris Hughes.

With close connections to leaders in politics, the Musicians' Union, intelligence agencies, secret paramilitaries and returned servicemen's leagues, Hughes was uniquely positioned to work these interlocking networks and realise an idealised nation 'pure' in blood, 'superior' in physical form, and unmatched in devotion to King and Empire. Ironically, to achieve this state of perfected Britishness, Hughes looked less to the Mother Country and more to Britain's rebellious offspring, the United States, the republic that repurposed British traditions of liberty, Anglo-Saxon exceptionalism and transatlantic slavery to advance its own ideas about race, modernity and progress. In forging links across the Pacific, Billy Hughes offered a few ideas of his own, while borrowing several proven tactics.

On the morning of Thursday, 29 March the influence of American ideas on Billy Hughes was front page news. Twenty-four hours earlier, they were harder to discern.

The reason was glaringly simple. On Wednesday, 28 March, Hughes was yesterday's man—outdated, obsolete and finished. But *before* his 'fall from political grace', *before* he became a miserable 'grouch', Billy Hughes was a three-term prime minister, a 'great world figure' followed by legions of devotees who believed, by charisma alone, he could 'swing civilization'.[1]

Since his fall from political grace, he was an object of amusement. Labor newspapers mocked him—never forgetting or forgiving the betrayal of the conscription referendums during the Great War. 'If I only were in power again,' read a parody diary, 'I'd ... use the War Precautions Act and declare all those who didn't vote for me were Germans, and get the vote disallowed.'[2]

Political pundits pitied him. Once lionised, the 'noisy barrackers' had 'ceased to follow "Billy"', commiserated the *Daily Telegraph*. 'Gone was the wild rush of the proletariat when their champion was preparing for the ring.' What remained was a frail old man ruminating about life and death—or at least, his romanticised version of it.[3]

As Hughes told it, his personal story embodied the epic hero cycle of British migration: the son of a humble Welsh carpenter arriving penniless in the 'land of opportunity'. The seeker in the guise of a frontier bushman, shearing sheep, driving cattle and forging iron—even though his most generous biographers conceded this was 'pure fantasy'.[4] But it was a powerful and enduring fabulism. A small, wiry man, with big ears, a craggy face and restless nervous energy, he could, at least, persuade his followers he was a fighter—even as he pivoted from left to right, from the champion of the worker to champion of the Digger.

For Billy Hughes was always fighting. Fighting to exalt the White working man, first within the Labor Party then the newly formed Nationalist Party. Fighting to send every able-bodied Australian man to battle the German Hun and save the British Empire. Fighting to win Australia a seat at the Treaty of Versailles, to secure Germany's colonial possessions in the South Pacific and block Japan's racial equality clause in the League of Nations charter. Fighting to exalt the returned Aussie Diggers—their jobs, farmland, honour, memory, even their New Guinea copra plantations. Fighting for the health of newborn White babies—the 'best emigrant' to fill the 'empty' continent. Fighting to realise Australia's 'destiny' as a White Dominion within the 'mighty' British Empire.

And after 1923, fighting with his cabinet colleagues in the Nationalist Party who secretly and overwhelmingly voted to remove him as leader and install the treasurer, Stanley Bruce.[5]

After seven tumultuous years as prime minister, Billy Hughes' exile to the backbenches burned him and he smouldered in uncharacteristic silence. Hughes had 'lost the pep and sting of a fighting politician' during the parliamentary session, remarked a correspondent. Dogged by rumours of ill-health, his public appearances were 'fleeting'. One physician diagnosed 'recurrent bouts of depression alternating with euphoria'.[6]

So, when in February 1924 Hughes accepted the English Speaking Union's invitation of a six-month American lecture tour, his colleagues responded with scepticism. The delusional grandeur of his promise to 'put Australia on the map' stirred much mirth. It would take 'a political revolution' before the fallen leader 'could hope to secure a strong following', chortled a politician. Even former allies wanted 'nothing' to do with him.[7]

Still, the reporter who waved Hughes off at the docks saw a man charged with the old 'fire' and 'vigour'. Hughes remained in buoyant spirits as he reached the West Coast and began explaining to audiences, several hundred at a time, why the Pacific and not the Atlantic was the 'storm centre' of the world.[8]

Hughes asked the people of Vancouver, Seattle, Portland, San Francisco and Los Angeles to imagine themselves on the 'threshold of a teeming world', the 'strategic centre of the modern world'. One side was alert, progressive, 'white' and 'English-speaking'. The other was awakening from a slumber; envious, overcrowded and Asian. Two sharply drawn sides with 'nothing in common'. An opposing force that was impossible to appease without humiliation or 'assimilate' without spawning an 'inferior' 'race'. 'Which side would ultimately dominate the Pacific?'[9]

Hughes' interpretation of history was largely a recitation of Australian defence policy, although the Manichaean clash he envisaged reached far beyond Japan's imperial ambitions. To 'safeguard the Pacific' and build the 'nucleus' of a 'new world', Hughes offered his White American audiences a twofold solution: firstly, a trade and defence alliance that would supplant the League of Nations and create an inviolable bond of English-speaking brothers. Secondly, a watertight immigration policy modelled on White Australia. A 'white speck' in an 'Asiatic sea' it may be, but 'nobody has got into Australia who we have wanted to keep out', he boasted.[10]

Hughes' timing was impeccable. He landed in the United States just as the Congress was hammering out the final details of the Johnson–Reed Bill, a draconian immigration package designed to preserve America's Nordic stock by barring virtually all migration from Asia and Eastern and Southern Europe. One sticking point was the longstanding 'gentleman's agreement' between the United States and Japan over the free movement of its people. Should a diplomatic treaty take precedence over border policy, ran the national debate.[11]

The newspapers owned by William Randolph Hearst emphatically said 'no' and in Billy Hughes saw an advocate with the gravitas of an elder statesman, wisdom of a modern sage and romance of a rugged frontiersman. 'Japan's expansion menaces white supremacy in the Pacific', read the headline of Hughes' lesson in 'the Antipodean method of stemming the rising tide of colour'.[12]

In Central Avenue, Los Angeles, the Black press followed the passage of a different piece of legislation. Most years, Southern mobs executed several dozen people and almost all victims were Black. The Dyer Bill would make lynching a federal offence, allowing federal authorities to intercede when state officials would not. (Ultimately, a Dixiecrat filibuster snuffed the bill.)[13] Sonny Clay's interest in these legislative battles is unknown, although the night Billy Hughes lectured in Los Angeles, Clay was a few blocks away, performing at Biltmore Hotel's Cinderella House, a gala event that revelled in cosmopolitan sophistication, drawing 'screen celebrities galore'.[14]

From Los Angeles, Billy Hughes travelled east to Dallas, Texas, arriving on Monday, 17 March for a four-night stopover, his longest so far. If Hughes did not know Dallas was a Ku Klux Klan town, home to the Imperial Wizard, he soon faced undeniable evidence. Since the previous Saturday, Dallas Klan 66 had been hosting a week-long Kolossal Karnival, drawing thousands of Klansmen from across Texas. On opening night, they had paraded through the downtown streets to a fiery cross in a city park. Each day following, different chapters took turns to march through the streets while a large cross illuminated with red electric globes 'could be seen for miles around Dallas, marking the Klan's dominance over the Dallas landscape', as one reporter wrote.[15]

Less visible were the river-bottom whippings, brandings and other forms of torture Dallas Klansmen doled out to adulterers, deviants, Papists, Hebrews, Negroes and miscegenators in a small grove of trees alongside a Black Baptist church. Local Black folk, huddled in their homes, heard victims cry out in pain.[16] Such sights and sounds had propelled a mass migration of Black Texans to California, including several members of the Sonny Clay Orchestra.

Dallas had more Klansmen per capita than any other American city: one out of three White Protestant men. The Klan's tendrils touched city politics, the criminal justice system, business, the press and clergy and, inevitably, the audience who attended Billy Hughes' two Dallas lectures.[17]

Hughes opened his talk with a celebration of Australia and America's 'similar ideals and objectives': two lands founded on Nordic prosperity and progress forged by a regenerative brand of frontier masculinity.[18]

The United States was a powerful world leader 'because of the essential daring, audacity, alertness, strength of its racial stock', approved Hughes. He paused and in his imitable style, swung from soaring optimism to apocalyptic doom. Hughes entreated his audience to 'preserve this heritage'. 'Weakening this strong fibre', diluting the right 'type of man' was the 'only danger' 'threatening this country'. 'Water that down, and the end is inevitable—you will fall.'[19]

Hughes then extended his listeners a lifeline. To ensure 'their own salvation', he called on 'men who have courage and that deathless tenacity of purpose' to be vigilant and attend to the smallest breach. 'Remain masters in your own household and establish, while you can, policies which preserve the priceless heritage of your great race.' In this quest, Australia can be a 'brother' to America 'for we are of the same blood'.[20]

Hughes' mix of horticultural metaphors, modern demography and old-time religion mirrored the vision advanced by the Imperial Wizard Hiram Evans six months earlier—a hotchpotch of divine laws, sacred covenants, rising human tides, moral fitness, inherited traits, eugenic degeneracy, unregulated immigration and unassimilable superior and inferior racial stocks. Only a 'deep and abiding respect for constituted authority', a 'higher temporal loyalty' would safeguard Western civilisation and 'insure' the 'nation's perfect and permanent development', Evans sermonised.[21] Surely then, Billy Hughes and the Klansmen of Texas recognised each other as 'kinsmen in tradition and ideals'.

On 21 March, Hughes bade farewell to Dallas, pushing on with the Midwestern and Northeastern leg of his tour. By the time he headed back across the Pacific, a stack of newspaper clippings measured his impact on the national conversation. Usually he preserved such clippings in a scrapbook—although several key moments are conspicuously missing from his papers in the National Library.[22]

So too, Hughes' success in putting White Australia on the American map was never fully appreciated by his parliamentary colleagues, largely because on his return, Hughes remained uncharacteristically quiet about his US adventures. At best he emphasised that the White dominions had found a 'natural champion and formidable ally' in the United States. They were most 'sympathetic' to Australia's 'vital interests' and peace in the Pacific depended on their shared 'destiny' and close 'friendship'. Why, he joked, 'the western American might even pass for a good Australian'.[23]

With that, Hughes returned to the backbench, his silence loud enough to keep political commentators wondering: What was he scheming? When would he launch his comeback? Hughes offered no clues, instead playing golf, opening school fetes and nostalgically recalling old times.[24]

But the pundits were right: Hughes was biding his time.

In December 1927, the former leader locked onto a topic close to his heart: Italian immigration and the threat to British White Australia.

Since Stanley Bruce came to power, the Nationalist Party had been accepting small numbers of Southern European migrants, about 12 per cent of total arrivals. These were exactly the type of dyke-cracking, fibre-weakening, stock-diluting breaches Hughes had warned of. He took particular offence at Bruce's comments that 'Australians should regard Europeans as just as white as themselves'. By Hughes' measure, Bruce's reckless policy was squandering the nation's 'priceless heritage' and would lead to an 'inevitable' 'fall'.[25]

In late February 1928, in a rousing address to a returned servicemen's club, Hughes anointed Australian aviator Bert Hinkler as an avatar of British exceptionalism. Days earlier, the airman had landed in Darwin after a sixteen-day solo flight. From his chiselled jaw to the engineering supremacy of his Avro Avian, Hinkler embodied all the 'qualities of the race—courage, endurance, and amazing skill', exulted Hughes. He had overcome 'the perils of the unknown' to make 'the British Empire what it is today'.[26] In truth, Hughes' triumph of heritage and race rested on one of two shaky premises: forgetting the aviator's father was born in Germany or including Teutons and Saxons in the Anglo-Saxon 'race'.[27]

Two weeks later, on 16 March, Billy Hughes was in Canberra, presenting a deputation on behalf of the Musicians' Union, pleading for the government to restrict all foreign musicians—and, as a corollary, reflecting on the matter of 'colored musicians'.[28]

A week later, the day of the Rowena Mansions 'raid', a gossipy column in Sydney's *Daily Telegraph* wondered if the 'remarkable little man' may have a 'comeback in the limelight'.[29] The same newspaper's high-pitched coverage of the 'nude' 'Negro orgy' looked like it might give Hughes his chance.

35
THIS BIT OF EARTH

Whether by serendipity or design, the Nationalist Party's annual conference was underway in Sydney on Wednesday, 28 March, the day two hundred faceless White men mysteriously congregated at Central Station to menace the Sonny Clay Orchestra.

That evening Billy Hughes made an unscheduled appearance at the assembly hall. As soon as he stepped through the door, a tremendous roar of cheers and clapping drowned out the debate on parliamentarian salaries. Handshakes and shoulder slaps punctuated his progress down the centre aisle. As he sauntered onto the stage, the audience rose to its feet shouting for him to speak. He obliged, unspooling what one reporter called a 'wonderful and vigorous fighting speech' that 'hurled brickbat after brickbat' at the leaders of his own party, the very men who had deposed him five years earlier. Observers compared his words to an exploding 'bomb' and a wild storm.[1]

He opened with a series of questions, abstract yet personal, charged with subtextual meaning. What do we stand against? What do we stand for? How much do we stand for it? Before inviting his audience to 'stand for something very definite'.

'We believe in White Australia—a British White Australia!' he declared, recalling the generations of British settlers who had transformed the 'primitive bush' into a land of prosperity, industry and progress, where no man was inferior to the next. For his audience, it was a familiar and comforting history—and for a seasoned orator, a moment ripe for a pivot. 'But our migration policy does not seem compatible with it.' This heritage was now under siege.[2]

His questions continued: 'To whom does this country belong?' 'Are we to take our orders from Mussolini?' 'Should we be subservient to Dago?' If the answer was 'no', then why were 'hundreds' of Italian migrants arriving each month. Why was there 'no end' to the 'Italians already here'? Each 'why' stirred unease in the listener, building tension as Hughes swelled to his punchline, the chorus of a popular song, well known to his audience: '*This bit of earth belongs to us!* It is for us to say who shall come in and who shall not come in!'[3]

The phrase chimed with the audience who responded with a barrage of cheers. And indeed, the sentiment echoed down the decades. In 2001, Prime Minister John Howard uttered remarkably similar words to defend his hard-line border control policies: 'We decide who comes to this country and the circumstances in which they come.'[4] Howard later claimed the line 'just came to me', although he grew up in a Digger enclave in Sydney's inner west. His father Lyall was an avid King and Empire patriot, war veteran, Returned Soldier's League member and, according to family members, likely a Guard militiaman or sympathiser.[5]

Galvanised by the crowd's enthusiasm, Hughes rehashed his doomsday predictions of White replacement: 'Unless the door is closed against undesirables now, it will never be closed.' The smallest leakage must be prevented, lest it swell to a flood and engulf the land. The result? 'Australia would experience the race problems which America has before her to-day.' 'America tried the "melting pot" theory and it failed,' he proclaimed. 'Negroes are now like gall stones in the bladder which cannot be cut out.'[6]

With that, Hughes turned his attentions to the 'players of jazz music' from the Sonny Clay Orchestra. 'Our own musicians have been boycotted in America,' he goaded, revisiting the Musicians' Union's exaggerated tale of Commonwealth Band humiliation. 'Now the Land of Liberty sends us these scum—these black beasts to entertain us and we have seen how they do it.'[7]

Hughes' allegation hung in the air, the unspoken details filled by lurid tabloid tales of Black lust and White slavery, and heroic fantasies of chivalry and honour.

'There was some talk about them going away on Saturday,' he ruminated, again building up to his punch. 'If that had happened in some American States, they would not have gone away on Saturday. *They would not have lived the night!* Are we going to tolerate such things?' 'Are we going to take all these things lying down?'[8]

It was an oblique call to arms, although the crowd's roar signalled they knew his meaning. By conflating the musicians' Blackness with the contested Whiteness of Southern Europeans, Hughes forged links between vigilante justice, frontier violence, fear of 'alien' invasion and the secret brotherhood of the Ku Klux Klan.

Perhaps knowing of the Rose Bay Digger's disgust for the war film *The Big Parade*, Hughes, in a crescendo of indignation, blasted Hollywood for daring to depict US soldiers as the heroes of the Western Front, before calling for a sweeping cinematic tribute to the glorious and indomitable spirit of the Australian soldier. Launching a soul-stirring eulogy to Anzac valour, British ingenuity and national destiny, he likened the Digger's tenacity and courage to the heroism of aviator Bert Hinkler—that special type of superior man who made it possible for the British Empire 'to win for itself advantage in all the fairest places of the earth'.[9]

The crowd 'cheered and cheered again', reported the *Daily Guardian*. 'Calls of "good old Billy" and "good on you, Little Digger" rang through the hall.' A *Daily Telegraph* photograph captured Hughes with arms raised, claiming victory.[10]

Billy Hughes attacking Italian immigrants and African American jazz musicians during a speech at the Nationalist Party Conference. (*Daily Telegraph*, State Library of NSW)

For Hughes' many supporters, this was a ripping riposte. As headlines read the following day, 'Fighting' Billy was 'himself again', 'in old time form'.[11] Few commentators were blind to his political ambitions—or his references to the Ku Klux Klan. In staging his 'comeback', Hughes lit 'the Fiery Cross' and revealed himself as 'the true spokesman of the Australian nation; magnificent, magniloquent', wrote *Smith's Weekly*. Hughes' 'threats of hell' made 'everybody' feel 'warm and happy', chuffed the writer, mixing trademark jocularity with a touch of introspection. Even 'staid, old Nationalist ladies enthusiastically cheered his pretty suggestions of n___r-lynchings'.[12]

A *Beckett's Budget* editorial was uncharacteristically ponderous, reflecting on the Darwinian struggle that underpinned the founding of the nation: 'Our forefathers, because of the numerical supremacy ... dispossessed the aboriginals ... and as our tenure is by right of conquest, so by our ability to defend, we must hold Australia.'[13]

Hughes' political colleagues, however, were livid. Sir Neville Howse called for Hughes' immediate expulsion, outraged by the suggestion he had 'undermined' the White Australia policy, denying issuing any 'instruction' the 'men should be lynched'.[14] Prime Minister Bruce denounced Hughes' words as 'totally and absolutely untrue', warning of the 'disastrous' impact on diplomatic relations. And indeed, the Italian Consul excoriated Hughes' 'childish, discourteous and vulgar utterances'.[15] The American Consul Ezra Lawton, however, remained silent—even after hearing Clay's account of the 'frame-up'.[16]

Amid the political fallout, Hughes stuck to 'his guns', his unflinching stance further mobilising his base.[17] The Melbourne branch of the Returned Soldiers' League 'heartily' welcomed 'every particular' detail of Hughes' 'brave' speech. A Brisbane club sent him a letter of congratulations.[18] Newspapers began a daily head count of the 'alien influx', the steady drumbeat intoning the threat of 'alien rule'. 'This bit of earth belongs to us/Pray God we keep it so!' read a poem in the *Daily Telegraph*.[19]

As most people knew, Hughes' slogan 'This bit of earth belongs to us' was the misquoted title of a well-known patriotic song, 'This Bit of the World Belongs to Us', composed by 'Dry Blower' Murphy to commemorate the 1908 visit of the US Navy's Great White Fleet. The following year, when a British Naval flotilla began patrolling the Pacific, Murphy changed the line 'keep the broad Pacific *clean* and free' to '*white* and free'.[20]

In 1916, when Prime Minister Hughes redefined the nation's war objectives to include the defence of White Australia, the song became meaningful in the context of the Great War. The catchphrase signalled Australia's 'right' to control Germany's colonial possessions in the Southwest Pacific to create a buffer between 'empty continent' and the 'yellow peril'.[21] And sometime between Hughes' condemnation of Italian migration and a Black American jazz band, the Little Digger repurposed the lyrics again. This time, the words upheld the myth of Anglo-Saxon exceptionalism, the cult of White supremacy and threat of vigilante violence.

Hughes claimed he improvised the speech in the heat of a spontaneous moment. In fact, he had scripted the epitaph several months earlier for the closing scene of the film *Birth of White Australia*. As the title suggested, the privately funded film borrowed heavily from DW Griffith's *Birth of a Nation*, the 1915 Hollywood box office sensation that sparked the revival of the Ku Klux Klan.[22]

Both American and Australian films mix historical drama with high romance. At its narrative core, *Birth of a Nation* was a White slavery miscegenation narrative set against the backdrop of the Civil War and Reconstruction: a gallant Confederate officer, elbowed and sidelined by 'Negro rule' raises a vigilante army to rescue a beautiful White woman held captive by a lascivious Black politician. In saving his sweetheart, the officer establishes a permanent, unofficial volunteer force to disarm Black soldiers and disenfranchise Black men.

The Australian version played out on the goldfields of Lambing Flat in 1860, centring on a fresh-faced White woman abducted by a villainous Chinese miner and rescued by her White suitor.[23] To protect White women from further outrages, the diggers club together and expel the Chinese. However, police thwart their plan, imprisoning the ringleaders and protecting the Chinese. As the inter-titles make clear, this was a travesty, a violation of natural law. 'You can't chain our mates up like dogs and let those yellow thieves go free,' protested one digger.

Indeed, the film's inter-titles spared no subtlety to drive home the political message: White working men had conquered this land, but government officials betrayed these rights when they punished the diggers for purging the Chinese 'invaders'. The implications were equally obvious. If the digger could not look to the government to defend hearth and home, they needed to make a stand for 'BRITISH WHITE AUSTRALIA'. To protect the virtue of his daughter, purity of his race, sovereignty of his nation, and dignity of his labour, the White settler needed to defy an unjust statutory law to honour a higher sacred law.

Hughes had encountered this new generation of White crusaders on his visit to Dallas in 1924. So too, the film reiterated the philosophy held dear by Guard leaders such as Major Jack Scott. It was hardly coincidental that *Birth of White Australia* was bankrolled by a consortium of graziers and politicians from the town of Young, where senior members of the Guard held sway in local government and the local Returned Soldiers' League.[24]

The film closed with views of modern-day Young, the site of Lambing Flat: its prosperous main street, robust agricultural economy, government buildings and war memorials to the fallen Anzacs. Into a garden stepped 'Fighting Billy' Hughes—'idol of the DIGGER and staunch advocate of British White Australia'. Repeating the same barbarians-at-the-gate argument heard at the Nationalist Party conference, he anointed the 'Digger' as the guardian of White Australia, protector of its sacred creed, defender of its moral essence. His speech concluded on the battle cry: 'THIS BIT OF THE WORLD BELONGS TO US.'[25]

Hughes' invocation at the Nationalist Party conference ultimately reached more people than the seldom-screened *Birth of White Australia*. News of the former leader's speech flashed across the Pacific. 'Under the rallying cry "White Australia"', Hughes led an attack on Italian migrants and Black entertainers. 'No incident in recent years has so stirred the Commonwealth,' read a widely syndicated Associated Press report, referring to the band's imminent deportation, although not Clay's accusations of a frame-up.[26] Still, the front page banner headline of the *Chicago Defender* screamed 'Australia Enforces Color Line Bar', naming Hughes as the leader of a 'widespread' 'exclusion movement' and 'white crusade'.[27]

Hughes' fighting words inspired Lothrop Stoddard—the best-selling American author of *The Rising Tide of Color Against White World-Supremacy* and rumoured Ku Klux Klan member—to reflect on the deep race solidarity between the two countries. 'Nowhere' was a 'race war' more likely than Australia, he told the two million readers of *Liberty* magazine. It was the 'center' of the 'storm'. And nowhere were the defences more robust. If 'Asiatics' dared breach this fortress, he contended, White Americans would join White Australians to repel this advance. The governments did not need to declare war for 'the guns would go off themselves'.[28]

The racial solidarity between the two nations complicated the simplistic knee-jerk anti-Americanism in Hughes' Bit of Earth speech. Indeed, Lothrop's response was part of a decades-long dialogue between thinkers in the two countries about colonial conquest, masculinity and nation-building. In 1868, Harvard zoologist Louis Agassiz explained the polygenic relationship between climate and race to Australian intellectual and politician Charles Pearson. Agassiz, in essence, believed Nordics and Africans to be separate species, the latter alien to American latitudes.[29] Pearson incorporated these ideas into his landmark 1893 'forecast', *National Life and Character*, contending the world's temperate zones were by 'natural law' the rightful home of the White race.[30] Theodore Roosevelt, in his treatise *American Ideals*, built on Pearson's valorisation of the Athenian citizen soldier, hopeful that a Lamarckian 'transmission of acquired characters' would revitalise a generation of foppish and pampered White men.[31] The intellectual lineage continued as Roosevelt's virile militarism and rugged frontier primitivism bolstered Hughes' claims that the true grit of the Anglo-Saxon race lay on the frontier and battlefield, beyond the frivolous fashions and labour-saving indulgences of modern life.[32]

For his part, Lothrop Stoddard's fantasy that White Australia was a Nordic paradise, home to 'vigorous' 'high grade' superior people made explicit the eugenic subtext in Hughes' White supremacist vision. For decades, historians had agonised over the 'law' that governed empire: if an empire rose, it was destined to fall and the rot *always* came from within.[33] As Stoddard told it, the science of eugenics could reverse Anglo-Saxon decline. Scientifically regulated reproduction could transform this cyclical pattern into an ascending trajectory. With enough political will, the millenarian quest for human perfectibility was within reach. 'Given a high type stock,' he predicted, '*a civilization might be immortal*' (his emphasis).[34] To his mind, Billy Hughes and White Australia was leading the way.

Hughes certainly read Stoddard's article, preserving two copies of the magazine. He also kept a newspaper file monitoring the fallout of his speech and the final page of a letter from a Washington, DC, man. But beyond that, Hughes' personal papers yield few insights.[35] So too, his many biographers have skated over this period of his career. Perhaps, it was just as Hughes wished. The gap in documentation about his ties to North American White supremacist groups was not accidental. As historian Donald Horne once noted, Hughes was prone to burning correspondence he construed as politically extreme.[36] However, two weeks after Hughes' speech, Prime Minister Bruce received a letter from the president of the Ku Klux Klan in Moose Jaw, Saskatchewan, thanking him for the government's 'able and definite stand' in preserving 'the heritage committed in your care'.[37]

The 'scalping knife' that Sonny Clay presumed to be in the hands of the Musicians' Union also bore the fingerprints of Billy Hughes, a man who wielded enormous influence. His connections to Major Longfield Lloyd and Federal Secretary Cecil Trevelyan ran deep. The patron and champion of the Returned Soldiers' League, the darling of newspaper magnates Ezra Norton and William Randolph Hearst, he could command audiences with Australian prime ministers and US presidents. Figures at the intersection of American eugenics and White supremacy, from Hiram Evans to Lothrop Stoddard, echoed his ideas.

Hughes deftly navigated the overlapping spheres of power to affirm predictions about the submergence of the White race and reassert a more militant British White Australia. Even though he never saw combat, Hughes' soaring oratory rekindled memories of masculine solidarity in the trenches and fanned the flames of righteous, if unconstitutional, rebellion. Through a wilful and destructive attack on his own party, Hughes officiated in rites to purify the race and rose from the ashes of political oblivion. In the raging debate that followed, a powerful martial fantasy sustained him: 'I am a battler. I have been in the forefront of many battles and I have always been a soldier.'[38]

36

FIT FOR THE TASK

Menacing mobs and high-pitch threats to lynch theatrical artists were not ends in themselves. Nor were bans on Black jazz musicians and restrictions on cultural practices. Instead, they were means to some people's end: a more perfect White Australia. However, sustained hostility to Black people was *not* the only path to this vision. Sections of the White population also required correction.

On Thursday, 29 March, an unusual advertisement appeared in the entertainment section of the Melbourne *Herald*. Three by four inches in size, the anonymous posting addressed the 'Youth of Melbourne':

> The future of this great continent lies in your hands.
> Your fathers have built it as a heritage for you.
> What are you going to do with it?
> You will have to make its laws.
> Regulate the lives of the citizens of to-morrow.
> Hold the scales of justice and punish the wrongdoer.
> Are you fit for the task?[1]

In those decades, eugenic meaning clung to the word 'fit', alluding to a system of genetic inheritance that could either advance or impede a

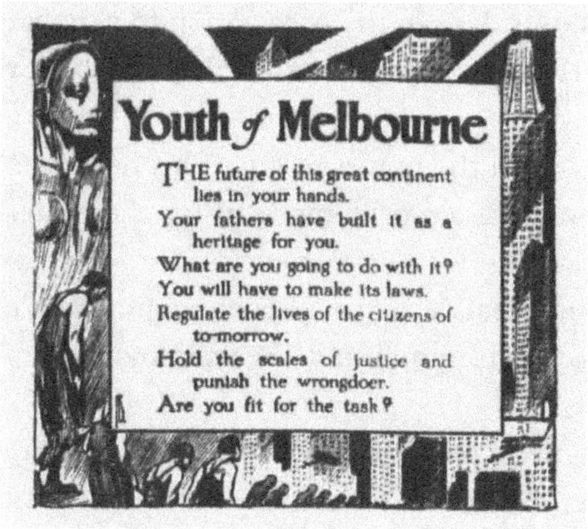

An anonymously posted message to the Youth of Melbourne (left); and Angela Booth, a moral purity crusader who served on the magistrate bench at the trial of the Rowena Mansions Five. (Melbourne *Herald*, State Library Victoria)

population's path to perfection. The statement, therefore, questioned the eugenic fitness of Melbourne's youth, casting doubt on their ability to uphold a sacred covenant founded in ancestral 'heritage' and maintained through law enforcement and other more personal forms of restraint and regulation. The dystopian artwork captured the author's pessimism (and owed a debt to Fritz Lang's soon-to-be-released futuristic film *Metropolis*): a line of worker drones trudging towards a modern, high-rise cityscape, searchlights scanning the skies. A hollow-eyed, sallow young woman headed the ghoulish procession, her beauty and vitality sapped by the urban night. Not lacking in material possessions, hers was a poverty of spirit.[2]

The author of this warning was unknown, although there were several candidates. Most were moral campaigners alarmed by the disposable income, personal freedom and sexual behaviour of young single women who lived independently of their families in the big bad city of Melbourne. Of these, one figure, Angela Booth, emerged as preoccupied uniquely with eugenics and unregulated youth. She herself held the scales of justice and punished the wrongdoer. That week, as justice of the peace on the bench of Melbourne's City Court, she had deliberated on the case of the five White women found in the company of the

Black musicians. As founder and president of the Association to Combat Social Evil she agonised over the upcoming generation's fitness for the task.[3]

'How are we to help youth to gain the power to guard his heritage?' she once asked. How could they make a world 'more fit for the better moulding of man'?[4]

By stamping out the forces of social decay while encouraging 'noble sport, frugal living, submission to discipline and the employment of control', she catechised.[5]

The challenge began with White women: as the mothers and future mothers of the nation and race, they could usher in a glorious era of spiritual, racial and social regeneration, or spawn a monstrous and dreary degeneration. She believed in perfection. She believed in annihilation.[6]

Tabloid newspapers delighted in lampooning post-menopausal social purity crusaders as frumpy, blue-shoed prigs spying lust and indecency at every turn. 'The Woeful Wail of a World-Weary Wowser', alliterated the *Truth*, ever ready to defend the working man's right to savour a cold beer in a swelter or pick the long-odds winner at the Melbourne Cup.[7] For all the scorn, Angela Booth made no efforts to defy the stereotype, happily inhabiting the caricatured soul of the World-Weary Wowser, the very type larrikin newspapers loved to hate—although in March 1928, more united them than divided them.

In contrast, Magistrate AA Kelley of Melbourne's City Court did not see someone mired in Victorian prudishness, but a modern woman versed in the latest scientific knowledge, expert in the 'modern method for the treatment of criminals', unblushing as she discussed miscegenation, drunkenness, prostitution, homosexuality and venereal disease.[8] Originally, the court appointed Angela Booth to assist with female cases, but her contribution was so much more. Since the advent of eugenics in the 1890s, she had kept abreast of US and British research. She had pondered Francis Galton's 'nurture and nature' debate over the influence of heredity and environment on people. She could quote Henry Maudsley's theory of degeneration (inferior inherited traits compounded over generations), Paul Popenoe's case for eugenic marriage, Rev. GP Merrick's twenty-year study of 16000 female prisoners, Margaret Sanger's call for contraception and equal wages, Havelock Ellis' views on sex impulse, and Charles Davenport's investigations into unrestrained female sexuality and feebleminded suggestibility.[9]

The sum of Booth's knowledge boiled down to one all-consuming issue: the unchecked reproduction of 'defective individuals'. Australia had watertight immigration laws that kept out 'undesirable' people, she argued, yet allowed 'mental defectives' inside the country to breed with impunity. Every day at the City Courts, she saw a procession of people who were 'unfit members of our community'. Data collated by Magistrate Kelley showed about half could be saved, while half proved resistant to rehabilitation. This second group displayed 'high levels of feeble mindedness'. Intelligence tests undertaken by her husband, Dr James Booth, at North Melbourne Children's Court confirmed the pattern, finding 43 per cent of juvenile offenders to be 'subnormal'. Worse, 'mental defectives' were highly fertile. In the course of her 'slum work', Angela Booth had come across 'an enormous number of feebleminded people with families of nine and ten'. Studies undertaken by Victoria's Inspector General for the Insane Dr William Ernest Jones showed 80 per cent of children born to one feebleminded parent bore the taints of feeblemindedness.[10] 'What is the outlook for the state if this is allowed to go on?' she petitioned.[11]

As a matter of urgency, she urged legislators to overturn the 'loose laws' and prevent these 'bad types' from reproducing. 'Mental defectives are a danger to the community,' she warned time and again. A 'diseased and morbid nature' was increasing the number of 'unintelligent human beings' who were 'weakening the human stock' and sapping 'the mass brainpower of the coming generation'. 'Its solution rested on the rise and fall of nations.'[12]

Her solution was self-supporting 'farm colonies for the segregation of the mentally unfit' with sterilisation as a precondition for discharge—a view supported by Dr Jones.[13] And although some fellow reformers found such proposals too 'autocratic' and extreme, many agreed 'unclean' Whites within the country's geographic borders were a 'national menace' creating a 'lax' environment that dragged down otherwise useful citizens.[14] As another campaigner pointed out, a 'really good clean Australia' was not 'merely white in skin, but white at heart'.[15]

Angela Booth looked forward to the passing of the Mental Deficiency Bill, which in March 1928 was poised to become state law. The bill had passed the lower house of Victoria's legislature and would soon be tabled in the upper house—or so she had been told. The politicians' dillydallying caused Booth much vexation. Once passed, the new laws would overhaul methods of crime prevention, empowering a magistrate or even a policeman to send a person to the Mental Deficiency Control Board and undergo evaluation. Already the bill's architect, Dr Jones, was preparing to circulate a 'Commonwealth Survey for Mental Deficiency' asking teachers to identify 'defective' school children better fitted for segregated farm colonies.[16]

Dr Jones had identified four grades of mental deficiency: idiots, imbeciles, feebleminded and moral defectives. This last group required very special diagnosis. As the minister of health told the Victorian parliament in 1926, 'moral defectives' were not necessarily 'mentally defective' so were tricky to spot, appearing so 'close' to 'normal' they often 'passed unnoticed' in the community. Their 'unfitness' manifested in 'vicious or criminal propensities' and 'unrestrained and deviant sexual activity'. Some were 'extraordinarily clever' although marked by 'no moral sense'. As such, they required 'care, supervision, and control for their own protection'.[17]

If Angela Booth had her way, all defendants would be examined for mental deficiency *before* they appeared in court. That way she could better distinguish the redeemable women trapped in a cycle of class poverty from the 'hopeless' 'moral degenerates'—and therein recommend a suitable punishment.[18]

By her measure, the five fashionable young women found consorting with the Black American musicians exhibited clear signs of environmentally induced racial degeneration. Their willpower had been weakened by the 'idleness' of leisure, their moral sense perverted by 'voluptuous reading', their ambitions corrupted by the 'pornography' of cinema and their vitality numbed by 'dance and sensuous music'.[19] Each screening of *Flesh and the Devil* or phonograph spin of 'The Good Bad Girl'—all readily available in Melbourne that week—allowed these young women to give free rein to their desires. And 'when the girl is free from customary restraints, her appetite once awakened, she gives as freely as the boy takes', read her diagnosis of modern ills in her carefully argued pamphlet 'The Prophylaxis of Venereal Disease'.[20]

Yet there remained a lingering doubt. Did the five women's 'disgraceful' behaviour reach beyond a morally corrupt marketplace to touch the very core of their being? Did a weak hereditary 'germ-plasm'—to use the scientific language of the period—condemn them as 'moral defectives'? Were they the 'weeds' in the 'social garden' displacing the flowers and robbing society 'of what might be perfect blooms'? If so these 'parasitic women must be placed under the same restraints as other anti-social and criminal classes'.[21]

To Booth's chagrin, the Magistrates Court could not yet address this complex set of issues. She conceded Magistrate Kelley had no option but to discharge the women, frustrated by a legal framework unable to tackle the 'enemy within'.

'The law is an ass,' she had announced the previous year. 'Many benevolent movements are afoot to reclaim the fallen, but we should be better off if the effort began when prevention was possible ... By removing from society harpies who batten on the unfortunate and weak.'[22]

Mrs Booth was not alone in her despair that the Rowena Mansions Five had walked free to return to their depraved lives. An *Argus* editorial 'deplored' the actions of 'white girls' who 'lamentably failed to live up to the Australian standard' and 'forget what is due to their racial origin'. 'What was lacking in the upbringing of these young people' that they would willingly 'associate on terms of less than equality with the coloured men on whom we claim the right to look down?' agonised the writer.[23]

A commentator in the *Bulletin* called for more censorship. Namely a ban on 'manifestly evil' Hollywood films that made 'bad types of Americans "interesting"'. 'Familiarising foolish virgins with the spectacle of colored heroes mauling white women about, contributed to the downfall of girls who took part in the beastly orgy in Melbourne,' he argued, plotting the women's degradation in three stages: '(1) n____r music; (2) n____r dances; (3) n____rs.'[24] Somehow, he suggested, Blackness needed to be excised from modern Australian leisure time culture.

The YWCA launched a 'Building Up Our Girls' campaign, a neo-classical body culture program promoting Greek Revival, folk, eurythmic and 'artistic' dance as a corrective to realign the twisted knees, sunken chests, distorted feet and moral disfigurement of the jazz dancer.[25] 'Perfect youthful bodies' were a 'door' to 'more spiritual things', assured one advocate of the body culture movement.[26]

The National Council of Women renewed calls for more policewomen to patrol streets, railway stations, parks, beaches and dance halls on the lookout for young women in moral danger. 'A policewoman's timely warning is invaluable to the girl who is more thoughtless than evil,' urged one advocate. The previous year, Commissioner Blamey had resisted their pleas. The 'Negro Orgy' brought new impetus to their campaign.[27]

The *Truth* Representative also lamented the shortcomings of the law. Authorities could deport the men, he argued, but who could protect White Australia from these dangerous women? 'No Act' made it 'an offense for a white girl to associate with a colored person', he complained.[28] To heighten a sense of urgency, the following week the *Truth* rehashed two old stories about 'promiscuous immorality' at Lake Tyers Aboriginal Mission, two hundred miles east of Melbourne. Growing numbers of 'half caste' men, afflicted with venereal disease and racial 'degeneration' were gravitating to Melbourne and 'finding joy' among the 'harpies of the slums', panicked the paper.[29] They demanded immediate action to prevent morally aberrant white women 'breeding *in* the colour'.

When General Blamey agreed to work with Major Lloyd to redress the infraction of 'Commonwealth policy', he, likely, had not foreseen that these efforts might imperil his vested interests in prostitution and gambling operations. But under pressure to take action, Blamey doubled the number of policewomen, from two to four, and set in motion a campaign to 'retrieve wayward girls from undesirable environments'.[30] To ensure the desired outcome, Blamey elected his plainclothes unit as best fitted to the task.

37
SAVING EDNA LANGDON

THE LAW WAS not finished with the 'wayward' women who had been acquitted so publicly. Inspector Hall of the plainclothes unit, professing to be scandalised by the 'startling revelations', authorised a clean-up operation to 'check the further growth of this menace'.[1] Over the following weeks, plainclothes police raided Fitzroy lodging houses and Little Bourke Street opium dens arresting over fifty 'girls' aged between fifteen and twenty-five, mostly on charges of vagrancy. The 'sensational raid' on Rowena Mansions had 'stirred' police to 'considerable activity', approved the *Sunday Times.* Contrary to previous claims of legal helplessness, police, in fact, had the power to 'save' 'jaded jazz fiends' from vice.[2]

In the City Court, Magistrate Kelley and Angela Booth heard each case, relying almost exclusively on police testimony to form judgements: the 'accused had been consorting with undesirable characters'. None were employed. Some were addicted to opium, others afflicted with venereal disease. Several were runaways. Their parents 'had been searching for them for some time', attested constables. Newspapers noted the defendants' 'obstinate and cheeky demeanour' and pronounced 'wayward character'.[3]

After a stern admonition, Kelley and Booth sent some young women back to their parents' care, never considering the situations they had fled. They sent many more to benevolent institutions where a matron would impose control and dispense frugal living. 'It is hoped that the campaign will result in a diminution of tender aged girls visiting the slums of the metropolis,' enthused one newspaper.[4]

Until the Mental Deficiency Bill was made law, Kelley and Booth were unable to refer offenders to the Mental Deficiency Control Board who could then identify and segregate the eugenically 'unfit'. However, the magistrate's sentencing pattern suggested a clever workaround. Kelley and Booth had devised a way of keeping these 'tender-aged girls' in semi-permanent states of remand at charitable institutions. Newspapers rarely noted a judgement of innocence or guilt or the length of the women's custodial sentences. At best, they mentioned a follow-up hearing in the coming weeks—yet that too often resulted in another deferred decision.

Kelley and Booth had been implementing this practice for some time, although in the previous six months, the language of eugenic unfitness had begun to inflect police testimony. One arresting officer described a 21-year-old woman charged with 'bad behaviour' as a 'revolting' and 'depraved' person who was 'mentally' and 'morally deficient', a 'menace to the male sex' and a 'danger to unsuspecting youth'. Remanded to a religious institution, she then vanished from court records.[5] Such cases were catnip for the *Truth.* In January 1928, they despaired that a morally deficient seventeen-year-old who had been held in a home for twelve months had returned to her 'fallen' life. Is she 'normal', they questioned. 'Men need to be protected from this new breed of predatory girls' who were 'completely devoid of moral sense'.[6]

On Thursday, 29 March, Edna Langdon may not have noticed the mysterious post in the *Herald* asking the Youth of Melbourne if they were 'fit for the task'. However, she surely knew the wide-eyed, bow-lipped winner of the Green Mill's Artist Model Competition was on the cover of *Table Talk* magazine. Edna once hoped she would be crowned 'Melbourne's Most Beautiful Model'. Studying the face of the pageant winner, she perhaps fathomed the gap between what had come to pass and what might have been.[7]

Certainly, Edna Langdon had some clue that Constables Saker and Dunn were looking for her. Earlier that day the policemen made a surprise visit to the Fitzroy home of Dorothy Davis and Dorothy McGowan. By the time they left, both girls agreed they would leave Melbourne by Saturday to take up an appointment in a country hotel.[8]

Edna Langdon and Nola Mackay somehow got word police had run the two Dorothys out of town and when Saker and Dunn paid a 'visit' to their flat, neither woman was home. According to the *Truth* Representative, 'police waited some time' before twigging that Langdon and Mackay were one step ahead of them.[9]

As Saker told it, he returned empty-handed to Russell Street headquarters only to find an arrest warrant for Edna Langdon waiting for him. Her stepfather, Leslie Langdon, had sent police a telegram asking them to detain his errant daughter until he arrived to claim her.[10]

Just how Edna Langdon ended up on the dummy carriage of a city-bound tram in the company of 'Ivy Day' is unclear, for they did not appear to be close friends. But by wild coincidence, Saker was driving down the same street and noticed Langdon and Day on the tram. He 'followed them in a car, arrested Edna Langdon and locked her up', again on a charge of vagrancy.[11] Her companion, 'Ivy Day' continued her journey—or perhaps alighted at the next stop and returned to the maid's quarters of the grazier's imposing city house, hoping her debt to the Victoria police had been settled.

Edna Langdon at Melbourne City Court: rearrested by police, then placed in a home for wayward girls, the court released her on condition she left Melbourne. (Melbourne *Truth*, State Library Victoria)

Edna Langdon again appeared in the City Court before Kelley and Booth, who remanded her to a Salvation Army home for wayward girls. Since 1923, the Victorian government had appointed the Salvation Army to 'provide for the treatment of such cases', and by late 1928 ran three centres in Melbourne for 'homeless women and women who have fallen into a life of crime'.[12]

Matrons oversaw a strict regime, convinced of the transformative power of close supervision, sparse food and hard physical labour. 'There is no excuse for any decent girl to be idle in Melbourne,' said Ensign Gladys Golding.[13] Over the next few days, Edna woke at dawn to attend church services, scrub the floors clean, then toil alongside other state wards in the home's commercial laundry—an acerbic brand of ablution designed less to cleanse and more to purify. Only her stepfather's appearance would release her. If he did not arrive, she would remain in the Salvation Army home, working for her keep in the laundry and training in domestic service until the court saw fit to release her.[14]

Nola Mackay was the only target of Saker's attentions who eluded his grasp. However, with the help of the *Truth* Representative, he would exact revenge.[15]

As the seasoned muckraker told it, he tracked down Nola Mackay's mother, showing up on her doorstep, possibly with Saker, likely plying her with questions. Nola's mother was a vulnerable woman with a long history of alcoholism and mental health issues. A decade earlier, her husband divorced her for adultery.[16] According to the measure of the Mental Deficiency Control Board, Mrs Mackay met several medical benchmarks of 'feeblemindedness'. Consistent with the eugenic 'laws' of inheritance, there was an 80 per cent certainty she had passed this condition on to her daughter Nola.

That Saturday, the *Truth* published their insider scoop, 'White Girls with Negro Lovers'. The exposé dwelled on the degraded state of each individual woman (except, of course, 'Ivy Day')—but reserved special umbrage for Nola Mackay. She was incorrigible, repeatedly visiting the

"Truth" has the Largest Nett Sales in the Southern Hemisphere

Truth

THE PEOPLES PAPER.

Why Suffer From Terrible Headaches? VIOPAKE LENSES

John Browning

182 Collins St. Cent. 1135 or 5348

WORK IT OUT FOR YOURSELF—

ARE YOU ABLE TO SAVE MONEY?

State Savings Bank

No. 1950 MELBOURNE, SATURDAY, MARCH 31, 1928 (TELS 2097, 4760) 16 PAGES 3d.

White Girls With Negro Lovers

Raid Discloses Wild Scene of Abandon

EASILY the biggest theatrical scandal in years was uncovered in the early hours of last Sunday morning, when police raided Rowena Mansions, in Nicholson-street, East Melbourne, and found members of Sonny Clay's Colored Idea revelling with young girls, most of them scantily clothed. For hours they had watched abandoned dancing and shocking happenings before the windows of the flat, and, on making their raid, discovered a worse condition within.

Flappers, Wine, Cocaine And Revels

BECAUSE there is no Act which makes it an offence for a white girl to associate with a colored person, police were powerless to convict the girls. Their charge of vagrancy fell down when the girls proved that they had means of support. A move is now on foot to frame an Act which will give the police such power.

Federal Cabinet will from now on ban all colored bands and entertainers from Australia.

The *Truth*'s insider account of the 'raid' on Rowena Mansions rested on lurid misrepresentations and a slanderous attack on Nola Mackay.

musicians' flat. She had led innocent Ivy Day down the path of depravity. She was dismissive of Constable Saker's authority.

And, alleged the *Truth,* she had a history of degenerate behaviour: 'One of the most disgraceful finds made by police during the raid was the diary of Nola McKay.' Given Saker and Dunn's long history of fabricating evidence, the diary was almost certainly fictional; the Sydney and Melbourne editions published different versions of the same passages. Nonetheless, it was a slanderous and humiliating attack on the 22-year-old dressmaker.

'No document could have been a more sweeping denunciation of the writer,' prefaced the *Truth,* hinting at 'putrid details and immoral ponderings', the bulk of which were 'unprintable'. The reporter, however, could reveal her 'numerous love affairs', of 'being in a _____ of a mess', of being 'illegally' treated by a doctor, of giving birth to a baby girl. Far from being chastened, Nola returned to leafy middle-class suburbs without an ounce of contrition.[17]

Also disclosed was Nola's 'love' for an unidentified 'black man', a 'Creole'—although none of the five musicians implicated in events claimed this highly particular ethnicity. The specifics of this alleged relationship varied in different editions of the *Truth*. 'He wants to marry me,' read the Melbourne version. In the Sydney edition, she planned to 'ask him to marry me'. Either way, Nola Mackay was ready to 'give up the white race'. The Sydney edition deemed her 'utterly without any moral sense whatever'—precisely the medical criteria for 'moral deficiency'.[18] Once the bill passed into law, Nola Mackay would be a candidate for detention, segregation and sterilisation.

There is no record of Nola Mackay's thoughts as she fled her hometown of Melbourne, abandoning her belongings, her friends and family, believing her mother had publicly renounced her. The charges came as a 'terrible shock', Mrs Mackay allegedly told the *Truth*. She was 'dumbfounded' her daughter would 'sink' to such a disgraceful level.[19] Nola's family offered no solace or support. Her father was deceased. Her beloved sister had also died several years earlier. Nor did she have a union, church or veteran's league to defend her. She faced the slander unprotected and alone.

Eventually she surfaced in the Western Australian mining town of Kalgoorlie where she worked as a secretary. In 1933, she married a miner and took his name.[20]

Despite assurances the plainclothes police were saving the wayward women of Melbourne, even representatives from the *Truth* hinted the 'clean-up' was a sham, more pantomime than police work.

A few weeks into the operation, Constable Saker arrested Bridget Mahoney, a notorious Melbourne madam and 'well-known habitué of the City Court', who trafficked in young women. On the witness stand, Saker offered the type of lurid through-the-window testimony beloved by tabloid reporters. Only this time, he assured the bench Bridget Mahoney had seen the error of her ways, surrendering her house of ill-repute and promising never to appear before the court again. Magistrate Kelley fined Mahoney £20 and 'she peeled off two tenners from a fat roll without blinking' then promptly returned to her old ways. Within two years she was back in court on an identical charge.[21]

With vested interests in prostitution and the cocaine trade, the plainclothes unit had no intention of biting the hand that fed it. Moreover, Constables Saker and Dunn were confident that police corruption was the one environmental factor Magistrate Kelley and Mrs Booth would *not* consider. No matter how many times Kelley headed corruption inquiries, he reliably ruled in the policemen's favour. When church groups complained to Inspector Hall that the menace of street solicitation was again on the increase, he resorted to old arguments, claiming loopholes in the law prevented police action.[22]

For years, rumours of systemic police corruption buzzed through the dining rooms of the Melbourne establishment. Around town, people knew Blamey's plainclothes unit as henchmen carrying out the chief's orders, with something for themselves on the side. In the City Court, Kelley and Booth heard defendants accuse plainclothes police of frame-ups, planting evidence, entrapment, persecution and dishing out the third degree. Time and again, they elected to ignore the policemen's subterranean world, allowing lies to pass as evidence.[23]

Kelley and Booth's wilful blindness to police graft was a means to an end, a prop holding up the fantasy that honourable people best 'fitted' for the job manned the criminal justice system. To acknowledge otherwise required them to give moral authority to delinquents, addicts and wayward women: the very people they branded 'morally deficient' and 'undesirable'. Rather than observe the wheels of law and order, Angela Booth fixed her attention on the germ plasm of young women like Edna Langdon and Nola Mackay, applying the eugenic laws of heredity to decide who would be purified and who would be sterilised. In doing so, she hoped to shepherd in a new era to befit a 'clean' White race.

PART XI

On Their Way

38

THE NON-STOP ENDURANCE DANCE RECORD

In the dormitory of the Salvation Army home for wayward girls, Edna Langdon had time to think back over the previous Saturday night. Until Constable Saker walked through the door, it had been an evening of music, laughter and dance but certainly nowhere close to the kaleidoscopic artist ball scene in *So This Is Paris*. Perhaps moments were tinged with disappointment, still feeling the sting of not winning the Artist Model Quest, not even securing a place, although hardly complaining. Still remembering Green Mill patrons cheering and shouting as she paraded on the Fountain of Life, her ambitions within reach. Still remembering the push-me pull-you steps of the Texas Tommy. Never forgetting the daily grind of life in a flimsy Broken Hill bungalow.

Edna Langdon had come a long way since arriving in Melbourne, mixing with celebrated American dance band musicians who wore plum suits, spoke in a poetic brand of English and taught her new dances that would soon spark a craze. It was a distance too far by the measure of people who saw in her restive desires for a modern, cosmopolitan and independent life, a de-centring of culture, a seismic shift that threatened to remake the world as they knew it.

Forces beyond her control were compelling her to unmake this world and return her to the town she fled. She was told her stepfather was on his way to collect her.[1]

On Monday, 1 April, Edna Langdon was again in the City Court before Magistrate Kelley and Angela Booth, JP—her third court appearance in five days. Her stepfather, Les Langdon, sat in the gallery. He was a silent man, unnervingly so for some members of his family, unable to tell if torment or rage festered beneath his detached visage. But it was a face Edna was, surely, grateful to see, if only because he was her ticket out of detention. Magistrate Kelley released her to Les Langdon's care on the strict condition she return to Broken Hill.[2]

Twenty-five years earlier, Les Langdon himself had stood in a similar court, marked a troubled child. Impervious to the thrashings of his mother, he kept running away, first from home, then probationary school, his head full of dreams of adventure. 'The lad was a good boy in many respects and was desirous of going to sea,' explained a farmer who sheltered the ten-year-old.[3] In 1914, Les Langdon succeeded, enlisting in the Australian Imperial Forces and crossing several oceans to reach the battlefields of the Western Front. But after eighty-two days of combat, he 'forfeited service' or in other words, ran away.[4] For years, Les Langdon lived in the shadows under an alias, at risk of being named and shamed as a deserter—although back in Broken Hill, his trespasses appeared to be almost forgiven. It was as if the town was a form of penance, a place to wait out the shame. Magistrate Kelley tasked him with escorting his stepdaughter into exile.

It was unclear whether Les Langdon recognised the woman sitting beside Magistrate Kelley. For Angela Booth, too, had lived in Broken Hill, and for much the same reason: for ten years, she had served out a penance.

In October 1896, 27-year-old Angela Plover had fled her Brisbane home with fellow reformer Dr James Booth, a married man. Booth swiftly divorced his wife, Amy, accusing her of adultery—a shame that drove her to suicide. Fourteen days after her death, Dr James Booth joined Angela Plover in holy matrimony and slunk off to Broken Hill.[5]

It had all the makings of a tasty tabloid treat: the unbecoming behaviour of a bastion of Brisbane blessedness. A world-weary wowser wild with wicked ways. Of course, the good people of Broken Hill knew none of this, the Booths successfully dodging the scrutiny of gossip columns and fashioning themselves as models of civic reform. They championed libraries, art galleries, mechanics institutes, imperial societies, nursing associations and music recitals.[6]

Even so, Angela Booth nursed no love for Broken Hill. It was a forsaken place of furious dust storms and violent thunderstorms, where 'oxide filth' from the mines leached into the town water supply. A city she condemned as so 'lacking in natural beauty' as to be more woe-begotten than England's 'slums', so 'destitute of natural attractions' to spawn children 'devoid of any moral sense'.[7]

Her allusions to a childhood in the slums hinted at a deeper secret in the heart of the 'world-weary wowser'. For Angela Booth's solidly respectable English Protestant exterior was an invention. She was born Elizabeth Plover, the child of an Irish Catholic dockworker, and raised in Liverpool's Scotland Road, surrounded by squalor, disease, violence, alcoholism, prostitution, gambling and bitter sectarianism.[8] The weight of statistics fingered her as degenerate. The Irish had an 'inherited susceptibility to mental illness', pronounced experts. Their 'incurable' criminality and promiscuity could be counted in Lancashire's insane asylums, prisons, brothels and syphilis wards. Her gender and class condemned her to menial occupations: if not a prostitute, then a domestic servant or street hawker, the very groups most likely to succumb to prostitution.[9]

By her own admission, Angela Booth had been 'acquainted with brothel life' from 'an early age'. She had been saved from 'indigent circumstances', likely by Protestant reformers in the Vigilance Association who subjected her to the same austere system of correction she now advocated for Melbourne's 'wayward girls'. When one saw the wretched child of the ghetto, 'one longs for the opportunity of giving them a chance', she wrote.[10]

Elizabeth Plover's free passage to Brisbane in 1890 proved her ticket to reinvention (she later described the ship's route through the Mediterranean as her 'tour of the continent'—before commencing what might be called her 'Imperial tour').[11] She landed in Queensland with a new name, religion and accent, moving undetected in the city's close-knit literary, progressive and esoteric circles, there meeting her future husband Dr James Booth. Both shared an interest in infectious diseases, telepathy, mesmerism, child welfare and women's education.[12] Both were disciples of Countess Wachtmeister, a high-ranking theosophist who drew on Buddhist and Brahmanic ideas to advance a history of celestial consciousness. Wachtmeister's lectures plotted an evolutionary ascent from 'shadowy' 'instinct' to 'vivified reason', ending with a prophesy about the immanent rise of a 'new race' blessed with 'divine intuition'. But this blessed race could only survive and flourish if the seeker made the 'low' 'disappear' and the 'high' pursue 'noble' ideals.[13] Filtering what they understood as the laws of karma through a eugenic Anglo-Saxonist lens, Angela Booth and her future husband pledged themselves to Wachtmeister's vision quest—even in the forlorn dustbowl of Broken Hill.

In banishing Edna Langdon back to a brown and charmless land, Angela Booth condemned the 'weed growth' to a terrain she believed was mostly fit for weeds—with a slim, but not insurmountable, hope of redemption. If Edna Langdon renounced the false beauty of sensual pleasure and pledged herself to the pursuit of discipline, thrift and noble ideals, she just might be saved. By exercising 'impulse control', by restraining and channelling her sexual energy, Booth believed Edna could power the mental and physical evolution of man and usher in a higher plane of civilisation. 'If it is possible for one, it is possible for all,' Angela Booth had once lectured, in an oblique reference to her own magnificent transformation.[14]

Edna Langdon did no such thing. Back in Broken Hill, she had no intention of labouring hard for scant wages as a domestic servant or drudge, waiting for a man of sufficient means to protect her. Perhaps, like Angela Booth, she drew sustenance from the expansive desert skies or found comfort in golden hills at sunset. So too, she may have been stirred by suffragist calls for equal wages and greater political representation. But mostly, Edna Langdon looked to Hollywood screen sirens and dance band music to explore new ways of hearing, relating, moving her body and tapping into the wider world.

Outside Broken Hill's picture palace, church ministers held prayer meetings to save the unrepentant. Inside, Norma Talmadge played Camille, a French courtesan in a world of vice, glamour, possibilities and tragedy. 'The world is mine! Paris is my footstool. I kick it over dancing with the wild winds of pleasure,' Camille penned in her diary.[15] As Leo Davis or Baby Lewis had possibly mentioned, actress Norma Talmadge was a Hollywood notable frequently seen slumming at the Apex Club.[16]

When Edna first left Broken Hill, a Musicians' Union strike had shut down the local Palais de Danse, essentially because some hometown musicians resented Big City players muscling in on what they believed was their territory—a position robustly supported by Federal Secretary Cecil Trevelyan. Their victory, however, was hollow. When the palladium reopened, dancers boycotted the band, resentful of the strong-armed tactics of a second-rate bully, and demanded the return of the exiled orchestra. Still, Edna Langdon resisted the temptation to enter the Palais' 'attractive girl competition', to be judged by the howl and holler of the crowd. But when a professional exhibition dancer named Bert Angus travelled to Broken Hill to break the world's non-stop dance record at the Palais, Edna Langdon signed up as a dance partner. The crowds returned for this test of endurance but the spirit of madcap excess had faded. In the face of spiralling unemployment—10 per cent and rising—the dance marathon's cash prizes came to symbolise a desperation that would only deepen, as the economy shifted from recession to a cruel and prolonged depression.[17]

Bert Angus danced non-stop for 142 hours, almost six days, setting a record broken in a Newcastle dance hall the following week. At the end of this gruelling marathon, Angus paid special tribute to Edna Langdon, for helping him survive a particularly 'bad spell' 'just before dawn' when his body shook and mind went blank and the pain in his stiff knee and chafed arms wracked his entire body. He could hear Edna call to him but in his delirium was unable to reply, haunted by particles of dust rising from the timber boards, trapped in a nightmarish hallucination. For hours on end, Edna shook him, kept him anchored, staving off a paranoid psychosis.[18] Although only eighteen, she had glimpsed this darkness. Edna knew what it took to endure.

39
SAILAWAY STREAMERS

DEPORTATION IS A legal process, borne of state authority and administered by bureaucrats. Anthropologists describe it as a ritual of public purification that symbolically excises from society qualities deemed unwanted and undesirable. On Saturday, 31 March 1928, Ivy Anderson and the ten members of the Sonny Clay Orchestra boarded a steamer bound for San Francisco. This official act of removal enabled bureaucrats and reporters to expedite a tidy denouement to a White Slavery miscegenation drama.[1] An *Argus* editorial titled 'A New Color Line' saw a reaffirmation of core national values:

> Whatever religion may have to say about all men being brothers the fact remains that no Australian regards the black man as his brother. Nor is that feeling to be regarded as wrong when it is concerned with the dignified assertion of our claim to retain Australia for people of white blood, and for them only.[2]

Frederick H Cumberworth, the political cartoonist with the *Evening News*, depicted a bridge spanning a body of water, connecting two lumps of rock: 'Australia' and 'America'. Along this bridge trudged a line of anthropoidal Black men in fancy white suits and hats, weighed down with luggage and musical instruments. 'The Color Line' read the title.[3]

The tag referred to the literal line of men and the Pacific Ocean, the watery boundary where Australia drew its colour line. The 'joke' lay in

The Color Line: A newspaper ink artist targets the gender, race, style and occupation of the musicians to mark them as 'undesirables'. (*Evening News*, State Library of NSW)

the disjunction between the musicians' modern suits and their subhuman appearance. For Cumberworth, they were the 'black beasts' of Hughes' speech draped in the veneer of civilisation, lusting after White status, women and privilege in cities far from their true 'home'. As viewers easily recognised, this 'home' was not the plantations of the Southern minstrel, but along with all the other primates in the Jungle, a fantasy land of cannibalism, maddening rhythms and primitive frenzied dance.[4]

'Negro jazz' may have brought the Jungle to White America, but the defenders of White Australia had determined this 'idea' would not cross its borders again. The four criteria Cumberworth used to mark this type as 'undesirable'—gender, race, style and occupation—mirrored the government's criteria for assessing the character of Black entertainers. The implication was clear: the White Australia policy not only kept out 'undesirable' people, but also 'undesirable' ideas about music, dance, masculinity, fashion and racial equality.

'On their way', ran the caption to the *Truth*'s front-page photograph of seven musicians waving goodbye. The jazzmen were going home and taking with them a set of 'ideas' which 'didn't suit Australia'.[5]

The noted historian Keith Hancock, who had been appalled by Hughes' 'crude' and 'offensive' lynching threats, applied a practical logic to justify the 'color line'. 'Reasonable Australians remember Australian Aborigines and confess they cannot trust themselves to be merciful and just in their dealings with a weaker people on their own soil,' he wrote. 'It is not merely a question of primitive fear, for they understand that ... racial war ... is none the less hateful if one race does all the lynching. What they fear is not their own physical conquest by another race, but the internal decomposition and degradation of their civilization.'[6]

Hancock, perhaps unintentionally, hit on the central paradox of the Australian experiment. In expelling the musicians, the nation's gatekeepers could deny their own frenzied primitivism and project themselves as civilised, rational, progressive and eminently practical. They needed to keep Australia White, not to save the race from contamination or promiscuous women from immorality, but to protect 'civilisation' from their own primitive and violent selves. The despised 'other' lay not beyond Australia's border but lurked in the heart of the most stoic race patriot. This national paradox played out in the swagger and doubt that characterised returned soldiers' legions and trade unions: the unshakable belief in their own biological and moral superiority coupled with a nagging sense of their economic and military vulnerability. Even the 'laws' of history dictated that British Empire would not always reign supreme. The rhetoric and practice of protectionism and vigilantism soothed these amorphous fears while expulsion and banishment maintained a facade of control.

Several Sydney papers noted that a similar drama was unfolding in faraway Vienna.[7] The target was cabaret dancer Josephine Baker, a figure famed throughout Australia, if only by reputation, as the 'toast of Paris', beloved by the 'creme of Parisian society', the 'idol' of a city that long defined Australian modernity and sophistication. Yet Austrian politicians, from 'Nationalists to Socialists', purporting to be offended by her scanty banana-skirt costumes and bodily contortions, united to banish her from the country. Slapping a punitive tax on her cabaret show, they forced her to abandon what was tipped to be a sell-out season.[8] Beneath the cries of immodesty and immorality lay anxieties startlingly similar to the Australian scandal: a perception that jazz music and dance distorted music, bodies and minds. A conviction that by some primitive and magical rite, the performance would obliterate a White individual's racial and national identity. A dread that as America's star was beginning to rise, Europe's was in decline. A conviction that degenerate art forms had highjacked consumer demand. A belief that a strong guiding hand could correct this aberration.[9]

What Sydney newspapers assumed to be a quirky coincidence was a global trend. By the outbreak of World War II, hostility to 'Negro jazz' and 'Negro culture' was a hallmark of authoritarian governments. By 1939, White South Africa, White Australia, Nazi Germany, Fascist Italy, Stalinist Russia, even Catholic Ireland had banned the entry of Black performers and the circulation of Black cultural practices.[10] The culture of the New Negro advanced an alternative brand of modernism that unsettled insular nationalism. By excising this particular expression of Blackness from modern leisure-time culture, Australian authorities sought to maintain the illusion of ethno-exceptionalism.

On the morning of Saturday, 31 March 1928, a number of customs officers were at Circular Quay, under instruction to intervene should 'difficulty' arise, but the scene that unfolded was not one they anticipated.[11] The theatre of ostracism did not run according to script.

The mood was festive. A throng gathered on the dock to give the passengers a hearty send-off. Amongst them were a photographer from the *Truth,* a reporter from the *Sun* and two dozen or so young women: some were 'colored', some White, all were 'smartly dressed'.

In the hour before the *Sierra* set sail, seven of the jazzmen lined up along the ship's deck rail. They tossed streamers, each unfurling a roll of crepe paper into the hands of the women on the wharf, each criss-crossed strand linking them together. 'They were a noisy crowd,' noted the reporter, 'laughing and joking and calling out to their friends.'

With a flamboyant disregard for the gravity of their deportation, the musicians and women shouted back and forth tips on 'how to remain in Australia'. Law enforcement officers were the source of much mirth—the *Sun* reporter learning he should keep a 'close eye' on Constable Saker (a tidbit not passed on in the Melbourne *Herald*'s reprint).[12]

Members of the Sonny Clay Orchestra aboard the San Francisco steamer mock the government's covert operation to ban them. (*Daily Telegraph*, State Library of NSW)

If the rest of the musicians' 'advice' continued to lampoon the efficiency of the Investigation Branch and Victoria police probe, the display was profoundly political in intent. For the musicians, it was an opportunity to expose the government's plan to rid the country of a modern African American sound and style and, somehow, remove the Blackness from Black art forms. For the Black Sydney women, it was a rare chance to mock publicly the posturing of the conquering race and pour scorn on the double standards that underlay the 'rules' of interracial sex. Their shouted words gave voice to a counter-narrative where Black ideas and practices powered the modern world—and perchance, one day, reconfigure the national conversation.

For the White women, their presence was a conscious act of defiance. After a week of moral hand-wringing and heated debate in the press, they remained unrepentant, shamelessly challenging the sacred creed upheld by political leaders, moral reformers, veteran associations and trade unionists.

Together they laughed, impervious to the condemnation of their enemies, savouring the final connection between dancer and dance band. The brief account in the *Sun* interpreted their antics as trivial and silly, while the *Truth* ignored them entirely, passing up a plum opportunity to angst about the moral bankruptcy of these jazz-crazed reprobates.[13]

Sailaway streamers brought a colourful jubilation to the beginning of a voyage, but they also brought tears. Crew hoisted the gangway and cast the cables loose. The funnel hooted, the engine whirred and the ship slipped almost imperceptibly from the dock. The tangle of streamers lengthened and one by one began to snap and flutter loose, floating down to the water—a ritualised breaking of the last tie, a farewell to people who may never see each other again.

But the ribbons of paper binding these individuals were more than material. This fragile web of 'wayward' and 'undesirable' people was making a modern cosmopolitan world. One day, this set of ideas would be strong enough to shake the forces that had shamed and banished them. Indeed, the expansion of this network would shape the trajectory of late twentieth-century culture, while the dreams of eugenicists, xenophobes and White supremacists would seem a flawed and foolhardy vision.

PART XII

The Quarantine Blues

40
SHAKE IT AND BREAK IT AND LET IT FALL

When Sonny Clay had accepted Harry Muller's offer to tour Australia, a web of events began to unfold that brought together a disparate collection of lives. Some folk connected by pushing and pulling through high-energy dances. Others clashed, commanded and colluded to orchestrate the band's removal. Once the storm had passed, each person continued on their path. The fallout of the tour was as fractured as each individual's journey.

Edna Langdon, for instance, moved to Brisbane in 1930 with her mother and sister and reverted to her original surname Ewart. She danced and played games at her coming-of-age party and debuted her sumptuously tailored dresses at local golf club dances. In 1936, she returned to Melbourne, and, for the next five decades, lived with her mother and near her sister in the St Kilda district. She remained single, moving in a world of extremely modern women. From Monday to Friday, she fashioned 'high class' clothing at her workshop in Kodak House, an elegant building that was something of a haven for Melbourne's women artists. At the Margaret MacLean Gallery on the ground floor, rolling exhibitions featured textile art, the needlework drawing inspiration from Japanese and Chinese embroiderers. Over the years, Edna apprenticed scores of young women. 'Excellent opportunities for capable girls,' read her job postings.[1]

During World War II, Edna volunteered as a servicewoman, likely working in intelligence, cryptography and telegraphy at the RAAF Wireless Transmitting Station. After the war, she spent weekends improving her handicap at the Albert Park golf course. One year she won the May Taylor Cup.[2]

Nola Mackay also returned to Melbourne after many decades in Kalgoorlie, Western Australia, and Launceston, Tasmania. Neither woman attracted even the smallest headline again.[3]

In less welcome ways, Sonny Clay's name also faded from the headlines. His reputation had been wounded by the Australian tour, though not fatally.

In April 1928, after three weeks at sea, the bandleader disembarked at San Francisco determined to present the 'true facts in the case', finding a sympathetic ear with several Black newspaper columnists. Billy Hughes was nothing more than an 'ex-umbrella mender', he sniped.[4]

Clay regrouped, albeit with a new crew of musicians, but still landed some enviable contracts in the Black show-business world. He returned to his old sporting haunts on the borderlands, first in Tijuana then with a plum residency at San Diego's Creole Palace, in the luxuriously appointed Douglass Hotel, backing the 'Harlem After Dark' burlesque. 'Oh boy, we had some times,' recalled a young saxophone player, remembering $500 tips, alcohol-fuelled excess and a fatherly bandleader in Sonny Clay who gave him another chance when he 'goofed up'—so long as he apologised.[5] Not long after, Clay teamed up with his idol Jack Johnson during the boxer's brief foray into the orchestra and cabaret game at Central Avenue's Dunbar Hotel. But really, Sonny Clay's show-business star would never again burn as bright. He was the guy who '*once* head[ed] the West's most widely known orchestra'.[6]

All musicians faced the double assault from the Depression and the introduction of sound motion pictures, although the squeeze was disproportionately borne by Black bands. Particularly so if they were the bandleader who 'messed up' in Australia' or drew 'girl trouble'. Bad luck plagued him. Brunswick records stopped releasing race records, leaving him with a stack of unreleased discs. His trumpeter died in a car crash just as he secured a residency in a San Bernardino ballroom—and his replacement didn't stick around for long; Clay was a 'heavy drinker' with a 'kinda big mouth', the new trumpeter recalled.[7]

In the mid-1910s, Sonny Clay prided himself on being ahead of the curve, on seeing change coming. Fifteen years later, he felt behind the pack, facing 'heavy competition' from a new generation of Black bandleaders pioneering Big Band, Swing and the Jump Blues. He soldiered on as a soloist, 'relying more and more on liquor to maintain some feeling of stability'. By the age of thirty-five, he was 'not in the best of health'. Still, colleagues were dazzled by his musical versatility—he could 'read anything'.[8]

Several younger members of the Colored Idea managed to keep a toehold in the business. Some even flourished. Leo Davis and Sonny Graven joined Les Hite's much celebrated big band, a fixture at Los Angeles' Cotton Club in the heart of Central Avenue, the crucible of the West Coast Sound and seat of a cultural renaissance. By the late 1930s, Davis turned his attentions to union organising although Graven remained on the bandstand, playing and recording with Louis Armstrong, Dexter Gordon and Charlie Mingus, and most notably Lionel Hampton's Swing Orchestra.[9] 'Band packs a terrific wallop from the minute it mounts the stand,' read a 1948 *Billboard* review. 'Spot is jam packed with kids who ... crowd the dance floor and jump to their hearts' content.'[10]

Baby Lewis was less fortunate. In 1936 he spent two seasons at Shanghai's Canidrome Ballroom with Buck Clayton's Orchestra before vanishing, somewhere in San Diego or Mexico. 'We never seemed to be able to find out what happened to him,' regretted Davis.[11]

The greatest success story belonged to Ivy Anderson—who soon changed her name to Ivie. According to Leo Davis, during the Australian tour, Anderson evolved from a comedienne and dancer into a remarkable vocalist. 'We were all surprised when she turned out to be such a good singer,' he recalled.[12] Her beguiling mix of dignified sophistication, technically imperfect vocals, playful scat singing and sardonic humour won her a headline spot at Club Alabam on Central Avenue. In 1932, Duke Ellington snared her for his big band. 'An extraordinary artist and an extraordinary person,' he wrote, recalling her performance of 'Stormy Weather' at the

London Palladium in June 1933. 'Tears streaming down her cheeks, Ivie did the most believable performance ever ... The audience and all the management brass broke down crying and applauding.'[13]

Sonny Clay followed his former colleagues' success, first with bitterness, then with a certain rapprochement as he recovered from alcoholism, saved, he recognised, by the love and wisdom of his second wife. He found steady work at the post office, ran a sideline first as a piano tuner, then as a pianist in a bar. He purchased a home in Watts, paid his income tax and did all those things Booker T Washington once advised back in Phoenix when Sonny Clay and his father marched with the Phoenix Famous Colored Young Men's Band.[14]

When jazz researcher John Bentley tracked him down in 1960 he encountered a 61-year-old who spoke in halting fragments, as if the bootleg liquor had taken its toll. Clay's answers jumped from describing notorious LA gamblers to a name-that-tune TV game show. He could name most songs from the first note, he assured Bentley—and, indeed, over the next two hours, demonstrated his deep knowledge of the American songbook.

At Bentley's prompting, he began with boogie-woogie, although Clay called it three tight chords on the left and 'anything that comes into your mind' on the right. The licks took him back to a church organ in his adolescent days when he tested the bounds of the sacred and the secular. His thoughts jumped to a San Diego sailor bar in the early 1940s when boogie 'was really getting into its prime'. He'd come home with his pockets loaded with money—'all I had to do was play the scales'.

Soon Bentley stopped asking questions, as if realising Clay's most coherent answers lay in his fingertips. 'When you're playing all night, these songs flow straight through me,' bantered Clay, mingling 'Suwanee River' into 'Old Man River', a Joplinesque rag into Gershwin's 'Summertime'. A high octave clambering riff called to mind the Mexican migrant workers who wheeled through Northwest Arizona each harvest with their sloping clarinets, valve trombones, guitars, flutes and piccolos. 'The Mexicans influenced me very much,' he reminisced, slipping into a *vals mexicano* rich with romantic flourish. And that 'Hebrew sound' in the early 1920s, he continued, why it almost reinvented the American songbook in a minor key. Although only recently did he fully appreciate the influence of circus music, recalling 'the roughnecks who used to put up the tents' singing 'shake it and break it and let it fall'.

Of course, he sampled his old mentor Jelly Roll Morton and a bunch of forgotten tunes that 'sold a lot of records'. The calculus of a businessman was never far away. People in the clubs liked the way he seemed to channel an entire orchestra through his two hands. Some nights 'you couldn't tell them I wasn't the best piano player in the world'.[15]

Sonny Clay at his Los Angeles home in 1942. (*Jazzfinder* magazine)

41
WHAT NOW?

In April 1928, The Four Covans wrapped up the remnants of the Colored Idea's tour with a farewell performance in Sydney. The moment the curtain rose, the audience greeted the whirlwind dance troupe with resounding cheers—a 'sympathy' applause, ventured Gayne Dexter. Since 'Sonny's banishment, theatregoers have apparently been doing a lot of thinking and readjustment'—aware that a hidden hand had engineered the scandal, aware they would not see a performer of Willie Covan's calibre in the foreseeable future.[1] Aware, too, that a local ban would do nothing to stop the next wave of African American musical innovation—only their experience of it.

By May, the *Truth* openly claimed credit for preventing 'two more dark bands' landing in Australia. By June, reviewers cheered the 'old negro melodies and jubilee choruses' of the 'N____r Minstrels', a 'refreshing jazz antidote' (in twelve years' time one of the blackfaced performers, Arthur Fadden, would become Australia's thirteenth prime minister).[2]

By November, Constable Harry Dunn's name was again at the centre of an alleged conspiracy. Five trade unionists accused him of framing them over the bombing of the Melbourne Greek Club.[3] So too, Constable Les Saker was back on his beat, hounding an Indigenous woman named Agnes Barnes. For years he had arrested her for petty offenses, one culminating in a ten-month custodial sentence. On her release in December 1928, Saker visited her employer, and had her sacked on the grounds of 'bad character'. Saker then re-arrested her for vagrancy. As he gave testimony in Melbourne City Court, Barnes drew a beer bottle from her coat and hurled it at him. Saker 'persecuted her because of her color', she told the magistrate.[4]

In an end-of-year review, Gayne Dexter's tones of remorse had grown louder as the long-term implications of life in a cultural quarantine sank in. The Colored Idea were the 'champion hard luck story', a show riding a 'big wave of popularity' that 'turned into a dumper', he rued.[5] Bill Maloney was more cutting, venting his spleen on the public: 'The much-maligned Sonny Clay' was 'playing to an audience not fully educated in the mysteries of the blues', he scorned.[6]

Twenty-five years passed before audiences would savour a trumpeter of Nini Coycault's stature. Or luxuriate in the finger-breaking strolls of Sonny Clay's piano. Or relish a drummer with Baby Lewis' electricity. Or behold a trombone player oozing with Sonny Graven's credentials. Almost a decade passed before a blues and scat vocalist matched the sophistication and invention of Ivy Anderson.[7]

The tours that never happened could be counted in the Black jazz troupes working the Asia-Pacific circuit. Wilbur's Blackbirds, the troupe almost contracted by Harry Muller, bypassed Sydney and headed straight to Singapore. They joined small knots of Black American performers who enlivened cafes, cabarets and hotels in port cities along the Asian archipelago. Manila was a particular stronghold. Shanghai then Bombay was home to piano 'genius' Teddy Weatherford, famed for his 'superb execution' of old classics and modern rag, jazz and blues.[8]

Far from denying professional opportunities to local orchestras, Black bandleaders recruited and trained local players who in turn seeded a national jazz sound. By the late 1930s, Filipino horn players rivalled Americans as Asia's preferred dance musicians.[9] Black jazz musicians formed the 'backbone' of Bombay's vibrant music scene whose influence spanned Indian classical music and future Bollywood soundtracks.[10]

Meanwhile, the Australian government only welcomed Black acts that evoked the cotton fields and days of slavery. In June 1929, authorities granted 'special permission' to tenor Walter Richardson to appear in the musical *Showboat*. Paul Robeson's rendition of 'Old Man River' had won accolades in London and Australians were keen to be part of the cultural moment, deaf to the subversive power Robeson brought to the lines 'What does he care if the land ain't free'.[11]

Richardson's wife Reginald Forsyth, keenly aware of Sonny Clay's fate, understood their warm welcome was conditional and temporary. 'We may watch Australia more than ever now,' she wrote in a letter to the *Chicago Defender*—although she had 'lots of fun' observing White Australia's 'unusual amount of interest' in the 'fashionable' 'Monte Carlo' 'suntan'. Cosmetic manufacturers released 'dark face powders' so that 'city girls' could have that 'popular outdoor look', she chuckled. One sales assistant admired her 'lovely shade', even more impressed to learn of her travels through the south of France.[12]

Meanwhile, bureaucrats exchanged memorandums and letters of acknowledgement clarifying the Richardsons' status and tracking their departure from the country. One singing trio complained that authorities treated them like 'criminals'. The Harmony Kings had toured the world but only in Australia did immigration officers confiscate their passports and require them to assemble in the purser's room as their ship left port.[13]

The economic collapse triggered by Wall Street's crash only increased Billy Hughes' gravitational pull on disaffected Diggers. 'Racial purity pays in the long run,' read his assurance in 1929, a theme he pursued with gusto. At war memorial dedications, Hughes reminded Diggers they 'had fought to keep Australia white'.[14] At a Returned Soldiers' League conference, he openly invoked White supremacy to amplify and intensify their grievances, while granting license to vigilante violence. Were the 'patriots' ready to 'do battle, and, if needs be die' to resist the 'alien element in our midst'? he asked.

> The enemy is within our gates and daily their daring grows, their numbers increase, and their power extends. Never was there a time when Australia was in need of stronger leadership and guidance.

> If that leadership is not to come from the men who fought with the AIF, where is the community to look for it?[15]

Three thousand delirious veterans cheered Hughes for five unbroken minutes. Among the crowd sat the upper echelons of the secret militia: Major Jack Scott, a newly elected league executive and Major General Sir Charles Rosenthal as well as the Viceroy Sir Dudley de Chair, and presumably his aide-de-camp, Major Longfield Lloyd.[16]

Hughes' words coincided with outbreaks of White violence across the country. Three months later, a bomb explosion at a West Melbourne boarding house endangered the lives of twenty Italian migrants. Weeks later two 'terrible explosions' ripped through the Greek Club, seriously injuring fifteen. Many more attacks in Melbourne, Sydney and North Queensland targeted Southern European migrants. Newspapers blamed the terror on industrial turmoil, underworld crime wars and an Italian proclivity for vendettas, but most incidents remained unsolved. The bombing of the Greek Club, in particular, seemed inexplicable, although one observer was moved to 'recall' Billy Hughes' 'warning' before reciting the White working man's credo: no Southern European should be in work while a Briton was unemployed.[17]

This was *not* the conclusion reached by Senior Constable Harry Dunn, the Victorian policeman whose investigation into the Greek Club bombing led to the imprisonment of five waterside workers—all members of a union who were the scourge of Police Commissioner Blamey. It was, however, one police frame-up decried by the labour movement, the focus of a decade-long campaign. Despite numerous parallels, at no point did unions or commentators compare events to the deportation of the Sonny Clay Orchestra. Quite the opposite. Political reporters like Hugh Buggy saw dance palaces and 'jazz babies' as 'far removed' from the 'hurly burly' of 'industrial wrangles', 'sectarian squabbles' and 'aggrieved returned soldiers'.[18]

By the time the alleged bombers gained early release, Dunn had been suspended from the force, the centre of too many corruption allegations. Many years earlier, his one-time partner Constable Les Saker had died after a 'short and painful' illness.[19]

So too, the deportation of the Sonny Clay Orchestra seemed like a blip when Musicians' Union Federal Secretary Cecil Trevelyan exploited the Depression to persuade James Scullin's Labor government to impose an embargo on *all* 'foreign' musicians. 'The fight is over,' Trevelyan announced. 'There are no orchestras of any foreign nationality here now.'[20] No more Italian opera companies. No more American dance bands. And no German Jewish conductors and virtuosos—no matter how many impressively pedigreed refugees sought asylum over the coming decade.[21]

Presented with the opportunity to accept outstanding players from the Vienna Philharmonic, Milan's La Scala and Berlin's State Opera, the Musicians' Union instead tightened membership qualifications, accepting only naturalised British subjects who had been resident for five years.[22] Spurned musicians decried the protectionist logic. 'What does ability count when the nationality and "race" are the pre-requisites for an existence even in this country!' complained violinist 'Tossy' Spivakovsky, as he left to pursue opportunities in the United States.[23] Those that remained took clerical and factory jobs, struck by the lack of imagination. In Germany, even the smallest cities funded their own orchestras, and the adoption of this model could enrich Australian musical culture—and create jobs. Professor Bernard Hines of Melbourne's Conservatorium shunned such ideas. The 'Jewish invasion' would compromise the 'distinctly British character of Australian musical life', he warned in a private letter.[24]

The cultural fortress, however, failed to create job security. The impact of sound motion pictures proved far more devastating than any touring band of 'foreigners'. The Musicians' Union shrank, yet still maintained an iron grip on the cultural sector—or, at least, remained a proxy for other gatekeepers' agendas—controlling the job market, crushing musical innovation and enterprise.

A column written by commercial artist and dance enthusiast Jim Russell charted the impact of bans on Black and 'foreign' musicians on Sydney's dance floors. In the 1920s, he had organised dance competitions at a Bondi Beach club where a 'jazz mad mob' mastered every modern step from the Charleston to the Heebie Jeebies. By 1933, however, he noted several fashionable Parisian dances—the Cuban Rumba, Argentinian Tango and Martinique Beguine—'didn't take' in Sydney, 'mainly' because the 'majority of orchestras' were unable to 'play suitable music' and struggled to master the Latin beat. By 1934, Russell noted a retreat into 'old time' music. 'Modern dancing' had lost its 'hold on the general public', he regretted. 'Shades of grandmother' appeared when orchestras struck up 'Daisy Daisy' and 'After the Ball is Over'. 'Old fogey' dances—the Foxtrot and waltz—dominated palladium floors.[25]

'Doldrums' was how music historian Andrew Bisset described the Australian music scene in the 1930s. Reviews of local jazz bands captured a mood of disappointment and feelings of inadequacy, feeding a syndrome eventually known as the cultural cringe. 'Incompetent' bandleaders playing 'below standard', sniped one critic. 'Too many dance bands' had 'mechanical rhythm and no swing', grumbled another. Commentators wondered if 'Imported Bands' would 'Boost Biz'? A music reporter grilled a visiting American conductor Ted Henkel about the popularity of 'colored bands'. Was it true they had worn out their novelty? Henkel replied in the negative; nothing could replace the 'real thing'.[26]

Even the *Australian Women's Weekly*, somewhat belatedly, recognised Swing as the 'musical fashion of the hour', listing America's 'swing maestros': Cab Calloway, Fats Waller, Benny Carter, Chick Webb, Duke Ellington. 'The new rage goes right back to the first principles of Negro music.'[27] Such reports amplified the niggling feeling that Australian musical culture was lagging behind the rest of the modern world. News of Duke Ellington's knock-out 1933 tour of England underscored the meagre musical consolations of being more British than the British. Reports detailed the enthusiasm of the Prince of Wales and rapturous superlatives from the 'musical intelligentsia'.[28]

It wasn't just music. The heavy hand of government paternalism obstructed other branches of modernism as officious upholders of taste began confidently exercising their powers. With a palpable sense of loss, Melbourne artist Alister Kershaw recalled the day authorities shut down Gino Nibbi's Leonardo Art Shop, the only bookstore stocking the works of the European avant-garde. 'No singing religious ever displayed more zeal than the Australian authorities when it came to looking after the moral well-being of their little chicks,' he lamented.[29] In the late 1930s, German Bauhaus photographer Wolfgang Sievers landed in Melbourne. 'Shocking' was his summation of the visual arts scene. 'I just couldn't grasp how backward it was. It was all mushy gumtrees and sentimental portraits.'[30] From artist Norman Lindsay to novelist Katharine Susannah Pritchard, the term 'cultural backwater' inflected debates about censorship and the arts.[31]

In 1935, Jim Russell drew an ink sketch for *Australian Music Maker and Dance Band News* that captured his longing for a world beyond the cultural quarantine. It showed a young White male musician seated beside his violin and saxophone, his chin resting in his palm, thinking. His feet were firmly planted on the island continent of 'Australia' but his head burst with the music of the world—'Dixie', 'Africa', 'Spain', 'America', 'England'. 'Little Man, What Now?' read the caption.[32] He could, like his friend and colleague Gayne Dexter, chase the action abroad and escape the country. Or he could crank up his scratchy phonographs and wonder.

LITTLE MAN, WHAT NOW?

'Little Man, What Now?' Ink artist and modern dance aficionado Jim Russell imagines the musical world beyond the cultural quarantine. (*Australian Music Maker and Dance Band News*)

42
BAGGING THE CAT

In 1949, Eugene Goossens, a British composer brought to Australia to lead the Sydney Symphony Orchestra, listed the many ways a 'ban on overseas players affects music here':

> a) The incontestable and absolute dearth of first-class Australian symphonic material.
> b) The shaky calibre of personnel ... which makes rehearsals and performances of anything but the most hackneyed works a major and hazardous adventure.
> c) A past heritage of mediocre teaching ... with a few notable exceptions, a generation of players lacking style and technical brilliance.
> d) The inability of many players ... to pass even the most elementary sight reading and oral tests.
> e) The almost total lack of first-class replacements for at least three of our orchestras.

His conclusions were brutal: 'A country musically strangled by reaction and narrow chauvinism ... In the cultural sense, Australia has experienced a major setback in her development.'[1]

Goossens soon suffered a setback of a personal nature. After nine years of turning Sydney audiences onto the modernist symphonies of

Stravinsky, Bartok, Ravel and Debussy, he was famously hounded out of the country, his reputation in tatters. His exit came courtesy of a sex scandal aided and abetted by a tabloid newspaper and a NSW vice squad detective fearful that 'foreigners'—even people with 'foreign'-sounding names—and their deviant ideas would destroy Australian society.[2]

Compelling parallels linked Eugene Goossens and Sonny Clay. Two musicians steeped in the traditions of modernism. A paying audience hungry for their offerings. An alliance of bureaucrats and organisations panicked by the degenerative effects of cosmopolitanism. A moral scandal aiming to destroy the careers and reputations of the targets.

These were not the only examples. In 1937 the Weinstraubs Syncopators, a dance and cabaret act popular in Weimar Berlin, arrived in Australia via Russia and Shanghai, some of the thousands of German Jewish refugees fleeing Nazism. Unusually, their contract at a high-end Italian restaurant had been approved directly by the minister, circumventing union rules.[3]

In June 1940, the Commonwealth Investigation Branch interned three of the six musicians as 'enemy aliens' without charge, without explanation. The musicians had no clue that a mysterious English businessman had appeared at a Paddington police station, accusing them of spying for the German army during their Russian tour. Or that days later, police received an anonymous letter that read: 'Looking for spies? Try the Weinstraubs.' Without investigating the allegations, authorities detained the musicians for fifteen months.[4]

When a review panel finally released bandleader John Kay, the Musicians' Union enlisted the help of the *Truth*, the Returned Soldiers' League and Investigation Branch to ensure he was not re-employed. The Syncopators were 'Nazis of the Nazi-ists', claimed a rival bandleader. Defeated, Kay accepted work as a mechanic.[5]

This shadowy alliance wielded significant power but it was *not* absolute—especially once British Singapore fell to the Japanese army in 1942 and turned Australia's policy agenda upside down. Fearing invasion, Prime Minister John Curtin looked to the United States for military support and, after initially balking, accepted that African American troops were a non-negotiable part of one million GIs who would help defend White Australia.[6]

The outsized impact of one servicemen's club in a shabby corner of Sydney—the Booker T Washington Club—offered a glimpse, writ small, into the disjunction between what the public desired and what policy-makers believed was best for them.

As Pansy Hickey, a seventeen-year-old textile worker from Redfern, told it, she usually socialised at the Aboriginal dance on Oxford Street, where an accordion and piano paced attendees through the 'old fashioned dances'. One night, she and several girlfriends learned of a dance at the Black servicemen's club in nearby Albion Street, so wrangled fake over-eighteen identification cards and wandered into the decrepit grandeur of the Booker T Washington Club. More than likely, she had never heard of the Great Educator Booker T Washington, although she would come to associate his name less with thrift and discipline and more the swinging hot rhythms of the 29th Quartermaster Band.[7]

'Oh! It was so exciting,' she later said, recalling the 'thrill' of learning to Jitterbug—'and I can say that we caught onto it really quick.' Unlike the 'old-fashioned' dances, the Jitterbug had no 'correct' steps, each American dance partner revealing a 'new and different' way to combine a shuffle, twist and rocking push and pull.[8]

For Pansy Hickey, each lesson reified a small yet profoundly modern idea: there was no rule which bound her to the trademarked steps of the ballroom masters. Each time a dancer added something of themselves, they staked a claim in its artistic conception. In doing so, they renegotiated the cultural contract, moving away from a relationship based on mastery and obedience to one approaching equality and democracy.

Pansy Hickey was a Wonnarua woman whose mother had been raised in a mission home, despatched to Cootamundra Girls' Home and consigned to domestic service. Pansy had been saved from this fate, her mother outmanoeuvring the Aboriginal Protection Board, keeping Pansy close to her culture and kinfolk. Still, Pansy survived on the margins of White society; her brother, a soldier, was barred from entering hotels 'for a drink with his army mates'. But at the Booker T Club, she sat at the centre of the world. The Black servicemen spoke with a poetic 'jive', applying it 'fluently' and sometimes romantically: 'They'd tell you you had eyes that looked like the stars.' They'd 'treat you as if you were very special'.

'They said lovely words of endearment that the Australian man didn't ... That in itself was a really great experience.' 'None of us girls had seen anything like it,' added her friend, Christine Hinton. 'It was unreal ... very, very beautiful.'[9]

Pansy, too, felt the Black GIs' pain when US military police summarily executed a Black soldier for a mild rule infraction. She tested her spirit of defiance, bluntly telling the White men who hovered outside the club that the unfairness of segregated facilities did not begin when they were denied entry.[10]

Over the coming decades, Pansy Hickey worked in Aboriginal health, education, theatre, welfare, culture and heritage. She fought discrimination and championed cultural knowledge, demanding Whites understand social reality through Aboriginal eyes. She was part of a wave of thinkers and activists who brought political force to Indigeneity and shifted the national conversation.[11]

When the 29th Quartermaster Band left for North Queensland, a local ensemble headed by Jim Somerville secured the spot on the dais—and expanded his musical horizons. Granted the 'freedom' to move beyond sheet music, to 'improvise', 'extend' and exaggerate, he played the blues at a 'fast clip' and 'Goodnight Sweetheart' 'very slow'. 'Certainly learnt a lot of things,' he mused.[12]

Merv Acheson, a sax player in Giles O'Sullivan's band, also spent 'some of the most musically rewarding nights' of his life at the Booker T Club. The fourteen-piece was a mix of Australian civilians and US servicemen: a Kansas City drummer direct from the musical crossroads at 18th and Vine, a trumpeter fresh from the Erskine Hawkins Orchestra at the Harlem Savoy. The club was a 'phenomenon', embodying 'all that was best in the music world', Acheson recalled. Often jam sessions at a harbour headland continued till dawn.[13]

A group of rough-edged adolescents from the neighbourhood, searching for a style to match their not-yet-fully-articulated modern rebellion, also gravitated to the Booker T Club. As several recalled in oral histories, they dedicated their leisure time to 'fraternising with the Negroes', showing up at the soldiers' preferred milk bars and barbershops to study as 'minutely as possible' their words, their walk, their army issue V discs and fashion.[14]

'Sydney's jitterbuggers were cutting the rug and bagging the cat to some purpose ... Some solid jive was going on,' a Darlinghurst kid in a brightly coloured, oversized zoot suit told a news reporter.[15] 'The idea that you could waste clothing' was like a 'kind of slap in the face to the powers that be', as if war-time rationing was someone else's problem, one Sydney zoot suiter later explained. Completing the performance was the rolling gait of the stroll—the component parts of an emergent subculture that, by some inexplicable lexical twist, assumed the name Bodgies and Widgies.[16]

The Booker T Club drew a suite of other Sydneysiders: local families, Australian soldiers, church ministers, aspiring actors and artists, and a mix of Aboriginal, Islander and White women, some assisting Red Cross administrators to organise their library and discussion programs. The lively atmosphere awoke one White volunteer to the cultivated dullness of Sydney life and the deadening hand of racial exclusion policies.[17]

Ideas once deemed heretical to White Australia entered the public discourse. At the New Theatre, a grassroots community playhouse, the club's director inaugurated a discussion about the contours of Black politics. Less formally, Black soldiers mixed with local artists at the Workers' Art Club. Soon after, the Sydney chapter of the Communist Party denounced racist dogma in the labour movement as 'the divide and rule policy of capitalism'. Even mainstream newspapers praised America's 'progressive' 'mingling of nationalities'. Or criticised the 'southern' practice of Jim Crow segregation. Or sought Black soldiers' views on the 1943 Harlem riots. Or introduced readers to the ideas of Frederick Douglass and Booker T Washington.[18]

The reception surprised both Black and White Americans. Before landing, White officers had warned Black troops to 'watch their step' because White Australians were 'dead against Negroes'. But to their collective astonishment, sections of the community—by no means all—confounded this perception. The spirit of fellowship baffled one US Army Colonel who found it 'paradoxical that the American Negro troops' had been received so warmly 'by outspoken advocates of "white supremacy"'.[19]

Still, die-hard defenders of White Australia lobbied strongly to stir moral panic, reprising a familiar litany of threats to White womanhood.

This time, wartime censorship dimmed their voices, promoting US–Australian unity over racial division.[20]

When US troops left Sydney in 1944, the Musicians' Union prohibition on 'colored' members and the government's 'character test' on Black performers remained. Yet Australia's brush with Black America had irrevocably altered the conversation. In the wake of the Nazi holocaust, the public recoiled from the language of eugenics and White supremacy. The privileging of Whiteness tested Cold War debates about Australia as a paragon of democracy, justice and equality. The idea that cultural anaemia was the price of racial homogeny gained traction. Commentators began skewering the narrow membership qualifications of the Musicians' Union. In the late 1940s, the government revisited its narrow British approach to immigration, accepting all Europeans as 'White', although it clung to the White Australia policy until 1973.[21]

In 1949 jazz musician and promoter Graeme Bell sneaked 65-year-old star trumpeter Rex Stewart into the country, 'forgetting' to mention his racial designation. Rapturous crowds greeted Stewart wherever he played. For years, he had toured with Ivy Anderson in the Duke Ellington Orchestra so was under no illusion about the power of the nation's gatekeepers—although few others remembered the fate of a travelling jazz orchestra in the battle between cosmopolitan moderns and crusading Anglo-Saxonists. Instead, audiences consumed and emulated—even mimicked and appropriated—a type of modernity fashioned by African America, as if they were the first to discover it.[22]

An Australian strain of White supremacy never disappeared. It was and remains a stubborn thread in the national tapestry—witnessed in unnecessarily cruel and dehumanising border policies, ignored calls for Indigenous restitution, White victimhood, a distorted warrior code among sections of the armed forces and the murderous violence of self-appointed White crusaders. But other voices have grown louder, promulgating new ideas, new ways to imagine and create a modern world.

In 1954, the Musicians' Union finally revoked their 'no colored' rule. A wave of tours by leading Black performers soon followed: Louis Armstrong, Ella Fitzgerald, Harry Belafonte, Nat King Cole, Paul Robeson,

Sammy Davis Jr, Chuck Berry, Little Richard and Chicago bluesman Big Joe Turner.[23] Their licks, shouts and swagger inspired the first generation of Australian rock and rollers, who copied, borrowed, even stole, cultural forms to tout themselves as 'originals'. The surge of creative energy it unleashed marked the starting point for most histories of Australian popular music. Racial and ethnic diversity and the free circulation of ideas, it transpired, fostered a vibrant national culture. Who ever would have thought it?

ACKNOWLEDGEMENTS

THIS PROJECT BEGAN with a question, formulated after watching *Red, White and Blues*, Mike Figgis' documentary about the transmission of the American blues to Britain and its re-importation back to the US. (Figgis' answer: in the years after World War II, a steady stream of Black rhythm and blues combinations came to the United Kingdom to entertain African American troops and a few local kids got wind of it.) How then, I wondered, did Australia, a country once synonymous with Whiteness, come to get the blues? In my search for answers, I stumbled upon Sam Hood's shot of the Sonny Clay Orchestra arriving at Circular Quay, the image forming the basis of my research, first as an essay, then article, thesis and now, a book. At the time, I never expected to stumble into political territory.

I am deeply indebted to the many people who assisted me on this journey. From the outset, Shane White, professor of US history at the University of Sydney, supported every phase of the project, closely reading each iteration. His steady encouragement has been invaluable, inspiring me to be a better historian and writer. I thank John O'Brien for his sharp and incisive comments and suggestions on the early drafts of this book. His expertise in screenwriting helped draw out the narrative. I also thank historians Richard Waterhouse and David Goodman for critiquing early versions of the project.

The research process brought me into contact with several genealogists and keepers of family knowledge who proved to be indispensable.

Many thanks to Jeffrey Fitzsimmons, genealogist of the Langdon clan, who helped me crack the riddle of Edna Langdon's identity. He shared family records and stories—and in response to my questions, spent many hours trawling through marriage indexes. For his enthusiasm and interest, I am deeply appreciative.

I had the enormous pleasure of speaking to several Indigenous elders, particularly from Dunghutti country, whose insights helped me piece together a picture of Aboriginal Sydney in the 1920s. I thank Uncle Bob Smith, Janet Smith, Sharin Gill, Jason Parkes, Dorsey Smith, Darius Neven and Veronica Neven for their generosity and knowledge. Special thanks to Aunty Katharine Boreham for her guidance and wisdom. I am also indebted to members of the La Perouse Land Council and community for their support, especially Chris Ingrey, Stacey Foster, Anne Martin and Dr Shayne Williams.

I am also indebted to the keepers of numerous archives. The good people at the Hogan Jazz Archive at Tulane University, Louisiana, made electronically available the handwritten notes of John Bentley's interview with Sonny Clay and the tapes of these interviews (after painstakingly restoring them). Thanks to Lori Schexnayder, Nicole Shibata and Dr Bruce Raeburn. Warm thanks to Chuck Haddix at the Marr Sound Archive at the University of Missouri, Kansas City, who directed me to Frank Driggs' interview with Leo Davis. In both instances, these oral histories exist because a small army of jazz enthusiasts had the foresight to interview a generation of African American performing artists. These researchers undertook this task without institutional support or sanction.

Staff and associates of the Victoria Police Museum Archive in Melbourne were of invaluable assistance. My gratitude to Caroline Oxley for locating and copying the service records of various police officers. My conversation with former detective and police historian Ralph Stavely was most illuminating. I also thank independent jazz historian Bill Egan who generously shared his research on Ivie Anderson and Willie Covan. Gratitude to Claudia Taranto at Radio National who tracked down the interview with Pansy Hickey—and Paula O'Connell who dug up what seems to be the only surviving image of Cecil Trevelyan, plus many details about his double life.

My appreciation extends to the librarians at the State Library of New South Wales who permitted me to photograph the original newspapers—although some proved too fragile. Luckily the scanned versions on Trove, while less detailed, provided an alternative. Over the course of this research, I benefited from the assistance of kind and helpful archivists and librarians at the National Archive of Australia, the National Library of Australia, the State Library Victoria, the Public Record Office of Victoria, the NSW State Archives and the many branches of the New York Public Library. Thanks also to the staff at the University of Sydney Library, particularly Rena McGrogan who arranged many inter-library loans.

My gratitude, too, to my colleagues in the Department of History at the University of Sydney, particularly Sophie Loy-Wilson for her insights into the tabloid preoccupation with city slums. In one-to-one meetings and group seminars, I valued the support, insights and ideas offered by Penny Russell, Kirsten McKenzie, Frances Clarke, Thomas Adams, Glenda Sluga, Richard White, Iain McCalman, Mark McKenna, Stephen Robertson, Barbara Caine, Michael McDonald, Andrew Fitzmaurice and Alison Bashford.

Several institutions financially supported this project. I am grateful to awards granted by the University of Sydney's Postgraduate Research Support Scheme as well as an essay prize offered by the NSW History Council. Later, a grant from the Literature Board of the Australia Council provided essential funding. Simply put: this book would not have been possible without their valuable assistance.

It's been a great pleasure to work with the crew at Melbourne University Publishing, particularly Louise Stirling, Duncan Fardon, Nathan Hollier, and the freelance editor Meaghan Amor, proofreader Eugenie Baulch and typesetter Pat Cannon. I have appreciated the feedback from the anonymous readers and the creativity and flair of the design and editorial teams.

Thanks to my yoga teachers, particularly my first teacher Eve Grzybowski, who literally straighten my spine, enabling me to endure long hours in the archive and at the computer. And most recently Paul Frechtling, who keeps encouraging me to test my limits.

I wish to thank my father Brendan, sister Paula and dear friend Veechi Stuart for their love, encouragement, wisdom and patience. Of course, the memory of my most literary mother, Mary, is never far away. And you, too, Breda. And finally, I thank my beloved family for keeping me grounded and inspired (and organising the bibliography as the deadline ticked closer): to my darling husband David and dearest daughters, Jasmine and Indigo. I will try not to bring up matters of history after seven o'clock.

BIBLIOGRAPHY

Manuscript Sources

Australia

National Archive of Australia, Canberra and Melbourne (NAA)
National Library of Australia Manuscript Collection, Canberra (NLA)
Noel Butlin Archives Centre, ANU, Canberra (NBAC)
NSW State Archives
Public Record Office of Victoria, Melbourne (PROV)
Registry of Births, Deaths and Marriages, Perth, Western Australia
Victoria Police Museum Archive, Melbourne (VPMA)

United States

Hogan Jazz Archive, Tulane University, Louisiana
Marr Sound Archive, University of Missouri, Kansas City
Schomburg Center for Research in Black Culture, New York Public Library, New York

Digital

A History of Aboriginal Sydney, www.historyofaboriginalsydney.edu.au
Ancestry.com
Australasian Legal Information Institute, UTS and UNSW Faculty of Law, www.austlii.edu.au/
Australian Broadcasting Corporation, www.abc.net.au/radionational
Australian Bureau of Statistics, abs.gov.au
Australian Dictionary of Biography, National Centre of Biography, Australian National University, adb.anu.edu.au/
Colonial Frontier Massacres, Australia, 1780–1930, c21ch.newcastle.edu.au/colonialmassacres/map
Dictionary of Sydney, dictionaryofsydney.org
Google Maps, google.com, maps.google.com.au/
Hansard, Parliament of Victoria, parliament.vic.gov.au
Internet Movie Database, IMDb, Amazon.com, www.imdb.com
The Yorta Yorta Dictionary App, yorta-yorta.wcclp.com.au

Periodicals and Newspapers, Australia

Advance! Australia
Advertiser (Adelaide, SA)
Advocate (Burnie, Tasmania)
Age (Melbourne, Victoria)
Albany Evening Herald
Argus (Melbourne, Victoria)
Armidale Chronicle
Armidale Express
Army News
Arrow
Australasian
Australian Aborigines Advocate (Sydney, NSW)
Australian Dance Band News (Sydney, NSW)
Australian Melody Maker and Dance Band News (Sydney, NSW)
Australian Women's Weekly (Sydney, NSW)
Australian Worker (Sydney, NSW)
Ballarat Courier (Victoria)
Barrier Daily Truth (Broken Hill, NSW)
Barrier Miner (Broken Hill, NSW)
Beaudesert Times (Queensland)
Beckett's Budget (Sydney, NSW)
Brisbane Courier (Queensland)
Brisbane Telegraph (Queensland)
Bulletin (Sydney, NSW)
Call News-Pictorial (Perth, WA)
Canberra Times (ACT)
Catholic Press (Sydney, NSW)
Chronicle (Adelaide, SA)
Country Life Stock and Station Journal (Sydney, NSW)
Cumberland Argus (Parramatta, NSW)
Daily Guardian (Sydney, NSW)
Daily Herald (Adelaide, SA)
Daily News (Perth, WA)
Daily Telegraph (Sydney, NSW)
Darwin Northern Standard (NT)
Dungog Chronicle (NSW)
Evening News (Sydney, NSW)
Everyones Magazine (Sydney, NSW)
Examiner (Launceston, Tasmania)
Farmer and Settler (Moree, NSW)
Fitzroy City Press
Geelong Advertiser (Victoria)
Glen Innes Examiner (NSW)
Gundagai Independent (NSW)
Herald (Melbourne, Victoria)
Horsham Times (Victoria)
Kiama Independent and Shoalhaven Advertiser (NSW)
Kilmore Free Press (Victoria)

Labor Call (Melbourne, Victoria)
Labor Daily (Sydney, NSW)
Lachlander and Condobolin and Western Districts Recorder (NSW)
Lang Lang Guardian (Victoria)
Law Institute Journal of Victoria (Melbourne, Victoria)
Leader (Melbourne, Victoria)
League (Melbourne, Victoria)
Mail (Adelaide, SA)
Mankind (Sydney, NSW)
Mercury (Tasmania)
Methodist Spectator (Melbourne, Victoria)
Moora Herald and Midland Districts Advocate (WA)
Morning Bulletin (Rockhampton, Queensland)
Morning Post (Cairns, Queensland)
Mount Alexander Mail (Castlemaine, Victoria)
National Advocate (Bathurst, NSW)
Newcastle Morning Herald (NSW)
New South Wales Police Gazette and Weekly Record of Crime (Sydney, NSW)
New Triad (Sydney, NSW)
North Western Courier (Narrabri, NSW)
Northern Standard (Darwin, NT)
Northern Territory Times and Gazette (Darwin, NT)
Perth Call (WA)
Prahran Telegraph (Melbourne, Victoria)
Professional Musician (Melbourne, Victoria)
Queanbeyan Age (ACT)
Queensland Times (Ipswich, Queensland)
Queenslander (Brisbane, Queensland)
Realm (Melbourne, Victoria)
Recorder (Port Pirie, SA)
Referee (Sydney, NSW)
Register (Adelaide)
Reveille (Sydney, NSW)
Singleton Argus (NSW)
Smith's Weekly (Sydney, NSW)
South Coast Times and Wollongong Argus (NSW)
Sport (Adelaide, SA)
Sun (Sydney, NSW)
Sunday Times (Perth, WA)
Sunraysia Daily (Mildura, Victoria)
Sydney Mail (NSW)
Sydney Morning Herald (NSW)
Table Talk (Melbourne, Victoria)
Townsville Daily Bulletin (Queensland)
Tribune (Sydney, NSW)
Truth (Melbourne, Victoria)
Truth (Perth, WA)
Truth (Sydney, NSW)
Undergrowth: A Magazine of Youth and Ideals (Sydney, NSW)

Uralla Times (NSW)
Victoria Police Gazette (Melbourne, Victoria)
Vision: A Literary Quarterly (Sydney, NSW)
Voice of the North (Newcastle, NSW)
Week (Brisbane, Queensland)
Weekly Times (Melbourne, Victoria)
Werribee Shire Banner (Victoria)
West Australian (Perth, WA)
Western Argus (Kalgoorie, WA)
Western Mail (Perth, WA)
Western Star and Roma Advertiser (Toowoomba, Queensland)

Periodicals and Newspapers, USA
Afro-American
Arizona Republican
Arizona Sentinel
Atlanta Constitution
Atlanta Daily World
Atlantic
Billboard
Bisbee Daily Review
Bisbee Herald
Brenham Banner
Brooklyn Daily Eagle
California Eagle
Chicago Daily Tribune
Chicago Defender
Corsicana Daily News
Crisis
Daily News
Dallas Daily Times Herald
Dallas Morning News
Denison Review
Dial
Down Beat
El Paso Herald
El Paso Times
Eugene Guard
Exhibitors Herald
Exhibitors Trade Review
Film Daily
Fort Worth Record
Fort Worth Telegram
Gaffney Ledger
Hamilton Ohio Journal News
Houston Post
Jazzfinder
Jazz Monthly
Jazz Research
Kansas City Star

Kingsport Times
La Grande Observer
Lead Daily Call
Liberty
Literary Digest
Logansport Pharos-Tribune
Los Angeles Evening Express
Los Angeles Record
Los Angeles Times
Melody
Minneapolis Star
Morning News
Motion Picture Magazine
Musical Quarterly
Nation
New Journal and Guide
New York Age
New York Sun
New York Times
New York Times Book Review and Magazine
New York Tribune
Oakland Tribune
Ogden Standard-Examiner
Philadelphia Tribune
Phoenix Tribune
Photoplay
Pittsburgh Courier
Pittsburgh Press
Post-Crescent
Radio Digest
San Bernardino County
San Francisco Chronicle
Santa Rosa Republican
Screenland
Seattle Daily Times
SS Stewarts Banjo and Guitar Journal
Star-Telegram
St Louis Globe Democrat
Sunset Magazine
Texan American
Topeka Plaindealer
Twin City Daily Sentinel
Urbana Daily Courier
Vanity Fair
Variety
Wall Street Journal
Washington Herald
Washington Post
Washington Times

Other Periodicals and Newspapers

Freeman's Journal (UK)

Irish News and Belfast Morning News (UK)

Manawatu Standard (NZ)

Montreal Gazette (Canada)

Northern Whig (UK)

Shields Daily Gazette (Tyne and Wear, UK)

Contemporary Material, Australia

——Annual Report 1926, Travellers' Aid Society of Victoria (Melbourne: The Society, A1927).

——Gymnastic Circus and Young Men's Christian Association of Melbourne, 'Official Souvenir Programme of the Second Annual Gymnastic Circus, December 6th, 1924 at 8 p.m.', (Melbourne: The Federated Press, 1924).

——*Miss Australia: A Quarterly Magazine* (Sydney), September 1926.

——Parliament of the Commonwealth of Australia: Report of the Royal Commission on the Moving Picture Industry in Australia (Canberra: Government Printer, 1928).

Atkinson, Meredith, *Capital and Labour: Co-operation or Class War?* (Sydney: Worker Education Association, 1918): 7.

Atkinson, Meredith, *The New Social Order: A Study of Post-War Reconstruction* (Sydney, NSW: Workers' Educational Association of Australia, 1919).

Bean, C.E.W., *The Story of Anzacs: An Historical Account of the Part Taken by Australia and New Zealand in the Great War, from the Outbreak in August 1914 until the Evacuation of Gallipoli in December 1915* (Melbourne: James Ingram and Sons, 1917).

Booth, Angela, *Voluntary Sterilization for Human Betterment* (Melbourne: Eugenics Society of Victoria, 1940).

Booth, James et al., *Teaching of Sex Hygiene: Report of a Conference Organized by the Workers' Educational Association of New South Wales, Sydney University, 1916* (Sydney: Burrows, 1917).

Booth, Mrs James, *The Payment of Women's Work* (Adelaide: A.E. Booth, 1916).

Booth, Mrs James, *Prostitution* (Sydney: William Applegate Gullick, Government Printer, 1917).

Booth, Mrs James et al., *The Prophylaxis of Venereal Disease: A Reply to Sir James Barrett* (Melbourne: Association to Combat the Social Evil, 1910).

Buley, E.C., *Glorious Deeds of Australasians in the Great War* (London: Andrew Melrose, 1916).

Gibson, N., *Jungle Justice: Victorian Police Scandals Exposed* (Melbourne: self-published, 1933).

Gurkha, N., *Graft: Startling Disclosures of Corruption into the Victorian Police Force* (Melbourne: self-published, 1930).

Hancock, Keith, *Australia* (London: Ernest Benn, 1930).

Hughes, W.M., *A Splendid Adventure: A Review of Empire Relations Within and Without the Commonwealth of Britannic Nations* (London: Ernest Benn Limited, 1929).

Hurley, Frank, *The Diaries of Frank Hurley, 1912–1941* (London; New York: Anthem Press, 2011).

Jerger, Charles, *Does Australia Stand for This?: The Case of Father Jerger* (Sydney: 1920).

Jones, William Ernest, *Report on Mental Deficiency in the Commonwealth of Australia* (Canberra: H.J. Green, Government Printer, 1929).

Lindsay, Jack, *Dionysos: Nietzsche Contra Nietzsche, An Essay in Lyrical Philosophy* (London: Fanfrolico Press, 1928).
Mackenzie, Compton, *Gallipoli Memories* (London: Cassell, 1929).
Monckton, J.B., *The Shuttle of Life* (London: Hutchinson & Co., 1928).
Murphy, 'Dryblower', *This Bit of the World Belongs to Us* (Melbourne: Allan & Co., 1914).
Nixon, Pamela, The Integration of a Half-Caste Community at La Perouse, N.S.W., Master's Thesis, University of Sydney, 1948.
Noble, Ralph A., 'Some Observations on the Treatment of the Feeble-Minded in Great Britain and America', *Medical Journal of Australia*, 12 July 1924.
Pearson, Charles, *National Life and Character: A Forecast* (London: Macmillan and Co., 1894).
Schuler, Phillip F.E., *Australia in Arms: A Narrative of the Australasian Imperial Force and Their Achievement at Anzac* (London: TF Unwin, 1916).
Scott, Ernest, *Australia during the War* (Sydney: Angus and Robertson, 1937).
Stewart, Jane A., 'Men of Today: William Morris Hughes', *Journal of Education*, 93:3, 20 January 1921.
Trevelyan, Cecil, *Fighting at the Dardanelles* (music) (Adelaide: Cawthorne, 1915).
Trevelyan, Cecil and Atterton, A.L., *Won't You Take a Gun?* (music) (Adelaide: Cawthorne, 1917).
Walsh, Phil K., *The Birth of White Australia* (1928), National Film and Sound Archive, Canberra.
Ward, Russel, *Australian Legend* (Melbourne: Oxford University Press, 1958).

Contemporary Writings, USA

——'Imperial Wizard Hiram Wesley Evans', *Texas One Hundred Per Cent American*, 22 February 1924: 1.
Adams, Brooks, *The Law of Civilization and Decay: An Essay on History* (New York: Macmillan, 1896).
Becker, H.S., 'The Professional Dance Musician and His Audience', *The American Journal of Sociology*, 57:2, 1951.
Bingham, Theodore A., *The Girl That Disappear: The Real Facts about the White Slave Trade* (Boston: R.G. Badger, 1911).
Bond, Max, *The Negro in Los Angeles* (San Francisco: R and E Research Associates, 1972).
Bowen, Louise de Koven, *The Public Dance Halls of Chicago* (Chicago: The Juvenile Protective Association of Chicago, 1917).
Curtis, Natalie, *Songs and Tales from the Dark Continent* (New York: G. Schirmer, 1920).
Dodge, Roger Pryor, *Hot Jazz and Jazz Dance* (New York: Oxford University Press, 1995).
Estabrook, Arthur H., *The Jukes in 1915* (District of Columbia: Carnegie Institution of Washington, 1916).
Evans, Hiram Wesley, *The Menace of Modern Immigration*, Bridwell Library, Special Collection: 17.
Goddard, Henry, *The Kallikak Family: A Study in the Heredity of Feeblemindedness* (New York: Macmillan, 1919).
Gordon, Leon, *White Cargo: A Play of the Primitive* (Boston: The Four Seas Company, 1925).
Gordon, Taylor, *Born to Be* (Seattle: University of Washington Press, 1975).
Grant, Madison, *The Passing of the Great Race: Or the Racial Basis of European History* (New York: C. Scribner's Sons, 1923).

Hamilton, Mary E., *The Policewoman: Her Service and Ideals* (New York: Frederick A. Stokes Co., 1924).
Hughes, Langston, 'The Negro Artist and the Racial Mountain', *Nation*, June 1926 cited in Karl Koenig, *Jazz in Print (1856–1929): An Anthology of Selected Early Readings in Jazz History* (Hillsdale, NY: Pendragon Press, 2002).
Hughes, Langston, 'The Folks at Home', *Esquire Magazine*, May 1934.
Hughes, Langston, *I Wonder as I Wander* (New York: Wang and Hill, 1964).
Hurston, Zora Neale, 'How It Feels to Be Colored Me', *The World Tomorrow* (May 1928).
Jordan, David Starr, *The Human Harvest: A Study of the Decay of Races through the Survival of the Unfit* (New York: Garland Pub., 1972 [c. 1907]).
Knowlton, Don, 'The Anatomy of Jazz', *Harper's*, March 1926.
Laubenstien, Paul Fritz, 'Jazz-Debit and Credit', *Musical Quarterly*, October 1928.
Lindsay, Vachel, *The Congo and Other Poems* (New York: The Macmillan Company, 1914).
Locke, Alain, *Race Contacts and Interracial Relations: Lectures of the Theory and Practice of Race* (Washington, DC: Howard University Press, 1916).
Locke, Alain, *The New Negro* (New York: Athenaeum, 1968 [c. 1925]).
McKay, Claude, 'Soviet Russia and the Negro', *Crisis*, January 1924.
Muse, Clarence, *The Dilemma of the Negro Actor* (Los Angeles: 1934).
Nott, Josiah et al., *Types of Mankind* (Philadelphia: Lippincott, Grambo & Co., 1854).
Roosevelt, Theodore, *American Ideals* (New York: G.F. Putman & Sons, 1898).
Sanger, Margaret, *Woman and the New Race* (New York: Brentano's, 1920).
Stoddard, Lothrop, 'White Australia—The Low-Pressure Center of the Globe', *Liberty*, May 1928.
Stoddard, Lothrop, *The Rising Tide of Color against White World-Supremacy* (New York: C. Scribner's Sons, 1921).
Stoddard, Lothrop, *The Revolt against Civilization: The Menace of the Under Man* (London: Chapman & Hall, 1922).
Stringham, Edwin J., '"Jazz" An Educational Problem', *Musical Quarterly*, April 1926.
Teasdale, Howard, Report and Recommendations of the Wisconsin Legislative Committee to Investigate the White Slave Traffic and Kindred Subjects (Democrat Printing Company, 1914).
Wells, Ida B., *Crusade for Justice: The Autobiography of Ida B. Wells* (Chicago: University of Chicago, 1972).
Young, Paul Campbell, 'Hypnotism', *Psychological Bulletin*, 23:1, 1926.
Young, Paul Campbell, 'A General Overview of the Literature on Hypnotism', *Psychological Bulletin*, 24, 1927.

Contemporary Writings, Britain

Committee on the Employment of Policewomen, Great Britain, Report of the Departmental Committee on the Employment of Policewomen (London: HMSO, 1924).
D'esterre, Neville, 'A Syncopated Apology (Part I)', *British Musician*, September 1928.
Frazer, Sir James George, *The Golden Bough: A Study in Magic and Religion* (abridged edition) (New York: The Macmillan Company, 1922).
Lawrence, D.H., *Kangaroo* (Cambridge: Cambridge University Press, 1994 [c. 1922]).
Lawrence, D.H. and Aldington, R., *The Spirit of Place: An Anthology Compiled from the Prose of D.H. Lawrence* (London: W. Heinemann, 1935).
Mackirdy, Olive Christian Malvery, *The White Slave Market* (London: S. Paul, 1912).

McDougall, William, *National Welfare and National Decay* (London: Methuen, 1921).

Trotter, W., *Instincts of the Herd in War and Peace* (London: T.F. Unwin Ltd, 1921).

Walker, Hugh, *The Literature of the Victorian Era* (Cambridge: Cambridge University Press, 1921).

Other Contemporary Writings

Gorky, Maxim, 'On the Music of the Degenerate', *Pravda*, 18 April 1928.

Memoirs and Oral Histories, Australia

Ball, W.M., *Intermittent Diplomat* (Melbourne: Melbourne University Press, 1988).

Buggy, Hugh, *The Real John Wren* (Camberwell, Vic: Widescope, 1977).

Carlyon, Norman D., *I Remember Blamey* (Melbourne: Macmillan, 1980).

Carlyon, Norman D., *The Flight of Steps* (Melbourne: N.D. Carlyon, 1986).

Kershaw, Alister, *Heydays: Memories and Glimpses of Melbourne Bohemia 1937–47* (North Ryde: Angus & Robertson, 1991).

Pearce, Marcella, *Melbourne Trade Hall Memories* (Melbourne: Trades Hall Council, 1997).

Pratt, Mel, *Journalism in the Thirties* (transcript of sound recording), Mel Pratt Collection, 1976, NLA ORAL TRC 121/85.

'The Merv Acheson Story', *Jazz Magazine*, March/April, 1982 and Summer/Autumn, 1986.

Tucker, Margaret, *If Everyone Cared: Autobiography of Margaret Tucker* (Sydney: Ure Smith, 1977).

Memoirs and Oral Histories, USA

Bentley, John, 'Sonny Clay: A Veritable Giant—Part 1', *Jazz Research*, November/December 1962.

Bentley, John, 'Sonny Clay: A Veritable Giant—Part 2', *Jazz Research*, January/February 1963.

Bentley, John and Miller, Ralph W., 'West Coast Jazz in the 1920s', *Jazz Monthly*, May 1961.

Bryant, Clora et al. (eds), *Central Avenue Sounds: Jazz in Los Angeles* (Berkeley: University of California Press, 1998).

Bushell, Garvin, *Jazz from the Beginning* (Ann Arbor: University of Michigan Press, 1990).

Clay, 'Sonny', Oral History Collection, Hogan Jazz Archive, Tulane University, Louisiana.

Davis, Leo McCoy, Frank Driggs Collection, Marr Sound Archive, University of Missouri, Kansas City.

Ellington, Duke, *Music Is My Mistress* (Garden City, NY: Doubleday, 1973).

Handy, W.C., *Father of the Blues: An Autobiography* (New York: Da Capo Press, 1991).

Lomax, Alan, *Mister Jelly Roll: The Fortunes of Jelly Roll Morton, New Orleans Creole and 'Inventor of Jazz'* (Berkeley: University of California Press, 2001)

Otis, J., and Lipsitz, G., *Listen to the Lambs* (Minneapolis: University of Minnesota Press, 2009) (reprint of W.W. Norton and Company, 1968).

Royal, Marshal with Gordon, Claire, *Marshal Royal, Jazz Survivor* (New York: Cassell, 1996).

Stewart, Rex and Gordon, Claire, *Boy Meets Horn* (Ann Arbor: University of Michigan Press, 1991).

Secondary Sources

Abbott, Lynn and Seroff, Doug, *Out of Sight: The Rise of African American Popular Music 1889–1895* (Jackson: University Press of Mississippi, 2002).

Abbott, Lynn and Seroff, Doug, *Ragged but Right: Black Traveling Shows, 'Coon' Songs and the Dark Pathway to Blues and Jazz* (Jackson: University Press of Mississippi, 2007).

Achebe, Chinua, 'An Image of Africa: Racism in Conrad's "Heart of Darkness"', *Massachusetts Review*, 18, 1977.

Addison, Heather, *Hollywood and the Rise of Physical Culture* (New York: Routledge, 2003).

Affeldt, Stefanie, 'A Paroxysm of Whiteness. "White" Labour, "White" Nation and "White" Sugar in Australia' in Wulf D. Hund et al. (eds), *Wages of Whiteness and Racist Symbolic Capital* (Berlin; Münster: LIT, 2010).

Affron, Charles, *Lillian Gish: Her Legend, Her Life* (New York: Scribner, 2001).

Alexander, Charles C., *The Ku Klux Klan in the Southwest* (Lexington: University of Kentucky Press, 1965).

Allen, Judith A., *Sex and Secrets: Crimes Involving Australian Women since 1880* (Melbourne: Oxford University Press, 1990).

Anderson, Fay and Trembath, Richard, *Witnesses to War: The History of Australian Conflict Reporting* (Melbourne: Melbourne University Press, 2011).

Anderson, Warwick, 'Ambiguities of Race: Science in the Reproductive Frontier of Australia and the Pacific between the Wars', *Australian Historical Studies*, 40:2, 2009.

Apel, Dora, *Imagery of Lynching: Black Men, White Women, and the Mob* (New Brunswick: Rutgers University Press, 2004).

Appelrouth, Scott, 'Body and Soul, Jazz in the 1920s', *American Behavioral Scientist*, 48:11, 2005.

Atkinson, J., '"Men of Colour": John Joseph and the Eureka Treason Trials', *Journal of Australian Colonial History*, 10:1, 2008.

Austin, Tony, 'Cecil Cook, Scientific Thought and Halfcastes in the Northern Territory, 1927–1939', *Aboriginal History*, 14:1, 1990.

Bakan, Michael B., 'Way Out West on Central: Jazz in the African American Community of Los Angeles before 1930' in Jacqueline Cogdell DjeDje and Eddie S. Meadows (eds), *California Soul: Music of African Americans in the West* (Berkeley: University of California Press, 1998).

Baldwin, Davarian L., 'Our Newcomers to the City: The Great Migration and the Making of Modern Mass Culture' in W. Fitzhugh Brundage (ed.), *Beyond Blackface: African Americans and the Creation of American Popular Culture, 1890–1930* (Chapel Hill: University of North Carolina Press, 2011).

Banner, L. W. et al., 'Biography as History', *American Historical Review*, 114:3, 2009.

Barlow, William, 'Black Music on Radio During the Jazz Age', *African American Review*, 29:2, 1995.

Bartley, Paula, *Prostitution: Prevention and Reform in England, 1860–1914* (United Kingdom: Routledge, 2000).

Bashford, Alison, *Imperial Hygiene: A Critical History of Colonialism, Nationalism, and Public Health* (New York: Palgrave Macmillan, 2004).

Bederman, Gail, *Manliness and Civilization: A Cultural History of Gender and Race in the United States, 1880–1917* (Chicago: University of Chicago Press, 1995).

Bell, James Harle, The La Perouse Aborigines, PhD Thesis, University of Sydney, 1960.

Bell, Roger and Bell, Phillip, *Americanization and Australia* (Sydney: UNSW Press, 1998).

Bellanta, Melissa, 'White Australia and Sonny Clay's Coloured Idea: The Story of an Ill-Fated Tour', *Extempore*, 2, 2009.

Bellanta, Melissa, 'Leary Kin: Australian Larrikins and the Blackface Minstrel Dandy', *Journal of Social History*, 42:3, 2009.

Bellanta, Melissa, 'Uncle Tom in the White Pacific: African-American Performances of the "Slave Sublime" in Late-colonial Australasia', *Journal of Colonialism and Colonial History*, 15:3, December 2014.

Bellanta, Melissa, *Larrikins: A History* (Brisbane: University of Queensland Press, 2012).

Berenstein, Rhona J., 'White Heroines and Hearts of Darkness: Race, Gender and Disguise in 1930s Jungle Films', *Film History*, 6:3, 1994.

Berman, Marshall, *All that is Solid Melts into Air: The Experience of Modernity* (London: Verso, 1985).

Best, Sue, 'Foundations of Femininity: Berlei Corsets and the (Un)making of the Modern Body', *Continuum*, 5:1, 1991.

Bisset, Andrew, *Black Roots, White Flowers: A History of Jazz in Australia* (Sydney: Golden Press, 1979).

Black, Edwin, *War against the Weak: Eugenics and America's Campaign to Create a Master Race* (New York: Four Walls Eight Windows, 2003).

Bland, Lucy, 'White Women and Men of Colour: Miscegenation Fears in Britain after the Great War', *Gender and History*, 17:1, 2005.

Bland, Lucy, *Banishing the Beast* (London: Penguin, 1995).

Bogle, Donald, *Bright Boulevards, Bold Dreams: The Story of Black Hollywood* (New York: One World Ballantine Books, 2005).

Bonnett, Alastair, 'From the Crises of Whiteness to Western Supremacism', *Australian Critical Race and Whiteness Studies Association Journal*, 1, 2005.

Booth, Marilyn and Burton, Antoinette (eds), *Journal of Women's History*, 21:3, 2009.

Brawley, Sean and Dixon, Chris, 'Jim Crow Downunder? African American Encounters with White Australia, 1942–1945', *Pacific Historical Review*, 71:4, 2002.

Brazil, John, 'Murder Trials, Murder and Twenties America', *American Quarterly*, 33:2, 1981.

Brok, A.J., 'The Commonwealth Investigation Branch in Western Australia 1919–1939', *Early Days: Journal of the Royal Western Australian Historical Society*, 12:6, 2006.

Brooks, Liam, The 1928 Waterfront Strike and the Fall of the Victorian Government, Honours Thesis, Faculty of Arts, Victoria University, 2008.

Brooks, Tim, *Lost Sounds: Blacks and the Birth of the Recording Industry, 1890–1919* (Urbana: University of Illinois Press, 2004).

Brown, Gavin, Presland, Gary and Stavely, Ralph, *In the Performance of Duty: The Murder and Assault of Victorian Police 1837–1988* (Melbourne: Police Historical Society, 1994).

Brown, Jayna, *Babylon Girls: Black Women Performers and the Shaping of the Modern* (Durham: Duke University Press, 2008).

Brown, Richard D., 'Microhistory and the Postmodern Challenge', *Journal of the Early Republic*, 23, 2003.

Brown, Richard Maxwell, 'Violence' in Clyde A. Milner II, Carol A. O'Connor and Martha Sandweiss (eds), *The Oxford History of the American West* (New York: Oxford University Press, 1994).

Brundage, W. Fitzhugh (ed.), *Beyond Blackface: African Americans and the Creation of American Popular Culture, 1890–1930* (Chapel Hill: University of North Carolina Press, 2011).

Brundage, W. Fitzhugh, *Lynching in the New South: Georgia and Virginia, 1880–1930*, (Urbana: University of Illinois Press, 1993).

Bruno, Franklin, 'James P. Johnson: From "Carolina Shout" to "The Charleston"', *Sound American*, www.soundamerican.org

Bryant, Clora et al. (eds), *Central Avenue Sounds: Jazz in Los Angeles* (Berkeley: University of California Press, 1998).

Bushell, Garvin, *Jazz from the Beginning* (Ann Arbor: University of Michigan Press, 1990).

Butcher, John G., *The British in Malaya, 1880–1941: The Social History of a European Community in Colonial South-East Asia* (New York: Oxford University Press, 1979).

Byrnes, Jason, 'The Body Snatchers—Peace Officers and the Peace Officers Act 1925', *Platypus Magazine*, 99, 2008.

Bythell, Duncan, 'The Brass Band in Australia: The Transplantation of British Popular Culture, 1850–1950', in Trevor Herbert (ed.), *Bands: The Brass Band Movement in the Nineteenth and Twentieth Centuries* (Buckingham: Open University Press, 1991).

Cain, Frank, *The Origins of Political Surveillance in Australia* (London: Angus and Robertson, 1983).

Cain, Frank, *The Australian Security Intelligence Organization: An Unofficial History* (London: F. Cass, 1993).

Caine, Barbara, *Biography and History* (New York: Palgrave Macmillan, 2010).

Campbell, E.D.C., *The Celluloid South: Hollywood and the Southern Myth* (Knoxville: University of Tennessee Press, 1981).

Cannadine, D., *Ornamentalism: How the British Saw Their Empire* (London: Penguin, 2001).

Card, Amanda, 'Art Dance, Burlesque and Body Culture: Negotiating Interwar Modernities' in Robert Dixon and Veronica Kelly (eds), *Impact of the Modern: Vernacular Modernities in Australia 1850–1969* (Sydney: Sydney University Press, 2008).

Carey, Jane, 'White Anxieties and the Articulation of Race: The Women's Movement and the Making of White Australia' in Jane Carey and Claire McLisky, *Creating White Australia* (Sydney: Sydney University Press, 2009).

Carney, Court, *Cuttin' Up: How Early Jazz Got America's Ear* (Lawrence: University Press of Kansas, 2009).

Carr, Julie, *The Captive White Woman of Gipps Land: In Pursuit of the Legend* (Melbourne: Melbourne University Press, 2001).

Cassells, Kyla, 'Politics and Meaning: Melbourne's Eight Hours Day and Anzac Day, 1928–1935', *Marxist Interventions*, 2, 2010.

Cassells, Kyla, '"I Love this Black Man": Race, Gender and Intimacy in Stories of the Sonny Clay Deportations, 1928', *Connections Made and Broken: Intimacy and Estrangement in Women's History*, Australian Women's History Network Symposium, 2011.

Cassells, Kyla, 'Dancing across the Colour Line: Race, Culture and White Australia in the 1920s', *Empire and International History*, The 4th International History Post-graduate Intensive, University of Sydney, July 2012.

Cathcart, Michael, The White Army of 1931: Origins and Legitimations, BA (Hons.), Dip. Ed., Australian National University, June 1983.

Cathcart, Michael, *Defending the National Tuckshop: Australia's Secret Army Intrigue of 1931* (Melbourne: McPhee Gribble/Penguin, 1988).

Centre City Development Corporation, *Downtown San Diego African-American Heritage*, San Diego, June 2004.
Chalmers, David Mark, *Hooded Americanism: The History of the Ku Klux Klan* (Durham: Duke University Press, 1987).
Chanin, Eileen and Miller, Steven, *Degenerates and Perverts: The 1939 Herald Exhibition of French and British Contemporary Art* (Melbourne: The Miegunyah Press, 2005).
Charters, Samuel, *A Trumpet around the Corner: The Story of New Orleans Jazz* (Jackson: University Press of Mississippi, 2008).
Chibnall, Steve, 'Whistle and Zoot: The Changing Meaning of a Suit of Clothes', *History Workshop*, 20, 1985.
Clare, John and Gail Brennan, *Bodgie, Dada and the Cult of Cool: A History of Australian Jazz* (Sydney: UNSW Press, 1995).
Clarke, Joan, *Dr Max Herz, Surgeon Extraordinary: The Human Price of Civil and Medical Bigotry in Australia* (Sydney: APCOL, 1976).
Clayton, Buck and Elliott, Nancy Miller, *Buck Clayton's Jazz World* (New York: Oxford University Press, 1987).
Clendinnen, Inga, *Dancing with Strangers* (Melbourne: Text Publishing, 2003).
Cohen, Harvey G., *Duke Ellington's America* (Chicago: University of Chicago Press, 2010).
Connor, John, *Anzac and Empire: George Foster Pearce and the Foundations of Australian Defence* (Cambridge; Melbourne: Cambridge University Press, 2011).
Conor, Liz, 'The Beauty Contestant in the Photographic Scene', *Journal of Australian Studies*, 71, 2001.
Conor, Liz, *The Spectacular Modern Woman: Feminine Visibility in the 1920s* (Bloomington: Indiana University Press, 2004).
Conor, Liz, '"Blackfella Missus Too Much Proud": Techniques of Appearing, Femininity, and Race in Australian Modernity' in Alys Eve Weinbaum et al. (eds), *The Modern Girl around the World: Consumption, Modernity, and Globalization* (Durham, NC: Duke University Press, 2008).
Cook, Susan C., 'Passionless Dancing and Passionate Reform: Respectability, Modernism and the Social Dancing of Irene and Vernon Castle' in William Washabough, *The Passion of Music and Dance: Body, Gender and Sexuality* (Oxford: Berg, 1998).
Corbould, Clare, 'Black Internationalism's Shifting Alliances: African American Newspapers, the White Australia Policy, and Indigenous Australians, 1919–1948', *History Compass*, 15:5, 2017.
Corbould, Clare, *Becoming African Americans: Black Public Life in Harlem, 1919–1939* (Cambridge, MA: Harvard University Press, 2009).
Cosgrove, Stuart, 'The Zoot-Suit and Style Warfare', *History Workshop*, 18, 1984.
Courtney, Susan, *Hollywood Fantasies of Miscegenation: Spectacular Narratives of Gender and Race, 1903–1967* (Princeton, NJ; Oxford: Princeton University Press, 2005).
Crawford, Richard, *The American Musical Landscape: The Business of Musicianship from Billings to Gershwin* (Berkeley: University of California Press, 2000).
Cripps, Thomas, *Slow Fade to Black: The Negro in American Film, 1900–1942* (New York: Oxford University Press, 1977).
Crombie, Isobel, *Body Culture: Max Dupain, Photography and Australian Culture, 1919–1939* (Melbourne: Images Publishing Group, 2004).
Crotty, Martin, 'The Anzac Citizen: Towards a History of the RSL', *Australian Journal of History and Politics*, 53:2, 2007.

Cullen, Frank et al., *Vaudeville, Old and New: An Encyclopedia of Variety Performers in America* (New York: Routledge, 2007).

Curthoys, Ann and Lake, Marilyn (eds), *Connected Worlds: History in Transnational Perspective* (Canberra: ANU Press, 2005).

Curthoys, Ann, 'White, British and European: Historicising Identity in Settler Societies' in Jane Carey and Claire McLisky (eds), *Creating White Australia* (Sydney: Sydney University Press, 2009).

Curtis, Bryan, 'D.W. Griffith in Black and White: Was the *Birth of a Nation* Director Really a Racist?', *Slate*, 3 January 2003.

Dangcil, Thomas, *Hollywood: 1900–1950 in Vintage Postcards* (Chicago: Arcadia Publishing, 2002).

Darian-Smith, Kate, Schaffer, Kay and Poignant, Roslyn, *Captive Lives: Australian Captivity Narratives* (London: Sir Robert Menzies Centre for Australian Studies, 1993).

Darian-Smith, K., '"Rescuing" Barbara Thomson and Other White Women: Captivity Narratives on Australian Frontiers' in K. Darian-Smith (ed.), *Text, Theory, Space: Land, Literature and History in South Africa and Australia* (London: Routledge, 1996).

Deacon, Desley, Russell, Penny and Woollacott, Angela, *Transnational Lives: Biographies of Global Modernity, 1700–Present* (Basingstoke: Palgrave Macmillan, 2010).

Dean, D.R. and Reynolds, J.A., *African American Historic Property Survey, City of Phoenix* (Phoenix: Athenaeum Public History Group, 2004).

De Graaf, L.B., 'The City of Black Angels: Emergence of the Los Angeles Ghetto, 1890–1930', *Pacific Historical Review*, 39:3, 1970.

Delson, Susan, *Dudley Murphy Hollywood Wild Card* (Minneapolis: University of Minnesota Press, 2006).

Dennett, Bruce, 'How Dixie Waltzed with Matilda: The Influence on Australia of Cinematic Images of the South', *The Mississippi Quarterly*, 63.3–4, 2010.

Diffee, Christopher, 'Sex and the City: The White Slavery Scare and Social Governance in the Progressive Era', *American Quarterly*, 57:2, 2005.

Dixon, Chris, 'Confronting the "Bulwark of White Supremacy": The African American Challenge to White Australia, 1941–1945', *The Journal of African American History*, 106:1 (Winter 2021).

Dixon, R., *Writing the Colonial Adventure: Race, Gender, and Nation in Anglo-Australian Popular Fiction, 1875–1914* (Cambridge: Cambridge University Press, 1995).

Dixon, Robert and Birns, Nicholas, *Reading across the Pacific: Australia–United States Intellectual Histories* (Sydney: Sydney University Press, 2010).

Dixon, Robert and Kelly, Veronica (eds), *Impact of the Modern: Vernacular Modernities in Australia 1870s–1960s* (Sydney: Sydney University Press, 2008).

Dormon, J. H., 'Shaping the Popular Image of Post-Reconstruction American Blacks: The "Coon Song" Phenomenon of the Gilded Age', *American Quarterly*, 40:4, 1988.

Dreyfus, Kay, 'The Foreigner, the Musicians' Union and the State in 1920s Australia: A Nexus of Conflict', *Music and Politics*, 3:1 (2009).

Dreyfus, Kay, *Silences and Secrets: The Australian Experience of the Weintraubs Syncopators* (Melbourne: Monash University Publishing, 2013).

Dümling, A., *The Vanished Musicians: Jewish Refugees in Australia* (Bern: Peter Lang, 2015).

Duncan, R. H., 'The Chinese and the Economic Development of Northern Baja California, 1889–1929', *Hispanic American Historical Review*, 74:4 (1994).

Dutton, David, 'The Commonwealth Investigation Branch and the Political Construction of the Australian Citizenry, 1920–40', *Labour History*, 75, 1998.
Dutton, David, *One of Us?: A Century of Australian Citizenship* (Sydney: UNSW Press, 2002).
Eklund, Erik, *Mining Towns: Making a Living, Making a Life* (Sydney: UNSW Press, 2012).
Ellinghaus, Katherine, 'Absorbing the "Aboriginal Problem": Controlling Interracial Marriage in Australia in the Late 19th and Early 20th Centuries', *Aboriginal History* 27 (2003).
Ellinghaus, Katherine, *Taking Assimilation to Heart: Marriages of White Women and Indigenous Men in the United States and Australia, 1887–1937* (Lincoln: University of Nebraska Press, 2006).
Epperson, Bruce D., *More Important than the Music: A History of Jazz Discography* (Chicago: University of Chicago Press, 2013).
Errington, Wayne and Van Onselen, Peter, *John Winston Howard: The Biography* (Melbourne: Melbourne University Press, 2007).
Evans, Nicholas M., *Writing Jazz: Race, Nationalism and Modern Culture in the 1920s* (New York; London: Garland, 2000).
Ewing, Adam, *The Age of Garvey: How a Jamaican Activist Created a Mass Movement and Changed Global Black Politics* (Princeton, NJ: Princeton University Press, 2014).
Farr, Finis, *Black Champion: The Life and Times of Jack Johnson* (London: Macmillan, 1964).
Fass, Paula, *The Damned and the Beautiful: American Youth in the 1920's* (New York: Oxford University Press, 1977).
Featherstone, Lisa, 'Sex Educating the Modern Girl: The Formation of New Knowledge in Interwar Australia', *Journal of Australian Studies*, 34:4, 2010.
Feimster, Crystal N., *Southern Horrors: Women and the Politics of Rape and Lynching* (Cambridge, MA: Harvard University Press, 2011).
Ferguson, Robert A., *The Trial in American Life* (Chicago: University of Chicago Press, 2007).
Finch, Lyn, 'Sexuality and Regulation', *Hecate*, 17:1, 1991.
Finnane, M., 'Controlling the "Alien" in Mid-Twentieth Century Australia: The Origins and Fate of a Policing Role', *Policing and Society*, 19:4, 2009.
Fischer, Gerhard, *Enemy Aliens: Internment and the Homefront Experience in Australia, 1914–1920* (Brisbane: University of Queensland Press, 1989).
Fitzgerald, John, *Big White Lie: Chinese Australians in White Australia* (Sydney: UNSW Press, 2007).
Fitzhardinge, L.F., *The Little Digger, 1914–1952: William Morris Hughes, a Political Biography, Volume 2* (Sydney: Angus & Robertson, 1979).
Fleming, E.J., *Paul Bern: The Life and Famous Death of the MGM Director and Husband of Harlow* (New York: McFarland & Company, 2009).
Foley, Neil, *The White Scourge: Mexicans, Blacks, and Poor Whites in Texas Cotton Culture* (Berkeley: University of California Press, 1997).
Frame, Tom, 'The Visit of the Great White Fleet', *Quadrant*, 30:8, 2008.
Frankenberg, Ruth, *White Women, Race Matters: The Social Construction of Whiteness* (London: Routledge, 1993).
Friedman, Ryan Jay, *Hollywood's African American Films: The Transition to Sound* (New Brunswick, NJ: Rutgers University Press, 2011).
Gates, Henry Louis and Higginbotham, Evelyn Brooks, *Harlem Renaissance Lives from the African American National Biography* (New York: Oxford University Press, 2009).

Gennari, John, *Blowin' Hot and Cool: Jazz and Its Critics* (Chicago: University of Chicago Press, 2006).

George-Graves, Nadine, *The Royalty of Negro Vaudeville: The Whitman Sisters and the Negotiation of Race, Gender and Class in African American Theatre, 1900–1940* (New York: St. Martin's Press, 2000).

Gibney, Matthew J. and Hansen, Randall (eds), *Immigration and Asylum: From 1900 to the Present, Volume 1* (Santa Barbara: ABC-CLIO, 2005).

Giddins, Gary, *Bing Crosby: A Pocketful of Dreams—the Early Years, 1903–1940* (Boston: Back Bay Books, 2002).

Giles, Paul, 'Antipodean American Literature: Franklin, Twain, and the Sphere of Subalternity', *American Literary History*, 20:1–2, 2008.

Gill, Christopher (ed.), *The Person and the Human Mind: Issues in Ancient and Modern Philosophy* (Oxford: Clarendon Press, 1990).

Ginzburg, Carlo, 'Microhistory: Two or Three Things That I Know About It', *Critical Enquiry*, 20, 1993.

Gioia, Ted, *West Coast Jazz: Modern Jazz in California, 1945–1960* (New York: Oxford University Press, 1992).

Golden, Eve, *Vernon and Irene Castle's Ragtime Revolution* (Lexington, KY: University Press of Kentucky, 2007).

Goldsby, Jacqueline, *A Spectacular Secret: Lynching in American Life and Literature*, (Chicago: University of Chicago, 2006).

Gonzales-Day, Ken, *Lynching in the West: 1850–1935* (Durham: Duke, 2006).

Goodall, Heather, *Invasion to Embassy: Land in Aboriginal Politics in New South Wales, 1770–1972* (Sydney: Allen & Unwin, 1996).

Goodall, Heather and Cadzow, Allison, *Rivers and Resilience: Aboriginal People on Sydney's Georges River* (Sydney: UNSW Press, 2009).

Goodman, David, *Gold Seeking: Victoria and California in the 1850s* (Sydney: Allen & Unwin, 1994).

Gorman, Daniel, 'Empire, Internationalism, and the Campaign against the Traffic in Women and Children in the 1920s', *Twentieth Century British History*, 19:2, 2009.

Grant, Stan and Rudder, John, *A New Wiradjuri Dictionary* (Canberra: Restoration House, 2010).

Gregory, James Noble, *The Southern Diaspora: How the Great Migrations of Black and White Southerners Transformed America* (Chapel Hill: University of North Carolina Press, 2005).

Gregson, Sarah, Foot Soldiers for Capital: The Influence of RSL Racism on Interwar Industrial Relations in Kalgoorlie and Broken Hill, PhD Thesis, University of New South Wales, 2003.

Gregson, Sarah and Crotty, Martin, 'The RSL: A Rejoinder', *Australian Journal of Politics and History*, 54:1, 2008.

Grittner, Frederick K., *White Slavery: Myth, Ideology, and American Law* (New York: Garland Publishing, 1990).

Gushee, Lawrence, 'New Orleans-Area Musicians on the West Coast, 1908–1925', *Black Music Research Journal*, 9:1 (1989).

Gushee, Lawrence, *Pioneers of Jazz: The Story of the Creole Band* (New York: Oxford University Press, 2005).

Haeusler, Peter, 'Progressivism and the Janus Face of "Efficient Citizenship": Meredith Atkinson and Australian Democracy', *Australian Journal of Politics and History*, 42:1, 1996.

Haldane, R., *The People's Force* (Melbourne: Melbourne University Press, 1995).

Hall, Richard, *Black Armband Days: Truth from the Dark Side of Australia's Past* (Sydney: Vintage, 1998).

Haney-López, Ian, *White by Law: The Legal Construction of Race* (New York: New York University Press, 1996).

Hanna, Judith Lynne, *To Dance Is Human: A Theory of Nonverbal Communication* (Austin: University of Texas Press, 1979).

Hannel, Susan L., 'The Influence of American Jazz on Fashion' in L. Welters and P.A. Cunningham (eds), *Twentieth-Century American Fashion* (Oxford: Berg, 2005).

Hardesty, Jacob, 'Canonic Constructions in Early 20th Century Music Appreciation Classes', *American Educational History Journal*, 38:1/2, 2011.

Hardie, Daniel, *Exploring Early Jazz: The Origins and Evolution of the New Orleans Style* (San Jose: Writers Club Press, 2002).

Harlan, Louis R. (ed.), *The Booker T. Washington Papers*, Vol. 3 (Urbana: University of Illinois Press, 1974).

Hartman, Saidiya, *Wayward Lives, Beautiful Experiments: Intimate Histories of Social Upheaval* (New York: W.W. Norton, 2019).

Haskins, Victoria, '"A Better Chance"? Sexual Abuse and the Apprenticeship of Aboriginal Girls Under the NSW Aborigines Protection Board', *Aboriginal History*, 28, 2004.

Haskins, Victoria, 'Domestic Service and Frontier Feminism: The Call for a Woman Visitor to "Half-Caste" Girls and Women in Domestic Service, Adelaide, 1925–1928', *Frontiers: A Journal of Women Studies*, 28:1–2, 2007.

Hawkins, C.M., A Compilation and Analysis of the Origins of the Foxtrot in White Mainstream America, Master of Arts Thesis, Brigham Young University, Department of Dance, 2002.

Haynes, Robert V., *A Night of Violence: The Houston Riot of 1917* (Baton Rouge: Louisiana State University Press, 1976).

Heap, Chad C., *Slumming: Sexual and Racial Encounters in American Nightlife, 1885–1940* (Chicago: University of Chicago Press, 2009).

Hebdige, Dick, *Subculture: The Meaning of Style* (New York: Routledge, 1991).

Heimann, Jim, *Out with the Stars: Hollywood Nightlife in the Golden Era* (New York: Abbeville Press, 1985).

Hench, Atcheson L., 'A Possible Clue to the Source of "Ballyhoo" and Some Queries', *American Speech*, 20:3, 1945.

Henriques, Fernando, *Children of Conflict: A Study of Interracial Sex and Marriage* (New York: Dutton, 1975).

Hentoff, Nat, 'For the Love of Ivie', *Jazz Times*, 31 May 2001.

Higham, Charles, *Ziegfeld* (London: W.H. Allen, 1973).

Hirst, John, *Sense and Nonsense in Australian History* (Melbourne: Black Inc., 2006).

Hobsbawn, Eric, *The Jazz Scene* (London: MacGibbon & Kee, 1959).

Hobsbawm, Eric, *Uncommon People: Resistance, Rebellion and Jazz* (London: Weidenfeld & Nicolson, 1998).

Homan, Shane and Mitchell, Tony, *Sounds of Then, Sounds of Now: Popular Music in Australia* (Hobart: ACYS, 2008)

Horak, Roman, '"We have become N_____s!": Josephine Baker as a Threat to Viennese Culture', *Strangers, Aliens and Foreigners Project*, Oriel College, Oxford, September 2010.

Horne, Donald, *In Search of Billy Hughes* (Melbourne: Macmillan, 1979).

Horne, Gerald, *Black and Brown: African Americans and the Mexican Revolution, 1910–1920* (New York: New York University Press, 2005).

Horner, D.M., *Blamey: The Commander-in-Chief* (Allen & Unwin, 1998).

Hughes, Aneurin, *Billy Hughes: Prime Minister and Controversial Founding Father of the Australian Labor Party* (Brisbane: John Wiley & Sons, 2005).

Hurley, Frank et al., *The Diaries of Frank Hurley, 1912–1941* (London; New York: Anthem Press, 2011).

Hustad, Donald Paul, 'Creation, Culture and the Music of the Spheres', *Choral Journal*, 47:9, March 2007.

Huyssen, Andreas, *After the Great Divide: Modernism, Mass Culture, Postmodernism* (Bloomington: Indiana University Press, 1986).

Irish, Paul, *Hidden in Plain View: The Aboriginal People of Coastal Sydney* (Sydney: NewSouth Publishing, 2017).

James, Jamie, *The Music of the Spheres: Music, Science, and the Natural Order of the Universe* (New York: Copernicus Press, 1995).

Jeater, Diana, 'Imagining Africans: Scholarship, Fantasy, and Science in Colonial Administration, 1920s Southern Rhodesia', *The International Journal of African Historical Studies*, 38:1, 2005.

Johnson, Bruce, *The Inaudible Music: Jazz, Gender and Australian Modernity* (Sydney: Currency Press, 2000).

Johnson, Dianne, *Sacred Waters: The Story of the Blue Mountains Traditional Owners* (Sydney: Halstead Press, 2006).

Johnson, Michael D., Wade H Hammond (1879–1957): Early Twentieth Century African American Military Bandmaster, PhD Thesis, Texas Tech University, 2004.

Jones, Ross, '"The Master Potter and the Rejected Pots": Eugenic Legislation in Victoria, 1918–1939', *Australian Historical Studies*, 29:113, 1999.

Jones, Ross, 'Brushing Some Dust Off the Wheels of Civilization: Ernest Jones and the 1928 Mental Deficiency Survey', *Australian Historical Studies*, 40:1, 2009.

Jules-Rosette, Bennetta and Njami, Simon, *Josephine Baker in Art and Life: The Icon and the Image* (Urbana: University of Illinois Press, 2007).

Keire, Mara L., 'The Vice Trust: A Reinterpretation of the White Slavery Scare in the United States, 1907–1917,' *Journal of Social History*, 35:1, 2001.

Keith, Jeanette, 'The Politics of Southern Draft Resistance, 1917–1918: Class, Race, and Conscription in the Rural South', *Journal of American History*, 87:4, 2000.

Kelley, Robin D.G., *Race Rebels: Culture, Politics and the Black Working Class* (New York: Maxwell Macmillan, 1994).

Kevles, Daniel J., *In the Name of Eugenics: Genetics and the Uses of Human Heredity* (New York: Knopf, 1985).

Kitch, Carolyn L., *The Girl on the Magazine Cover: The Origins of Visual Stereotypes in American Mass Media* (Chapel Hill: University of North Carolina Press, 2001).

Kline, Wendy, *Building a Better Race: Gender, Sexuality, and Eugenics from the Turn of the Century to the Baby Boom* (Berkeley: University of California Press, 2001).

Koenig, Karl (ed.), *Jazz in Print 1856–1929: An Anthology of Selected Early Readings in Jazz History* (Hillsdale, NY: Pendragon Press, 2002).

Koritz, Amy, *Culture Makers: Urban Performance and Literature in the 1920s* (Urbana, IL: University of Illinois Press, 2009).

Kun, Josh, 'Tijuana and the Borders of Race' in W. Deverell (ed.), *The Blackwell Companion to Los Angeles* (Oxford: Blackwell Publishing Company, 2010).

Kurashige, Scott, *The Shifting Grounds of Race: Black and Japanese Americans in the Making of Multiethnic Los Angeles* (Princeton, NJ; Woodstock: Princeton University Press, 2008).

Laird, Pamela Walker, *Advertising Progress: American Business and the Rise of Consumer Marketing* (Baltimore, MD: John Hopkins University Press, 1998).

Lake, Marilyn, 'The Power of Anzac' in M. McKernan and M. Browne (eds), *Australia: Two Centuries of War and Peace* (Canberra: Allen & Unwin Australia, 1988).

Lake, Marilyn, 'Mission Impossible: How Men Gave Birth to the Australian Nation—Nationalism, Gender and Other Seminal Acts', *Gender* and *History*, 4:3, 1992.

Lake, Marilyn, 'Frontier Feminism and the Marauding White Man,' *Australian Frontiers: Journal of Australian Studies*, 49, 1996.

Lake, Marilyn, 'Childbearers as Rights-Bearers: Feminist Discourse on the Rights of Aboriginal and Non-Aboriginal Mothers in Australia, 1920–1950', *Women's History Review*, 8:2, 1999.

Lake, Marilyn, 'The White Man under Siege: New Histories of Race in the Nineteenth Century and the Advent of White Australia', *History Workshop Journal*, 58, 2004.

Lake, Marilyn, *A Divided Society: Tasmania During World War I* (Melbourne: Melbourne University Press, 1975).

Lake, Marilyn, and Damousi, Joy (eds), *Gender and War: Australians at War in the Twentieth Century* (Cambridge: Cambridge University Press, 1995).

Lake, Marilyn and Reynolds, Henry, *Drawing the Global Colour Line: White Men's Countries and the Question of Racial Equality* (Melbourne: Melbourne University Press, 2008).

Lake, Marilyn, Reynolds, Henry, McKenna, Mark and Damousi, Joy, *What's Wrong with ANZAC? The Militarisation of Australian History* (Sydney: UNSW Press, 2010).

Lamothe, Daphne, *Inventing the New Negro: Narrative, Culture and Ethnography* (Philadelphia: University of Pennsylvania Press, 2008).

Lane, Terence, *Australian Impressionism* (Melbourne: National Gallery of Victoria, 2007).

Langum, David J., *Crossing over the Line: Legislating Morality and the Mann Act* (Chicago: University of Chicago Press, 1994).

Latham, Angela J., *Posing a Threat: Flappers, Chorus Girls and other Brazen Performers of the American 1920s* (Hanover and London: Wesleyan University Press, 2000).

Lefferts, Peter M., 'U.S. Army Black Regimental Bands and the Appointments of Their First Black Bandmasters', *Black Music Research Journal*, 33:2, Fall 2013.

Leggio, James, *Music and Modern Art* (New York: Routledge, 2002).

Leider, Emily W., *Myrna Loy: The Only Good Girl in Hollywood* (Berkeley: University of California Press, 2011).

Lemire, Elise Virginia, *'Miscegenation': Making Race in America* (Philadelphia: University of Pennsylvania Press, 2002).

Lemke, Sieglinde, *Primitivist Modernism: Black Culture and the Origins of Transatlantic Modernism* (New York: Oxford University Press, 1998).

Levin, Floyd, *Classic Jazz: A Personal View of the Music and the Musicians* (Berkeley: University of California Press, 2000).

Lewis, Earl and Ardizonne, Heidi, *Love on Trial: An American Scandal in Black and White* (New York: W.W. Norton, 2001).

Lissarrague, Amanda and Muurrbay Aboriginal Language and Culture Co-operative, and Many Rivers Aboriginal Language Centre, *Dhanggati Grammar and Dictionary with Dhanggati Stories* (Nambucca Heads: Muurrbay Aboriginal Language and Culture Co-operative, 2007).

Lock, Graham, *Blutopia: Visions of the Future and Revisions of the Past in the Work of Sun Ra, Duke Ellington, and Anthony Braxton* (Durham: Duke University Press, 1999).

Lomax, Alan, *Mister Jelly Roll: The Fortunes of Jelly Roll Morton, New Orleans Creole and 'Inventor of Jazz'* (Berkeley: University of California Press, 2001).

Londey, Peter, 'A Possession Forever: Charles Bean, the Ancient Greeks, and Military Commemoration in Australia', *Australian Journal of Politics and History*, 53:3, 2007.

Louis, Les, 'The RSL and the Cold War 1946–50', *Labour History*, 74, 1998.

Luckingham, Bradford, *Phoenix: The History of a Southwestern Metropolis* (Tucson: University of Arizona Press, 1989).

Lupkin, Paula, *Manhood Factories: YMCA Architecture and the Making of Modern Urban Culture* (St Paul: University of Minnesota Press, 2010).

Malnig, Julie, 'Two Stepping to Glory: Social Dance and the Rhetoric of Social Mobility' in Ann Cooper Albright and Ann Dils (eds), *Moving History/Dancing Cultures: A Dance History Reader* (Middletown, CT: Wesleyan University Press, 2001).

Martin, Carol J., *Dance Marathons: Performing American Culture of the 1920s and 1930s* (Jackson: University Press of Mississippi, 1994).

Martinez, Julia, 'Asian Workers in Pre-War Port Darwin: Exclusion and Exemption', *Maritime Studies*, 109, 1999.

Matthews, Jill Julius, *Dance Hall and Picture Palace: Sydney's Romance with Modernity* (Sydney: Currency Press, 2005).

Maynard, John, 'Frederick Maynard and the Australian Aboriginal Progressive Association (AAPA): One God, One Aim, One Destiny', *Aboriginal History*, 21, 1997.

Maynard, John, '"In the Interests of Our People": The Influence of Garveyism on the Rise of Australian Aboriginal Political Activism', *Aboriginal History*, 29, November 2011.

Maynard, John, *Fight for Liberty and Freedom: The Origins of Australian Aboriginal Activism* (Canberra: Aboriginal Studies Press, 2007).

McBernie, Grant, 'The Importance of Being Well Bred' in Marilyn Lake and Kelly Farley (eds), *Double Time: Women in Victoria, 150 Years* (Melbourne: Penguin Books, 1985).

McCarthy, Albert J., *Big Band Jazz* (New York: Berkley Publishing Corporation, 1977).

McConville, Chris, 'Waterfront Unionism in Three Ports: Buenos Aires, Melbourne and San Francisco, 1919–1934', *Australian Labour History Reconsidered*, 1999.

McGregor, Craig, 'Growing Up (Uncool): Pop Music and Youth Culture in the 50's and 60's' in Philip Hayward (ed.), *From Pop to Punk to Postmodernism: Popular Music and Australian Culture from the 1960s to the 1990s* (Sydney: Allen & Unwin, 1992).

McGregor, Russell, '"Breed out the colour" or the Importance of Being White', *Australian Historical Studies*, 33:120, 2002.

McKernan, Michael, *The Australian People and the Great War* (Melbourne: Thomas Nelson, 1980).

McKernan, Michael, *All in! Australia During the Second World War* (Melbourne: Nelson, 1983).

McNeil, William H., *Keeping Together in Time: Dance and Drill in Human History* (Cambridge, MA: Harvard University Press, 1995).

McQueen, Humphrey, *Social Sketches of Australia* (Brisbane: University of Queensland Press, 2004).

McWhirter, Cameron, *Red Summer: The Summer of 1919 and the Awakening of Black America* (New York: Henry Holt & Co., 2011).

Meaney, Neville, '"The Yellow Peril": Invasion Scare Novels and Australian Political Culture' in Ken Stewart (ed.), *The 1890s: Australian Literature and Literary Culture* (Brisbane: University of Queensland Press, 1996).

Meaney, Neville, *A History of Australian Defence and Foreign Policy, 1901–23, Volume 2, Australia and World Crisis, 1914–1923* (Sydney: Sydney University Press, 2009).

Menand, Louis, 'Morton, Agassiz, and the Origins of Scientific Racism in the United States', *The Journal of Blacks in Higher Education*, 34, 2001–02.

Merriman, Alan, *The Anthropology of Music* (Evanston, IL: Northwestern University Press, 1976 [c. 1964]).

Metzger, Barbara, 'Towards an International Human Rights Regime during the Interwar Years' in Kevin Grant, Philippa Levine and Frank Trentmann (eds), *Beyond Sovereignty: Britain, Empire and Transnationalism, c. 1880–1950* (Basingstoke: Palgrave Macmillan, 2007).

Miller, James, *Koori: A Will to Win* (Sydney: Angus & Robertson, 1985).

Miller, Mark, *Some Hustling This! Taking Jazz to the World, 1914–1929* (Toronto: Mercury Press, 2005).

Milner, Greg, *Perfecting Sound Forever: An Aural History of Recorded Music* (New York: Faber and Faber, 2009).

Monk, Ray, 'Life without Theory: Biography as an Exemplar of Philosophical Understanding', *Poetics Today*, 28:3, 2007.

Moore, Andrew, *The Secret Army and the Premier: Conservative Paramilitary Organisations in New South Wales 1930–32* (Sydney: UNSW Press, 1989).

Moreira-Almeida, Alexander, Angelica de Almeida, Francisco Neto, 'History of "Spiritist Madness" in Brazil', *History of Psychiatry*, 16:1, March 2005.

Morison, Patricia, *Jt Wilson and the Fraternity of Duckmaloi* (Amsterdam; Atlanta: Rodopi, 1997).

Morpeth, Neil, 'Avatism, Utopian Longings and Jack Lindsay: An Essay on the Nietzschean Presences and Hellenic Pasts' in Martin Crotty, John Germov and Grant Rodwell (eds), *Race for a Place: Eugenics, Darwinism and Social Thought and Practice in Australia* (Newcastle: University of Newcastle, 2000).

Morton Jr, David L, *Sound Recording: The Life Story of a Technology* (Baltimore, MD: John Hopkins University Press, 2006).

Morton, James and Robinson, Russell, *Shotgun and Standover: The Story of the Painters and Dockers* (Sydney: Pan Macmillan, 2010).

Musser, Charles, 'Why Did Negroes Love Al Jolson and The Jazz Singer?: Melodrama, Blackface and Cosmopolitan Theatrical Culture', *Film History*, 23:2, 2011.

Nader, Laura (ed.), *Naked Science: Anthropological Inquiry into Boundaries, Power, and Knowledge* (New York: Routledge, 1996).

Nails, June, *White Captives: Gender and Ethnicity on the American Frontier* (Canberra: UNC Press, 1993).

Nicholls, Glenn, *Deported: A History of Forced Departures from Australia* (Sydney: University of New South Wales Press, 2007).

Nieman, Donald G., 'African Americans and the Meaning of Freedom: Washington County, Texas as a Case Study, 1865–1886', *Chicago-Kent Law Review*, 70:2 (1994).

Nugent, Maria, 'An Economy of Shells: A Brief History of La Perouse Aboriginal Women's Shell-Work and its Markets, 1880–2010' in Natasha Fijn et al. (eds), *Indigenous Participation in Australian Economies II: Historical Engagements and Current Enterprises* (Canberra: ANU Press, 2012).

Nugent, Maria, *Botany Bay: Where Histories Meet* (Sydney: Allen & Unwin, 2005).

O'Connor, Desmond, 'Declared Black: Confrontation between Italian and Anglo-Celtic Workers in Port Adelaide, 1928–1932', *Australian Labour History Reconsidered*, 1999.

Orbison, Charles Edward, 'Fighting Bob' Shuler and KGEF: The Silencing of a Radio Crusader, Thesis, August 1975, University of North Texas.

Paisley, Fiona, *Loving Protection? Australian Feminism and Aboriginal Women's Rights, 1919–1939* (Melbourne: Melbourne University Press, 2000).

Parsons, Timothy, *The African Rank-and-File: Social Implications of Colonial Military Service in the King's African Rifles, 1902–1964* (Portsmouth, NH: Heinemann, 1999).

Pascoe, Peggy, *What Comes Naturally: Miscegenation Law and the Making of Race in America* (Oxford; New York: Oxford University Press, 2009).

Pastras, Philip, *Dead Man Blues: Jelly Roll Morton Way Out West* (Berkeley: University of California Press, 2001).

Paulin, Diana Rebekkah, *Imperfect Unions: Staging Miscegenation in U.S. Drama and Fiction* (Minneapolis: University of Minnesota Press, 2012).

Pegram, T.R., *One Hundred Per Cent American: The Rebirth and Decline of the Ku Klux Klan, in the 1920s* (Lanham, MD: Ivan R. Dee, 2011).

Peiss, Kathy Lee, *Cheap Amusements: Working Women and Leisure in Turn-of-the-Century New York* (Philadelphia: Temple University Press, 1986).

Peiss, Kathy Lee, *Hope in a Jar: The Making of America's Beauty Culture* (New York: Henry Holt & Company, 1998).

Perry, Elisabeth I., '"The General Motherhood of the Commonwealth": Dance Hall Reform in the Progressive Era', *American Quarterly*, 37:5, 1985.

Petersen, R.C., *Peter Jackson: A Biography of the Australian Heavyweight Champion, 1860–1901* (Jefferson, NC: McFarland & Co., 2011).

Petersen, Vibeke Rützou, *Women and Modernity in Weimar Germany: Reality and Its Representation in Popular Fiction* (New York: Berghahn Books, 2001).

Pope, Joan, 'Dalcroze Eurhythmics: Interaction in Australia in the 1920s', *Australian Journal of Music Education*, 2, 2010.

Pybus, Cassandra, *Black Founders: The Unknown History of Australia's First Black Settlers* (Sydney: UNSW Press, 2006).

Quinland, M., 'Bellbrook, My Father's Country', *Aboriginal History*, 7:1, 1983.

Radano, Ronald, 'Hot Fantasies: American Modernism and the Idea of Black Rhythm' in Ronald Radano and Philip V. Bohlman (eds), *Music and the Racial Imagination*, (Chicago: University of Chicago Press, 2000).

Ramsey, Guthrie P. Jr., *Race Music: Black Cultures from Bebop to Hip-Hop* (Berkeley: University of California Press, 2003).

Ramsland, John, '"A Gladiator Caste Envied by All Men, Adored by All Women": The Surf Life Saver and Mythical Beach Iconography in New South Wales', *ISAA Review*, 10:1, 2011.

Regester, Charlene, 'Stepin Fetchit: The Man, the Image, and the African American Press', *Film History*, 6:4, 1994.

Reiger, Kerreen M., *The Disenchantment of the Home: Modernizing the Australian Family 1880–1940* (Melbourne: Oxford University Press, 1985).

Reynolds, Henry, *The Other Side of the Frontier: Aboriginal Resistance to the European Invasion of Australia* (Melbourne: Penguin Books, 1982).

Reynolds, Henry, *Nowhere People* (Melbourne: Viking, 2005).

Riesman, Bob, *I Feel So Good: The Life and Times of Big Bill Broonzy* (Chicago: University of Chicago Press, 2012).

Riverol, A.R., *Miss America Pageant Before, After and in Spite of Television* (Bowling Green: Bowling Green State University Popular Press, 1992).

Roberts, Randy, *Papa Jack: Jack Johnson and the Era of White Hopes* (New York: Collier Macmillan, 1983).
Rodwell, Grant, '"The Sense of Victorious Struggle": The Eugenic Dynamic in Australian Popular Surf-culture, 1900–50', *Journal of Australian Studies*, 23:62, 1999.
Rogin, Michael Paul, *Blackface, White Noise: Jewish Immigrants in the Hollywood Melting Pot* (Berkeley: University of California Press, 1996).
Ross, Sara, '"Good Little Bad Girls": Controversy and the Flapper Comedienne', *Film History*, 13:4, 2001.
Rouget, Gilbert and Biebuyck, Brunhilde, *Music and Trance: A Theory of the Relations between Music and Possession* (Chicago: University of Chicago Press, 1985).
Royal, Marshal, *Marshal Royal, Jazz Survivor* (New York: Cassell, 1996).
Ruggiero, Guido, *Binding Passions: Tales of Magic, Marriage, and Power at the End of the Renaissance* (New York: Oxford University Press, 1993).
Runstedtler, Theresa, *Jack Johnson, Rebel Sojourner: Boxing in the Shadow of the Global Color Line* (Berkeley: University of California Press, 2012).
Russell, Penny, 'Ornaments of Empire? Government House and the Idea of English Aristocracy in Colonial Australia', *History Australia*, 1:2, 2004.
Salamone, Frank A., *The Culture of Jazz: Jazz as Critical Culture* (Lanham: The Rowman & Littlefield, 2008).
Sales, Peter M., 'White Australia, Black Americans: A Melbourne Incident, 1928', *Australian Quarterly*, 46:4, 1974.
Saunders, Kay, 'Conflict between the American and Australian Governments over the Introduction of Black Servicemen into Australia during World War Two', *Australian Journal of Politics and History*, 33, 1987.
Saunders, Kay and Daniels, Roger, *Alien Justice: Wartime Internment in Australia and North America* (Brisbane: University of Queensland Press, 2000).
Schantz, E.M., 'All Night at the Owl: The Social and Political Relations of Mexicali's Red Light District, 1913–1925' in Andrew Grant Wood (ed.), *On the Border: Society and Culture between the United States and Mexico* (Oxford: SR Books, 2004).
Schedvin, C.B., *Australia and the Great Depression: A Study of Economic Development and Policy in the 1920s and 1930s* (Sydney: Sydney University Press, 1970).
Schickel, Richard, *D.W. Griffith: An American Life* (New York: Simon and Schuster, 1984).
Schoener, Allon, *Harlem on My Mind: Cultural Capital of Black America, 1900–1966* (New York: Dell Publishing Company, 1979).
Schudson, Michael, *The Power of News* (Cambridge, MA: Harvard University Press, 1996).
Scott, Ellen C., *Cinema Civil Rights: Regulation, Repression, and Race in the Classical Hollywood Era* (New Brunswick, NJ: Rutgers University Press, 2015).
Scott, Ernest, *Australia during the War* (Sydney: Angus and Robertson, 1937).
Sears, A., 'Fortified Silos or Interconnected Webs: The Relationship between History and other Subjects in the Curriculum' in Ian Davies (ed.), *Debates in History Teaching* (New York: Routledge, 2011).
Segrave, Kerry, *Vision Aids in America: A Social History of Eyewear and Sight Correction since 1900* (Jefferson, NC: McFarland, 2011).
Sengstock, Charles A., *That Toddlin' Town: Chicago's White Dance Bands and Orchestras, 1900–1950* (Urbana: University of Illinois Press, 2004).
Shack, William A., *Harlem in Montmartre: A Paris Jazz Story between the Great Wars* (Berkeley: University of California Press, 2001).

Shaw, Arnold, *The Jazz Age: Popular Music in the 1920s* (New York: Oxford University Press, 1987).

Shuler, Robert, *Fighting Bob Shuler of Los Angeles* (Indianapolis: Dog Ear Publishing, 2011).

Singer, Barry, *Black and Blue: The Life and Lyrics of Andy Razaf* (New York: Maxwell Macmillan International, 1992).

Spencer, J.M. (ed.), 'On Jazzology: A Rapsody', *Sacred Music of the Secular City: From Blues to Rap* (Durham: Duke University Press, 1992).

Spencer, Paul, *Society and the Dance: The Social Anthropology of Process and Performance*, (Cambridge; New York: Cambridge University Press, 1985).

Stearns, Marshall and Stearns, Jean, *Jazz Dance: The Story of American Vernacular Dance* (New York: Macmillan, 1968).

Stephen, Ann et al. (eds), *Modern Times: The Untold Story of Modernism in Australia* (Sydney: The Miegunyah Press and Powerhouse Publishing, 2008).

Stewart, Rex, *Boy Meets Horn* (Ann Arbor: University of Michigan Press, 1991).

Stoddard, Tom, *Jazz on the Barbary Coast* (Chigwell: Storyville, 1982).

Stokes, Melvyn, *D.W. Griffith's* The Birth of a Nation*: A History of 'the Most Controversial Motion Picture of All Time'* (New York: Oxford University Press, 2007).

Stoler, Ann Laura, 'Carnal Knowledge and Imperial Power' in Michaela di Leonardo (ed.), *Gender at the Crossroads of Knowledge* (Berkeley: University of California Press, 1991).

Strobel, Margaret, *European Women and the Second British Empire* (Bloomington: Indiana University Press, 1991).

Sturma, Michael, *South Sea Maidens: Western Fantasy and Sexual Politics in the South Pacific* (Westport, CT: Greenwood Press, 2002).

Sullivan, Jack, *New World Symphonies: How American Culture Changed European Music* (New Haven: Yale University Press, 1999).

Sutcliffe, M., 'Sonny Clay and the Coloured Idea,' *Australian Record and Music Review*, 35, 1997.

Sweeney, Fionnghuala, *Afromodernisms: Paris, Harlem and the Avant-Garde* (Edinburgh: Edinburgh University Press, 2013).

Tabili, Laura, '"Women of a Very Low Type": Crossing Racial Boundaries in Imperial Britain' in Laura Frader and Sonya O. Rose (eds), *Gender and Class in Modern Europe* (Ithaca: Cornell University Press, 1996).

Taylor, Alex, *Perils of the Studio: Inside the Artistic Affairs of Bohemian Melbourne* (Melbourne: Australian Scholarly Publishing, 2007).

Taylor, L.D., 'The Wild Frontier Moves South: U.S. Entrepreneurs and the Growth of Tijuana's Vice Industry, 1908–1935', *The Journal of San Diego History*, 48:3, 2002.

Taylor, Quintard et al., *Seeking El Dorado: African Americans in California* (Seattle: University of Seattle Press, 2001).

Taylor, Yuval and Austen, Jake, *Darkest America: Black Minstrelsy from Slavery to Hip-Hop* (New York: W.W. Norton, 2012).

Thompson, E.P., *The Making of the English Working Class* (London: Gollancz, 1963).

Thomson, Alistair, '"Steadfast until death?" C.E.W. Bean and the Representation of Australian Military Manhood', *Australian Historical Studies*, 23:93, 1989.

Ting Yi Lui, Mary, 'Saving Young Girls from Chinatown: White Slavery and Woman Suffrage, 1910–1920', *Journal of the History of Sexuality*, 18:3, 2009.

Toll, Robert C., *Blacking Up: The Minstrel Show in Nineteenth Century America* (New York: Oxford University Press, 1974).

Torgovnick, Marianna, *Gone Primitive: Savage Intellects, Modern Lives* (Chicago: University of Chicago Press, 1990).

Turner, Victor, *The Anthropology of Performance* (New York: PAJ Publications, 1986).

Tyler, Bruce M., 'Black Jive and White Repression', *Journal of Ethnic Studies*, 16:4, 1989.

Tyler, Edward Stovall, *Paris Noir: African Americans in the City of Light* (Boston: Houghton Mifflin, 1996).

Usher, Jim (ed.), *The Argus: Life and Death of a Newspaper* (Melbourne: Jim Usher, 1999).

Vanderwood, P.J., *Satan's Playground: Mobsters and Movie Stars at America's Greatest Gaming Resort* (Durham: Duke University Press, 2010).

Van Straten, Frank, *Huge Deal: The Fortunes and Follies of Hugh D. McIntosh* (Melbourne: Lothian Books, 2004).

Van Straten, Frank, *Tivoli* (Melbourne: Lothian, 2003).

Volk, Terese M., 'Anne Shaw Faulkner Oberndorfer (1877–1948): Music Educator for the Homemakers of America', *Journal of Historical Research in Music Education*, 29:1, 2007.

Waldren, Christopher, *The Many Faces of Judge Lynch: Extralegal Violence and Punishment in America* (Basingstoke: Palgrave Macmillan, 2002).

Walker, David, 'Modern Nerves, Nervous Moderns: Notes on Male Neurasthenia: Artists, Doctors and Human Energy, 1870/1929', *Australian Cultural History*, 6, 1987.

Walker, David, *Anxious Nation: Australia and the Rise of Asia 1850–1939* (Brisbane: University of Queensland Press, 1999).

Wallis, Brian, 'Black Bodies, White Science: Louis Agassiz's Slave Daguerreotypes', *American Art*, 9:2, 1995.

Walton, R.D., 'Feeling for the Jugular: Japanese Espionage at Newcastle 1919–1926', *Australian Journal of Politics and History*, 32:1, 2008.

Ward, Geoffrey C., *Unforgivable Blackness: The Rise and Fall of Jack Johnson* (New York: A.A. Knopf, 2004).

Warhaft, Sally, *Well May We Say: The Speeches that Made Australia* (Melbourne: Black Inc., 2004).

Waterhouse, Richard, *From Minstrel Show to Vaudeville: The Australian Popular Stage, 1788–1914* (Sydney: UNSW Press, 1990).

Waterhouse, Richard, *Private Pleasures, Public Pleasures: A History of Australian Popular Culture since 1788* (South Melbourne: Longman, 1995).

Waterhouse, Richard, *The Vision Splendid: A Social and Cultural History of Rural Australia* (Perth: Curtin University Books, 2005).

Watkins, Clifford Edward, *Showman: The Life and Music of Perry George Lowery* (Jackson: University Press of Mississippi, 2003).

Watkins, Mel, *Stepin Fetchit: The Life and Times of Lincoln Perry* (New York: Pantheon Books, 2005).

Weinbaum, Alys Eve, 'Racial Masquerade: Consumption and Contestation of American Modernity' in Alys Eve Weinbaum et al. (eds), *The Modern Girl around the World: Consumption, Modernity, and Globalization* (Durham, NC: Duke University Press, 2008).

Wells, Jeff, *Boxing Day: The Fight that Changed the World* (Sydney: Harper Collins, 1998).

Whitaker, Matthew C., 'The Rise of Black Phoenix: African-American Migration, Settlement and Community Development in Maricopa County, Arizona 1868–1930', *Journal of Negro History*, 85:3, Summer 2000: 197–209.

Whitaker, Matthew Corey, In Search of Black Phoenicians: African American Culture and Community in Phoenix, Arizona, 1868–1940, Master's Thesis, Arizona State University, 1997.

White, Luise, *Speaking with Vampires: Rumour and History in Colonial Africa* (Berkeley: University of California Press, 2000).

White, Shane and White, Graham, *Stylin': African American Expressive Culture from Its Beginnings to the Zoot Suit* (Ithaca, NY: Cornell University Press, 1998).

Whiteoak, John, 'Popular Music, Militarism, Women, and the Early Brass Band in Australia', *Australasian Music Research*, 6, 2001.

Williams, Gregory Paul, *The Story of Hollywood: An Illustrated History* (Los Angeles: BL Press LLC, 2011).

Williams, John F., *ANZACS, the Media and the Great War* (Kensington, NSW: UNSW Press, 1999).

Williams, John Frank, *The Quarantined Culture: Australian Reactions to Modernism, 1913–1939* (New York: Cambridge University Press, 1995).

Williamson, Karina, 'From Heavenly Harmony to Eloquent Silence: Representations of World Order from Dryden to Shelley', *Review of English Studies*, 55:221, 2004.

Wilson, Jeremiah Moses, *Creative Conflict in African American Thought* (New York: Cambridge University Press, 2004).

Woollacott, Angela, 'White Colonialism and Sexual Modernity: Australian Women in the Early Twentieth Century Metropolis' in Antoinette Burton (ed.), *Gender, Sexuality and Colonial Modernities* (New York: Routledge, 1999).

Woolley, C., *Arresting Women: A History of Women in Victoria Police* (Melbourne: Victoria Press, 1997).

Work, David, 'Enforcing Neutrality: the Tenth US Cavalry Band', *Western Historical Quarterly*, 40:2 (2008).

Young, Robert J.C., *Colonial Desire: Hybridity in Theory, Culture and Race* (New York: Routledge, 1995).

Zeitz, Joshua, *Flapper: A Madcap Story of Sex, Style, Celebrity, and the Women Who Made America Modern* (New York: Crown Publishers, 2006).

NOTES

Prologue: The Frame-Up

1 W.M. Hughes, *A Splendid Adventure: A Review of Empire Relations Within and Without the Commonwealth of Britannic Nations* (London: Ernest Benn Limited, 1929): 364.
2 'Advertising', Sydney *Truth*, 22 Jan. 1928: 23.
3 'Val Haltren's Men Lose Twice', *Oakland Tribune*, 22 Jun. 1908: 9.
4 'Sonny Clay's Parting Shot', *Everyones*, 4 Apr. 1928: 6.
5 'From Australia', *Chicago Defender*, 10 Mar. 1928: 7.
6 Sonny Clay, Oral History Collection, Hogan Jazz Archive, Tulane University, Louisiana.
7 'Sonny Clay's Plantation Band Turns *Sierra* into Jazz Ship', *Everyones*, 25 Jan. 1928: 39.
8 Sam Hood, *The Colored Idea Band of Sonny Clay Arrives in Sydney*, 19 Jan. 1928, Hood Collection, State Library of NSW. 'The Colored Idea Band of Sonny Clay Arrives in Sydney, 1928 / Sam Hood', Hood Collection part II / B: Photographic prints, State Library of NSW.
9 'Colored Entertainers', *Daily Telegraph*, 21 Jan. 1928: 22.
10 Major Longfield Lloyd, Report: 'Negro Orchestra—Lately at the Tivoli Theatre Sydney', 24 Feb. 1928, NAA B741 V/4718.

Chapter 1 The Education of Sonny Clay

1 D.R. Dean and J.A. Reynolds, *African American Historic Property Survey, City of Phoenix* (Phoenix: Athenaeum Public History Group, 2004); John Bentley, 'Sonny Clay: A Veritable Giant—Part 1', *Jazz Research* (Nov/Dec 1962): 7–8; 'Washington to Be Here', *Arizona Republican*, 21 Sept. 1911: 5 [Henceforth *AR*]; 'Booker T Washington', *AR*, 23 Sept. 1911: 2.
2 'Emancipation Day at Eastlake Park', *AR*, 11 Jun. 1911: 6; 'Band Social', *AR*, 9 Apr. 1911: 4.
3 'They Organize', *Brenham Banner*, 24 Jul. 1880: 2 [Henceforth *BB*]; 'The Congressional Nomination', *BB*, 5 Aug. 1880: 2; *BB*, 1 Oct. 1880; 'Seranade', *BB*, 7 Oct. 1889: 3; 'Owl Barbecue', *BB*, 26 Jul. 1878: 3; 'Watrousville Convention', *BB*, 31 Aug. 1878: 3; *BB*, 30 Sept. 1880: 3; 'Garfield Club', *BB*, 7 Aug. 1880: 2.
4 'Colored Band', *AR*, 9 Apr. 1911: 6; *AR*, 11 Jun. 1911: 6.

5 Donald G. Nieman, 'African Americans and the Meaning of Freedom: Washington County, Texas as a Case Study, 1865–1886', *Chicago-Kent Law Review*, 70:2 (1994): 541–82.
6 *BB*, 9 Dec. 1886: 7; *BB*, 16 Dec. 1886: 2; 'Mental Anguish', *BB*, 2 Dec. 1897: 9.
7 Bradford Luckingham, *Phoenix: The History of a Southwestern Metropolis* (Tucson: University of Arizona Press, 1989): 40–68.
8 Matthew Corey Whitaker, In Search of Black Phoenicians: African American Culture and Community in Phoenix, Arizona, 1868–1940, Master's Thesis, Arizona State University, 1997.
9 Louis R. Harlan (ed.), *The Booker T. Washington Papers*, Vol. 3 (Urbana: University of Illinois Press, 1974): 583–587.
10 'Liberty Is on the Way', *AR*, 11 Sept. 1911: 5.
11 Harlan, *The Booker T. Washington Papers*, Vol. 3: 583–587; 'White City in the Park', *AR*, 20 Sept. 1911: 3; 'Advertisement: This Is the Real Thing', *AR*, 22 Sept. 1911: 7; 'Leader Gives Good Advice', *AR*, 22 Sept. 1911: 9; 'Perished in Awful Crush', *AR*, 22 Sept. 1911: 3; *AR*, 9 Aug. 1911: 4; 'Day's Event at Eastside Lake', *AR*, 24 Sept. 1911: 4.
12 'Booker T Washington', *AR*, 23 Sept. 1911: 2.
13 Bruce D. Epperson, *More Important than the Music: A History of Jazz Discography* (Chicago: University of Chicago Press, 2013).
14 William Clay, *1900* US Federal Census, *Houston Ward 1, Harris, Texas*, Ancestry.com.
15 W.C. Handy, *Father of the Blues: An Autobiography* (New York: Da Capo Press, 1991): 136.
16 Taylor Gordon, *Born to Be* (Seattle: University of Washington Press, 1975): 119.
17 Clifford Edward Watkins, *Showman: The Life and Music of Perry George Lowery* (Jackson: University Press of Mississippi, 2003); Lynn Abbott and Doug Seroff, *Ragged but Right: Black Traveling Shows, 'Coon' Songs and the Dark Pathway to Blues and Jazz* (Jackson: University Press of Mississippi, 2007): 206.
18 'Coast Dope', *Chicago Defender*, 29 Sept. 1923: 7.
19 'Southwest Facing a Circus Famine', *AR*, 19 Apr. 1915: 4; 'Fifty, Fifty, Fifty', *AR*, 20 Oct. 1916: 9; Abbott and Seroff, *Ragged but Right*: 176.
20 Tim Brooks, *Lost Sounds: Blacks and the Birth of the Recording Industry, 1890–1919* (Urbana: University of Illinois Press, 2004): 407, 428.
21 Bentley, 'Sonny Clay, Part 1': 7–8; Sonny Clay, Oral History Collection, Hogan Jazz Archive, Tulane University, Louisiana.
22 Bob Riesman, *I Feel So Good: The Life and Times of Big Bill Broonzy* (Chicago: University of Chicago Press, 2012).
23 Dean and Reynolds, *African American Historic Property Survey*: 63–64; Bentley, 'Sonny Clay, Part 2': John Bentley, *Jazz Research*, Jan/Feb. 1963, 13–14; 'Colored Graduates Are Given Banquet', *AR*, 11 Jun. 1919: 8.
24 Sonny Clay, Oral History Collection, Hogan Jazz Archive; 'Sonny Clay in Retrospect', *Jazzfinder*, Sept. 1948: 3–6; Bentley, 'Sonny Clay, Part 1': 7–8; Bentley, 'Sonny Clay, Part 2': 13–14.
25 Garvin Bushell, *Jazz from the Beginning* (Ann Arbor: University of Michigan Press, 1990): 1–2.
26 Handy, *Father of the Blues*: 167.
27 For examples of conversion to Modernism, see: Neville D'esterre, 'A Syncopated Apology (Part l)', *British Musician*, Sept. 1928; Jack Sullivan, *New World Symphonies: How American Culture Changed European Music* (New Haven: Yale University Press,

1999): 194; Frank A. Salamone, *The Culture of Jazz: Jazz as Critical Culture* (Lanham: Rowman & Littlefield Publishing Group, 2008): 53.

28 Bentley, 'Sonny Clay, Part 1': 7–8; Sonny Clay, Oral History Collection, Hogan Jazz Archive.

29 'Advertisement', *AR*, 21 Jun. 1917: 2; 'Advertisement', *AR*, 28 Dec. 1917: 4.

30 Bentley, 'Sonny Clay, Part 1': 6–7; Sonny Clay, Oral History Collection, Hogan Jazz Archive.

31 'Advertisement', *AR*, 17 Sept. 1918: 8; 'Advertisement', *AR*, 20 Sept. 1918: 12; Sonny Clay, Oral History Collection, Hogan Jazz Archive; 'Advertisement', *AR*, 3 Jun. 1919: 16.

32 'Plantation Days', *Daily Telegraph*, 25 Jan. 1928; Bentley, 'Sonny Clay, Part 2': 13–14; William Roger Campbell 'Sonny' Clay, Find A Grave, http://www.findagrave.com/cgi-bin/fg.cgi?page=gr&GRid=122706922.

33 Dean and Reynolds, *African American Historic Property Survey*: 24–25; *AR*, 27 Nov. 1917; 'Commencement of High School', *AR*, 29 May 1919: 16; 'Requisites for High School Graduate', *AR*, 3 Jun. 1919: 6; 'Colored Graduates Are Given Banquet', *AR*, 11 Jun. 1919: 8.

34 *AR*, 18 Sept. 1910, cited in Matthew C. Whitaker, 'The Rise of Black Phoenix: African-American Migration, Settlement and Community Development in Maricopa County, Arizona 1868–1930', *Journal of Negro History*, 85:3 (Summer 2000): 197–209.

35 Bradford Luckingham, *Minorities in Phoenix: A Profile of Mexican American, Chinese American, and African American Communities, 1860–1992* (Tucson: University of Arizona Press, 1994): 140; 'Advertisement', *AR*, 11 Nov. 1917: 10.

Chapter 2 Independence Day

1 'Send Reinforcements To Border', *Arizona Republican*, 28 Jun. 1919: 2 [Henceforth *AR*]; 'Trying to Quell Sonora Yaquis', *El Paso Herald*, 14 Feb. 1916: 5; David Work, 'Enforcing Neutrality: The Tenth US Cavalry Band', *Western Historical Quarterly*, 40:2: 179–200; 'Buffalo Soldiers Part II', *History Illustrated: A Magazine of the Fort Huachuca Museum* 2, 1999: 73–75; Peter M. Lefferts, 'U.S. Army Black Regimental Bands and the Appointments of Their First Black Bandmasters', *Black Music Research Journal* 33:2 (Fall 2013): 151–175.

2 Michael D. Johnson, Wade H Hammond (1879–1957): Early Twentieth Century African American Military Bandmaster, PhD Thesis, Texas Tech University, 2004; 'Rebels Abandon North Sonora Field', *Bisbee Daily Review*, 5 Oct. 1912: 8.

3 'Tenth Cavalry Band to Arrive Tonight', *AR*, 27 Jun. 1919: 14; 'Riverside Park', 'Twelve Planes Take Place in Air Tournament', *AR*, 25 Jun. 1919: 12.

4 *Phoenix Tribune*, 28 Dec. 1918; *Phoenix Tribune*, 14 Jun. 1919, cited in Gerald Horne, *Black and Brown: African Americans and the Mexican Revolution, 1910–1920* (New York: New York University Press, 2005): 111.

5 'Cavalry Band Plays Tonight', *AR*, 29 Jun. 1919: 5; 'Tenth Cavalry Band to Arrive Tonight', *AR*, 27 Jun. 1919: 14; 'Tenth Cavalry Troops Engage Bisbee Police', *AR*, 4 Jul. 1919: 1; 'Bisbee Quiet after Negro Troop Riot', *AR*, 5 Jul. 1919: 10; 'Five Wounded in Street', *Bisbee Daily Review*, 4 Jul. 1919: 10; 'Riot Follows Mob', *AR*, 31 Aug. 1919: 1; Cameron McWhirter, *Red Summer: The Summer of 1919 and the Awakening of Black America* (New York: Henry Holt & Co., 2011).

6 'Racial Outbreaks', *AR*, 4 Aug. 1919: 4.

7 *Phoenix Tribune*, 28 Dec. 1918; 'The Real Causes of the Two Race Riots', *Crisis*, Feb. 1920: 56–62; National Association for the Advancement of Colored People,

The Tenth Annual Report of the NAACP for the Year 1919; Neil Foley, *The White Scourge: Mexicans, Blacks, and Poor Whites in Texas Cotton Culture* (Berkeley: University of California Press, 1997): 4; Gerald Horne, *Black and Brown: African Americans and the Mexican Revolution, 1910–1920* (New York: New York University Press, 2005).

8 *California Eagle*, 6 Dec. 1919, cited in Quintard Taylor et al., *Seeking El Dorado: African Americans in California* (Seattle: University of Seattle Press, 2001): 165.

9 Advertisement printed in *Gale's Magazine*, an IWW periodical published in Mexico City, cited in Randy Roberts, *Papa Jack: Jack Johnson and the Era of White Hopes* (New York: Collier Macmillan, 1983): 212; 'Jack Idolized in Mexico', *Chicago Defender*, 10 May 1919: 11; 'Make J. Johnson Hero in Mexico', *Chicago Tribune*, 16 Apr. 1919: 20; 'Jack Johnson Now Thrives as Medicine Man', *Chicago Tribune*, 21 Apr. 1919: 19; 'Refused Johnson', *Chicago Defender*, 12 Jul. 1919: 1.

10 Finis Farr, *Black Champion: The Life and Times of Jack Johnson* (London: Macmillan, 1964): 218–220; Geoffrey C. Ward, *Unforgivable Blackness: The Rise and Fall of Jack Johnson* (New York: A.A. Knopf, 2004): 397.

Chapter 3 Across the River Styx: Sonny Clay's Tijuana

1 John Bentley, 'Sonny Clay: A Veritable Giant—Part 2', *Jazz Research*, Jan./Feb. 1963: 13–14; E.M. Schantz, 'All Night at the Owl: The Social and Political Relations of Mexicali's Red Light District, 1913–1925' in *On the Border: Society and Culture between the United States and Mexico*, ed. Andrew Grant Wood (Oxford: SR Books, 2004): 91–144; L.D. Taylor, 'The Wild Frontier Moves South: U.S. Entrepreneurs and the Growth of Tijuana's Vice Industry, 1908–1935', *Journal of San Diego History*, 48:3 (2002); P.J. Vanderwood, *Satan's Playground, Mobsters and Movie Stars at America's Greatest Gaming Resort* (Durham and London: Duke University Press, 2010): 72–76.

2 'Governor Esteban Cantu', *Arizona Sentinel*, 18 Oct. 1917: 1; 'Plan Great Casino Below Line', *Los Angeles Times*, 20 Apr. 1919: II 1.

3 'Liquor Flows at Tijuana', *Denison Review*, 4 Feb. 1920: 1.

4 'The Drought and Tia Juana', *New York Times*, 6 Jun. 1920: 69.

5 *New York Times*, 6 Jun. 1920: 69; 'In Tia Juana', *Los Angeles Times*, 2 Aug. 1925: B5.

6 *Denison Review*, 4 Feb. 1920: 1; 'Tia Juana, Wickedest Town', *Twin City Daily Sentinel*, 20 Jan. 1921: 8.

7 Bentley, 'Sonny Clay, Part 2': 13–14; 'Troop Transfer', *Bisbee Herald*, 3 Jan. 1919: 4; 'Governor Cantu Issues Iron-Clad Order', *Arizona Sentinel*, 15 Nov. 1917: 4; 'Federals Kill, Loot, the Desert Post', *Arizona Republican*, 9 Sept. 1919: 2; 'Some Mexican Slayings that Were Hushed Up', *Chicago Tribune*, 17 Sept. 1919: 10; Jaurez in Revolt without Fighting', *New York Times*, 4 May 1920: 1; Robert H. Duncan, 'The Chinese and the Economic Development of Northern Baja California, 1889–1929', *Hispanic American Historical Review*, 74:4 (Nov. 1994): 615–647.

8 *Los Angeles Times*, 20 Apr. 1919: II 1; 'Gaming Resort Online Closed', *Ogden Standard*, 26 Sept. 1920: 1; Schantz, 'All Night at the Owl': 91–144; Clora Bryant et al. (eds), *Central Avenue Sounds: Jazz in Los Angeles* (Berkeley: University of California Press, 1998): 82, 94.

9 Bentley, 'Sonny Clay, Part 2': 13–14.

10 'Coast Dope', *Chicago Defender*, 5 Apr. 1924: 7.

11 'Race Track Gossip', *Chicago Defender*, 31 Mar. 1934: 17; 7 Sept. 1925: 14.

12 'San Diego Boasts of Nite Club', 1 Apr. 1939: 20; 'Coast Stage Stars Shine', *Chicago Defender*, 24 Aug. 1935: 7; Centre City Development Corporation, *Downtown San Diego African-American Heritage*, San Diego, June 2004: 28.
13 Josh Kun, 'Tijuana and the Borders of Race', *The Blackwell Companion to Los Angeles* in ed. W. Deverell (Oxford: Blackwell Publishing Company, 2010): 313–326; Schantz, 'All Night at the Owl': 106–109.
14 'Kennel Man Sees Great Things Ahead Hereabout', *The Rounder*, year unknown, cited in Schantz, 'Meretricious Mexicali': 103.
15 'Coast Dope', *Chicago Defender*, 24 Jul. 1922: 8; *Chicago Defender*, 1 Jul. 1922: 8.
16 'Coast Dope', *Chicago Defender*, 11 Mar. 1922: 8.
17 Cited in Philip Pastras, *Dead Man Blues: Jelly Roll Morton Way Out West* (Berkeley: University of California Press, 2001): 79–80.
18 Alan Lomax, *Mister Jelly Roll: The Fortunes of Jelly Roll Morton, New Orleans Creole and 'Inventor of Jazz'* (Berkeley: University of California Press, 2001): 116, 160, 227; Garvin Bushell, *Jazz from the Beginning* (Ann Arbor: University of Michigan Press, 1990): 43.
19 Lomax, *Mister Jelly Roll*: 164.
20 Lomax, *Mister Jelly Roll*: 116, 160, 227. 'People ... thought I was one of the movie stars, I had so many clothes.'
21 John Bentley, 'Sonny Clay: A Veritable Giant—Part 1', *Jazz Research*, Nov/Dec. 1962: 6–7.
22 Bentley, 'Sonny Clay, Part 2': 13–14; Pastras, *Dead Man Blues*: 108–122.
23 Dorothy Clay 1921–1921, Find A Grave, https://www.findagrave.com/memorial/9783596/verbena-g_-clay
24 'Coast Dope', *Chicago Defender*, 17 Jul. 1920; 19 Sept. 1921; 15 Oct. 1921; 1 Jul. 1922; 7 Oct. 1922.
25 *New York Tribune*, 21 Jul. 1920: 19.
26 'Jack Johnson Returns to US', *Chicago Tribune*, 21 Jul. 1921; 'Jack Johnson Returns from Exile', *Chicago Defender*, 24 Jul. 1920: 1; 'Jack Johnson Is Jailed Here Despite Protest', *Los Angeles Times*, 21 Jul. 1920: II 1.
27 Kun, 'Tijuana and the Borders of Race': 319–320.

Chapter 4 South Central Avenue, Los Angeles

1 Numerically speaking, White Southern immigration far exceeded Black. See James Noble Gregory, *The Southern Diaspora: How the Great Migrations of Black and White Southerners Transformed America* (Chapel Hill: University of North Carolina Press, 2005); Scott Kurashige, *The Shifting Grounds of Race: Black and Japanese Americans in the Making of Multiethnic Los Angeles* (Princeton, NJ; Woodstock: Princeton University Press, 2008); also see Chapter 1, Ted Gioia, *West Coast Jazz: Modern Jazz in California, 1945–1960* (New York: Oxford University Press, 1992); J. Max Bond, *The Negro in Los Angeles* (San Francisco: R and E Research Associates, 1972).
2 Clora Bryant et al. (eds), *Central Avenue Sounds: Jazz in Los Angeles* (Berkeley: University of California Press, 1998): 24.
3 Between 1882 and 1968, forty-three lynchings took place in California. Forty-one of the victims were designated 'white'. Two were Black. See: *Table: Lynchings: by State and Race, 1882–1968*, from research completed at Berea College in January 1999 for the Charles Chesnutt Digital Library. http://faculty.berea.edu/browners/chesnutt/classroom/lynchings_table_state.html (accessed 2 Feb. 2018).

4 Bond, *The Negro in Los Angeles*: 52; L.B. De Graaf, 'The City of Black Angels: Emergence of the Los Angeles Ghetto, 1890–1930', *Pacific Historical Review*, 39:3 (1970): 323–352.
5 *Los Angeles Times*, 12 Feb. 1909.
6 Philip Pastras, *Dead Man Blues: Jelly Roll Morton Way Out West* (Berkeley: University of California Press, 2001): 79–80; Garvin Bushell, *Jazz from the Beginning* (Ann Arbor: University of Michigan Press, 1990): 43.
7 Tom Stoddard, *Jazz on the Barbary Coast* (Berkeley: Heyday Books, 1982): 26.
8 For example: Papa Mutt, Wade Whaley, Dink Johnson, Ernest Coycault. Lawrence Gushee, 'New Orleans-Area Musicians on the West Coast, 1908–1925', *Black Music Research Journal*, 9:1 (1989): 1–18.
9 'Coast Dope', *Chicago Defender*, 20 Nov. 1920: 15.
10 John Bentley, 'Sonny Clay: A Veritable Giant—Part 2', *Jazz Research*, Jan./Feb. 1963: 13–14; 'Dancing Demons', *Los Angeles Times*, 5 Apr. 1925: D16.
11 Sonny Clay, Oral History Collection, Hogan Jazz Archive, Tulane University, Louisiana.
12 'Advertisement', *San Francisco Chronicle*, 6 Aug. 1923: 6; 'Advertisement', *Post-Crescent*, 8 Jul. 1924: 10.
13 Bentley, 'Sonny Clay, Part 2': 13–14.
14 Marshal, Royal, *Marshal Royal: Jazz Survivor* (New York: Cassell, 1996): 18–20.
15 Johnny Otis and George Lipsitz, *Listen to the Lambs* (Minneapolis: University of Minnesota Press, 2009): 96.
16 'Coast Dope', *Chicago Defender*, 1 Nov. 1924: 7.
17 'Coast Dope', *Chicago Defender*, 10 Jan. 1925: 6.
18 Leo McCoy Davis, Frank Driggs, Oral History Collection, Tape 77, Marr Sound Archive, University of Missouri, Kansas City.
19 'Advertisement: The Royal Star Athletic Club', *California Eagle*, 7 Nov. 1922; 'Coming Events', *California Eagle*, 25 Nov. 1922: 6.
20 *California Eagle*, 12 Feb. 1926: 4; Michael B. Bakan, 'Way Out West on Central: Jazz in the African American Community of Los Angeles before 1930' in *California Soul: Music of African Americans in the West*, eds Jacqueline Cogdell DjeDje and Eddie S. Meadows (Berkeley: University of California Press, 1998): 43.
21 'Val Haltren's Men Lose Twice', *Oakland Tribune*, 22 Jun. 1908: 9; Samuel Charters, *A Trumpet Around the Corner: The Story of New Orleans Jazz* (Jackson: University Press of Mississippi, 2008): 102, 223; Daniel Hardie, *Exploring Early Jazz: The Origins and Evolution of the New Orleans Style* (San Jose: Writers Club Press, 2002): 103.
22 'Sonny Clay in Retrospect', *Jazzfinder*, Sept. 1948.
23 Court Carney, *Cuttin' Up: How Early Jazz Got America's Ear* (Lawrence: University Press of Kansas, 2009):106–114; Albert J. McCarthy, *Big Band Jazz* (New York: Berkley Publishing Corporation, 1977): 172–173.
24 Royal, *Marshal Royal, Jazz Survivor*: 18.
25 Donald Bogle, *Bright Boulevards, Bold Dreams: The Story of Black Hollywood* (New York: One World Ballantine Books, 2005): 73–74.
26 Stoddard, *Jazz on the Barbary Coast*: 100.
27 'Sex Pictures Are on the Wane', *Motion Picture Magazine*, Jul. 1925: 28–32.
28 'Sinners in Silk', *Exhibitors Trade Review*, 14 Sept. 1924.
29 'Circe the Enchantress', *Screenland*, May 1926: 94.
30 Bentley, 'Sonny Clay, Part 2': 13–14.

31 'Rivoli', *Exhibitors Trade Review*, 29 Oct. 1921: 1553; 'Camera Trick Used in Dante's *Inferno*', *Kingsport Times*, 4 Jan. 1925: 6; 'The Snob Coming', *Eugene Guard*, 21 Mar. 1925: 8.
32 'Circe', *Variety*, 10 Dec. 1924: 35.
33 'The Other Mae Murray', *Motion Picture Magazine*, Jul. 1923: 90.
34 'Lincoln Perry Writes', *Chicago Defender*, 27 Aug. 1927, cited in Mel Watkins, *Stepin Fetchit: The Life and Times of Lincoln Perry* (New York: Pantheon Books, 2005): 20.
35 'Filmland Goes Harlem', *Fort Worth Telegram*, 17 Jul. 1929: 12.
36 E.J. Fleming, *Paul Bern: The Life and Famous Death of the MGM Director and Husband of Harlow* (New York: McFarland & Company, 2009): 242, 263.
37 'A Jungle Lorelei', *Photoplay*, Jul. 1929: 40.
38 Langston Hughes, 'The Negro Artist and the Racial Mountain', *The Nation*, Jun. 1926, cited in Karl Koenig, *Jazz in Print (1856–1929): An Anthology of Selected Early Readings in Jazz History* (Hillsdale, NY: Pendragon Press, 2002): 478–479.
39 Ronald Radano, 'Hot Fantasies: American Modernism and the Idea of Black Rhythm' in *Music and the Racial Imagination*, eds Ronald Radano and Philip Bohlman (Chicago: University of Chicago Press, 2000): 459–480.
40 'In Defense of Jazz and Its Makers', *New York Times*, 13 Mar. 1927: 22.
41 Michael Paul Rogin, *Blackface, White Noise: Jewish Immigrants in the Hollywood Melting Pot* (Berkeley: University of California Press, 1996): 4.
42 Clarence Muse, *The Dilemma of the Negro Actor* (Los Angeles: 1934).
43 W.E.B. Du Bois, 'The Strivings of the Negro People', *The Atlantic*, Aug. 1897. https://www.theatlantic.com/magazine/archive/1897/08/strivings-of-the-negro-people/305446/
44 Andy Razaf, cited in Barry Singer, *Black and Blue: The Life and Lyrics of Andy Razaf* (New York: Maxwell Macmillan International, 1992): 51.
45 Alain Locke (ed.), *The New Negro* (New York: Athenaeum, 1968): 3–16.
46 'Coast Dope', *Chicago Defender*, 18 Feb. 1928.
47 'Coast Dope', *Chicago Defender*, 1 Nov. 1924: 7.
48 'Coast Dope', *Chicago Defender*, 10 Jan. 1925: 6.
49 'The Musician's Protective Union', 23 Apr. 1926: 10.
50 'California News', *Pittsburgh Courier*, 20 Feb. 1926: 5.
51 'Radio Ball', *Pittsburgh Courier*, 20 Mar. 1926: 5.

Chapter 5 The Lost Angels

1 'KNX-Pacific 337', *Radio Digest*, 17 Jan. 1925: 7.
2 'Dancing Demons Play and Write Jazz Music', *Los Angeles Times*, 5 Apr. 1925: D16; 'Demoniacal Dance Demons Demonstrate', *Los Angeles Times*, 12 Apr. 1925: 22.
3 'Los Angeles', *Variety*, 11 Nov. 1927: 60.
4 Sonny Clay, Oral History Collection, Hogan Jazz Archive, Tulane University, Louisiana; 'Sonny Clay in Retrospect', *Jazzfinder*, Sept. 1948: 3–6.
5 'Coast Dope', *Chicago Defender*, 23 May 1925: 7.
6 'Radio', *La Grande Observer*, 9 Jul. 1925: 3.
7 'Advertisement: Brunswick Records', *Santa Rosa Republican*, 22 Aug. 1925: 4.
8 'California News', *Pittsburgh Courier*, 6 Mar. 1926: 15.
9 'The Wolf. Eh! What?', *California Eagle*, 12 Feb. 1926: 8.
10 'Coast Dope', *Chicago Defender*, 15 May 1926: 7.
11 'Coast Dope', *Chicago Defender*, 10 Oct. 1925: 6.
12 John Bentley and Ralph W. Miller, 'West Coast Jazz in the 1920s', *Jazz Monthly*, May 1961.

13 John Bentley, 'Sonny Clay: A Veritable Giant—Part 1', *Jazz Research*, Nov./Dec. 1962: 7–8; John Bentley, Sonny Clay: A Veritable Giant—Part 2', *Jazz Research*, Jan./ Feb. 1963: 13–14.
14 Sonny Clay, Oral History Collection, Hogan Jazz Archive.
15 'Griffith Has Set Re-Enchantment to Music', *Arizona Republican*, 23 Apr. 1916: 6; Gerald Horne, *Black and Brown: African Americans and the Mexican Revolution, 1910–1920* (New York: New York University Press, 2005): 181.
16 Richard Schickel, *D.W. Griffith: An American Life* (New York: Simon and Schuster, 1984).
17 Bentley, 'Sonny Clay, Part 2': 13–14.
18 Charles Affron, *Lillian Gish: Her Legend, Her Life* (New York: Scribner, 2001): 88.
19 Bryan Curtis, 'D.W. Griffith in Black and White: Was the *Birth of a Nation* Director Really a Racist?', *Slate*, 3 Jan. 2003.
20 Ziegfeld's cable to the *New York Times*, cited in Charles Higham, *Ziegfeld* (London: W.H. Allen, 1973): 104.
21 Alys Eve Weinbaum, 'Racial Masquerade: Consumption and Contestation of American Modernity' in *The Modern Girl around the World: Consumption, Modernity, and Globalization*, eds Alys Eve Weinbaum et al., (Durham, NC: Duke University Press, 2008): 120–146.
22 Robert Shuler, *Fighting Bob Shuler of Los Angeles* (Indianapolis: Dog Ear Publishing, 2011): 108.
23 Sonny Clay, Oral History Collection, Hogan Jazz Archive.
24 Rex Stewart, *Boy Meets Horn* (Ann Arbor: University of Michigan Press, 1991):177–178; 'California News', *Pittsburgh Courier*, 6 Mar. 1926: 15; Duke Ellington, *Music Is My Mistress* (Garden City, NY: Doubleday, 1973): 124; 'Plantation Days', *Daily Telegraph*, 25 Jan. 1928: 7.
25 Clora Bryant et al. (eds), *Central Avenue Sounds: Jazz in Los Angeles* (Berkeley: University of California Press, 1998): 55, 115, 241.
26 Garvin Bushell, *Jazz from the Beginning* (Ann Arbor: University of Michigan Press, 1990): 96.
27 'Coast Dope', *Chicago Defender*, 10 Mar. 1923: 8; 'Coast Dope', *Chicago Defender*, 17 Mar. 1923: 7.
28 J. Max Bond, *The Negro in Los Angeles* (San Francisco: R. and E. Research Associates, 1972).
29 Marshal Royal, *Marshal Royal, Jazz Survivor* (New York: Cassell, 1996): 20.

Chapter 6 The Best Box Office Judge in Australia

1 'In California with Harry Muller', *Everyones*, 6 Jan. 1926: 34; 'Theatre Gossip', Sydney *Truth*, 17 Feb. 1924: 5.
2 'Harry Muller', *Everyones*, 5 Aug. 1925: 45.
3 *Film Weekly*, cited in 'Palmerston North Show Business Doyen Lived a Life among the Stars', *Manawatu Standard*, 17 Aug. 2019.
4 'Vaudeville Outlook Bright, says Muller', *Everyones*, 25 Jan. 1928: 1.
5 Adelaide *Mail*, 21 Jun. 1913: 12.
6 'With Harry Muller in San Francisco', *Everyones*, 7 Apr. 1926: 10.
7 'With Harry Muller in San Francisco', *Everyones*, 7 Jul. 1926: 52.
8 'In Los Angeles with Harry P. Muller', *Everyones*, 18 Nov. 1925: 14.
9 'With Harry Muller in San Francisco', *Everyones*, 7 Apr. 1926: 10.
10 ibid.
11 'In California with Harry Muller', *Everyones*, 6 Jan. 1926: 34.

12 'Harry P. Muller in San Francisco', *Everyones*, 7 Oct. 1925: 24.
13 'In Los Angeles with Harry P. Muller', *Everyones*, 18 Nov. 1925: 14.
14 'With Harry Muller in San Francisco', *Everyones*, 18 Aug. 1926: 38.
15 'In California with Harry Muller', *Everyones*, 6 Jan. 1926: 34.
16 'In Los Angeles with Harry P. Muller', *Everyones*, 18 Nov. 1925: 14.
17 'In Los Angeles with Harry P. Muller', *Everyones*, 18 Nov. 1925: 14.
18 *Parliament of the Commonwealth of Australia: Report of the Royal Commission on the Moving Picture Industry in Australia* (Canberra: Government Printer, 1928): 3.
19 'Cinema Industry Trends Admissions and Key Events, 1901–1932', *Screen Australia*, https://www.screenaustralia.gov.au/fact-finders/cinema/industry-trends/historical-admissions/1901-1932
20 'Have You Booked Miss 1928?', *Everyones*, 4 Jan. 1928: 17–18. For discussion of leisure and the Australian modern working girl see: Jill Julius Matthews, *Dance Hall & Picture Palace: Sydney's Romance with Modernity* (Sydney: Currency Press, 2005): 79–100; Liz Connor, *The Spectacular Modern Woman* (Bloomington: Indiana University Press, 2004): 209–223.
21 'Brilliant Society and Jazz Drama', *Exhibition Trade Review*, 18 Oct. 1924: 42.
22 'In Los Angeles with Harry P. Muller', *Everyones*, 18 Nov. 1925: 14.
23 Dr Woolsey Martin, the pastor at the Hollywood Methodist Church, cited in Gregory Paul Williams, *The Story of Hollywood: An Illustrated History* (Los Angeles: BL Press LLC, 2011): 108.
24 Advertisement, *Kansas City Star*, 1 Jan. 1922: 9.
25 *Pittsburgh Press*, 25 Jul. 1920: 73.
26 *Washington Herald*, 27 Aug. 1920: 6.
27 'In Los Angeles with Harry P. Muller', *Everyones*, 18 Nov. 1925: 14; Charles Edward Orbison, 'Fighting Bob' Shuler and KGEF: The Silencing of a Radio Crusader, Thesis, Master of Science, August 1975, University of North Texas.
28 Ellen C. Scott, *Cinema Civil Rights: Regulation, Repression, and Race in the Classical Hollywood Era* (New Brunswick, NJ: Rutgers University Press, 2015).
29 'Girls Properly Clothed', Melbourne *Herald*, 17 Jan. 1922: 5.
30 Atcheson L. Hench, 'A Possible Clue to the Source of "Ballyhoo" and Some Queries', *American Speech*, 20:3 (1945): 184–186.
31 'With Harry Muller in San Francisco', *Everyones*, 7 Jul. 1926: 52.

Chapter 7 The Real Charleston

1 'Harry Muller', *Everyones*, 5 Aug. 1925: 45.
2 'Harry P Muller in San Francisco', *Everyones*, 7 Oct. 1925: 24.
3 'Our Chicago Letter by Bob Conkey', *Everyones*, 9 Dec. 1925: 33.
4 *Kingsport Times*, 23 Mar. 1926: 4.
5 Franklin Bruno, 'James P. Johnson: From "Carolina Shout" to "The Charleston"', *Sound American*, https://soundamerican.org/issues/alien/james-p-johnson-carolina-shout-charleston
6 *Minneapolis Star*, 11 Mar. 1927: 17; *Ogden Standard-Examiner*, 1 Nov. 1925: 23; *Kingsport Times*, 23 Mar. 1926: 4; *Logansport Pharos-Tribune*, 31 Dec. 1925: 1.
7 Marshall Stearns and Jean Stearns, *Jazz Dance: The Story of American Vernacular Dance* (New York: Macmillan New York, 1968): 249.
8 'James P. Johnson by Tom Davin', *Jazz Review*, 2:2 (July 1959): 11–13.
9 *New York Age*, 5 Jan. 1924: 2.
10 *Daily News*, 23 Nov. 1923: 9.
11 *Daily Mail*, 28 Mar. 1926: 11.

12 '*Sally, Irene and Mary* (1925) Restoration Trailer', *George Eastman Museum*, https://youtu.be/14r1-Jy3Gcl
13 'The Charleston', *Everyones*, 21 Jul. 1926: 60; *Everyones*, 15 Dec. 1926: 111.
14 Buddy Brown, 'Coast Dope', *Chicago Defender*, 11 Jun. 1927.
15 For an overview of Cato's career see: Henry Louis Gates and Evelyn Brooks Higginbotham, *Harlem Renaissance Lives from the African American National Biography* (New York: Oxford University Press, 2009): 109–111.
16 Sydney *Sun*, 22 Jul. 1926: 2; Sydney *Sun*, 23 Jul. 1926; Sydney *Sun*, 25 Jul. 1926: 35.
17 'The Southern Revue', *Sunday Times*, 5 Dec. 1926: 27; 'Theatre Royal, Celebrity Vaudeville', Adelaide *Advertiser*, 4 Oct. 1926.
18 'Sydney Theatres', *Everyones*, 28 Jul. 1926: 41.
19 'Astute Tivoli Management', Melbourne *Truth*, 21 Aug. 1926: 11.
20 'Minto Cato Writes', *Chicago Defender*, 6 Nov. 1926: 7.
21 'The Tivoli', *Sydney Morning Herald*, 26 Jul. 1926: 6.
22 'Miss Mills Is a Reason for Buying Seats', *Chicago Daily Tribune*, 20 Aug. 1924: 17; 'Elmer Praises WGN Program', *Chicago Daily Tribune*, 15 Aug. 1928; 'Story of Negro Will Be Told in Music Pageant', *Chicago Daily Tribune*, 16 Aug. 1934. Also see: Arnold Shaw, *The Jazz Age: Popular Music in the 1920s* (New York: Oxford University Press, 1987): 88–92.
23 'The Theatre and Its People', *Table Talk*, 9 Sept. 1926: 2.
24 'Astute Tivoli Management', Melbourne *Truth*, 21 Aug. 1926; 'Celebrity Vaudeville', Adelaide *Register*, 4 Oct. 1926.
25 'Romance and Henry Santrey', *Everyones*, 23 Jun. 1926: 41; 'Continued Success', Adelaide *Register*, 25 Nov. 1926: 13; 'Santrey's Band Arrived on August 23rd', *Everyones*, 11 Aug. 1926: 50.
26 'Mr Santrey's Orchestra', *Sydney Morning Herald*, 23 Aug. 1926: 12; 'Harry Muller's American Letter', *Everyones*, 21 Jul. 1926: 66.
27 'Radio and Jazz', *Queanbeyan Age*, 9 Sept. 1926: 4.
28 'The Meaning of Jazz', Adelaide *Advertiser*, 15 Nov. 1926: 7.
29 Edwin J. Stringham, '"Jazz" An Educational Problem', *Musical Quarterly*, Apr. 1926; Paul Whiteman, 'In Defense of Jazz and Its Makers', *New York Times*, 13 Mar. 1927.
30 'Santrey's Midnight Revels', *Everyones*, 8 Sept. 1926: 56.

Chapter 8 Testing the Waters

1 SS *Sierra*, April 1928, Image 7, California, Passenger and Crew Lists, 1882–1957, Ancestry.com; 'Lincoln Perry's Letter', *Chicago Defender*, 14 Jan. 1928: 6.
2 In 1925, Bing Crosby launched his career in *The Syncopation Idea*.
3 'Loew's State Has Elaborate Colored Revue', *Los Angeles Times*, 4 Apr. 1927: A7.
4 'Lincoln Perry's Letter', *Chicago Defender*, 29 Oct. 1927: 8; 'Theatre Royal', Adelaide *Advertiser*, 4 Oct. 1926: 14.
5 'Lincoln Perry's Letter', *Chicago Defender*, 23 Jul. 1927: 6.
6 Marshall Stearns and Jean Stearns, *Jazz Dance: The Story of American Vernacular Dance* (New York: Macmillan New York, 1968): 249. For a film clip of Willie Covan performing with 'US Kid' Thompson see: *Newsreel: Eccentric Steps* (1925), British Pathe Pictures, http://www.britishpathe.com/video/eccentric-steps/query/01000100 (accessed 6 Oct. 2020).
7 Stearns and Stearns, *Jazz Dance*: 176.
8 William Hann appeared in Noble Sissle's groundbreaking *Shuffle Along* (1921) and *Chocolate Dandies* (1925); Tim Brooks, *Lost Sounds: Blacks and the Birth of the Recording Industry 1890–1919* (Urbana: University of Illinois Press, 2004): 453–469.

9 'Coloured Emperors of Harmony', *Brisbane Courier*, 15 Sept. 1927: 16.
10 'From Australia', *Chicago Defender*, 10 Mar. 1928: 7.
11 'Australia', Sydney *Sun*, 20 Aug. 1944: 4; 'Letter from the Antipodes', *Chicago Defender*, 28 Apr. 1923: 13.
12 Cassandra Pybus, *Black Founders: The Unknown History of Australia's First Black Settlers* (Sydney: UNSW Press, 2006).
13 J. Atkinson, '"Men of Colour": John Joseph and the Eureka Treason Trials', *Journal of Australian Colonial History*, 10:1 (2008): 75–98.
14 Richard Waterhouse, *From Minstrel Show to Vaudeville: The Australian Popular Stage, 1788–1914* (Sydney: UNSW Press, 1990): 61–79.
15 'Miss Bessie Campbell', *SS Stewarts Banjo and Guitar Journal*, Feb./Mar. 1897: 2; 'Obituary: Hosea Easton', *Critic*, 8 Jul. 1899: 14.
16 Melissa Bellanta, 'Uncle Tom in the White Pacific: African-American Performances of the "Slave Sublime" in Late-colonial Australasia', *Journal of Colonialism & Colonial History*, 15:3 (Dec. 2014): n/a.
17 'The Fisk Jubilee Singers', *Mount Alexander Mail*, 4 Oct. 1887: 2.
18 'Drysdale', *Geelong Advertiser*, 15 Apr. 1895: 4; 'Aboriginal Music', *Kiama Independent and Shoalhaven Advertiser*, 15 Mar. 1887: 4.
19 Lynn Abbott and Doug Seroff, *Out of Sight: The Rise of African American Popular Music 1889–1895* (Jackson: University Press of Mississippi, 2002): 119–141.
20 'Jim Harris Writes', *Topeka Plaindealer*, 11 Aug. 1899: 4.
21 Abbott and Seroff, *Out of Sight*: 131.
22 'The Stage', *Indianapolis Freeman*, 29 Jul. 1899: 5; 'Tom Logan Writes', *Topeka Plaindealer*, 29 Sept. 1899: 2.
23 Waterhouse, *From Minstrel Show to Vaudeville*: 148–149; for examples of Australian enthusiasm for African American performers see: 'Tivoli Vaudeville', *Argus*, 8 Dec. 1924; 'A Big Show', *Cairns Morning Post*, 3 Mar. 1900.
24 'Victoria', *Sydney Morning Herald*, 24 Jan. 1879; 'Hosea Easton's Funeral', *Evening News*, 26 Jun. 1899; 'Theatrical Maintenance Case', *Fitzroy City Press*, 23 Mar. 1900: 3.
25 R.C. Petersen, *Peter Jackson: A Biography of the Australian Heavyweight Champion, 1860–1901* (Jefferson, NC: McFarland & Co, 2011).
26 'Reception to Jack Johnson', *Referee*, 30 Jan. 1907: 7.
27 Theresa Runstedtler, *Jack Johnson, Rebel Sojourner: Boxing in the Shadow of the Global Color Line* (Berkeley: University of California Press, 2012): 31–67.
28 'Jack Johnson Arrives, A Warm Reception', *Sydney Morning Herald*, 30 Oct. 1908: 10.
29 'Emperors of Harmony', *Chicago Defender*, 14 Jan. 1928.
30 'Vaudeville Outlook Bright, says Muller', *Everyones*, 25 Jan. 1928: 1.
31 For examples see: Collector of Customs files of 'J L Smith—American Negro ex Moeraki 1.6.1923—Departed S.S. Makura, 2.8.1923', NAA B13, 1923/10153 and 'Four Colored Artists', NAA C&E 1925/15659.
32 Immigration Branch, *Book of Precedents*, 1912–1933, NAA Item No A1823: 4.
33 Letter: Walter M. Marks MP to Senator George Pearce, Minister for Home & Territories Department, 11 Jan. 1923, NAA A1, 1923/2723.
34 Home & Territories Department Memorandum No 23/1190, 9 Feb. 1923; Letter: Secretary, Minister for Home & Territories to JC Bendrodt, 2 Feb. 1923, NAA A1, 1923/2723.
35 'In Honolulu', *Chicago Defender*, 5 Jul. 1924: 6.
36 'California News', *Pittsburgh Courier*, 6 Mar. 1926.

37 Letter: J.C. Bendrodt to Mr Maclaren, Home & Territories Department, Melbourne, 16 Jan. 1923, NAA A1, 1923/2723.
38 Home & Territories Department Memorandum No 23/1190, 9 Feb. 1923.
39 'Australian Musicians Object', Adelaide *Advertiser*, 2 Sept. 1924: 16; 'Imported Jazz Bands', Broken Hill *Barrier Miner*, 2 Sept. 1924: 4.
40 For example, see: 'Rebuke to Mr Hughes', Sydney *Sun*, 30 Mar. 1928; 'Storm in Nationalist Camp', Burnie *Advocate*, 31 Mar. 1928.
41 'Sonny Clay's Parting Shot', *Everyones*, 4 Apr. 1928: 6.
42 For discussion of entry requirements see: Alison Bashford, *Imperial Hygiene: A Critical History of Colonialism, Nationalism, and Public Health* (New York: Palgrave Macmillan, 2004): 137–166.
43 Letter: Department Home & Territories to the Manager, Tivoli Theatre, Melbourne, 12 Jan. 1928, NAA A1, 1929/4892.
44 'Sonny Clay's Parting Shot', *Everyones*, 4 Apr. 1928: 6.
45 ibid.
46 Frank Hill, 'Plays & Players', *Daily Guardian*, 23 Jan. 1928: 8.
47 'Coast Dope', *Chicago Defender*, 17 Sept. 1927: 7.
48 'Here and There', *Afro-American*, 3 Dec. 1927: 8.
49 'Lincoln Perry's Letter', *Chicago Defender*, 29 Oct. 1927: 8.
50 'Coloured Comedy', *Daily Guardian*, 19 Jan. 1928.
51 Letter: J.C. Bendrodt to Mr Maclaren, Home & Territories Department, Melbourne, 16 Jan. 1923, NAA A1, 1923/2723; Cecil Trevelyan, *Musician Union of Australia Rules* (Melbourne: Labor Call Press, 1927), MUA NBAC E156/1.

Chapter 9 My Blue Heaven

1 'The Plantation Band in Sonny Clay's New Idea', *Daily Guardian*, 14 Jan. 1928; Sydney *Truth*, 25 Dec. 1927: 11; 'Coloured Comedy', *Daily Guardian*, 19 Jan. 1928; 'Sonny Clay's Idea', *Table Talk*, 16 Feb. 1928: 22; 'Stage Pars and Points', Sydney *Truth*, 8 Jan. 1928: 11; 'Advertisement: Colored Idea', *Daily Telegraph*, 20 Jan. 1928: 10.
2 'Sonny Clay', *Beckett's Budget*, 20 Jan. 1928: 23; 'Tivoli Novelty', Sydney *Truth*, 22 Jan. 1928: 23; *Daily Guardian*, 14 Jan. 1928; *Everyones*, 11 Jan. 1928: 40.
3 'Sonny Clay's Plantation Band Turns *Sierra* into Jazz Ship', *Everyones*, 25 Jan. 1928: 39.
4 *Everyones*, 25 Jan. 1928: 39; 'Newspapers Don't Like Publicity Men', *Everyones*, 10 Nov. 1926; 'Stories in Black and White', *Everyones*, 5 Sept. 1928: 5; Dexter's father, Robert, wrote under the pseudonym 'Pilot' for sporting newspaper *The Referee*.
5 *Everyones*, 25 Jan. 1928: 39; Ronald Radano, 'Hot Fantasies: American Modernism and the Idea of Black Rhythm' in *Music and the Racial Imagination*, eds Ronald Radano and Philip Bohlman (Chicago: University of Chicago Press, 2000): 459–480.
6 For example, see: *The Mercury*, 31 Mar. 1928; 'New York', Adelaide *Register*, 16 Nov. 1927; 'Majestic Theatre', Adelaide *Register*, 3 Dec. 1924. Examples of these films include: *Wolf's Clothing* (1927) and *New York* (1928). Also see Ryan Jay Friedman, *Hollywood's African American Films: The Transition to Sound* (New Brunswick, NJ: Rutgers University Press, 2011): 28–56.
7 'So This Is an Australian Who Roused Commission's Ire in "So This Is Paris"', *Everyones*, 4 Jan. 1928: 8; 'Commissions Comment Booms "So This Is Paris"', *Everyones*, 31 Aug. 1927: 40.

8 'Camera Tricks. Walking in Clouds', *Armidale Chronicle*, 3 Sept. 1927: 4.
9 *Everyones*, 25 Jan. 1928: 39.
10 'Woman's World', *News*, 7 Mar. 1928: 7; Sydney *Sun*, 5 Jul. 1930: 3; Sydney *Sun*, 8 Feb. 1933: 10.
11 'Sydney Is Australia's Chief Art Centre', *Daily Telegraph*, 25 Sept. 1927: 16; *Daily Telegraph*, 1 Dec. 1927: 7, 11; *Daily Telegraph*, 11 Sept. 1927: 28; Ann Stephen, Philip Goad and Andrew McNamara (eds), *Modern Times: The Untold Story of Modernism in Australia* (Sydney: The Miegunyah Press and Powerhouse Publishing, 2008).
12 M. Andre Lhote, 'Cubism', in *Undergrowth: A Magazine of Youth and Ideals*, eds Nancy A. Hall and Dore Hawthorne, Mar–Apr 1928; *Undergrowth*, Jan–Feb 1927; *Undergrowth*, May–June 1927.
13 'Will Do As We Like', *Daily Telegraph*, 6 Sept. 1927: 22; 'Artists Hold High Revelry', *Daily Telegraph*, 6 Sept. 1927: 3.
14 'In Oxford Bags', Sydney *Sun*, 2 Jun. 1925: 12; 'Abduction', *New South Wales Police Gazette and Weekly Record of Crime*, 26 Jan. 1927: 54; 'News & Notes', *Uralla Times*, 8 Nov. 1926: 4; 'Money in Paper Selling', *Daily Examiner*, 15 Nov. 1926: 4; 'Coogee Casino's K.B. Clientele', Sydney *Truth*, 16 May 1926: 11; 'Trousers Will Be Tighter This Winter', *Uralla Times*, 21 May 1928: 4; 'A Bundle of Letters', Sydney *Sun*, 16 Sept. 1925: 8.
15 *Arrow*, 11 Sept. 1931: 16; *Beaudesert Times*, 12 Jul. 1929: 9; *Arrow*, 13 Jan. 1933: 27; for example of illustration see: *The Referee*, 9 Apr. 1936: 1; *The Referee*, 23 Jul. 1936: 1; *Labor Daily*, 27 Jun. 1929: 7; *Sydney Morning Herald*, 30 Jul. 1929: 5.
16 'Colored Idea', Sydney *Sun*, 22 Jan. 1928: 23.
17 'Australia', *Variety*, 29 Feb. 1928: 2.
18 Sydney *Truth*, 22 Jan. 1928: 23; 'Great Business at Tivoli', *Daily Guardian*, 14 Jan. 1928; 'The Music Box', *Everyones*, 29 Feb. 1928: 43; 'Sonny Clay Looks Good for Long Run at Sydney Tivoli', *Everyones*, 25 Jan. 1928: 41.
19 'Colored Stars Shine', *Labor Daily*, 31 Jan. 1928: 6; 'The Tivoli', *Sydney Morning Herald*, 23 Jan. 1928: 7; *Labor Daily*, 31 Jan. 1928: 6; *Everyones*, 25 Jan. 1928: 41.
20 *Sydney Morning Herald*, 23 Jan. 1928: 7; Sydney *Truth*, 22 Jan. 1928: 23.
21 'Ivy Anderson', *Beckett's Budget*, 17 Feb. 1928: 23; *Ivie Anderson*, Radio station CKMO, Vancouver, BC, 27 Sept. 1947. Interviewed by Bill Hill (unissued); Sydney *Truth*, 22 Jan. 1928: 23; *Everyones*, 25 Jan. 1928: 41.
22 Sydney *Sun*, 22 Jan. 1928: 5; 'Sonny Clay's Team Makes a Hit', *Daily Telegraph*, 23 Jan. 1928: 7; 'Dancing Times', *Table Talk*, 23 Feb. 1928: 20; *Labor Daily*, 31 Jan. 1928: 6; Sydney *Truth*, 22 Jan. 1928: 23; 'Black Basso', *Sunday Times*, 29 Jan. 1928: 17.
23 Sydney *Truth*, 22 Jan. 1928: 23.
24 'Broadcasting', *Newcastle Morning Herald*, 31 Jan. 1928: 6; 'Broadcasting', *Sydney Morning Herald*, 28 Jan. 1928: 4; 'Advertisement', *Sydney Morning Herald*, 28 Jan. 1928: 12; *Evening News*, 23 Jan. 1928; *Daily Guardian*, 23 Jan. 1928; Sydney *Sun*, 20 Feb. 1928; 'The Music Box', *Everyones*, 12 Dec. 1928: 107.

Chapter 10 The Jazzing Spheres

1 'Colored Jazz', Sydney *Truth*, 22 Jan. 1928: 23.
2 'Sonny Clay's Plantation Band Turns *Sierra* into Jazz Ship', *Everyones*, 25 Jan. 1928: 39.
3 'Toujours Jazz', *The Dial*, Aug. 1923: 93, 99.
4 'Advertisement: *Romance of Runnibede*', *Beckett's Budget*, 17 Feb. 1928: 19.

5 Julie Carr, *The Captive White Woman of Gipps Land: In Pursuit of the Legend* (Melbourne: Melbourne University Press, 2001); June Nails, *White Captives: Gender and Ethnicity on the American Frontier* (Canberra: UNC Press, 1993).
6 'Bombs Burst When Dexter Said Australians Lacked Screen Beauty', *Everyones*, 9 Nov. 1927: 5; 'Sonny Clay Looks Good for Long Run at Sydney Tivoli', *Everyones*, 25 Jan. 1928: 41.
7 'Hislop Drops Bomb for Musicians' Union', *Everyones*, 1 Feb. 1928: 43; 'Imported Musicians', *Sydney Morning Herald*, 3 Mar. 1928: 18; 'Insulting Australia', *Everyones*, 14 Sept. 1927: 4; 'How Wicked Is Hollywood?', *Everyones*, 14 Sept. 1927: 5; 'Vaudeville Outlook Bright, Says Muller', *Everyones*, 25 Jan. 1928: 3; 'Dancing Around', *Everyones*, 11 May 1927: 39.
8 '"Patriots" Don't Pay for Aust Film', *Everyones*, 8 Feb. 1928: 20.
9 'How Will the Censor Board Be Chosen?', *Everyones*, 23 May 1928: 4; 'So This Is an Australian Who Roused Commission's Ire in "So This is Paris"', *Everyones*, 4 Jan. 1928: 8; 'A Film Trade Commission Is Not Wanted Here, Mr Hays', *Everyones*, 25 Jan. 1928: 5; 'The Annual Insult', *Everyones*, 2 May 1928: 1.
10 *Everyones*, 9 Nov. 1927: 5.
11 'Physical Culture', *Age*, 14 Aug. 1923: 6; Charles Pearson, *National Life and Character: A Forecast* (London: Macmillan and Co., 1894): 165, 231; YMCA, *Official Souvenir Programme of the Second Annual Gymnastic Circus* (Melbourne: The Federated Press, 1924); *March to Nationhood* (Movietone News, 1938).
12 Keith Hancock, *Australia* (London: Ernest Benn, 1930): 78.
13 *Everyones*, 9 Nov. 1927: 5.
14 Jack Lindsay, *Dionysos: Nietzsche Contra Nietzsche, An Essay in Lyrical Philosophy* (London: Fanfrolico Press, 1928). Also see: Neil Morpeth, 'Avatism, Utopian Longings and Jack Lindsay: An Essay on the Nietzschean Presences and Hellenic Pasts', in *Race for a Place: Eugenics, Darwinism and Social Thought and Practice in Australia: Proceedings of the History & Sociology of Eugenics Conference, University of Newcastle, 27–28 April 2000*, ed. Martin Crotty, John Germov and Grant Rodwell (Callaghan, NSW: Faculty of Arts and Social Science, University of Newcastle, 2000): 35–45.
15 'Modernism in Art', *New Triad*, 11 Nov. 1927: 9; 'Melbourne Listens to Gershwin', *New Triad*, 1 Mar. 1928: 42.
16 'The Spirit of Jazz', *Argus*, 6 Jul. 1926: 5.
17 'Twisted Legs', Sydney *Sun*, 27 Feb. 1928: 1.
18 'Jazz Swept Over World like Disease', Sydney *Sun*, 25 Jan. 1928: 1; 'Young Folk Raise Hell in Modern Sodom', Sydney *Sun*, 25 Jan. 1928: 1; 'Do High Heels Destroy Beauty of Figure', *Daily Telegraph*, 28 Feb. 1928: 23; 'Our Moral Standards', *Sunday Times*, 9 Sept. 1923; 'Australia's Unemployed Soldiers', *The League*, 29 Apr. 1922: 1.
19 'Jazz Means Back to the Jungle', *Argus*, 31 Aug. 1937: 10.
20 James Leggio, *Music and Modern Art* (New York: Routledge, 2002): 100. Also see: Donald Paul Hustad, 'Creation, Culture and the Music of the Spheres', *Choral Journal*, 47:9 (March 2007): 22–32; Karina Williamson, 'From Heavenly Harmony to Eloquent Silence: Representations of World Order from Dysden to Shelley', *Review of English Studies*, 55:221 (2004): 527–544; Jamie James, *The Music of the Spheres: Music, Science, and the Natural Order of the Universe* (New York: Copernicus Press, 1995).
21 'Apotheosis of Jazz', *Bulletin*, 5 Jan. 1928: 34.

22 'Coloured Ideas', *Smith's Weekly*, 28 Jan. 1928: 7; I am indebted to insights offered by the following scholars: Ronald Radano, 'Hot Fantasies: American Modernism and the Idea of Black Rhythm' in *Music and the Racial Imagination*, ed. Ronald Radano and Philip Bohlman (Chicago: University of Chicago Press, 2000): 459–480; Chinua Achebe, 'An Image of Africa: Racism in Conrad's "Heart of Darkness"', *Massachusetts Review*, 18 (1977); Marianna Torgovnick, *Gone Primitive: Savage Intellects, Modern Lives* (Chicago: University of Chicago Press, 1990); Dianne Jeater, 'Imagining Africans: Scholarship, Fantasy, and Science in Colonial Administration, 1920s Southern Rhodesia', *The International Journal of African Historical Studies*, 38:1 (2005): 1–26.

Chapter 11 A Comparative Vacation

1 *Beckett's Budget*, 10 Feb. 1928: 1, 16; 17 Feb. 1928: 12; 2 Mar. 1928: 23.

2 'Minto Cato Writes', *Chicago Defender*, 6 Nov. 1926: 7; 'A Letter from Australia', *Chicago Defender*, 2 Oct. 1926: 8; 'Tivoli, Sydney', *Everyones*, 1 Feb. 1928: 44; 'A Letter from Australia', *Chicago Defender*, 2 Oct. 1926: 8; 'Sonny Clay', *Referee*, 8 Feb. 1928: 17.

3 Leo McCoy Davis, Tape 76 Frank Driggs Collection; 'Leo Davis Band Forging to Front', *Chicago Defender*, 30 Mar. 1940: 20.

4 Leo McCoy Davis, Tape 293, Frank Driggs Collection.

5 ibid.

6 'Tilly Devine', *Labor Daily*, 23 Apr. 1925: 6; 'A Pretty Barmaid on a Murder Charge', *Evening News*, 19 Oct. 1927: 13; *Chicago Defender*, 2 Oct. 1926: 8.

7 'Writes Interesting Story of Australia', *Chicago Defender*, 12 Apr. 1930: 15; *Chicago Defender*, 25 Jan. 1930: 6; 'Australia: As I Saw It', *Chicago Defender*, 20 Nov. 1920: 16.

8 'Population of Sydney', *Barrier Miner*, 4 Nov. 1930: 1; 'Southern Europeans as Migrants', *Age*, 5 Apr. 1928: 11; *Chicago Defender*, 25 Jan. 1930: 6.

9 'A Letter from the Antipodes', *Chicago Defender*, 28 Apr. 1923: 13; *Chicago Defender*, 20 Nov. 1920: 16; 'Modern Horse Racing Owes Much to Australian Methods', *Chicago Defender*, 31 Dec. 1927: 8; 'Stories in Black and White', *Everyones*, 5 Sept. 1928: 5.

10 'A Letter from Australia', *Chicago Defender*, 2 Oct. 1926: 8; 'A Letter from the Antipodes', *Chicago Defender*, 28 Apr. 1923: 13; *Chicago Defender*, 6 Nov. 1926: 7.

11 Census of the Commonwealth of Australia, 30 June 1933, Part XII—Race, (Canberra: Commonwealth Govt Printer, 1933): 907, 920–922. The 1933 census counted a total of twelve unmarried West Indian 'half-caste' women between the ages of fifteen and thirty in New South Wales. Another nine were of African American descent.

12 John Maynard, 'Frederick Maynard & The Australian Aboriginal Progressive Association (AAPA): One God, One Aim, One Destiny', *Aboriginal History*, 21 (1997): 1–13. Also see: John Maynard, *Fight For Liberty and Freedom: The Origins of Australian Aboriginal Activism* (Canberra: Aboriginal Studies Press, 2007): 27.

13 *The Voice of the North*, 10 Oct. 1927; *Chicago Defender*, 28 Apr. 1923: 13; Adam Ewing, *The Age of Garvey: How a Jamaican Activist Created a Mass Movement and Changed Global Black Politics* (Princeton, NJ: Princeton University Press, 2014); Prince Marc Kojo Tovalou Houènou, 'The Problem of Negroes in French Colonial Africa' cited in J. Ayo Langley, *Ideologies of Liberation in Black Africa, 1856–1970*

(London: Rex Collings, 1979); John Maynard, 'In the Interests of Our People: The Influence of Garveyism on the Rise of Australian Aboriginal Political Activism', *Aboriginal History*, 29 (Nov. 2011).

14 'The Universal Brotherhood of Man', Sydney *Truth*, 17 Mar. 1927: 8; Fionnghuala Sweeney, *Afromodernisms: Paris, Harlem and the Avant-Garde* (Edinburgh: Edinburgh University Press, 2013): 3.

15 *Chicago Defender*, 28 Apr. 1923: 13.

16 Robert S. Abbott, 'My Trip Abroad: Xiii Kojo of Dahomey', *Chicago Defender*, 1 Feb. 1930: 1; 'My Trip Abroad: The Colored American in Paris', *Chicago Defender*, 23 Nov. 1929: 1; 'British Columbia Follows Australia in Color Ban', *Chicago Defender*, 3 Jan. 1925: 4; 'Launch Desperate Attempt to Keep Australia White', *Chicago Defender*, 11 Jul. 1925: A1; 'Want White Australia', *Chicago Defender*, 4 Feb. 1922: 1; 'Australia Makes Fight to Be White', *Chicago Defender*, 25 Mar. 1922: 22; 1; 'Australians Work to Make Their Land White', *Chicago Defender*, 26 Aug. 1922: 3. Also see Clare Corbould, 'Black Internationalism's Shifting Alliances: African American Newspapers, the White Australia Policy, and Indigenous Australians, 1919–1948', *History Compass*, 15:5, e12366 (2017); Chris Dixon, 'Confronting the "Bulwark of White Supremacy": The African American Challenge to White Australia, 1941–1945', *The Journal of African American History*, 106:1 (Winter 2021).

17 'A Letter from the Antipodes', *Chicago Defender*, 5 May 1923: 13; *Chicago Defender*, 6 Nov. 1926: 7.

18 For example, see 'Celluloid Boomerangs', *Urbana Daily Courier*, 26 Feb. 1910; 'On Principle of Boomerang', *Lead Daily Call*, 20 Jan. 1920; 'Why the Boomerang Returns to the Thrower', *Hamilton Ohio Journal News*, 18 Dec. 1922: 11; *Washington Times*, 23 Oct. 1918.

19 *Brooklyn Daily Eagle*, 21 May 1922: 81; *Post Crescent*, 16 May 1923: 4; *Atlanta Constitution*, 7 Mar. 1920: 7; *Gaffney Ledger*, 14 Aug. 1928: 1; 'The Boomerang', *Chicago Defender*, 15 Oct. 1927: A2; 'The Burden: A Romance of the South Synopsis', *Chicago Defender*, 29 Apr. 1922: 14; 'Lily White Trees', *Chicago Defender*, 28 Feb. 1920: 2.

20 'American Tourists "Must See" Aborigines', *Sydney Morning Herald*, 24 Dec. 1929: 9.

21 *Australian Aborigines Advocate*, 31 Aug. 1925; *Australian Aborigines Advocate*, 30 Sept. 1925; Jeff Wells, *Boxing Day: The Fight that Changed the World* (Pymble, NSW: Harper Collins, 1998).

22 Maria Nugent, 'An Economy of Shells: A Brief History of La Perouse Aboriginal Women's Shell-Work and Its Markets, 1880–2010', in *Indigenous Participation in Australian Economies II: Historical Engagements and Current Enterprises*, ed. Natasha Fijn et al. (Canberra: ANU Press, 2012).

23 *Freemans Journal*, 30 Sept. 1920; 'Aboriginal Display at La Perouse', *Mankind*, 1 Mar. 1931; *Sunday Times*, 22 Jan. 1928; 'Tragic Letter', Sydney *Truth*, 22 Jan. 1928: 23.

24 'Negroes Arrive in Sydney', Sydney *Sun*, 29 Mar. 1928: 2.

25 'Federal Ban on Negroes', Melbourne *Herald*, 28 Mar. 1928: 1.

Chapter 12 American Boomerang

1 Census of the Commonwealth of Australia, 30 June 1933, Part XII—Race, (Canberra: Commonwealth Govt Printer, 1933): 907, 920–922. [Hereafter: 1933 Census—Race].

2 Jorma Pohjanpalo, 'La Perouse 1928', Jorma Pohjanpalo Collection of Photographs of Sydney and Queensland, 1928–1931, National Library of Australia, http://

nla.gov.au/nla.obj-152625695; also see: 'Gillum Moore, Charlie Golden, Jane Timbery and Local Children', *A History of Aboriginal Sydney*, https://www.historyofaboriginalsydney.edu.au/south-coastal/1880s (accessed 20 Apr. 2019).

3 The 1921 census counted 39 females and 42 males. By 1933, the population had grown to 71 and 68 respectively—and would continue to grow. By 1947, the community had doubled in size. Census of the Commonwealth of Australia, 2–4 April 1921, Part V—Race (Melbourne: Acting Govt Printer, 1921): 298–99, 322–24; Pamela Nixon, The Integration of a Half-Caste Community at La Perouse, N.S.W., Master's Thesis, University of Sydney, 1948; James Harle Bell, The La Perouse Aborigines, PhD Thesis, University of Sydney, 1960; Maria Nugent, *Botany Bay: Where Histories Meet* (Sydney: Allen & Unwin, 2005); *Freemans Journal*, 30 Sept. 1920; *Evening News*, 16 Jan. 1928; *Sydney Morning Herald*, 5 Jan. 1922; *Australian Aborigines Advocate*, 31 Jun. 1927; Margaret Tucker, *If Everyone Cared: Autobiography of Margaret Tucker* (Sydney: Ure Smith, 1977): 136.

4 *Australian Aborigines Advocate*, 31 Mar. 1926. 'The enemy of souls has agents at work everywhere. They teach erroneous doctrine and thus, confuse the minds of the dark folk. Others paint pictures of imaginary grievances and dupe the native folk into forming organisations which they assert will have the effect of immediate emancipation.'

5 *Sydney Morning Herald*, 4 Apr. 1928; *Sydney Morning Herald*, 11 Jun. 1928; *Australian Aborigines Advocate*, 31 Mar. 1928; *Sydney Morning Herald*, 14 Feb. 1928; *Sydney Morning Herald*, 10 Feb. 1928; *Evening News*, 16 Jan. 1928. The mayor's supporters agreed that the seaside resort was 'too valuable ... to tolerate unsightly shacks'. For revocation of Aboriginal land in 1920s see: Heather Goodall, *Invasion to Embassy: Land in Aboriginal Politics in New South Wales, 1770–1972* (Sydney: Allen & Unwin, 1996): 194–199; 'La Perouse Aboriginal Protest', *Sydney Morning Herald*, 4 Apr. 1928; *Sydney Morning Herald*, 4 Mar. 1928; *Sydney Morning Herald*, 4 Feb. 1928.

6 *Sydney Morning Herald*, 2 Oct. 1928; *Sydney Morning Herald*, 16 Feb. 1928.

7 *Sydney Morning Herald*, 29 Oct. 1924; 1933 Census—Race; 'Aboriginal Girls as Domestic Servants', *Sydney Mail*, 24 May 1922: 22; AWB Photographs, NRS 30, Aborigines Welfare Board, 1883–1969, NSW State Records and Archives; 1916 amendments to Aboriginal Protection Act cited in James Miller, *Koori: A Will to Win* (Sydney: Angus & Robertson, 1985): 147. Also see: Victoria Haskins, '"A Better Chance"? Sexual Abuse and the Apprenticeship of Aboriginal Girls Under the NSW Aborigines Protection Board', *Aboriginal History*, 28 (2004), 33–58; Fiona Paisley, *Loving Protection? Australian Feminism and Aboriginal Women's Rights, 1919–1939* (Melbourne: Melbourne University Press, 2000).

8 Miller, *Koori: A Will to Win*: 163.

9 'Aborigines', *Sydney Morning Herald*, 29 Oct. 1924: 12.

10 Tucker, *If Everyone Cared*: 90, 123.

11 Tucker, *If Everyone Cared*: 65.

12 Tucker, *If Everyone Cared*: 129.

13 Tucker, *If Everyone Cared*: 86, 132–134.

14 'Worst Storm Since Easter Gales', *Daily Telegraph*, 11 Feb. 1928: 5; 'Collars Wilted; Storm Brought Relief', *Daily Telegraph*, 11 Feb. 1928: 3; 'Steamy Weather', Sydney *Sun*, 10 Feb. 1928: 6.

15 Paul Irish, *Hidden in Plain View: The Aboriginal People of Coastal Sydney* (Sydney: NewSouth Publishing, 2017): 45–46, 72, 127; Amanda Lissarrague, Muurrbay Aboriginal Language and Culture Co-operative and Many Rivers Aboriginal

Language Centre, *Dhanggati Grammar and Dictionary with Dhanggati Stories* (Nambucca Heads: Muurrbay Aboriginal Language and Culture Co-operative, 2007): 180; Sharon Atkinson and WCC Language Program, *The Yorta Yorta Dictionary App*, yorta-yorta.wcclp.com.au; Stan Grant and John Rudder, *A New Wiradjuri Dictionary* (Canberra: Restoration House, 2010).

16 *Australian Aborigines Advocate*, 31 Mar. 1928; Russell McGregor, '"Breed Out the Colour": The Importance of Being White', *Australian Historical Studies*, 33 (120): 286–302; Katherine Ellinghaus, 'Absorbing the "Aboriginal Problem": Controlling Interracial Marriage in Australia in the Late 19th and Early 20th Centuries', *Aboriginal History* 27 (2003): 183–207.

17 'Studio Portrait of Aboriginal Serviceman, Believed to Be 1271 Private (Pte) Thomas Williams, D Company, 33rd Battalion, of Coonamble, NSW, with His Daughter Sophie', P01758.001, Australian War Memorial; Heather Goodall and Allison Cadzow, *Rivers and Resilience: Aboriginal People on Sydney's Georges River* (Sydney: UNSW Press, 2009): 125; Dianne Johnson, *Sacred Waters: The Story of the Blue Mountains Traditional Owners* (Sydney: Halstead Press, 2006): 53; *Sydney Morning Herald*, 31 May 1931; 'Salt Pan Creek', *Evening News*, 17 Oct. 1925; 1933 Census—Race.

18 *Geelong Advertiser*, 15 Apr. 1895: 4; *Kiama Independent*, 15 Mar. 1887: 4; Goodall and Cadzow, *Rivers and Resilience*: 120–122; 130–132; *Sydney Morning Herald*, 7 Nov. 1924; Sydney *Truth*, 14 Feb. 1926; Sydney *Truth*, 3 Jun. 1928; *Evening News*, 20 Mar. 1928.

19 *Daily Guardian*, 7 May 1925; 'Australian Aboriginal Progressive Association', *Macleay Chronicle*, 7 Oct. 1925: 4; 'Natives in Conference', *North Western Courier*, 25 Feb. 1926: 6.

Chapter 13 Major Lloyd's Investigation Branch

1 Longfield Lloyd, Investigation Branch, NSW Office, *Annual Report*, 2 Jul. 1923, NAA A9650, Folder 4; *Annual Report*, 1 Jul. 1924, NAA A9650, Folder 5.

2 Lloyd, *Annual Report*, 1923; *Annual Report*, 1924, NAA A9650.

3 William M. Hughes, Letter to Major Longfield Lloyd, 14 Feb. 1934 & 13 Sept. 1935, E.E. Longfield Lloyd Papers, NLA MS 2887.

4 'Catty Communications', *Smith's Weekly*, 16 Aug. 1930: 11; 'Near and Far', *Sydney Morning Herald*, 5 May 1925: 4.

5 Lloyd, *Annual Report*, 1923.

6 *West Australian*, 24 Mar. 1953: 2; *Sydney Morning Herald*, 3 Aug. 1923: 10.

7 Lloyd, *Annual Report*, 1923; *Annual Report*, 1924.

8 For overview of the Investigation Branch see: Frank Cain, *The Origins of Political Surveillance in Australia* (London: Angus and Robertson, 1983): 188–227; David Dutton, *One of Us: A Century of Australian Citizenship* (Sydney: UNSW Press, 2002): 105–129; David Dutton, 'The Commonwealth Investigation Branch and the Political Construction of the Australian Citizenry, 1920–40', *Labour History*, 75 (1998): 155–174; M. Finnane, 'Controlling the "Alien" in Mid-Twentieth Century Australia: The Origins and Fate of a Policing Role', *Policing and Society*, 19:4 (2009): 442–467; A.J. Brok, 'The Commonwealth Investigation Branch in Western Australia 1919–1939', *Early Days: Journal of the Royal Western Australian Historical Society*, 12:6 (2006): 670–685.

9 Lloyd, *Annual Report*, 1923; Lloyd, *Annual Report*, 1924.

10 Commonwealth of Australia 1928 Yearbook Section 10 (B) (Canberra: Commonwealth Government Printer, 1927): 925–927.

11 Jason Byrnes, 'The Body Snatchers: Peace Officers and the Peace Officer's Act 1925', *Platypus Magazine*, Jul. 2008: 28–31; *Singleton Argus*, 3 Dec. 1925: 2.
12 Major Longfield Lloyd, Report: 'Negro Orchestra—Lately at the Tivoli Theatre Sydney', 24 Feb. 1928, NAA B741 V/4718.
13 'The Inquiry', *Cumberland Argus*, 17 Oct. 1896: 4; *Government Gazette of the State of New South Wales*, 24 May 1904: 4300; 17 Apr. 1907: 2250; 'Evading Income Tax', *Sydney Morning Herald*, 13 Apr. 1921: 12; 'Can Sue for Damages', *Labor Daily*, 8 Mar. 1927: 6.
14 'Heart of Man', Sydney *Truth*, 13 Feb. 1927: 13; 'Gold Mining Leases', Sydney *Sun*, 12 Jul. 1928: 13; 'Alleged Conspiracy', *Singleton Argus*, 1 Nov. 1928: 3.
15 'Roving Commission for Govt Officer', *Barrier Miner*, 14 Nov. 1941: 3; 'The Malay Peninsula Today', *Sydney Morning Herald*, 30 Mar. 1912: 7; John G. Butcher, *The British in Malaya, 1880–1941: The Social History of a European Community in Colonial South-East Asia* (Kuala Lumpur: Oxford University Press, 1979): 97–125; Timothy Parsons, *The African Rank-and-File: Social Implications of Colonial Military Service in the King's African Rifles, 1902–1964* (Portsmouth, NH: Heinemann, 1999): 106–115. Parsons noted that the regiment attracted two types of officer: one who sought 'adventure, hunting and combat experience'; the other, 'inferior men unwanted by their parent unit'.
16 'Jacob Johnson', *Sydney Morning Herald*, 8 Sept. 1931: 10; 'Jacob Johnson', *Sydney Morning Herald*, 18 Sept. 1931: 10; 'Jacob Johnson', *Sydney Morning Herald*, 16 Sept. 1931: 11; 'Jacob Johnson', *Sydney Morning Herald*, 11 Sept. 1931.
17 W.M. Ball, *Intermittent Diplomat* (Melbourne: Melbourne University Press, 1988): 272–273; David Walker, *Anxious Nation: Australia and the Rise of Asia 1850–1939* (Brisbane: University of Queensland Press, 1999): 221.
18 Lloyd, Eric Edwin Longfield: Service Number—W1253, B2455, NAA; 'His Best Friends', *Glen Innes Examiner*, 8 Jul. 1915: 5; 'Corporal-Bugler Alfred R. Wardrop', *Sunday Times*, 29 Aug. 1915: 9; Phillip F.E. Schuler, *Australia in Arms: A Narrative of the Australasian Imperial Force and Their Achievement at Anzac* (London: TF Unwin, 1916): 300.
19 Gerhard Fischer, *Enemy Aliens: Internment and the Homefront Experience in Australia, 1914–1920* (Brisbane: University of Queensland Press, 1989); Michael McKernan, *The Australian People and the Great War* (Melbourne: Thomas Nelson, 1980): 150–177; Ernest Scott, *Australia during the War* (Sydney: Angus and Robertson, 1937): 105–167; John Connor, *Anzac and Empire: George Foster Pearce and the Foundations of Australian Defence* (Melbourne: Cambridge University Press, 2011): 104–106; Neville Meaney, *A History of Australian Defence and Foreign Policy, 1901–23, Volume 2, Australia and World Crisis, 1914–1923* (Sydney: Sydney University Press, 2009): 34–35.
20 Kay Saunders and Roger Daniels, *Alien Justice: Wartime Internment in Australia and North America* (Brisbane: University of Queensland Press, 2000): 50; Joan Clarke, *Dr. Max Herz, Surgeon Extraordinary: The Human Price of Civil and Medical Bigotry in Australia* (Sydney: APCOL, 1976): 110.
21 Paech and Wenke's File, MP367/1, 567/3/4154, NAA: 25, 26, 30, 31, 32, 105; Ian Turner, *Industrial Labour and Politics* (Canberra: ANU Press, 1965): 104, 97–121.
22 Paech and Wenke's File, MP367/1, 567/3/4154, NAA.
23 David Dutton, *One of Us: A Century of Australian Citizenship*, (Sydney: UNSW Press, 2002): 95.
24 Fischer, *Enemy Aliens*: 302; 'German Agitator', *Sydney Morning Herald*, 5 Jun. 1920: 13.

25 'Friday, July 20, 1920', *Argus*, 23 Jul. 1920: 6; Charles Jerger, *Does Australia Stand For This?: The Case of Father Jerger* (Sydney: 1920) NLA, <http://nla.gov.au/nla.obj-76428244>
26 Letter: Hughes to Lloyd, 14 Feb. 1934, E.E. Longfield Lloyd Papers, NLA MS 2887.
27 *Sydney Morning Herald*, 8 Sept. 1931: 10.

Chapter 14 The 'Black Menace'

1 'Sonny Clay's Parting Shot', *Everyones*, 4 Apr. 1928: 6.
2 Major Longfield Lloyd, Report: 'Negro Orchestra—Lately at the Tivoli Theatre Sydney', 24 Feb. 1928, NAA B741 V/4718.
3 Charles Pearson, *National Life and Character: A Forecast* (London: Macmillan and Co., 1894): 16–17.
4 Australia, Parliament 1901: 4807.
5 See *Vagrancy Act (NSW) 1902*.
6 Immigration Branch, *Book of Precedents*, 1912–1933, NAA Item No A1823: 4.
7 'La Warra Up-to-Date', *Leader*, 11 Jun. 1928: 1.
8 'Boxers and Color Line', Sydney *Truth*, 6 Mar. 1927: 1;'Fans Delighted', Sydney *Sun*, 7 Jun. 1927: 5; '40 Imported Boxers Have Visited Sydney', *Sunday Times*, 2 Jan. 1927: 6; 'They're Off', *Sunday Times*, 6 Feb. 1927: 6.
9 'Coloured Boxers', Sydney *Sun*, 8 Mar. 1927: 4; 'Chasing Out the Chinese. Letting in the Negro', *Evening News*, 11 Nov. 1927: 10; 'Girls Who Ignore the Color Line Disgrace the City', Sydney *Truth*, 8 Mar. 1927: 13.
10 Sydney *Truth*, 8 Mar. 1927: 13; 'Coloured Boxers', Sydney *Sun*, 8 Mar. 1927: 4; 'Another Negro Fighter', Sydney *Truth*, 24 Apr. 1927: 1; 'Rust and Rot', Sydney *Truth*, 19 Jun. 1927: 5.
11 Sydney *Truth*, 24 Apr. 1927: 1; Sydney *Truth*, 19 Jun. 1927: 5.
12 'Protection as a National Policy White v Colored Labor', Sydney *Truth*, 21 Jun. 1896: 3; 'Slavery in the West', Sydney *Truth*, 9 Jun. 1901: 3; 'Australia for the White Race', Sydney *Truth*, 11 Oct. 1896: 4.
13 'The Private Lives of Sydney Men', *Sydney Morning Herald*, 7 Mar. 1981: 41.
14 In contrast to the *Sydney Morning Herald*'s coverage of Royal Commission into Jacob Johnson, October 1931; 'Obituary Ezra Norton', *Canberra Times*, 6 Jan. 1967: 6.
15 'Black Fighters Should Meet Black Adversaries', Sydney *Truth*, 17 Mar. 1927: 2.
16 'Sonny Jim Boxer', Sydney *Truth*, 17 Mar. 1927: 22.
17 Sydney *Truth*, 8 Mar. 1927: 13; 'The Universal Brotherhood of Man', Sydney *Truth*, 17 Mar. 1927: 22.
18 *Barrier Miner*, 30 May 1927: 1; 'Squires Creditable Showing', *Brisbane Courier*, 25 Jul. 1927: 9; 'Boxers', Sydney *Truth*, 7 Aug. 1927; 'Coloured Boxers', Sydney *Sun*, 24 Aug. 1927: 12.
19 'Stadium', *Sydney Morning Herald*, 27 Aug. 1927: 20; 'Truth Boxers', Sydney *Truth*, 28 Aug. 1927: 1.
20 'New South Wales', *Barrier Miner*, 1 Sept. 1927: 4; 'Sunny Jim Williams', *Referee*, 14 Sept. 1927: 10; 'The Color Line in Boxing', *Evening News*, 29 Aug. 1927: 6; 'Exodus of Imported Fighter', *Labor Daily*, 15 Sept. 1927: 2; 'White Australia?', Sydney *Truth*, 9 Oct. 1927: 4; 'Boxing', *Australian Worker*, 22 Jun. 1927: 9.
21 'Hall Dutch?', Sydney *Truth*, 23 Oct.1927: 24.
22 'Black Boxers', Sydney *Truth*, 23 Oct. 1927: 24.
23 'Rise of the White Gladiator', *Smith's Weekly*, 8 Oct. 1927: 8.
24 Pearson, *National Life and Character*: 16–17.

Chapter 15 Synchronising Operations

1 'Riverina Flood', *Examiner*, 18 Feb. 1928: 9; 'The Music Box', *Everyones*, 8 Feb. 1928: 44; 'Advertising', Melbourne *Herald*, 15 Feb. 1928: 9.
2 'Tivoli Melbourne', *Everyones*, 22 Feb. 1928: 43; 'A Colored Idea', Melbourne *Herald*, 28 Feb. 1928: 10; 'The Music Box', *Everyones*, 29 Feb. 1928: 43; 'Colored Idea—A Popular One', Melbourne *Herald*, 21 Feb. 1928: 13.
3 George McFarland Beaconsfield Longmore informant and Jacob Johnson defendant, NAA: SP185/1, 23880/15; 'Roving Commission for Government Officer', *Barrier Miner*, 14 Nov. 1941: 3; 'Jacob Johnson', *Sydney Morning Herald*, 8 Sept. 1931: 10; 'Jacob Johnson', *Sydney Morning Herald*, 11 Sept. 1931; 'The Johnson Case', *Sydney Morning Herald*, 21 Feb. 1929: 11.
4 '"Jerry" Jackson's Gold Trail', Sydney *Truth*, 21 Oct. 1928: 20; 'Heart of Man', Sydney *Truth*, 13 Feb. 1927: 13.
5 Major Longfield Lloyd, Report: 'Negro Orchestra—Lately at the Tivoli Theatre Sydney', 24 Feb. 1928, NAA B741 V/4718.
6 Lloyd, 'Negro Orchestra', V/4718; Longfield Lloyd, Investigation Branch, NSW Office, *Annual Report*, 2 Jul. 1923, NAA A9650, Folder 4; *Annual Report*, 1 Jul. 1924, NAA A9650, Folder 5.
7 Lloyd, 'Negro Orchestra', NAA B741 V/4718.
8 ibid.
9 Confidential Letter: Major H.E. Jones, IB Director, to General T. Blamey, Chief Commissioner of Police, Victoria, 1 Mar. 1928, NAA V/4718.
10 'Immigration: General Blamey's Views', *Sydney Morning Herald*, 18 Jun. 1925: 8.
11 'The Pacific', *Sydney Morning Herald*, 26 Aug. 1921: 6.
12 For example, Mrs Earnest Scott, 'Victoria League', *The Australasian*, 20 Aug. 1927: 60; Major Wilfred Kent-Hughes, see: *Argus*, 27 Dec. 1927: 6; *Argus*, 24 Jul. 1926: 7 cited in Geoff Spencely, '"The Minister of Starvation": Wilfred Kent Hughes, Fascism and the Unemployment Relief (Administration) Act', *Labour History*, 81 (2001): 137.
13 John Hetherington, *Blamey* (Melbourne: Cheshire, 1954): 64.
14 'Immigration: General Blamey's Views', *Sydney Morning Herald*, 18 Jun. 1925: 8.
15 File: 'Saker, Leslie Barton, Register No 6415', *Record of Conduct and Service*, Victoria Police Museum Archive; File: 'Dunn, Harry Spencer, Register No 5552', *Record of Conduct and Service*, Victoria Police Museum Archive.
16 Sydney *Truth*, 22 Jan. 1928: 23.
17 'Coon-Can Band', Melbourne *Truth*, 25 Feb. 1928: 12.
18 'A Colored Idea', Melbourne *Herald*, 28 Feb. 1928: 10.
19 'Colored Folk Introduce New Idea', *Age*, 18 Feb. 1928: 17.
20 'Sonny Clay's Colored Idea', *Table Talk*, 1 Mar. 1928: 39; Melbourne *Herald*, 21 Feb. 1928: 13.
21 '"Black Bottom" Saves Him', Melbourne *Truth*, 3 Mar. 1928: 10.

Chapter 16 The Carlyon Touch

1 Keith Hancock, *Australia* (London: Ernest Benn, 1930): 35; Henry Goddard, *The Kallikak Family: A Study in the Heredity of Feeblemindedness* (New York: Macmillan, 1919); Arthur H. Estabrook, *The Jukes in 1915* (District of Columbia: Carnegie Institution of Washington, 1916).
2 'Prominent Personalities', *Table Talk*, 21 Jul. 1927: 15.
3 By personal correspondence with Mark De Leon.
4 Norman D. Carlyon, *The Flight of Steps* (Melbourne: ND Carlyon, 1986): 108–110.

5 Norman D. Carlyon, *I Remember Blamey* (Melbourne: Macmillan, 1980): 1.
6 'Prominent Personalities', *Table Talk*, 21 Jul. 1927: 1; *Australasian*, 20 Aug. 1927: 60; 'A Melbourne Futurist', *Age*, 13 Aug. 1929: 7; 'Max Meldrum in America', *Age*, 11 Jul. 1928: 16; 'Tradition in Art', *Argus*, 17 Sept. 1927: 8.
7 *Table Talk*, 1 May 1924: 14; Melbourne *Herald*, 3 Jan. 1924: 3.
8 *Bulletin*, 20 Aug. 1925: 37.
9 'Melbourne Chatter', *Bulletin*, 22 Apr. 1926: 28.
10 'Sensational Raid at Carlyon's Hotel', Melbourne *Herald*, 6 Feb. 1926: 13; 'Dramatic Police Raid', *Age*, 1 Feb., 1926: 9.
11 'Dancing Times', *Table Talk*, 6 Jul. 1922: 13.
12 Immigration Branch, *Book of Precedents*, 1912–1933, NAA Item No A1823: 4; Home & Territories Department Memorandum No 23/1190, 9 Feb. 1923; Letter: from Secretary, Minister for Home & Territories, to J.C. Bendrodt, 2 Feb. 1923, NAA A1, 1923/2723; Home & Territories Department Memorandum No 23/368, 1 Nov. 1923.
13 Carlyon, *The Flight of Steps*: 108; NAA 4A156/8/7, Aug. 1924 cited in Kay Dreyfus, *Silences and Secrets: The Australian Experience of the Weintraubs Syncopators* (Clayton: Monash University Publishing, 2013): 79; Ronald Radano, 'Hot Fantasies: American Modernism and the Idea of Black Rhythm' in *Music and the Racial Imagination*, eds Ronald Radano and Philip V. Bohlman (Chicago: University of Chicago Press, 2000): 462.
14 'Dancing Times', *Table Talk*, 2 Apr. 1925: 29; 30 Apr. 1925: 13; 7 May 1925: 13; Melbourne *Herald*, 14 Mar. 1925: 17; 20 Apr. 1925: 18; Carlyon, *The Flight of Steps*: 108.
15 Carlyon, *The Flight of Steps*: 108, 118; 'Prominent Personalities', *Table Talk*, 21 Jul. 1927: 15.
16 'Dancing Times', *Table Talk*, 19 Apr. 1928: 45; 'And Voices Objection to the Charleston', Melbourne *Truth*, 10 Apr. 1926: 11; Eric J. Sheldon, 'Where Will It All End?', *Australian Music Maker and Dance Band News*, 1 Dec. 1933: 14–15; Carlyon, *The Flight of Steps*: 108.
17 '*Sally, Irene and Mary* (1925) Restoration Trailer', George Eastman Museum, https://youtu.be/14r1-Jy3GcI; Empress Picture Theatres Short Reel: Lesson Number 6; 'The Charleston', Sydney *Sun*, 6 Aug. 1926: 2; 'The Charleston', *Everyones*, 21 Jul. 1926: 60; *Everyones*, 15 Dec. 1926: 111; 'Dancing Times', *Table Talk*, 23 Sept. 1926: 20.
18 '*Truth*'s New Dancing Experts Laughs at the Charleston Twisters', Melbourne *Truth*, 24 May 1926: 12.
19 'Dancing Times', *Table Talk*, 30 Sept. 1926: 14; 'News and Notes from Melbourne Dance Resorts', *Table Talk*, 2 Feb. 1928: 43; 'Dancing Times', *Table Talk*, 26 May 1928: 18.
20 '*Truth*'s New Dancing Experts Laughs at the Charleston Twisters', Melbourne *Truth*, 24 May 1926: 2.
21 'Dancing Times', *Table Talk*, 9 Feb. 1928: 14; 'Dancing Times', *Table Talk*, 8 Mar. 1928: 20; 'Dancing Times', *Table Talk*, 2 Feb. 1928: 43; '*Truth*'s New Dancing Expert Laughs at the Charleston Twisters', Melbourne *Truth*, 24 May 1926: 12; 'And Voices Objection to the Charleston', Melbourne *Truth*, 10 Apr. 1926: 11.
22 'His New Ex and Lady Somers Hear of Charleston', Melbourne *Truth*, 3 Jul. 1926: 11; 'Jazzing Around', Melbourne *Truth*, 19 Jun. 1926: 11; 'And Voices Objection to the Charleston', Melbourne *Truth*, 10 Apr. 1926: 11; 'Dancing Times', *Table Talk*, 23 Sept. 1926: 20.

23 'Prominent Personalities', *Table Talk*, 21 Jul. 1927: 15; *Everyones*, 8 Sept. 1926: 51; 'In and About Melbourne', Melbourne *Truth*, 4 Sept. 1926: 10; 'Health Commission, Dance Hall', *Argus*, 1 Jun. 1926.
24 Melbourne *Truth*, 23 Sept. 1926: 11; 'Green Mill Dance Palais', *Argus*, 8 Sept. 1926: 26; 'Green Mill Opening', Melbourne *Truth*, 11 Sept. 1926: 11; 'Dancing Times', *Table Talk*, 16 Sept. 1926: 18.
25 'Dancing Times', *Table Talk*, 26 Jan. 1928: 53.
26 For example: 'Dancing Times', *Table Talk*, 7 May 1925: 13; 21 Aug. 1924: 45; 'Melbourne's Green Mill Uses Movie Methods', *Everyones*, 5 Oct. 1927; 'Music at the Mill', *Table Talk*, 2 Sept. 1926: 20.
27 'Prominent Personalities', *Table Talk*, 21 Jul. 1927: 15.

Chapter 17 A Sterling Advertisement for Australian Girlhood

1 D.H. Lawrence, *Kangaroo* (Cambridge: Cambridge University Press, 1994): 100, 342; D.H. Lawrence and Richard Aldington, *The Spirit of Place: An Anthology Compiled from the Prose of D.H. Lawrence* (London: W. Heinemann, 1935): 100, 244.
2 Erik Eklund, *Mining Towns: Making a Living, Making a Life* (Kensington: UNSW Press, 2012): 35–68.
3 'Miss Australia', *Barrier Miner*, 6 Sept. 1927: 4; 'Miss Australia', *Barrier Miner*, 8 Sept. 1927; *Miss Australia: A Quarterly Magazine*, Sept. 1926; 'Miss Australia: A Nation's Quest', *National Museum of Australia Friends Magazine*, 18:1 (2007); Liz Conor, *The Spectacular Modern Woman* (Bloomington: Indiana University Press, 2004): 293; Marion Brooke, 'Mills, Beryl Lucy (1907–1977)', *Australian Dictionary of Biography*, National Centre of Biography, Australian National University, http://adb.anu.edu.au/biography/mills-beryl-lucy-11130/text19821 (accessed 19 Jun. 2020).
4 'Hollywood Greets Miss Australia', *Everyones*, 20 Oct. 1926; 'Miss Australia for Lecture Tour', *Everyones*, 11 Nov. 1926; 'Miss Australia', *Barrier Miner*, 12 Sept. 1927.
5 For example, see: *In a Shantung Garden*.
6 'Miss Australia for Lecture Tour', *Everyones*, 11 Nov. 1926; 'Miss Australia', *Barrier Miner*, 7 Sept. 1927.
7 For discussion of feminine beauty in the 1920s see: Angela J. Latham, *Posing a Threat: Flappers, Chorus Girls and Other Brazen Performers of the American 1920s* (Hanover and London: Wesleyan University Press, 2000): 104–107; Conor, *The Spectacular Modern Woman*: 116.
8 'Miss Australia, 1926', *Barrier Miner*, 19 Nov. 1927; 'Miss Australia', *Barrier Miner*, 12 Sept. 1927; 'Miss Beryl Mills Makes Pretty Bride', *Morning Bulletin*, 26 Mar. 1928.
9 'Girl Truants Found in City', Melbourne *Truth*, 16 Jul. 1927: 9; *Annual Report 1926*, Travellers' Aid Society of Victoria (Melbourne: The Society, 1927).
10 Edna Madeline Ewart, *England & Wales, Christening Index, 1530–1980*; Arthur William Ewart, *England & Wales Death Index: 1916–2005*, 1918, Q3-July-Aug-Sept, E, Image 19; *England & Wales, National Probate Calendar (Index of Wills and Administration) 1961–1941*, 1918, E, Ew, Image 1, Ancestry.com; by personal correspondence with Leslie Langdon's great-nephew, Jeffrey Fitzsimmons.
11 'Advertising', *Barrier Miner*, 19 Sept. 1924: 2; 'Amusements', *Barrier Miner*, 24 Sept. 1924: 2.
12 Edna Madeline Ewart, Australian Electoral Roll 1903–1980, Victoria 1937: Fawkner, Prahran, F, Entry #3564, Ancestry.com; 'Advertisement', *Argus*, 20 Oct. 1945; 'Sequel to Flat Raid', *Argus*, 30 Mar. 1928: 16.

13 'Musicians Dispute at Broken Hill', *Everyones*, 24 Aug. 1927: 53; 'Dispute at the Palais', *Barrier Daily Truth*, 30 Sept. 1926; 'Trouble at the Palais Is Temporarily Settled', *Barrier Daily Truth*, 1 Oct. 1926.
14 'Dancing Times', *Table Talk*, 12 Jan. 1928: 14; 'Pictures-Plus-Dancing Dropped at Cairo, St Kilda', *Everyones*, 4 Jan. 1928: 6.
15 'Affray at Green Mill', *Argus*, 22 Mar. 1928: 3; 'Three Frocks and Coat', *Argus*, 12 Feb. 1927: 14; 'Fur Coat Transactions', *Argus*, 2 Apr. 1927: 11.
16 'Dancing Times', *Table Talk*, 9 Feb. 1928: 14; 'Fight Pictures at Green Mill', *Everyones*, 23 Nov. 1927: 30; 'In and About Melbourne', *Truth*, 9 Sept. 1926: 10; 'Dancing Times', *Table Talk*, 15 Mar. 1928.
17 'Danced for 69 Hours', *Argus*, 20 Aug. 1927: 34; 'Newspaper Attacks Stopped Non-Stop Dance', *Everyones*, 7 Sept. 1927: 52.
18 'Notes and Comments', *Labor Call*, 25 Aug. 1927: 8.
19 'Glorifying the Australian Girl', *Everyones*, 19 Nov. 1926: 20; 'Film Girl Search', *Record*, 20 Nov. 1926: 8.
20 'Dancing Times', *Table Talk*, 10 Feb. 1927: 22; 'Jazz the Rage', *Film Daily*, 13 Jan. 1924: 2.
21 'Looking Backward', *Gundagai Independent*, 11 Apr. 1927: 3; 'Dancing Times', *Table Talk*, 7 Apr. 1927: 22.
22 'Miss Phyllis Gibbs', *Brisbane Telegraph*, 25 Oct. 1928: 14; 'For Women', *Evening News*, 31 Mar. 1927: 18.
23 'A Model Affair', *Table Talk*, 12 Jan. 1928: 14; *Everyones*, 18 Jan. 1928: 32; 'Advertisement', *Table Talk*, 26 Jan. 1928: 53.
24 Alex Taylor, *Perils of the Studio: Inside the Artistic Affairs of Bohemian Melbourne* (Melbourne: Australian Scholarly Publishing/State Library of Victoria, 2007): 175; Angela J. Latham, *Posing a Threat: Flappers, Chorus Girls and Other Brazen Performers of the American 1920s* (Hanover and London: Wesleyan University Press, 2000): 104–108; 'Dancing Times', *Table Talk*, 2 Feb. 1928: 43; 'Commissions Comment Booms "So This Is Paris"', *Everyones*, 31 Aug. 1927: 40; 'A Model Affair', *Table Talk*, 12 Jan. 1928: 14.
25 'Advertisement', *Table Talk*, 26 Jan. 1928: 53.
26 *Everyones*, 15 Feb. 1928: 12; 'Dancing Times', *Table Talk*, 26 Jan. 1928: 53; 'Dancing Times', *Table Talk*, 1 Mar. 1928: 24; '*Sally, Irene and Mary* (1925) Restoration Trailer'; 'Bathing Beauty Joins "The Passing Show"', 1923, cited in Jonas Westover, *The Shuberts and Their Passing Shows: The Untold Tale of Ziegfeld's Rivals* (New York: Oxford University Press, 2016): 96.
27 'Dancing Times', *Table Talk*, 1 Mar. 1928, 24; Ann Stephen, 'The Body at the Scene of Modernism' in *Modern Times: The Untold Story of Modernism in Australia*, eds Ann Stephen, Philip Goad and Andrew McNamara (Melbourne: The Miegunyah Press, 2008): 44–55, 219.
28 'Dancing Times', *Table Talk*, 26 Jan. 1928: 53.
29 'Advertisement', Melbourne *Herald*, 25 Jan. 1928: 9.

Chapter 18 Miss 1928

1 'Advertising', Melbourne *Herald*, 17 Jan. 1928: 9; 'Unmarried Women: What Is a Fair Wage?', Adelaide *Advertiser*, 6 Sept. 1927: 15; 'Negro Orgy', Sydney *Sun*, 27 Mar. 1928: 12; *Everyones*, 7 Mar. 1928: 22; 'Green Mill Advertisement', Melbourne *Herald*, 27 Feb. 1928: 9.
2 Adolph Zukor, *The Public Is Never Wrong* (New York, Putnam, 1953): 245.
3 'Advertising', Melbourne *Herald*, 27 Feb. 1928: 9–10.

4 Based on a survey of films advertised in *Everyones* magazine between 1926 and 1929, images of women swooning or unconscious in their lover's protective arms include: *The Sea Beast* (1 Sept. 1926: 13), *Cobra* (1 Sept. 1926: 9), *His Jazz Bride* (26 Jan. 1927: 17), *After Midnight Revels* (16 Feb. 1927: 42). Cautionary and titillating tales about young women's pursuit of hedonistic pleasures included *Cabaret* (26 Feb. 1927: 53), *Twinkletoes* (2 Mar. 1927: 15), *Three Weeks in Paris* (9 Mar. 1927: 8), *Camille* (6 Jul. 1927: 1), *Jazz* (27 Jul. 1927: 42), *The Show Girl* (12 Oct. 1927: 37), *Come to My House* (2 May 1928: 11).
5 *Bulletin*, 12 Jan. 1928: 13; for other examples see: *Bulletin*, 21 Mar. 1928: 15; *Bulletin*, 5 Jan. 1929: 15.
6 'Are You Synthetic?', *Daily Telegraph*, 4 Dec. 1927: 4.
7 'The Tired Business Man', *Lachlander and Condobolin and Western Districts Recorder*, 4 Jan. 1922: 9; 'A Smart Ensemble for Business Girls', *Sport*, 23 Mar. 1928: 15; 'The Girls of Today', *Table Talk*, 12 Jan. 1928: 19.
8 'Have You Booked Miss 1928?', *Everyones*, 4 Jan. 1928: 17–18.
9 'Dancing Times', *Table Talk*, 1 Mar. 1928: 24; Melbourne *Truth*, 18 Feb. 1928: 12.
10 *Everyones*, 7 Mar. 1928: 22.
11 'Dancing Time', *Table Talk*, 15 Mar. 1928: 16; 'Tivoli Circuit', *Everyones*, 12 Dec. 1928: 142.
12 '"Realism" in Art', *Argus*, 22 Feb. 1928: 24; 'In Town and Out', Melbourne *Herald*, 18 Jul. 1923: 8; 'Victoria League', *Australasian*, 20 Aug. 1927: 60; 'New Year's Eve in Paris', *Age*, 19 Feb. 1927: 29; 'Moving Pictures', *Australasian*, 21 Jul. 1928: 21; 'Paris Notes', *Age*, 30 Jan. 1926: 30; 'Sonny Clay Receives Commendatory Letter', *California Eagle*, 11 May 1928: 10; 'Social', *Table Talk*, 21 Aug. 1924: 38; 'Concert at Yannathan', *Lang Lang Guardian*, 9 May 1917: 2; 'Tivoli Advertisement', Melbourne *Herald*, 20 Mar. 1928: 9; 'Tivoli Turn Please', Melbourne *Herald*, 13 Mar. 1928: 19.
13 Adelaide *Advertiser*, 6 Mar. 1928: 15; *Australasian*, 10 Mar. 1928: 18.
14 Melbourne *Herald*, 6 Mar. 1928: 9; 'Advertisement', *Sun News Pictorial*, 5 Mar. 1928: 2.
15 'Filmland Goes Harlem', *Chicago Daily Tribune*, 7 Jul. 1929.
16 Clora Bryant et al. (eds), *Central Avenue Sounds: Jazz in Los Angeles* (Berkeley: University of California Press, 1999): 56; Marshal Royal, *Marshal Royal, Jazz Survivor* (New York: Cassell, 1996): 20; 'Advertisement', *Argus*, 3 Mar. 1928: 38; 'Advertisement', *Sun News Pictorial*, 5 Mar. 1928: 24; *Darwin Northern Standard*, 10 Feb. 1931: 1.
17 'Cubist Sweaters', Adelaide *Chronicle*, 1 Oct. 1927: 70; Jill Matthews, *Dance Hall & Picture Palace: Sydney's Romance with Modernity* (Sydney: Currency Press, 2005).

Chapter 19 Jazz Night

1 'White Girls with Negro Lovers', Melbourne *Truth*, 31 Mar. 1928: 1; Cablegram: Cecil Trevelyan, Federal Secretary, MUA, to Tom Carlyon, Green Mill, undated, MUA NBA E156/2/5(ii).
2 Letter: John J. Davoren, Solicitor, Broken Hill, to Cecil Trevelyan, Oct. 1926, MUA NBA E156/8/7; 'Smiles for Australia', *Daily Telegraph*, 20 Jan. 1928: 8; 'Grand Opera: Signor Gonzales Arrives', Sydney *Sun*, 22 Feb. 1928: 17; 'Italian Musicians Not Wanted', *Daily Telegraph*, 1 Mar. 1928: 7; Kay Dreyfus, *Silences and Secrets: The Australian Experience of the Weintraubs Syncopators* (Clayton: Monash University Publishing, 2013): 83.
3 'Music and Labor', *Everyones*, 7 Mar. 1928: 4.

4 *Australasian*, 26 May 1928: 14; *Chronicle*, 24 Mar. 1928: 71; Also see: Barbara Herrnstein Smith, *Contingencies of Value: Alternative Perspectives for Critical Theory* (Cambridge, MA: Harvard University Press, 1988).
5 'Dancing Times', *Table Talk*, 26 Jan. 1928: 53.
6 'Green Mill', *Argus*, 14 Oct. 1926; 'Sunday Concerts', *Argus*, 7 Oct. 1926: 12; Norman D. Carlyon, *The Flight of Steps* (Melbourne: ND Carlyon, 1986): 111; 'Sensational Raid at Carlyon's Hotel', Melbourne *Truth*, 6 Feb. 1926: 13.
7 *Everyones*, 12 Dec. 1928: 107.
8 'Dancing Times', *Table Talk*, 22 Mar. 1928: 39; 'Dancing Times', *Table Talk*, 26 Jan. 1928: 53; Carlyon, *The Flight of Steps*: 107–108.
9 'Jazz Night', *Bulletin*, 28 Aug. 1929: 11.
10 For examples, see: 'In Darkest Africa', *Sydney Morning Herald*, 21 Aug. 1928: 6; 'Witchcraft—Strange African Beliefs', *Sydney Morning Herald*, 10 Oct. 1928: 7; 'Belief in Witchcraft', *Kilmore Free Press*, 8 Sept. 1927: 2; 'Black Magic: Superstition in Africa', Adelaide *Advertiser*, 29 Nov. 1929: 26; Diana Jeater, 'Imagining Africans: Scholarship, Fantasy, and Science in Colonial Administration, 1920s Southern Rhodesia', *The International Journal of African Historical Studies*, 38:1, 2005: 1–26.
11 Vachel Lindsay, *The Congo and Other Poems* (New York, The Macmillan Company, 1914); 'Poetry Recital', *Brisbane Courier*, 17 May 1930: 26; 'A "Cymbalist"', Melbourne *Herald*, 23 Apr. 1921: 12; 'Poetry and Dance', *Daily Telegraph*, 25 Oct. 1933: 17. Also see Marianna Torgovnick, *Gone Primitive: Savage Intellects, Modern Lives* (Chicago: University of Chicago Press, 1990): 9.
12 James George Frazer, *The Golden Bough: A Study in Magic and Religion* (New York: The Macmillan Company, 1922): 50.
13 Natalie Curtis, *Songs and Tales from the Dark Continent* (New York: G. Schirmer, 1920).
14 For example, see: Samuel Chotzinoff, 'Jazz: A Brief History—A Consideration of Negro Harmonies and Modern Dance Music', *Vanity Fair*, June 1923; Arthur S. Garbett, 'Why You Like Jazz', *Sunset Magazine*, March 1924; for analysis of American media's portrayal of jazz as the devil's music see Alan Merriman, *The Anthropology of Music* (Evanston, IL: Northwestern University Press, 1964): 241–244.
15 For other examples, see 'Modern Music Is an Expression of Modern Thought', *Australian Dance Band News*, 1 Dec. 1932: Z6–7; Paul Fritz Laubenstien, 'Jazz—Debit and Credit', *Musical Quarterly*, Oct. 1928: 614; *Evening News*, 25 Jan. 1928: 11; Andreas Huyssen traces this anxiety in terms of mass culture and femininity, describing a White male fear of 'engulfing femininity' and being 'devoured by commodification' whereas 'fortified and stable ego boundaries ... represent the *sine qua non* of male psychology in the bourgeois order'. Andreas Huyssen, *After the Great Divide: Modernism, Mass Culture, Postmodernism* (Bloomington: Indiana University Press, 1986): 53.
16 For example, see Langston Hughes' poems 'Danse Africaine' (1922) and 'Jazzonia' (1924); Paul Colin's series of graphic images of Josephine Baker, 1922; paintings include *Makeup Through the Window* by Koga Harue (1930), *Bal Jeunesse* by Palmer C. Hayden, 1927; *Teaching Old Dogs New Tricks*, John Held, Jr, 1926; *Aspiration*, Aaron Douglas, 1936.
17 For examples, see: *Sanders of the River* (1935), *Aloma of the South Sea* (1927), *A Dangerous Woman* (1929), *The Devil Dancer* (1927), *Ingagi* (1930), *Trader Horn* (1931); Jayna Brown, *Babylon Girls: Black Women Performers and the Shaping of the Modern* (Durham: Duke University Press, 2008): 231.

18 Paul Campbell Young, 'A General Overview of the Literature on Hypnotism', *The Psychological Bulletin*, 24 (1927): 540–560; Paul Campbell Young, 'Hypnotism', *The Psychological Bulletin*, 23:1 (1926): 506–519; Wendy Kline, *Building a Better Race: Gender, Sexuality, and Eugenics from the Turn of the Century to the Baby Boom* (Berkeley: University of California Press, 2001).
19 Howard Teasdale, Report and Recommendations of the Wisconsin Legislative Committee to Investigate the White Slave Traffic and Kindred Subjects (Democrat Printing Company, 1914): 103; Ruth M. Alexander, *The 'Girl Problem': Female Sexual Delinquency in New York, 1900–1930* (Ithaca: Cornell University Press, 1995).
20 'Physical Displays by Children', *Argus*, 16 Sept. 1922: 9; Meredith Atkinson, *Capital and Labour: Co-operation or Class War?* (Sydney: Worker Education Association, 1918): 7; Peter Haeusler, 'Progressivism and the Janus Face of "Efficient Citizenship": Meredith Atkinson and Australian Democracy', *Australian Journal of Politics & History*, 42:1 (1996): 24–38.
21 Scott Appelrouth, 'Body and Soul, Jazz in the 1920s', *American Behavioral Scientist*, 48:11 (2005): 1499–1501.
22 Cecil Trevelyan, *Musicians' Union of Australia Rules* (Melbourne: Labor Call Press, 1927), MUA NBA E156/1; 'Foreign Musicians Displacing Australians', *Sydney Morning Herald*, 15 Mar. 1928: 22; 'Aussies Out in the Cold', *Labor Daily*, 17 Mar. 1928: 1; W.H.S. Lamble, *Leafet: What Is Australia Worth to You?* undated, MUA NBA E156/1/1.
23 'Dancing Times', *Table Talk*, 29 Mar. 1928: 49.
24 'White Girls with Negro Lovers', Melbourne *Truth*, 31 Mar. 1928: 1.

Chapter 20 Cecil Trevelyan's Questions of Principle

1 *Irish News and Belfast Morning News*, 10 Jul. 1900: 1.
2 'Sad Fatality at Whitehead', *Northern Whig*, 12 Jul. 1900: 5; 'Manager of the Belfast Empire Theatre Drowned', *Freeman's Journal*, 12 Jul. 1900.
3 'Sanderson v Sanderson', *Shields Daily Gazette*, 21 Jun. 1904: 4.
4 Passenger List, SS *Medic*, Liverpool to Sydney, 3 Sept. 1900, Ancestry.com
5 'Sanderson v Sanderson', *Shields Daily Gazette*, 21 Jun. 1904: 4.
6 'Musician's Champion', *Cairns Post*, 3 Sept. 1935: 6.
7 'Personal', Adelaide *Mail*, 1 Mar. 1913: 5; Kay Dreyfus, *Silences and Secrets: The Australian Experience of the Weintraubs Syncopators* (Clayton: Monash University Publishing, 2013): 69; 'Question of Testing', *Daily Herald*, 20 Jul. 1912: 6; 'A Violinist's Dismissal', Adelaide *Advertiser*, 17 Oct. 1912: 14; 'Musicians' Union', Adelaide *Register*, 23 Jul. 1912: 10.
8 Cecil Trevelyan, 'Fighting at the Dardanelles' (music), (Adelaide: Cawthorne, 1915); Corporal F.A.C. George, letter dated 18 April 1915, AWM/IDRL 310 cited in Dale James Blair, 'An Army of Warriors, These Anzacs': Legend and Illusion in the First AIF, PhD Thesis, Victoria University of Technology, July 1998: 95.
9 'General News', Adelaide *Advertiser*, 27 Jul. 1917: 6; Cecil Trevelyan and A.L. Atterton, 'Won't You Take a Gun?' (music), (Adelaide: Cawthorne, 1917).
10 For discussion of Hughes' wartime speeches see Chapter 5, 'The British Race Has Found Its Soul' in John F. Williams, *ANZACS, the Media and the Great War* (Sydney: UNSW Press, 1999): 98–110.
11 'Labor in Conclave', Sydney *Sun*, 2 Jun. 1918: 2; 'Musicians' Union', *Argus*, 16 Apr. 1918: 4; 'The Procession', *Age*, 17 Apr. 1918: 10; 'Enemy Aliens', Sydney *Truth*, 21 Apr. 1918: 4; 'Trades Hall Pro-German?', *Geelong Advertiser*, 23 Apr. 1918: 4; 'Labour Split', *Daily Telegraph*, 25 May 1918: 7; Dreyfus, *Silences and Secrets*: 67.

12 'No German Band!', Adelaide *Mail*, 1 Feb. 1919: 2.
13 'Musicians' Union Objects to Importations', Melbourne *Herald*, 27 Mar. 1928: 5; R.D. Patton, *Constitution Rules and By-Laws of the Musicians' Union of Australia*, (NSW District, 1921); Secretary's Report, *Minutes for the Federal Conference of the MUA*, 1918, MUA NBAC E156/6/1; 'Deputation to Prime Minister', *Professional Musician*, Mar. 1928: 9; Cecil Trevelyan, *Musicians' Union of Australia Rules*, (Melbourne: Labor Call Press, 1927); Minutes: Ninth Session, 11 Nov. 1927; General Secretary, 20th Session, 28 Nov. 1924, MUA NBAC E156/6/2.
14 Minutes: Twelfth Session, 14 Nov. 1927, Importation of Musicians: 16 MUA NBAC E156/6/2.
15 ibid.
16 'Musicians' Union Starts War on American Players', *Everyones*, 19 Oct. 1927: 41.
17 Letter: J.C. Bendrodt, Manager, Palais Royale, to Cecil Trevelyan, 4 Sept. 1924; Trevelyan to Bendrodt, 4 Oct. 1924; Cecil Trevelyan, Federal Secretary, Musicians' Union of Australia, Letter to J.C. Bendrodt, 14 Oct. 1924, MUA NBAC E156/2/5 (ii).
18 Letter: Musicians' Union District Secretary to Directors J.C. Williamson, Melbourne, 17 May 1924, MUA NBAC E156 2/5i -2/6lb.
19 'Hislop Drops Bomb for Musicians' Union', *Everyones*, 1 Feb. 1928, 43.
20 Letter: J.C. Bendrodt, Manager, Palais Royale, to Cecil Trevelyan, 4 Sept. 1924.
21 Letter: Trevelyan to Bendrodt, 4 Oct. 1924, MUA NBAC E156/2/5 (ii); 'Imported Musicians' Union's Complaint', *Sydney Morning Herald*, 3 Mar. 1928: 18; Letter: Trevelyan to J.C. Williamson's Grand Opera Orchestra, 1 May 1928, MUA NBAC E156 2/5i -2/6lb; Letter: Trevelyan in Kalgoorie to Lambel in Melbourne, 1 May 1928, MUA NBAC E156 2/5i -2/6lb.
22 Letter: Trevelyan to Bendrodt, 4 Oct. 1924, MUA NBAC E156/2/5 (ii).
23 Cited in Dreyfus, *Silences and Secrets*: 68.
24 Dreyfus, *Silences and Secrets*: 57, 86.

Chapter 21 War on American Players

1 'What's on at the Shows', *Perth Call*, 28 Oct. 1927: 6; 'Lincoln Perry's Letter', *Chicago Defender*, 29 Oct. 1927: 8; 'Musicians' Union Starts War on American Players', *Everyones*, 19 Oct. 1927: 41.
2 'Mr Baille's Reply', *Mercury*, 22 Feb. 1928: 3; John Whiteoak, 'Popular Music, Militarism, Women, and the Early "Brass Band" in Australia', *Australasian Music Research* (2001): 27; Duncan Bythell, 'The Brass Band in Australia: The Transplantation of British Popular Culture, 1850–1950' in *Bands: The Brass Band Movement in the Nineteenth and Twentieth Centuries*, ed. Trevor Herbert (Buckingham: Open University Press, 1991): 145–164.
3 Program: The Australian Commonwealth Silver Band, National Library of Australia; 'Australian Commonwealth Band', *Morning Bulletin*, 19 Nov. 1927: 6; between them, the players had won over 350 medals.
4 'Labor: Imported Bands', Adelaide *Advertiser*, 18 Oct. 1927: 17; 'Commonwealth Band', *Mercury*, 22 Feb. 1928: 3; 'A Musical Treat for Werribee: Famous Band to Appear', *Werribee Shire Banner*, 31 May 1928: 5.
5 Photograph: Australian Commonwealth Band, *Professional Musician*, Feb. 1928; *Werribee Shire Banner*, 31 May 1928: 5; 'The Showman's Corner', *Everyones*, 11 Jan. 1928: 33.
6 'How Australian Musicians Are Treated in America', *Professional Musician*, Mar. 1928.
7 Leaflet: 'What Is Australia Worth to You?', Noel Butlin Archive E/156.

8 'Debarred', *Sydney Morning Herald*, 6 Feb. 1928: 11; 'No Retaliation', *Sydney Morning Herald*, 8 Feb. 1928: 16.
9 'Musicians Ask Mr Bruce for Embargo', *Everyones*, 21 Mar. 1928: 38; Notes of an Interview at Parliament House, 16 Mar. 1928, NAA CP362/2; 'Deputation to Prime Minister', *Professional Musician*, Mar. 1928: 9.
10 'White Girls with Negro Lovers', Melbourne *Truth*, 31 Mar. 1928: 1.
11 Letter from Roland S. Browne, Investigation Branch, Victoria, to Major Harold Jones, Director, Investigation Branch, Canberra, 13 Mar. 1928, NAA V/4718.
12 'By Force', Sydney *Sun*, 27 Jun. 1927: 11; 'World Peace', *Sydney Morning Herald*, 28 Jun. 1927: 10; 'Fighting for Our Ideals', Melbourne *Herald*, 27 Jun. 1927: 4; 'Doctrine of World Peace', *Age*, 28 Jun. 1927: 9.
13 'Deputation to Prime Minister', Mar. 1928: 9.
14 'Notes of an Interview at Parliament House', 16 Mar. 1928, NAA CP362/2.
15 Memorandum: Cecil Trevelyan. Musicians' Union of Australia Federal Office, 15 May 1925, Noel Butlin Archive E/156; 'Deputation to Prime Minister', Mar. 1928: 9.
16 'Notes of an Interview at Parliament House', 16 Mar. 1928, NAA CP362/2; 'Federal Ban on Negro Bands, Mr Bruce Will Act', Melbourne *Herald*, 28 Mar. 1928: 1; 'Deputation to Prime Minister', Mar. 1928: 9.
17 'Everyone and Everybody', *Labor Daily*, 20 Sept. 1926: 4.
18 'Melbourne Day by Day', Burnie *Advocate*, 24 Mar. 1928: 5; 'Green Mill Advertisment', *Sun News Pictorial*, 5 Mar. 1928: 28.
19 Letter: Roland S. Browne to Major Harold Jones, Director, Investigation Branch, Canberra, 13 Mar. 1928, NAA V/4718.

Chapter 22 Constable Saker Tells the Truth

1 Saker v Saker, Supreme Court of the State of Victoria, Divorce Case Files, Melbourne, Case # 1929/25, 22 Jan. 1929, VPRS283/P0002/134.
2 ibid.
3 ibid.
4 John Hetherington, *Thomas Blamey* (Melbourne: Oxford University Press, 1974): 53.
5 'Victoria Police Inquiry', *Barrier Miner*, 19 Nov. 1924: 1; 'Police Hornet's Nest Stirred', Melbourne *Truth*, 22 May 1926: 14.
6 Bill Patey, 'Police Round Memories, 1947–54' in *The Argus: Life & Death of a Newspaper*, ed. Jim Usher (St Andrews, Victoria: Jim Usher, 1999): Mel Pratt et al., *Journalism in the Thirties*, (transcript of sound recording), Mel Pratt Collection, 1976, NLA ORAL TRC 121/85, J:3:1/14–16.
7 'An Opium Raid', *Age*, 24 Dec. 1927: 10; 'Unlawful Games', *Argus*, 28 Feb. 1925: 29; 'Dramatic Police Raid', *Age*, 1 Feb. 1926: 9; 'Alleged Illegal Betting', *Argus*, 12 Jan. 1925: 14; 'Italian Club Raided', *Argus*, 30 Mar. 1925: 12; 'Police Spring a Surprise', *Age*, 24 Feb. 1929: 10; 'Arrested on Motor-Launch', *Argus*, 20 Jan. 1928: 13; 'USA Seaman Arrested', Melbourne *Herald*, 24 Feb. 1928: 2; 'Sequel to Raid', *Argus*, 28 Feb. 1928: 27; 'Man with Rifle', *Weekly Times*, 19 Feb. 1927: 12.
8 'Hidden Haunts of Vice', Melbourne *Truth*, 2 May 1927: 6.
9 'How Do They Live?', Melbourne *Truth*, 2 May 1927: 6.
10 'Hidden Haunts of Vice', Melbourne *Truth*, 5 Feb. 1927: 6.
11 'Sinister Happening while Melbourne Sleeps', Melbourne *Truth*, 21 May 1927.
12 Pratt et al., *Journalism in the Thirties*: J:3:1/14–16.

13 For discussion of the 'Badge 80 Affair' see R. Haldane, *The People's Force* (Melbourne: Melbourne University Press, 1995): 197; D.M. Horner, *Blamey: The Commander-in-Chief* (St Leonards, NSW: Allen & Unwin, 1998): 75–83; 'Stolen Police Medal', *Argus*, 20 Nov. 1925: 10; 'The Blamey Papers', *Argus*, 30 Nov. 1953: 8; '"Mum" Tracy Defends General Blamey', *Smith's Weekly*, 16 Oct. 1926: 3.
14 'Putting the Blame on Blamey', Sydney *Truth*, 29 Nov. 1925: 16.
15 Hetherington, *Thomas Blamey*: 57.
16 Pratt et al., *Journalism in the Thirties*: J:3:1/14–16; for discussion of sensationalism in newspapers of the 1920s see Michael Schudson, *The Power of News* (Cambridge, MA: Harvard University Press, 1996): 37–112; John Brazil, 'Murder Trials, Murder and Twenties America', *American Quarterly*, 33:2 (1981): 163–184.
17 'Bomb Gang Contains International Crooks', Melbourne *Truth*, 8 Dec. 1928, p. 1: Gavin Brown, Gary Presland and Ralph Stavely, *In the Performance of Duty: The Murder and Assault of Victorian Police 1837–1988* (Melbourne: Police Historical Society, 1994): 154–156.
18 'For Meritorious Service', *Geelong Advertiser*, 30 Jun. 1923: 3; 'Melbourne for Law Breaking', *Smith's Weekly*, 21 Jun. 1924: 3; 'Police Valor Badges', *Weekly Times*, 27 Nov. 1926: 5; 'McIver Libel Action', Melbourne *Herald*, 27 Sept. 1929: 3; *Victoria Police Gazette*, 27 Feb. 1930: 207.
19 'Police Commissioner's Evidence at Inquiry', Melbourne *Herald*, 13 Nov. 1933: 12; 'Valor Badge Police Attacked', Melbourne *Herald*, 18 Nov. 1926: 1; 'Sharp Words', Melbourne *Herald*, 11 Dec. 1922: 3.
20 N. Gurkha, *Graft: Startling Disclosures of Corruption into the Victorian Police Force*, 2nd edition (self-published, May 1930); 'Corruption and Graft Rampant in Melbourne', *Smith's Weekly*, 31 May 1924: 3.
21 'The Blamey Papers No 2', *Argus*, 30 Nov. 1953: 7.
22 'Police Commissioner's Evidence at Inquiry', Melbourne *Herald*, 13 Nov. 1933: 12; *Past Pattern, Future Directions: Victoria Police and the Problem of Corruption and Serious Misconduct* (Victorian Government Printer, 2007); Hetherington, *Thomas Blamey*: 58–9.
23 'Disturbance at Oakleigh', *Argus*, 16 Jan. 1925: 8; 'Police and Civilians', *Age*, 13 Feb. 1926: 19; 'He Was Seen from the Churchyard', Melbourne *Herald*, 15 Dec. 1928; 'Dramatic Police Raid', *Age*, 1 Feb. 1926: 9.
24 'The Blamey Papers', *Argus*, 30 Nov. 1953: 8; Michael Cathcart, The White Army of 1931: Origins and Legitimations, BA (Hons), Dip. Ed., Australian National University, June 1983: 95.
25 Court of Petty Sessions, Magistrates City Court Register, 23–24 Feb. 1928, VPRS 1665: 47–48; 'The Opium Habit', *Geelong Advertiser*, 6 Dec. 1927: 6; 1; 'An Opium Raid', *Age*, 24 Dec. 1927: 10; 'An Opium Den', *Age*, 14 Feb. 1928: 15; 'Six Chinese in Court', *Argus*, 23 Nov. 1927; 'Chinese House Raided', *Argus*, 31 Jan. 1927: 12; 'Opium Dealer Fined £50', *Horsham Times*, 14 Sept. 1926: 4.
26 Court of Petty Sessions, Magistrates City Court Register, 23–24 Feb. 1928, VPRS 1665: 47–48.
27 File: 'Saker, Leslie Barton, Register No 6415', Record of Conduct and Service, Victoria Police Museum Archive; File: 'Dunn, Harry Spencer, Register No 5552', Record of Conduct and Service, Victoria Police Museum Archive; Major Longfield Lloyd, Report: 'Negro Orchestra—Lately at the Tivoli Theatre Sydney', 24 Feb. 1928, NAA B741 V/4718.

Chapter 23 Women Who Bite Policemen

1 'The Private Life of Sydney's Wildest Man', *Sydney Morning Herald*, 13 Mar. 1981: 9.
2 *Sydney Morning Herald*, 9 Mar. 1981: 10.
3 *Bulletin*, 30 Nov. 1982: 69; 'Ezra Norton: A Strange, Abrupt, Ruthless Man', *Sydney Morning Herald*, 4 Sept. 1982: 30; Valerie Lawson, 'Norton, Ezra (1897–1967)', *Australian Dictionary of Biography*, National Centre of Biography, Australian National University.
4 *Sydney Morning Herald*, 4 Sept. 1982: 30.
5 John Osburn, 'The Dramaturgy of the Tabloid: Climax and Novelty in a Theory of Condensed Forms', *Theatre Journal*, 46:4 (1994): 507–522.
6 'Civilization: Not an Exclusive Possession', Perth *Truth*, 22 Oct. 1927: 1.
7 'A Black-Out for Sonny Clay's Noisome N_____s', Sydney *Truth*, 1 Apr. 1928: 13; Confidential Letter: Major H.E. Jones, IB Director, to General T. Blamey, Chief Commissioner of Police, Victoria, 1 Mar. 1928, NAA V/4718.
8 'Sonny Clay's Parting Shot', *Everyones*, 4 Apr. 1928: 6; Letter: Inspector Roland S. Browne to Major Jones, Director, Investigation Branch, Canberra, 13 Mar. 1928, NAA V/4718.
9 Sydney *Truth*, 1 Apr. 1928: 13.
10 ibid.; Letter: Inspector Roland S. Browne to Major Jones, Director, Investigation Branch, Canberra, 13 Mar. 1928, NAA V/4718; Confidential Letter: J. Musgrave, Collector of Customs, Victoria, to The Secretary, H&T Dept, Canberra, 28 Mar. 1928, NAA 1923/10153.
11 Sydney *Truth*, 1 Apr. 1928: 13; 'Raid on Flat', *Argus*, 28 Mar. 1928: 21; 'Negro Undesirables', Melbourne *Herald*, 27 Mar. 1928: 1; 'White Girls; Negroes', Sydney *Evening News*, 27 Mar. 1928: 11.
12 'Advertising', Melbourne *Herald*, 19 Mar. 1928: 9.
13 Sydney *Truth*, 1 Apr. 1928: 13; 'Raid on Negroes Flat', *Ballarat Courier*, 28 Mar. 1928: 8; 'Pictures-Plus-Dancing Dropped at Cairo, St Kilda', *Everyones*, 4 Jan. 1928; 'Dancing Times', *Table Talk*, 12 Jan. 1928: 14; 'Hinkler Re-Broadcast in London', Melbourne *Herald*, 22 Mar. 1928: 2; 'Advertising', Melbourne *Herald*, 21 Mar. 1928: 8; 'Melbourne Day by Day', Burnie *Advocate*, 24 Mar. 1928: 5; 'Advertisement', *Sun News Pictorial*, 5 May 1928: 28.
14 Report of L.B. Saker, Constable 6415, Victoria Police, Melbourne, 27 Mar. 1928, NAA V/4718.
15 Bill Patey, 'Police Round Memories, 1947–54' in *The Argus: Life & Death of a Newspaper*, ed. Jim Usher (St Andrews, Victoria: Jim Usher, 1999).
16 Melbourne *Truth*, 24 Mar. 1928: 12.
17 Sydney *Truth*, 1 Apr. 1928: 13.

Chapter 24 Silk Petticoats and Mauve Pyjamas

1 'White Girls with Negro Lovers', Melbourne *Truth*, 31 Mar. 1928: 1.
2 Report of L.B. Saker, Constable 6415, Victoria Police, Melbourne, 27 Mar. 1928, NAA V/4718.
3 'Negroes Blame White Girls', *Daily Guardian*, 30 Mar. 1928.
4 'A Black-Out for Sonny Clay's Noisome N_____s', Sydney *Truth*, 1 Apr. 1928: 13.
5 Melbourne *Truth*, 31 Mar. 1928: 1.
6 ibid.
7 'Raid on Negroes Flat', *Ballarat Courier*, 28 Mar. 1928: 8.
8 Melbourne *Truth*, 31 Mar. 1928: 1.

9 'Raid on a Flat', *Age*, 27 Mar. 1928: 21.
10 'White Girls; Negroes', Sydney *Evening News*, 27 Mar. 1928: 11.
11 'Negro Orgy: White Girls on Vagrancy Charges', Sydney *Sun*, 27 Mar. 1928: 12; Melbourne *Herald*, 27 Mar. 1928: 5.
12 'Black "Boys" and White Girls', *Beckett's Budget*, 30 Mar. 1928: 7.
13 ibid.
14 Douglas Flamming, *Bound for Freedom: Black Los Angeles in Jim Crow America* (Berkeley: University of California Press, 2005): 211; Donald Bogle, *Bright Boulevards, Bold Dreams: The Story of Black Hollywood* (Philadelphia: Running Press Adult, 2019): 74.
15 Clora Bryant et al. (eds), *Central Avenue Sounds: Jazz in Los Angeles* (Berkeley: University of California Press, 1998): 130, 157.
16 'Black "Boys" and White Girls', *Beckett's Budget*, 30 Mar. 1928: 7.
17 Bryant et al., *Central Avenue Sounds*: 56; Marshal Royal, *Marshal Royal, Jazz Survivor* (New York: Cassell, 1996): 20; David Lewis, 1920 US Federal Census, Bexar, Texas, San Antonio Ward 6, Ancestry.com; Buck Clayton and Nancy Miller Elliott, *Buck Clayton's Jazz World* (New York: Oxford University Press, 1987): 66.
18 'Complaints Concerning Negroes', Adelaide *Advertiser*, 26 Mar. 1928: 13.
19 'A Black-Out for Sonny Clay's Noisome N______s', Sydney *Truth*, 1 Apr. 1928: 13.
20 Pops Foster and Tom Stoddard, *Pops Foster: The Autobiography of a New Orleans Jazzman as Told to Tom Stoddard* (Berkeley: University of California Press, 1971): 132.
21 'Dorothy Anderson', *Prahran Telegraph*, 27 May 1927: 5.
22 'Raid on a Flat', *Age*, 27 Mar. 1928: 21.
23 On 5 December 1928, Trixie Ross' name appears on Magistrates City Court Register; Charge: Vagrancy; Decision: Discharged. VPRS 1665: 193; 'Possession of Drugs', *Argus*, 12 Dec. 1928: 24; 'He Was Seen from the Churchyard', Melbourne *Truth*, 15 Dec. 1928.
24 FD-CASS-76, Leo Davis Sound Recording, 1977, Frank Driggs Collection, Marr Sound Archive, University of Missouri, Kansas City.

Chapter 25 Tooth and Law

1 Court of Petty Sessions, 25 Mar. 1928, Magistrates City Court Register, Melbourne, VPRS 1665, 193.
2 'Complaints Concerning Negroes', Adelaide *Advertiser*, 26 Mar. 1928: 13.
3 'A Black-Out for Sonny Clay's Noisome N______s', Sydney *Truth*, 1 Apr. 1928: 17; 'Sonny Clay's Parting Shot', *Everyones*, 4 Apr. 1928: 6.
4 Marcella Pearce, *Melbourne Trade Hall Memories* (Melbourne: Trades Hall Council, 1997): 40–42; Report of L.B. Saker, Constable 6415, Victoria Police, Melbourne, 27 Mar. 1928, NAA V/4718; 'Negro Theatrical Artists', *Age*, 28 Mar. 1928: 12; 'Negro Undesirables', Melbourne *Herald*, 27 Mar. 1928: 5.
5 *Age*, 28 Mar. 1928: 12; 'Raid on Flat', *Argus*, 28 Mar. 1928: 21.
6 'Negro Theatre Artists and White Firls in Flat', Melbourne *Herald*, 26 Mar. 1928: 3.
7 Letter: Inspector, Investigation Branch, Melbourne, to the Director, Investigation Branch, Canberra, 28 Mar. 1928, NAA No V/4718.

Chapter 26 The Eight Hour Day

1 'Real Significance of Eight Hours Day', *Labor Call*, 22 Mar. 1928: 1.
2 'Advertisement: Order of Procession', *Labor Call*, 22 Mar. 1928: 8; 'Eight Hour Day', *Weekly Times*, 31 Mar. 1928: 11; Kyla Cassells, 'Politics and Meaning: Melbourne's Eight Hours Day and Anzac Day, 1928–1935', *Marxist Interventions*, 2 (2010):

79–108; Michael Cathcart, The White Army of 1931: Origins and Legitimations, B.A. (Hons), Dip. Ed., Australian National University, Jun. 1985: 64, 67.

3 'The Industrialists' Case', *Brisbane Courier*, 14 Nov. 1923: 8.

4 'Raid on a Flat', *Age*, 26 Mar. 1928: 10.

5 'Complaints Concerning Negroes', Adelaide *Advertiser*, 26 Mar. 1928: 13; 'A Flat Raided', Adelaide *Advertiser*, 26 Mar. 1928: 13.

6 'Negro Theatre Artists and White Girls in Flat', Melbourne *Herald*, 26 Mar. 1928: 3; 'No More Negro Entertainers', Sydney *Sun News*, 28 Mar. 1928: 26; *Professional Musician*, 1928: 20; Norman D. Carlyon, *The Flight of Steps* (Melbourne: N.D. Carlyon, 1986): 107–108.

7 Melbourne *Herald*, 26 Mar. 1928: 3; Detective Inspector Gleeson, Report: 'Sonny Clay' Company of Negro Musicians, 28 Mar. 1928, NAA File 1923/10153.

8 'Quick Action Follows Negro Party', *Daily Telegraph*, 27 Mar. 1928: 3.

9 Melbourne *Herald*, 26 Mar. 1928: 3.

10 ibid.

11 ibid.

12 'Negroes and White Girls', Adelaide *Advertiser*, 28 Mar. 1928: 10; 'The Color Line', *Age*, 27 Mar. 1928: 10; 'White Girls; Negroes', *Evening News*, 27 Mar. 1928: 11; 'Negroes and White Girls', Adelaide *Chronicle*, 31 Mar. 1928: 37.

13 'Negro Undesirables', Melbourne *Herald*, 27 Mar. 1928: 1; Adelaide *Chronicle*, 31 Mar. 1928: 37.

14 'Raid on Flat', *Argus*, 28 Mar. 1928: 21; *Age*, 27 Mar. 1928: 10; 'Govt Demands Party Action against Mr Hughes', Melbourne *Herald*, 30 Mar. 1928: 1.

15 Letter: Director, Investigation Branch, to J.G. Maclaren, Secretary Home & Territories Department, Canberra, 27 Mar. 1928, NAA Ref 27/21825.

16 Adelaide *Advertiser*, 26 Mar. 1928: 13; Adelaide *Chronicle*, 31 Mar. 1928: 37.

Chapter 27 A Young Woman in Trouble

1 'Ararat', *Age*, 15 May 1925: 21; 'The Late Mr Kirkpatrick', *Leader*, 23 Dec. 1916: 8; *Australasian*, 28 Jan. 1928: 12.

2 'Young Woman in Trouble', *Prahran Telegraph*, 27 May 1927: 5; 'Girl Given Chance to Reform', *Prahran Telegraph*, 10 Jun. 1927: 6.

3 *Prahran Telegraph*, 27 May 1927: 5.

4 *Who's Who in the World of Women, Victoria Australia* (Melbourne: Reference Press Association, 1934); 'Cars and Their Owners', *Table Talk*, 15 July 1926: 35; *Australasian*, 28 Jan. 1928: 12; *Australasian*, 18 Sept. 1920.

5 'The Color Line', *Age*, 27 Mar. 1928: 10.

6 For examples of goggles in popular culture see: 'Advertisement for "Very Confidential"', *Everyones*, 11 Jan. 1928: 44. The sketch shows two young women in an open plane in leather caps and aviator goggles on their foreheads. 'Advertisement for "Now We're in the Air"', *Everyones*, 29 Feb. 1928: 14. A comedy featuring Louise Brooks wearing aviator goggles. 'Very Confidential', *Everyones*, 11 Jan. 1928: 44; 'Now We're in the Air', *Everyones*, 29 Feb. 1928: 14; 'Mrs Miller and Captain Lancaster', *Table Talk*, 5 May 1928: 9.

7 'The Color Line', *Age*, 27 Mar. 1928: 10.

8 'Girls and Their Negro Friends in the Nude', *Northern Territory Times*, 27 Mar. 1928: 2.

9 'Impudent Negroes Repeat Orgy with White Girls', *Daily Guardian*, 27 Mar. 1928: 1.

10 'White Girls; Negroes', *Evening News*, 27 Mar. 1928: 11.

11 *Evening News*, 27 Mar. 1928: 11; 'Raid on Flat', *Argus*, 28 Mar. 1928: 21; 'Negro Theatrical Artists', *Age*, 28 Mar. 1928: 12; 'Raid on Negroes' Flat Described', Melbourne *Herald*, 27 Mar. 1928: 5; 'White Girls with Negro Lovers', Melbourne *Truth*, 31 Mar. 1928: 1; 'Pictures-Plus-Dancing Dropped at Cairo, St Kilda', *Everyones*, 4 Jan. 1928: 6.
12 'A Black-Out for Sonny Clay's Noisome N_____s', Sydney *Truth*, 1 Apr. 1928: 13; 'White Girls with Negro Lovers', Melbourne *Truth*, 31 Mar. 1928: 1.
13 'Negro Orgy', Sydney *Sun*, 27 Mar. 1928: 12.
14 Sydney *Sun*, 27 Mar. 1928: 12; *Evening News*, 27 Mar. 1928: 11; Sydney *Truth*, 1 Apr. 1928: 13; *Age*, 28 Mar. 1928: 12.
15 'Treatment of Criminals', *Age*, 15 Mar. 1929: 11.
16 *Beckett's Budget*, 30 Mar. 1928: 7.

Chapter 28 Judicial Theatre

1 'Mr. Thomas Latham', *Argus*, 18 Jul. 1938: 9; 'Mr Thomas O'Callaghan', *Argus*, 2 Sept. 1931: 6; 'Raid on Flat', *Argus*, 28 Mar. 1928: 21; 'Negro Orgy', Sydney *Sun*, 27 Mar. 1928: 12; 'Girl Faints When Hears Police Story', *Daily Telegraph*, 28 Mar. 1928: 2; 'Negro Theatrical Artists', *Age*, 28 Mar. 1928: 12.
2 Report of L.B. Saker, Constable 6415, Victoria Police, Melbourne, 27 Mar. 1928, NAA V/4718.
3 For discussion of vagrancy law and prostitution see Judith A. Allen, *Sex & Secrets: Crimes Involving Australian Women Since 1880* (Melbourne: Oxford University Press, 1990): 91–92.
4 'Shattering Lives', *Argus*, 31 Dec. 1925: 9.
5 Melbourne *Truth*, 5 May 1928: 14.
6 'Black "Boys" and White Girls', *Beckett's Budget*, 30 Mar. 1928: 7; 'White Girls; Negroes', *Evening News*, 27 Mar. 1928: 11.
7 *Argus*, 28 Mar. 1928: 21; *Beckett's Budget*, 30 Mar. 1928: 7; Sydney *Sun*, 27 Mar. 1928: 12.
8 Sydney *Sun*, 27 Mar. 1928: 12.
9 *Age*, 28 Mar. 1928: 12; 'Raid on Negroes Flat', *Ballarat Courier*, 28 Mar. 1928: 8; Sydney *Sun*, 27 Mar. 1928: 12.
10 *Beckett's Budget*, 30 Mar. 1928: 7; Sydney *Sun*, 27 Mar. 1928: 12; *Ballarat Courier*, 28 Mar. 1928: 8.
11 *Evening News*, 27 Mar. 1928: 11; Sydney *Sun*, 27 Mar. 1928: 12; *Argus*, 28 Mar. 1928: 21; *Ballarat Courier*, 28 Mar. 1928: 8.
12 'Police News', *Argus*, 3 Nov. 1925: 33. For instances of defendants claiming that PC Saker abused police power see: 'Police and Civilians', *Age*, 13 Feb. 1926: 19; 'Disturbance at Oakleigh', *Argus*, 16 Jan. 1925; 'Police Allege Ringing-in', *Argus*, 3 Nov. 1925; 'Fought Like a Man', *West Australian*, 12 Sept. 1925; 'Woman Complains of Police', *Argus*, 4 Jul. 1928; 'He Was Seen from the Churchyard', Melbourne *Truth*, 15 Dec. 1928.
13 N. Gibson, *Graft: Startling Disclosures of Corruption into the Victorian Police Force* (Melbourne: self-published, 1930); Neil Gibson, *Jungle Justice: Victorian Police Scandals Exposed* (Melbourne: self-published, 1933).
14 'Graft Charges', *Sydney Morning Herald*, 10 Oct. 1933: 9; Office of Police Integrity, *Past Pattern, Future Directions: Victoria Police and the Problem of Corruption and Serious Misconduct* (Melbourne: Victorian Government Printer, 2008).
15 'White Girls with Negro Lovers', Melbourne *Truth*, 31 Mar. 1928: 1; *Beckett's Budget*, 30 Mar. 1928: 7.

16 *Beckett's Budget*, 30 Mar. 1928: 7; *Ballarat Courier*, 28 Mar. 1928: 8.
17 'Raid on Negroes' Flat Described', Melbourne *Herald*, 27 Mar. 1928: 5.
18 *Beckett's Budget*, 30 Mar. 1928: 7.
19 *Age*, 28 Mar. 1928: 12.
20 Report of L.B. Saker, Constable 6415, Victoria Police, Melbourne, 27 Mar. 1928, NAA V/4718; Pops Foster and Tom Stoddard, *Pops Foster: The Autobiography of a New Orleans Jazzman as Told to Tom Stoddard* (Berkeley: University of California Press, 1971): 132.
21 *Argus*, 28 Mar. 1928: 21.
22 'Impudent Negroes Repeat Orgy with White Girls', *Daily Guardian*, 27 Mar. 1928: 1; Sydney *Sun*, 27 Mar. 1928: 12.
23 Such as 'Cabaret', *Everyones*, 26 Feb. 1927: 53; 'Twinkletoes', *Everyones*, 2 Mar. 1927: 15; 'Three Weeks in Paris', *Everyones*, 9 Mar. 1927: 8; 'Jazz', *Everyones*, 27 Jul. 1927: 42; 'The Show Girl', *Everyones*, 12 Oct. 1927: 37; 'Come to My House', *Everyones*, 2 May 1928: 11; 'Camille', *Everyones*, 6 Jul. 1927: 1. 'Tye Kee's Visitors'.
24 Melbourne *Herald*, 27 Jan. 1903: 2; Melbourne *Herald*, 27 Mar. 1928: 5; 'How Florrie Fell', Melbourne *Truth*, 8 Jan. 1927: 12.
25 *Age*, 28 Mar. 1928: 12; Melbourne *Herald*, 27 Mar. 1928: 5.
26 *Beckett's Budget*, 30 Mar. 1928: 7.
27 'Black Plague', *Daily Guardian*, 27 Mar. 1928; Melbourne *Herald*, 27 Mar. 1928: 5; Ivy Day, a housemaid, earned 30 shillings a week. Dorothy McGowan, a housemaid, earned 35 shillings. For discussion of women's wages in 1920s see: Jill Julius Matthews, *Dance Hall & Picture Palace: Sydney's Romance with Modernity* (Sydney: Currency Press, 2005): 84–96; Kathy Lee Peiss, *Cheap Amusements: Working Women and Leisure in Turn-of-the-Century New York* (Philadelphia: Temple University Press, 1986): 51–55.
28 *Beckett's Budget*, 30 Mar. 1928: 7; *Daily Guardian*, 27 Mar. 1928: 1; *Evening News*, 27 Mar. 1928: 1.
29 *Age*, 28 Mar. 1928: 12; *Ballarat Courier*, 28 Mar. 1928: 8.
30 Sydney *Truth*, 1 Apr. 1928: 13.

Chapter 29 A Captive Audience

1 For studies of miscegenation in the interwar period see: Liz Conor, '"Blackfella Missus Too Much Proud": Techniques of Appearing, Femininity, and Race in Australian Modernity' in *The Modern Girl Around the World: Consumption, Modernity, and Globalization*, ed. Alys Eve Weinbaum (Durham, NC: Duke University Press, 2008); Lucy Bland, 'White Women and Men of Colour: Miscegenation Fears in Britain After the Great War', *Gender and History*, 17:1 (2005): 29–61; Laura Tabili, '"Women of a Very Low Type": Crossing Racial Boundaries in Imperial Britain' in *Gender and Class in Modern Europe*, eds Laura Frader and Sonya O. Rose (Ithaca: Cornell University Press, 1996): 165–90; Earl Lewis and Heidi Ardizonne, *Love on Trial: An American Scandal in Black and White* (New York: W.W. Norton, 2001).
2 'Advertisement', *Everyones*, 19 May 1926: 24–26; for discussion of Hurley's career see: Frank Hurley, Robert Dixon and Christopher Lee, *The Diaries of Frank Hurley, 1912–1941* (London; New York: Anthem Press, 2011). Also, see: Michael Sturma, *South Sea Maidens: Western Fantasy and Sexual Politics in the South Pacific* (Westport, CT: Greenwood Press, 2002).
3 Leon Gordon, *White Cargo: A Play of the Primitive* (Boston: The Four Seas Company, 1925); Liz Conor, *The Spectacular Modern Woman: Feminine Visibility in the 1920s*

(Bloomington: Indiana University Press, 2004): 196–198; Gerald Martin Bordman, *The Concise Oxford Companion to American Theatre* (New York: Oxford University Press, 1987): 659; 'The Theatre and Its People', *Table Talk*, 9 Sept. 1926; 'Theatre Royal—"White Cargo"', *Sydney Morning Herald*, 10 Nov. 1928. For discussion of colonial concubinage see: Ann Laura Stoler, 'Carnal Knowledge and Imperial Power' in *Gender at the Crossroads of Knowledge*, ed. Michaela di Leonardo (Berkeley: University of California Press, 1991): 51–101.

4 *Townsville Daily Bulletin*, 3 May 1927: 3; *Brisbane Courier*, 7 May 1926: 17.

5 'The Black Madame Butterfly', *Smith's Weekly*, 21 Jan. 1928: 10. Also see: Marilyn Lake, 'Frontier Feminism and the Marauding White Man', *Journal of Australian Studies*, 49 (1996): 12–20.

6 'Betsy', *Australian Aborigines Advocate*, 1 Jul. 1928: 3; 'Betsy', *Australian Aborigines Advocate*, 1 Aug. 1928: 10.

7 *Sydney Morning Herald*, 12 May 1927: 5; for discussion of pro-Aboriginal policies within Women's Movement see: Victoria Haskins, 'Domestic Service and Frontier Feminism: The Call for a Woman Visitor to "Half-Caste" Girls and Women in Domestic Service, Adelaide, 1925–1928', *Frontiers: A Journal of Women Studies*, 28:1–2 (2007): 124–164.

8 'Massacre', *Sydney Morning Herald*, 8 Mar. 1927: 11; Kate Auty, 'Patrick Bernard O'Leary and the Forrest River Massacres, Western Australia: Examining "Wodgil" and the Significance of 8 June 1926', *Aboriginal History*, 28 (2004): 122–155.

9 Bill Wilson and Justin O'Brien, '"To Infuse a Universal Terror": A Reappraisal of the Coniston Killings', *Aboriginal History*, 27 (2003): 59–78.

10 *Evening News*, 17 May 1923; Fred Maynard, AAPA, *To the Royal Commission on the Constitution* (a handwritten note), 22 Feb. 1928, NAA.

11 Census of the Commonwealth of Australia, 30 June 1933, Part XII—Race, (Canberra: Commonwealth Govt Printer, 1933): 907, 920–922. For discussion of 'half-caste' population in interwar period see: Warwick Anderson, 'Ambiguities of Race: Science on the Reproductive Frontier of Australia and the Pacific Between the Wars', *Australian Historical Studies*, 40:2 (2009): 143–160; Tony Austin, 'Cecil Cook, Scientific Thought and Half-Castes in the Northern Territory, 1927–1939', *Aboriginal History*, 14:1 (1990): 104–122.

12 'Native Race Dying Rapidly', *Australian Aborigines Advocate*, 31 May 1927: 6.

13 'Sink of Immorality', Sydney *Truth*, 21 Nov. 1926: 19; Russel Ward, *Australian Legend* (Melbourne: Oxford University Press, 1958).

14 J.B. Monckton, *The Shuttle of Life* (London: Hutchinson & Co., 1928).

15 'Migrant Girl Saved from White Slavers', *Smith's Weekly*, 21 Jan. 1928: 9.

16 'Lying Afghans, Horrible Fate of Women Who Marry Them', Adelaide *Advertiser*, 30 Mar. 1913: 10.

17 'The White Slave Traffic', *Northern Territory Times and Gazette*, 26 Feb. 1914: 8.

18 'Negro Bands in Australia', *Age*, 2 Apr. 1928: 12.

19 'Raid on Flat', *Argus*, 28 Mar. 1928: 21.

20 Keith Hancock, *Australia* (London: Ernest Benn, 1930): 66.

21 Charles Pearson, *National Life and Character: A Forecast* (London: Macmillan and Co., 1894): 16–17.

Chapter 30 The Sydney Express

1 Clora Bryant et al. (eds), *Central Avenue Sounds: Jazz in Los Angeles* (Berkeley: University of California Press, 1999): 386.

2 'Negro Undesirables', Melbourne *Herald*, 27 Mar. 1928: 1; Detective Inspector Gleeson, Report: 'Sonny Clay' Company of Negro Musicians, 28 Mar. 1928, NAA File 1923/10153; Letter: Inspector, Investigation Branch, Melbourne, to the Director, Investigation Branch, Canberra, 28 Mar. 1928, NAA No V/4718; Andrew McLeod, 'On the Origins of Consorting Laws', *Melbourne University Law Review*, 37: 1 (2013): 103; 'Negroes Leaving Australia', *Argus*, 28 Mar. 1928: 21; *Age*, 27 Mar. 1928: 10; 'Negro Orgy: White Girls on Vagrancy Charges', Sydney *Sun*, 27 Mar. 1928: 12.
3 Claude McKay, 'Soviet Russia and the Negro', *Crisis*, Jan. 1924: 117.
4 Melbourne *Herald*, 27 Mar. 1928: 1; Cecil Trevelyan, *Musicians' Union of Australia Rules* (Melbourne: Labor Call Press, 1927), MUA NBA E156/1; 'Federal Ban on Negro Bands', Melbourne *Herald*, 28 Mar. 1928: 1; 'Deputation to Prime Minister', *Professional Musician*, Mar. 1928: 9; 'Mr Bruce and the Professors', Melbourne *Herald*, 27 Mar. 1928: 5.
5 Melbourne *Herald*, 27 Mar. 1928: 5.
6 ibid.
7 *Ivie Anderson*, Radio station CKMO, Vancouver, BC, 27 Sept. 1947. Interviewed by Bill Hill (unissued).
8 'Ivie Anderson's Tips to Vocalists', *Down Beat*, 15 Jul. 1942: 31; 'For the Love of Ivie', *Jazz Times*, 31: 1–5: 170; Harvey G. Cohen, *Duke Ellington's America* (Chicago: University of Chicago Press, 2010): 196.
9 'Photograph', *Beckett's Budget*, 28 Jan. 1928: 7; 10 Feb. 1928: 1, 13, 16; 2 Mar. 1928: 23.
10 'Sonny Clay's Parting Shot', *Everyones*, 4 Apr. 1928: 6; Rex Stewart, *Boy Meets Horn* (Ann Arbor: University of Michigan Press, 1991): 178; 'Plantation Days', *Daily Telegraph*, 25 Jan. 1928: 7.
11 'White Girls with Black Men', *Labor Daily*, 26 Mar. 1928: 1; *Argus*, 28 Mar. 1928: 21.
12 'The Musical Bunch', *Chicago Defender*, 5 May 1928: 6.
13 *Methodist Spectator*, 4 Apr. 1928: 331.
14 'Stars that Shine', *Chicago Defender*, 12 May 1928: 6.
15 'Negro Artists', Sydney *Sun*, 17 Apr. 1928: 11.
16 'Ivie Anderson's Tips to Vocalists', *Down Beat*, 15 Jul. 1942: 31.

Chapter 31 British Justice

1 'Jazz Band Negroes Reach Sydney', Melbourne *Herald*, 28 Mar. 1928: 1.
2 Melbourne *Herald*, 28 Mar. 1928: 1; 'Sonny Clay's Negroes', *Age*, 29 Mar. 1928: 10; 'Sonny Clay's Parting Shot', *Everyones*, 4 Apr. 1928: 6; *California Eagle*, 11 May 1928: 2; '"A Frame-Up" Negro Band's Protest', *Canberra Times*, 29 Mar. 1928: 1.
3 *Canberra Times*, 29 Mar. 1928: 1.
4 'Sonny Clay's Parting Shot', *Everyones*, 4 Apr. 1928: 6.
5 Ida B. Wells, *Crusade for Justice: The Autobiography of Ida B. Wells*, (Chicago: University of Chicago, 1972): 71. Also see Crystal Nicole Feimster, *Southern Horrors: Women and the Politics of Rape and Lynching* (Cambridge, MA: Harvard University Press, 2011); Peggy Pascoe, *What Comes Naturally: Miscegenation Law and the Making of Race in America* (Oxford, New York: Oxford University Press, 2009): 157, 168.
6 1860 US Federal Census Slave Schedules, Ancestry.com
7 By personal correspondence with Mark Lomax, Pasadena, California.

8 J. Wells, *Boxing Day: The Fight that Changed the World* (Sydney: Harper Collins, 1998); Theresa Runstedtler, *Jack Johnson, Rebel Sojourner: Boxing in the Shadow of the Global Color Line* (Berkeley: University of California Press, 2012).
9 Cited in Geoffrey C. Ward, *Unforgivable Blackness: The Rise and Fall of Jack Johnson* (New York: A.A. Knopf, 2004): 139.
10 'A Black Outlook', *Bulletin*, 14 Mar. 1928: 41.
11 'Negroes Arrive in Sydney', Sydney *Sun*, 29 Mar. 1928: 2; Melbourne *Herald*, 28 Mar. 1928: 1.
12 Kirsten McKenzie, *Scandal in the Colonies: Sydney and Cape Town, 1820–1850* (Melbourne: Melbourne University Press, 2006): 8.
13 'How Some Whites Demean the Purity of Their Colour', Melbourne *Truth*, 18 Aug. 1926: 9.
14 See Ilaria Vanni, 'The Archive and the Contact Zones: The Story of Stan Loycurrie and Jack Noorywauka, Performers at the 1929 Australian Aboriginal Art Exhibition, Melbourne', *Journal of Australian Studies*, 38:3 (2014): 314–330.
15 'Impudent Negroes', *Daily Guardian*, 27 Mar. 1928: 1; Melbourne *Herald*, 28 Mar. 1928: 1.
16 Shane White and Graham White, *Stylin': African American Expressive Culture from Its Beginnings to the Zoot Suit* (Ithaca, NY: Cornell University Press, 1998).
17 Langston Hughes, 'Home', *The Ways of White Folks* (New York: Knopf, 1934).
18 'Dame Margaret Greville', *Northern Times*, 25 Jun. 1927: 4.
19 'Sonny Clay's Parting Shot', *Everyones*, 4 Apr. 1928: 6; 'How Australian Musicians Are Treated in America', *Professional Musician*, Mar. 1928; 'A One-Sided Whine from Little America', *Australasian Band and Orchestra News*, 26 Sept. 1927: 2.
20 *Minutes of Quarterly General Meeting*, 27 Jan. 1928; 12 Apr. 1928, MUA NBAC E7, 1/8–10.
21 Letter: Inspector, Investigation Branch, Melbourne, to the Director, Investigation Branch, Canberra, 28 Mar. 1928, NAA V/4718; 'Negro Undesirables', Melbourne *Herald*, 27 Mar. 1928: 1; 'Negroes Leaving Australia', *Argus*, 28 Mar. 1928: 21; *Age*, 27 Mar. 1928: 10.

Chapter 32 Citizen Soldier

1 'Negroes from Melbourne Flat on Their Way Home', *Daily Guardian*, 27 Mar. 1928: 11; 'Negroes Arrive in Sydney', Sydney *Sun*, 29 Mar. 1928: 2; 'Sonny Clay Returns', *Daily Telegraph*, 29 Mar. 1928: 3.
2 FD-CASS-76, Leo Davis Sound Recording, 1977, Frank Driggs Collection, Marr Sound Archive, University of Missouri, Kansas City; W.C. Handy, *Father of the Blues: An Autobiography* (New York: Da Capo Press, 1991); Equal Justice Initiative, *Lynching in America: Documented African American Racial Terror*, https://lynchinginamerica.eji.org
3 Dora Apel, *Imagery of Lynching: Black Men, White Women, and the Mob* (New Brunswick: Rutgers University Press, 2004): 37; Jacqueline Goldsby, *A Spectacular Secret: Lynching in American Life and Literature* (Chicago: University of Chicago, 2006).
4 *Daily Telegraph*, 29 Mar. 1928: 10.
5 ibid.: 3.
6 Emory Tolnay Stewart and E.M. Beck, *A Festival of Violence: An Analysis of Southern Lynchings, 1882–1930* (Urbana: University of Illinois Press, 1995); Henry Reynolds, *The Other Side of the Frontier: Aboriginal Resistance to the European Invasion of Australia* (Melbourne: Penguin Books, 1982); Lyndall Ryan et al.,

Colonial Frontier Massacres, Australia, 1780–1930, c21ch.newcastle.edu.au/colonialmassacres/map

7 Report, Roland Browne to Major Jones, Commonwealth Investigation Branch, 8 Feb. 1931, NAA CRS A369.

8 Michael Cathcart, The White Army of 1931: Origins and Legitimations. BA (Hons.), Dip. Ed., Australian National University, June 1983: 1, 63, 70, 74, 84.

9 Andrew Moore, *The Secret Army and the Premier: Conservative Paramilitary Organisations in NSW 1930–32* (Sydney: UNSW Press, 1989); John Hetherington, *Blamey* (Melbourne: Cheshire, 1954).

10 Military Intelligence Report S80, NAA SP1141/1/13 cited in Moore, *The Secret Army*: 17.

11 Robert Darroch, 'The Man Behind Australia's Secret Army', *Bulletin*, 20 May 1980: 58–70.

12 Robert Darroch, *DH Lawrence's 99 Days in Australia* (Sydney: Svengall Press, 2017): 53; Letter: D.H. Lawrence to Catherine Carswell, 22 Jun. 1922 cited in Robert Darroch, *Kangaroo*'s Secret Army Research notes. http://www.dhlawrencesocietyaustralia.com.au; Andrew Moore interviewed a Mrs Jeffery who recalled that at bridge parties on the North Shore in the 1930s Jack Scott had been 'ribbed' over his portrayal as Jack Callcott in *Kangaroo*.

13 D.H. Lawrence, *Kangaroo* (London: Martin Secker, 1923): 40, 97, 112.

14 Lawrence, *Kangaroo*: 111; Col. Eric Campbell, *The Rallying Point*, cited in Darroch, 'The Man Behind Australia's Secret Army': 63–64; Scott, W.J.R., B2455, NAA: 6, 30, 53; Andrew Moore, 'Scott, William John (1888–1956)', *Australian Dictionary of Biography*, National Centre of Biography, Australian National University.

15 'Insult to British Flag', *Daily Telegraph*, 2 May 1921: 5; 'May Day', *Sydney Morning Herald*, 2 May 1921: 9; 'The A.L.P. and Domain Doings', *Australian Worker*, 12 May 1921: 3; Don Rawson, 'Political Violence in Australia', *Dissent* (Autumn 1968).

16 'Soldiers' Protest', *Sydney Morning Herald*, 9 May1921: 9; 'Rosenthal', *Catholic Press*, 9 Jun. 1921: 25; 'King and Empire', *Daily Telegraph*, 20 Jul. 1920: 5.

17 Darroch, *DH Lawrence's 99 Days in Australia*: 54.

18 Cited in Frank Cain, *The Origins of Political Surveillance in Australia* (London: Angus and Robertson, 1983): 208 and Moore, *The Secret Army*: 49.

19 NAA file with 'stray' note written by Longfield Lloyd dated 22 Jan. 1921 cited in Darroch, 'The Man Behind Australia's Secret Army': 66.

20 Eric Campbell, *The Rallying Point* cited in Darroch, 'The Man Behind Australia's Secret Army': 63–64.

21 Lawrence, *Kangaroo*: 209.

22 ibid.: 94, 97.

23 'White Australia and How It Is Possible', *The League*, 31 Jan. 1922: 8; 'The Colour Line', *The League*, 28 Feb. 1922: 6.

24 'Twelfth Annual Federal Congress', *The Reveille*, 21 Jan. 1928: 5; *The Realm*, 30 Jun. 1923: 7; 'Congress Agenda', *The League*, 31 Jul. 1922: 16–17; *The Reveille*, 21 Jan. 1929.

25 *The League*, 31 Mar. 1922: 36.

26 'Negro Bands in Australia', *Age*, 2 Apr. 1928: 12.

27 Lawrence, *Kangaroo*: 234, 324.

28 'Way They Have in the Army', *Evening News*, 21 Apr. 1926: 15; 'Lord Allenby', *Sydney Morning Herald*, 20 Jan. 1926: 17; 'Day of Ideals', *Daily Telegraph*, 23 Apr. 1923: 6.

29 'Returned Soldiers', *Daily Examiner*, 11 Aug. 1927: 5; 'Diggers' Row', *Evening News*, 10 Aug. 1927: 3; 'Storm Among the "Diggers"', *Daily Telegraph*, 10 Aug. 1927: 13; '"The Big Parade" not Objectionable', *Everyones*, 28 Jul. 1926: 5.
30 'The Last Resort of Nationalists', *Australian Worker*, 19 May 1921: 5; 'The A.L.P. and Domain Doings', *Australian Worker*, 12 May 1921: 3.
31 'Men Who Fought', *National Advocate*, 26 Aug. 1929: 3.
32 For discussion of Hughes' wartime speeches see John F. Williams, *ANZACS, the Media and the Great War* (Sydney: UNSW Press, 1999): 98–110.
33 'Anzac Day', *Daily Telegraph*, 26 Apr. 1927: 8; 'Rose Bay League', *Sydney Morning Herald*, 26 Apr. 1927: 14.
34 'Physical Culture', *Age*, 14 Aug. 1923: 6.
35 E.C. Buley, *Glorious Deeds of Australasians in the Great War* (London: Andrew Melrose, 1916): 59–61.
36 Compton Mackenzie, *Gallipoli Memories* (London: Cassell, 1929): 65–66; C.E.W. Bean, *The Story of Anzacs: An Historical Account of the Part Taken by Australia and New Zealand in the Great War, from the Outbreak in August 1914 until the Evacuation of Gallipoli in December 1915* (Melbourne: James Ingram and Sons, 1917): 4–8; also see Alistair Thomson, 'Steadfast until Death? C.E.W. Bean and the Representation of Australian Military Manhood', *Australian Historical Studies*, 23: 93 (1989): 466–467.
37 'Australian Poetry. Greek Traits', *Sydney Morning Herald*, 24 Dec. 1926: 13.
38 *The League*, 31 Mar. 1922: 36; Peter Londey, 'A Possession Forever: Charles Bean, the Ancient Greeks, and Military Commemoration in Australia', *Australian Journal of Politics and History*, 53:3 (2007): 344–359; see also Donald Horne, *In Search of Billy Hughes* (Melbourne: Macmillan, 1979): 148–153.
39 Londey, 'A Possession Forever': 347.
40 J.A.R. McKellar, 'Marathon', *New Triad*, 1 May 1928: 21; 'Sane Mind, Sane Body', *New Triad*, 10 May 1923: 8.

Chapter 33 The Character Test

1 'Nationalist Forces Rally', *Daily Telegraph*, 29 Mar. 1928: 10; 'Sonny Clay's Negroes', *Age*, 29 Mar. 1928: 10; 'Negroes from Melbourne Flat on Their Way Home', *Daily Guardian*, 29 Mar. 1928.
2 'Sonny Clay's Parting Shot', *Everyones*, 4 Apr. 1928: 6.
3 Mel Pratt et al., *Journalism in the Thirties* (transcript of sound recording), Mel Pratt Collection, 1976, NLA ORAL TRC 121/85, p. J:3:1/5; 'No More Negro Entertainers', *Sun*, 29 Mar. 1928: 2; 'Ban on Negroes, Federal Ministry's Decision', *Argus*, 29 Mar. 1928; 'Federal Ban on Negro Bands, Mr Bruce Will Act', Melbourne *Herald*, 28 Mar. 1928: 1.
4 'Notes of an Interview at Parliament House', 16 Mar. 1928, NAA CP362/2.
5 Letter: Department of Home & Territories to J.C. Williamson & Co., Sydney, 2 Apr. 1928, NAA Ref 27/21825. An identical letter was also sent out to Stadiums Ltd, J.C. Williamson & Co. Melbourne, Fullers Theatre Sydney.
6 Melbourne *Herald*, 28 Mar. 1928: 1.
7 'Australia to See "Blackbirds"', *Afro-American*, 23 Jun. 1928: 9; Samuel Charters, *A Trumpet Around the Corner: The Story of New Orleans Jazz* (Ukraine: University Press of Mississippi, 2008); 'Coast Dope', *Chicago Defender*, 21 Mar. 1928: 7.
8 'Musicians' Union Objects to Importations', Melbourne *Herald*, 27 Mar. 1928; 'Second Musicians' Union Deputation Presented by W.M. Hughes', 10 May 1928,

NAA D596 1928/6104; 'Deputation to Prime Minister', *Professional Musician*, Mar. 1928: 9.

9 'Negro Ban', *Sun*, 31 Mar. 1928: 3; 'Ban on Negroes, Australia's Business', Melbourne *Herald*, 31 Mar. 1928: 4.

10 'Negro Ban', *Sun*, 31 Mar. 1928: 3; *Evening News*, 30 Mar. 1928: 3.

11 'Musicians Ousted from Australia', *Pittsburgh Courier*, 14 Apr. 1928: 5.

12 'The Musical Bunch', *Chicago Defender*, 5 May 1928: 6; 'To American Pressmen', *California Eagle*, 11 May 1928: 2.

13 'Sonny Clay's Negroes', *Age*, 29 Mar. 1928: 10.

14 'Negro Ban', *Sun*, 31 Mar. 1928: 3; 'Ban on Negroes, Australia's Business', Melbourne *Herald*, 31 Mar. 1928: 4.

15 'Sonny Clay's Parting Shot', *Everyones*, 4 Apr. 1928: 6.

16 'Stories in Black-and-White', *Everyones*, 5 Sept. 1928: 5.

Chapter 34 Storm Centre

1 'The Case of Mr Wm Hughes', *Daily Telegraph*, 6 Jul. 1925: 4.

2 'Diary of Billy Hughes', *Labor Call*, 3 Sept. 1925: 12.

3 'Mr Hughes Grows Reflective', *Daily Telegraph*, 21 Sept. 1927: 4.

4 L.F. Fitzhardinge, *The Little Digger, 1914–1952: William Morris Hughes, A Political Biography, Volume 2* (Sydney: Angus & Robertson, 1964): 17; 'Plea Made for Australia', *Los Angeles Times*, 14 Mar. 1924: 1.

5 'R.S. & S.I. League', *South Coast Times and Wollongong Argus*, 2 Mar. 1928: 18; 'The Future World of Six Great Nations', *New York Times*, 30 Mar. 1924: XX4; Jane A. Stewart, 'Men of Today: William Morris Hughes', *Journal of Education*, 20 Jan. 1921, 93:3: 63–64.

6 Cited in Fitzhardinge, *The Little Digger, 1914–1952*: 530; 'Mr. Wm. Hughes, M.H.R.', *Moora Herald and Midland Districts Advocate*, 16 Jul. 1925: 4.

7 'Always a Fighter', *Brisbane Telegraph*, 21 Feb. 1924: 4.

8 ibid.; 'Mr Hughes Leaves', Melbourne *Herald*, 2 Feb. 1924: 1; 'Sees Pacific Nation', *Seattle Daily Times*, 6 Mar. 1924: 12; 'American Tour', *Brisbane Telegraph*, 7 Mar. 1924: 8; 'Former Premier Here', *Seattle Daily Times*, 6 Mar. 1924: 12.

9 'Japanese Excluded', *Washington Post*, 13 Apr. 1924: 1; 'The Race Issue', *Albany Evening Herald*, 31 Mar. 1924: 2; 'Ex-Premier of Australia Here', *Los Angeles Evening Express*, 13 Mar. 1924: 13.

10 'St. Louis Globe-Democrat', 22 Mar. 1924: 4; 'Regrets Treaty Delay', *New York Times*, 24 Mar. 1924: 27; 'Asks Us to Know Australia Better', *New York Times*, 3 Apr. 1924: 3; 'Multiplying Asiatic Millions Are Grave World Problem', *Fort Worth Record*, 18 May 1924: 44; 'How Asiatics Are Barred in Australia', *Fort Worth Record*, 25 May 1924: 43.

11 See: Marilyn Lake and Henry Reynolds, *Drawing the Global Colour Line: White Men's Countries and the Question of Racial Equality* (Melbourne: Melbourne University Press, 2008): 284–309; Daniel Okrent, *The Guarded Gate: Bigotry, Eugenics, and the Law That Kept Two Generations of Jews, Italians, and Other European Immigrants Out of America* (New York: Scribner, 2020); Jia Lynn Yang, *One Mighty and Irresistible Tide: The Epic Struggle over American Immigration, 1924–1965* (New York: W.W. Norton & Company, 2020).

12 'Japan's Expansion Menaces White Supremacy in the Pacific', *Fort Worth Record*, 20 Apr. 1924: 38; 'How Australia Keeps Out the Asiatics', *Los Angeles Record*, 19 Mar. 1924: 10; *Los Angeles Evening Express*, 13 Mar. 1924: 1, 13.

13 'Bill H.R.1 the Dyer Anti-Lynching Bill', *The Crisis*, Feb. 1924: 164.
14 'Film Folk Turn Out', *Exhibitors Herald*, 22 Mar. 1924: 40.
15 *El Paso Times*, 18 Mar. 1924: 3; 'Imperial Wizard Hiram Wesley Evans', *Texas One Hundred Per Cent American*, 22 Feb. 1924: 1; 'Corsicana and Ennis Klansmen at Carnival', *Corsicana Daily News*, 21 Mar. 1924: 13; 'Big Klan Parade as Carnival Opens', *Dallas Morning News*, 17 Mar. 1924: 9; Shaun David Henry, The Klan and the Craft: An Analysis of Masonic Dual Members with the Ku Klux Klan in Dallas, 1920–1926, Master of Arts Thesis, University of Texas, Dallas, 2017; Mark N. Norris, Saving Society through Politics: The Ku Klux Klan in Dallas Texas in the 1920s, PhD Dissertation, University of North Texas, Dec. 1997; Darwin Payne, 'When Dallas Was the Most Racist City in America', *D Magazine*, Jun. 2017; Ku Klux Klan: Kolossal Karnival: Dallas, Texas, 15–22 March 1924, *Ku Klux Klan Ephemera Collection*, Online Archive of America, oac.cdlib.org.
16 'The Real Black Menace', *Texan American*, 5 Jan. 1923: 1 cited in Norris: 123; *Dallas Daily Times Herald*, 2 Apr. 1921, cited in Norris: 121; 'Mayor Urges that Klan Disband and that City Employees Renounce It', 7 Apr. 1922: 1, cited in Norris: 130; 'Woman Ordered to Leave City Under Pain of Thrashing', *Star-Telegram*, 23 Mar. 1922: 1; 'Assault and Death Threat Told Police by Wife of Victim', *Star-Telegram*, 25 Mar. 1922: 1; 'Bellhop Accused of Insult to Women', *Star-Telegram*, 2 Apr. 1921: 1; Darwin Payne, *Big D: Triumphs and Troubles of an American Supercity in the 20th Century* (Dallas: Three Forks Press, 1994): 73–74; 'Possibly Many Floggings South of Dallas in Last Few Months', *Morning News*, 28 Mar. 1922: 2; 'Home of Mob Victim Guarded while Police Comb Dallas for Gang', *Star-Telegram*, 21 Mar. 1922: 1.
17 Henry, The Klan and the Craft.
18 'Mr Hughes Talks to U.S.A.', Melbourne *Herald*, 19 Mar. 1924: 7; *Los Angeles Evening Express*, 13 Mar. 1924: 1, 13.
19 'War Premier of Australia Addresses Dallas Club', *Houston Post*, 21 Mar. 1924: 3.
20 'Sees Pacific Nation', *Seattle Daily Times*, 3 Jul. 1924: 28; 'War Premier of Australia Addresses Dallas Club', *Houston Post*, 21 Mar. 1924: 3.
21 Hiram Wesley Evans, *The Menace of Modern Immigration*, Bridwell Library, Special Collection: 17.
22 Papers of William Morris Hughes, NLA MS 1358, Series 26, 1924 Tour of the USA, 1923–24.
23 'Former Premier of Australia will Be Guest Here Today', *St Louis Globe Democrat*, 21 Mar. 1924: 3; 'Premier Hughes to Lecture', *Chicago Daily Tribune*, 22 Mar. 1924: 19; 'American Tour', *Brisbane Telegraph*, 7 Mar. 1924: 8; 'Japanese Excluded in Immigration Bill', *Washington Post*, 13 Apr. 1924: 1; 'U.S. Bungled Japanese Exclusion Bill', *Chicago Daily Tribune*, 26 Jun. 1924: 12; 'Advises U.S. and Australia', *Chicago Daily Tribune*, 27 Aug. 1924: 10; 'Cotton Prospects', *Sunraysia Daily*, 30 Aug. 1924: 3; 'South Africa and Australia Favor Guidance of U.S.', *Chicago Daily Tribune*, 15 Nov. 1924: 9; 'They Have Roads in America!', *Daily Telegraph*, 26 Aug. 1924: 6; 'Boiled Down', *Country Life Stock and Station Journal*, 5 Sept. 1924: 1.
24 'Town Talk', *Daily Telegraph*, 8 Jan. 1925: 1; 'Mr. Wm. Hughes, M.H.R.', *Moora Herald and Midland Districts Advocate*, 16 Jul. 1925: 4; 'Referendum', *Daily Telegraph*, 14 Aug. 1926: 7; 'Newspaper Specials', *Wall Street Journal*, 24 Jul. 1924: 9; 'New Fibre Board Industry', *Daily Telegraph*, 17 Jun. 1927: 27; *Daily Telegraph*, 14 May 1928: 1; 'Said That', *Wingham Chronicle and Manning River Observer*, 2 Mar. 1928: 7.

25 'Southern Europeans as Migrants', *Age*, 4 Apr. 1928: 11; 'Immigration Policy Attacked', *Daily Telegraph*, 30 Sept. 1927: 3; 'Sees Pacific Nation', *Seattle Daily Times*, 3 Mar. 1924: 28.
26 'Hughes' Tribute', Sydney *Sun*, 1 Mar. 1928: 13; 'French Praise', *Brisbane Courier*, 22 Feb. 1928: 15; 'Magnificent', *Brisbane Courier*, 23 Feb. 1928: 19.
27 Hinkler encouraged this perception, boasting 'everything in his Avro-Avian' was 'of British make—even the air in its tires', Burnie *Advocate*, 24 Mar. 1928: 5.
28 'Aussies Out in the Cold', *Labor Daily*, 17 Mar. 1928: 1.
29 'The Voice of the City', *Daily Telegraph*, 24 Mar. 1928: 7.

Chapter 35 This Bit of Earth

1 'Hughes Slates Bruce Govt and Mussolini', *Daily Guardian*, 27 Mar. 1928: 1; 'Storm Bursts at National Party Conference', *Daily Telegraph*, 31 Mar. 1928: 1; 'Hughes' Bomb in Nationalist Camp', *Evening News*, 30 Mar. 1928: 3.
2 'Mr Hughes on Australia for Australians', *Age*, 29 Mar. 1928: 10; 'Mussolini's Orders and "Black Beasts" of America', *Daily Telegraph*, 29 Mar. 1928: 3.
3 *Age*, 29 Mar. 1928: 10; *Daily Telegraph*, 29 Mar. 1928: 3; *Daily Guardian*, 27 Mar. 1928: 1.
4 Transcript of the Prime Minister, The Hon. John Howard MP, Address at the Launch of a Stronger Tasmania Policy, Launceston, Tasmania, 2 Nov. 2001, PM Transcripts, Department of Prime Minister and Cabinet, https://pmtranscripts.pmc.gov.au/release/transcript-12332
5 Wayne Errington and Peter van Onselen, *John Winston Howard: The Biography* (Melbourne: Melbourne University Press, 2007); Milton Cockburn, 'What Makes Johnny Run?', *Sydney Morning Herald*, 7 Jan. 1989; 'The Secret Howard Plantations', *Sydney Morning Herald*, 10 Jun. 2006; Transcripts: 'John Howard: Questions from the Audience', *Counterpoint*, Radio National, 1 Nov. 2010, https://www.abc.net.au/radionational/programs/counterpoint/john-howard-questions-from-the-audience/2982818
6 *Age*, 29 Mar. 1928: 10.
7 *Daily Telegraph*, 29 Mar. 1928: 6.
8 'Mr Hughes Attacks Migration Policy', Melbourne *Herald*, 28 Mar. 1928: 1.
9 'Hughes Tribute', Sydney *Sun*, 1 Mar. 1928: 13.
10 *Daily Telegraph*, 31 Mar. 1928:1.
11 *Daily Telegraph*, 29 Mar. 1928: 3.
12 'Man of the Week', *Smith's Weekly*, 7 Apr. 1928: 13.
13 'Black "Boys" and White Girls', *Beckett's Budget*, 6 Apr. 1928: 4.
14 'Govt Demands Party Action Against Mr Hughes', Melbourne *Herald*, 30 Mar. 1928: 1.
15 'Hughes' Statement "Totally and Absolutely Untrue"', *Daily Telegraph*, 30 Mar. 1928: 3.
16 'Sonny Clay's Negroes', *Age*, 29 Mar. 1928: 10.
17 *Daily Telegraph*, 30 Mar. 1928: 3.
18 'Returned Soldiers Commend Mr. Hughes', *Brisbane Courier*, 4 Apr. 1928: 5.
19 'This Bit of Earth Belongs to Us', *Daily Telegraph*, 30 Mar. 1928: 6; 'Southern Europeans as Migrants', *Age*, 4 Apr. 1928: 11; 'Foreign Influx', *Canberra Times*, 11 Jul. 1928: 1.
20 'Dryblower' Murphy, *This Bit of the World Belongs to Us* (Melbourne: Allan & Co., 1914); nla.gov.au/nla.mus-an5725216

21 Neville Meaney, *A History of Australian Defence and Foreign Policy, 1901–23, Volume 2, Australia and World Crisis, 1914–1923* (Sydney: Sydney University Press, 2009): 56–76; Marilyn Lake, A *Divided Society: Tasmania during World War I* (Melbourne: Melbourne University Press, 1975): 73–75.
22 'Mr Hughes' Denial', Burnie *Advocate*, 2 Apr. 1928: 5; Lacey Percival and Phillip K. Walsh, *The Birth of White Australia* (Dominion Films, 1928), National Film and Sound Archive, Canberra.
23 For discussion of *Birth of a Nation* and the Ku Klux Klan see: David Mark Chalmers, *Hooded Americanism: The History of the Ku Klux Klan* (Durham: Duke University Press, 1987): 22–27.
24 'Australian Films', *Sydney Morning Herald*, 23 Feb. 1927: 16; Captain C.G. Prescott was a city alderman, the president of the local RSSILA and a 'senior member' of the secret paramilitary. In 1931, Prescott would be elected mayor. Andrew Moore, *The Secret Army and the Premier: Conservative Paramilitary Organisations in New South Wales 1930–32* (Sydney: UNSW Press, 1989): 128.
25 'Birth of White Australia', *Leader*, 15 May 1929: 6. For discussion about depiction of Aboriginal people in *Birth of White Australia*, see Bruce Dennett, 'How Dixie Waltzed with Matilda: The Influence on Australia of Cinematic Images of the South', *The Mississippi Quarterly*, 63:3–4 (2010): 493–510.
26 'Australians Trying to Bar Colored Race', *San Francisco Chronicle*, 29 Mar. 1928; 'Coast Dope', *Chicago Defender*, 14 Apr. 1928; *Montreal Gazette*, 29 Mar. 1928; *New York Sun*, 29 Mar. 1928; *New York Times*, 29 Mar. 1928.
27 'Australia Enforces Color Line Bar', *Chicago Defender*, 7 Apr. 1928: 1.
28 Lothrop Stoddard, 'White Australia—The Low-Pressure Center of the Globe', *Liberty*, May 1928: 37–41; 'Australia, the Storm Centre', Adelaide *Register*, 23 May 1928: 9.
29 Marilyn Lake and Henry Reynolds, *Drawing the Global Colour Line: White Men's Countries and the Question of Racial Equality* (Melbourne: Melbourne University Press, 2008): 55; Hugh Walker, *The Literature of the Victorian Era* (Cambridge: Cambridge University Press, 1921): 81; Josiah Nott, George R. Gliddon, Samuel George Morton, Louis Agassiz et al., *Types of Mankind* (Philadelphia: Lippincott, Grambo & Co., 1854); also see: Brian Wallis, 'Black Bodies, White Science: Louis Agassiz's Slave Daguerreotypes', *American Art*, 9:2 (1995): 39; Louis Menand, 'Morton, Agassiz, and the Origins of Scientific Racism in the United States', *The Journal of Blacks in Higher Education*, 34 (2001–02): 110–113.
30 Charles Pearson, *National Life and Character: A Forecast* (London: Macmillan and Co., 1894): 16–17; see: Marilyn Lake, 'The White Man under Siege: New Histories of Race in the Nineteenth Century and the Advent of White Australia', *History Workshop Journal*, 58 (2004): 41–62; Alastair Bonnett, 'From the Crises of Whiteness to Western Supremacism', *Australian Critical Race and Whiteness Studies Association Journal*, 1 (2005): 8–20; Lake and Reynolds, *Drawing the Global Colour Line*: 94–113.
31 Theodore Roosevelt, *American Ideals* (New York: G.F. Putman & Sons, 1898): 116.
32 For critique of Roosevelt's brand of masculinity see: Gail Bederman, *Manliness and Civilization: A Cultural History of Gender and Race in the United States, 1880–1917* (Chicago: University of Chicago Press, 1995): 170–214; Neville Meaney, *A History of Australian Defence and Foreign Policy, 1901–23, Volume 2, Australia and World Crisis, 1914–1923* (Sydney: Sydney University Press, 2009): 263. For examples of speeches see: 'We Turned Our Back on the Purifying Waters of Self Sacrifice' in

Well May We Say: The Speeches that Made Australia, ed. Sally Warhaft (Melbourne: Black Inc., 2004): 74–81; John F. Williams, *ANZACS, the Media and the Great War* (Sydney: UNSW Press, 1999): 98–110.

33 Brooks Adams, *The Law of Civilization and Decay: An Essay on History* (New York: Macmillan, 1896); William McDougall, *National Welfare and National Decay* (London: Methuen, 1921); Pearson, *National Life and Character*; Lothrop Stoddard, *The Revolt against Civilization: The Menace of the Under Man* (London: Chapman & Hall, 1922).

34 Stoddard, *The Revolt against Civilization*: 25.

35 Letter: Unnamed man to W.M. Hughes, 3 Apr. 1928, Hughes Collection, NLA MS 1358, Series 32, Subseries 2, Folder 26.

36 Donald Horne, *In Search of Billy Hughes* (Melbourne: Macmillan, 1979): 168.

37 'Ku Klux Klan re "White Australia"', 9 Apr. 1928, NAA A458, 745/1/333.

38 'Government Demands Party Action against Mr Hughes', Melbourne *Herald*, 30 Mar. 1928: 1.

Chapter 36 Fit for the Task

1 'Youth of Melbourne', Melbourne *Herald*, 29 Mar. 1928: 7.

2 'Metropolis', *Argus*, 2 Apr. 1928: 14.

3 Melbourne *Herald*, 29 Mar. 1928: 7.

4 Mrs James Booth, *Prostitution* (Sydney: William Applegate Gullick, Government Printer, 1917): 37.

5 Booth, *Prostitution*: 24.

6 See Kerreen M. Reiger, 'The Rational Management of Sex' in *The Disenchantment of the Home: Modernizing the Australian Family 1880–1940* (Melbourne: Oxford University Press, 1985): 190–200.

7 'A Bathurst B-r-r!', Sydney *Truth*, 17 Jul. 1921: 6.

8 'Treatment of Criminals', *Age*, 15 Mar. 1929: 11.

9 'Honorary Justices', *Argus*, 12 Jul. 1923: 8. From 1895, Booth was a member of the Australasian Association of the Advancement of Science. 'Garden Party at Government House', *Brisbane Courier*, 14 Jan. 1895: 7; 'Society for Prevention of Cruelty', *Brisbane Courier*, 9 Apr. 1896: 7; 'Mesmeric Entertainments', *Brisbane Courier*, 2 Jun. 1896: 7; Booth, *Prostitution*; Mrs James Booth et al., *Teaching of Sex Hygiene: Report of a Conference Organized by the Workers' Educational Association of New South Wales, Sydney University, 1916* (Sydney: Burrows, 1917); Mrs James Booth et al., 'The Prophylaxis of Venereal Disease: A Reply to Sir James Barrett' (Melbourne: Association to Combat the Social Evil, 1910); Angela Booth, *Voluntary Sterilization for Human Betterment* (Melbourne: Booth, James, & Eugenics Society of Victoria, 1940).

10 'Health of the People', *Argus*, 13 Oct. 1921: 7; Booth, *Voluntary Sterilization for Human Betterment*: 4; 'Treatment of Criminals', *Age*, 15 Mar. 1929: 11; 'Death of Dr. James Booth', *Barrier Miner*, 8 Aug. 1944: 2; William Ernest Jones, *Report on Mental Deficiency in the Commonwealth of Australia* (Canberra: H.J. Green, Government Printer, 1929): 15.

11 'Yarra Bend Must Go', Melbourne *Herald*, 14 Aug. 1923: 6.

12 Jones, *Report on Mental Deficiency*: 15; Melbourne *Herald*, 14 Aug. 1923: 6; 'National Federation Aims', *Argus*, 15 Aug. 1923: 8; 'Breeding Disease', *Age*, 14 Aug. 1924: 8; 'A Woman's Melbourne Letter', *Western Mail*, 5 Jul. 1918: 28; Booth, *Voluntary Sterilization for Human Betterment*: 4; 'Yarra Bend Must Go', Melbourne *Herald*, 14 Aug. 1923: 6.

13 'National Federation', *Argus*, 9 Sept. 1922: 28; 'Some Observations on the Treatment of the Feeble-Minded in Great Britain and America', *Medical Journal Association*, 12 Jul. 1924: 36.

14 William Ernest Jones, unpublished, handwritten diaries, written between 1938 and 1954. Royal Melbourne Hospital Health Services Library, incorporating the Victorian Mental Health Library, Parkville, Melbourne. Pages unnumbered, but see under '1921' cited in Ross Jones, 'Brushing Some Dust off Wheels of Civilization: Ernest Jones and the 1928 Mental Deficiency Survey', *Australian Historical Studies*, 40:1 (2009): 67; 'Breeding Disease', *Age*, 14 Aug. 1924: 8; 'Health Week', *Argus*, 11 Oct. 1923: 4; Jane Carey and Claire McLisky, *Creating White Australia* (Sydney: Sydney University Press, 2009): 195–213. For discussion of eugenic clauses in Australia's Immigration Act, see: Alison Bashford, *Imperial Hygiene: A Critical History of Colonialism, Nationalism, and Public Health* (New York: Palgrave Macmillan, 2004): 137–166.

15 Comment made by Judge Walter Bevan. 'Wanted—A Real White Australia', *Sunday Times*, 26 Jun. 1927: 6.

16 Jones, *Report on Mental Deficiency*: 3; Jones, 'Brushing Some Dust off the Wheels of Civilization': 63–78.

17 Hansard, Parliament of Victoria, VPD 172, 6 Oct. 1926: 1854–1855.

18 Booth, *Voluntary Sterilization for Human Betterment*: 4.

19 Booth, *Prostitution*: 21; 'Advertisement', Sydney *Sun*, 23 Mar. 1928: 3; 'Advertisement', *Evening News*, 27 Mar. 1928: 11; Paul Ash, 'The Good Bad Girl' (Sydney: J Albert & Son, 1926).

20 Booth et al., 'The Prophylaxis of Venereal Disease': 10.

21 Booth, *Prostitution*: 32, 37.

22 'The Law Is an Ass', *Record*, 16 Jul. 1927: 4.

23 'A New Color Line', *Argus*, 9 Apr. 1928: 14.

24 'The Decadence We Import', *Bulletin*, 4 Apr. 1928: 9.

25 'Building Up Our Girls', *Australian Women's Mirror*, 10 Apr. 1928: 11; 'Twisted Legs, the Degradation of Jazz', Sydney *Sun*, 27 Feb. 1928; 'Do High Heels Destroy Beauty of Figure', *Daily Telegraph*, 28 Feb. 1928: 23. For discussion of Australian body culture movement see: Isobel Crombie, *Body Culture: Max Dupain, Photography and Australian Culture, 1919–1939* (Melbourne: National Gallery of Victoria, 2004); Amanda Card, 'Art Dance, Burlesque and Body Culture: Negotiating Interwar Modernities' in *Impact of the Modern: Vernacular Modernities in Australia 1850–1969*, eds Robert Dixon and Veronica Kelly (Sydney: Sydney University Press, 2008): 18–37.

26 'The Kingdom of Youth', *Advance Australia*, 1 May 1927.

27 'Women Police', Adelaide *Advertiser*, 21 Aug. 1924; 'Women's Activities', *Argus*, 25 Feb. 1927; 'Women's Activities', *Argus*, 17 Nov. 1927; 'Policewomen Praised', *Argus*, 8 Jun. 1927: 17; C. Woolley, *Arresting Women: A History of Women in Victoria Police* (Melbourne: Victoria Press, 1997).

28 'White Girls with Negro Lovers', Melbourne *Truth*, 31 Mar. 1928: 1.

29 'Mission Scandal', Melbourne *Truth*, 18 Jun. 1927: 15; 'Terrible Tyers', Melbourne *Truth*, 12 Dec. 1927: 11; 'Lake Tyres Misbehaviour', Melbourne *Truth*, 7 Apr. 1928: 16; the *Truth* made no mention of the primary trigger behind this demographic shift. Aboriginal Protection Board strategies mostly removed young Aboriginal women, leaving a disproportionately high number of young men on the missions. As Russell McGregor has pointed out, strategies to 'breed out the

colour' overwhelmingly focused on pairing Aboriginal women with white men. See: McGregor, '"Breed Out the Colour": Or the Importance of Being White', 286–302.

30 'Irresponsible Girls', *Canberra Times*, 7 Apr. 1928: 4.

Chapter 37 Saving Edna Langdon

1 'Irresponsible Girls', *Canberra Times*, 7 Apr. 1928: 4.
2 'Girls in Flats', *Sunday Times*, 1 Apr. 1928: 3; 'Street Walking Girls', *Age*, 31 Mar. 1928: 15; 'Lodging Houses, Raided', *Barrier Miner*, 31 Mar. 1928: 1; 'A Melbourne Clean-Up', *Daily Telegraph*, 31 Mar. 1928: 2; 'Dope Worries Police', Melbourne *Truth*, 21 Jul. 1928; 'How Do They Live?', Melbourne *Truth*, 2 May 1927: 6; Court of Petty Sessions, Magistrates City Court Register, 31 Mar. – 11 Apr. 1928, VPRS 1665: 193–203.
3 *Age*, 31 Mar. 1928: 15.
4 'Irresponsible Girls', *Canberra Times*, 7 Apr. 1928: 4.
5 'Depraved Girl, Charge of Bad Behavior', Melbourne *Truth*, 19 Nov. 1927: 7; *Argus*, 29 Oct. 1927: 37.
6 'Melbourne's Young Girls Who Drift into Life's Black Waters', Melbourne *Truth*, 14 Jan. 1928: 14; 'A Very Precocious Flapper', Melbourne *Truth*, 24 Dec. 1927: 6.
7 *Table Talk*, 29 Mar. 1928: 1.
8 'White Girls with Negro Lovers', Melbourne *Truth*, 31 Mar. 1928: 1.
9 Melbourne *Truth*, 31 Mar. 1928: 1.
10 'Melbourne Flat Raid', *Barrier Miner*, 30 Mar. 1928: 1; 'Sequel to Flat Raid', *Argus*, 30 Mar. 1928: 16.
11 Court of Petty Sessions, Magistrates City Court Register, 30 Mar. 1928, VPRS 1665, 193.
12 *Argus*, 6 Oct. 1927: 13; 'Home for Wayward Girls', *Argus*, 17 Mar. 1923: 25; 'Presbyterian Assembly', *Argus*, 11 Nov. 1920: 5.
13 'New Australians', *Argus*, 13 Jan. 1928: 5.
14 'Home for Wayward Girls', *Argus*, 17 Mar. 1923: 25; 'Father Asks Police to Hold Young Girl', Melbourne *Herald*, 30 Mar. 1928: 7; also see Paula Bartley, *Prostitution: Prevention and Reform in England, 1860–1914* (London: Routledge, 2000); Lyn Finch, 'Sexuality and Regulation', *Hecate*, 17:1 (1991): 43–50.
15 Melbourne *Truth*, 31 Mar. 1928: 1.
16 McKay vs McKay VPRS 283/PO, unit 212, Case No. 1913/46.
17 Melbourne *Truth*, 31 Mar. 1928: 1.
18 'A Black-Out for Sonny Clay's Noisome N_____s', Sydney *Truth*, 1 Apr. 1928: 17.
19 Melbourne *Truth*, 31 Mar. 1928: 1.
20 Registry of Births, Deaths and Marriages, Perth, WA, Certificate of Marriage, Michael Fox and Nola Mackay, Boulder, Western Australia, 1 Apr. 1933.
21 Melbourne *Truth*, 5 May 1928: 14; *Argus*, 18 Sept. 1930: 10.
22 'Social Reform Campaign', *Argus*, 3 Aug. 1928: 14.
23 Mel Pratt et al., *Journalism in the Thirties* (transcript of sound recording), Mel Pratt Collection, 1976, NLA ORAL TRC 121/85, p. J:3:1/5; Adelaide *Advertiser*, 29 Dec. 1928: 11.

Chapter 38 The Non-Stop Endurance Dance Record

1 Saidiya Hartmann, *Wayward Lives, Beautiful Experiments: Intimate Histories of Social Upheaval* (New York: W.W. Norton & Company, 2019).

2 'Wayward Girls', Melbourne *Herald*, 2 Apr. 1928: 23.
3 'Thrashing of No Avail', Adelaide *Register*, 8 Oct. 1903: 4; 'A Youthful Wanderer', Adelaide *Advertiser*, 8 Oct. 1903: 6; 'The Port Boat Mystery Solved', Adelaide *Advertiser*, 8 Oct. 1903: 6; 'Harbouring a State Child', Adelaide *Advertiser*, 15 Jun. 1906: 7.
4 NAA: A9300, LANGDON L. A.
5 'A Pretty Wedding', *Sydney Morning Herald*, 16 Jan. 1897: 7; *Brisbane Courier*, 25 Dec. 1896; 'Prevention of Cruelty Society', *Brisbane Courier*, 11 Dec. 1896: 2; Booth vs Booth 1896/2377, NSW State Records.
6 'Death of Dr Booth', *Barrier Miner*, 4 Aug. 1944; 'Victoria League', *Barrier Miner*, 19 Nov. 1909: 4; 'From Broken Hill', *Adelaide Observer*, 7 May 1910: 4, 5; 'Broken Hill', Adelaide *Register*, 30 Apr. 1910: 14; 'Mother's Day', *Barrier Miner*, 13 May 1912: 5; 'YMCA', *Barrier Miner*, 26 Jan. 1914: 2.
7 'A Plea for the Children of the Barrier', *Barrier Miner*, 16 Mar. 1912: 5.
8 Elizabeth Plover, 1871 UK Census, 2nd Floor, 5th Court, 19 St Martins Street, Municipal Ward of Scotland Ecclesiatical District; 1881 UK Census, 294 Scotland Road, Liverpool, Ancestry.com
9 Paula Bartley, *Prostitution: Prevention and Reform in England, 1860–1914* (London: Routledge, 2000).
10 Cited in Grant McBernie, 'The Importance of Being Well Bred' in *Double Time: Women in Victoria, 150 Years*, eds Marilyn Lake and Kelly Farley (Melbourne: Penguin Books, 1985): 312–321.
11 Passenger List: Eliza Plover, SS *Jumna*, 15 Jun. 1890; 'Local and General News', *Queensland Times*, 30 Sept. 1890: 4.
12 'Psychical Research', *Week*, 29 Dec. 1893: 12; 'Neglected Children', *Brisbane Courier*, 5 Jul. 1895: 4, 5; 'Children's Hospital Ball', *Brisbane Courier*, 19 Jul. 1895: 5–6.
13 'Woman's World', *Brisbane Courier*, 18 Oct. 1895: 6; 'Theosophical Society', *Brisbane Courier*, 3 Oct. 1895: 4; 'Lecture by Countess Wachtmeister', *Queenslander*, 19 Oct. 1895: 747; 'Countess Wachtmeister', *Daily Telegraph*, 6 Sept. 1895: 3.
14 Mrs James Booth, *Prostitution* (Sydney: William Applegate Gullick, Government Printer, 1917): 37.
15 'Camille', *Everyones*, 6 Jul. 1927: 1; 'Church Notes', *Barrier Miner*, 22 Sept. 1928: 3; 'Lenard's Pictures', *Barrier Miner*, 19 Apr. 1928: 3; 'Camille', *Variety*, 31 Dec. 1926.
16 Marshal Royal, *Marshal Royal, Jazz Survivor* (New York: Cassell, 1996): 27; Clora Bryant et al. (eds), *Central Avenue Sounds: Jazz in Los Angeles* (Berkeley: University of California Press, 1998): 38.
17 'Broken Hill Palais Dispute', Adelaide *Register*, 21 Jul. 1927: 12; 'Broken Hill Palais De Dance', *Sydney Morning Herald*, 2 Aug. 1927: 10; 'Attractive Girl Competition at the Palais De Danse', *Barrier Miner*, 1 May 1928: 3; 'Johnson's Pictures', *Barrier Miner*, 30 May 1928: 2; 'Endurance Dancing', *Barrier Miner*, 20 Jun. 1928: 2; 'Endurance Dancing', *Barrier Miner*, 21 Jun. 1928: 1; 'Endurance Dancing', *Barrier Miner*, 26 Jun. 1928: 2; 'Personal Notices', *Barrier Miner*, 26 Jun. 1928: 1; C.B. Schedvin, *Australia and the Great Depression: A Study of Economic Development and Policy in the 1920s and 1930s* (Sydney: Sydney University Press, 1970).
18 'Endurance Dancing', *Barrier Miner*, 19 Jun. 1928: 2; 'After 150 Hours Dancing', *Call News-Pictorial*, 3 Aug. 1928: 2; 'Endurance Dancing', *Armidale Express*, 26 Jun. 1928: 1; 'Endurance Dancing Bert Angus's New Record', *Barrier Miner*, 25 Jun. 1928: 2.

Chapter 39 Sailaway Streamers

1 David Dutton, 'The Commonwealth Investigation Branch and the Political Construction of the Australian Citizenry, 1920–40', *Labour History*, 75 (1998): 164; 'Shipping Intelligence', *Daily Telegraph*, 2 Apr. 1928: 17.
2 'A New Color Line', *Argus*, 9 Apr. 1928: 14.
3 'The Color Line', *Evening News*, 30 Mar. 1928: 3.
4 See: Chinua Achebe, 'An Image of Africa: Racism in Conrad's "Heart of Darkness"', *Massachusetts Review*, 18 (1977).
5 Photograph, *Truth*, 8 Apr. 1928: 1.
6 W. Keith Hancock, *Australia* (London: Ernest Benn, 1930): 75.
7 'Josephine Baker', *Daily Telegraph*, 26 Mar. 1928: 7; 'Jazz Grand Opera in Vienna', *Daily Guardian*, 27 Mar. 1928.
8 'A Dusky Star', Melbourne *Herald*, 2 Mar. 1929: 17; 'Paris Notes', *Age*, 28 Feb. 1928: 9; Bennetta Jules-Rosette and Simon Njami, *Josephine Baker in Art and Life: The Icon and the Image* (Urbana: University of Illinois Press, 2007): 163.
9 Roman Horak, '"We Have Become N____rs!": Josephine Baker as a Threat to Viennese Culture', *Strangers, Aliens and Foreigners Project*, Oriel College, Oxford, Sept. 2010, www.inter-disciplinary.net/at-the-interface/diversity-recognition/strangers-aliens-and-foreigners/
10 'Minto Cato Writes', *Chicago Defender*, 6 Nov. 1926; *Pittsburgh Courier*, 14 Apr. 1928; Rudiger Ritter, 'Jazz in Moscow under Stalinism' in *Jazz and Totalitarianism*, ed. Bruce Johnson (New York: Routledge, 2017): 50–66; Maxim Gorky, 'On the Music of the Degenerate', *Pravda*, 18 Apr. 1928: 2; 'Nazi Veto on Jazz', *Examiner*, 13 Dec. 1935: 17; 'Jazz Banned', *Sydney Morning Herald*, 15 Oct. 1935: 11; 'No More Jazz to Be Played in Germany', *Argus*, 15 Oct. 1935: 9; 'Across the Pond', *Chicago Defender*, 8 May 1937: 21; 'Leon Abbey's Swing Band', *Chicago Defender*, 19 Dec. 1936: 20; Cathal Brennan, 'The Anti-Jazz Campaign', *The Irish Story*, 1 Jul. 2011, https://www.theirishstory.com/2011/07/01/the-anti-jazz-campaign/
11 Memorandum: Collector of Customs to Assistant Secretary, Department of Home and Territories, 31 Mar. 1928, NAA 27/21825; 'Noisy Farewell', Sydney *Sun*, 31 Mar. 1928.
12 Sydney *Sun*, 31 Mar. 1928; 'Negro Bandsmen Sail from Sydney', Melbourne *Herald*, 31 Mar. 1928.
13 Sydney *Truth*, 8 Apr. 1928: 1; Sydney *Sun*, 31 Mar. 1928.

Chapter 40 Shake It and Break It and Let It Fall

1 'Golf Brisbane', *Courier-Mail*, 22 Nov. 1933: 18; 'Brisbane Coming Out Party', *Brisbane Courier*, 26 Feb. 1931: 17; Wife's Debts', *Barrier Miner*, 1 Nov. 1930; *Courier-Mail*, 29 Jun. 1935: 20; Australian Electoral Roll, Brisbane 1936, Ancestry.com; 'Artist with a Needle Show', *Argus*, 9 Nov. 1937: 2; *Argus*, 1 Dec. 1945; Classified Advertisements, *Argus*, 20 Oct. 1945.
2 'Buffet Dinner Last Night at Servicewomen's Club', *Argus*, 27 Feb. 1947: 8; 'On the Home Front—Australian Servicewomen in World War Two', Virtual War Memorial Australia, 2015, vwma.org.au; Australian Electoral Roll, Victoria 1937 and Victoria 1980, Ancestry.com; 'Associates Results, Albert Park', *Argus*, 18 Jun. 1947: 27.
3 Australian Electoral Roll 1903–1980, Tasmania 1949 and Victoria 1963, Ancestry.com
4 'Sonny Clay Receives Commendatory Letter', *California Eagle*, 11 May 1928: 10; 'Sonny Clay Back in US', *California Eagle*, 4 May 1928: 2.

5 *California Eagle*, 8 Jun. 1928:10; Peter Vacher, *Swingin' on Central Avenue: African American Jazz in Los Angeles* (Lanham: Rowman & Littlefield, 2015): 110; 'The Musical Bunch', *Chicago Defender*, 18 Aug. 1928: 6.
6 'Jack Johnson's Cabaret Opens Tonight', *California Eagle*, 9 Oct. 1931:10; 'Up and at 'Em', *Variety*, 30 Apr. 1930: 62; '"Bandana Land" Clicks on Pacific Coast', *New Journal and Guide*, 19 Apr. 1930: 9; 'Da-Da-De-Do!', *Pittsburgh Courier*, 10 Nov. 1928: A1; 'Stars that Shine', *Chicago Defender*, 10 Nov. 1928: 6; 'Behind the Scenes', *California Eagle*, 5 Jun. 1931: 10.
7 'In Hollywood', *Afro-American*, 26 Mar. 1932: 8; Vacher, *Swingin' on Central Avenue*: 15, 194; 'Two Bands to Battle in Dances', *San Bernardino County*, 10 Nov. 1931: 5; John Bentley and Ralph W. Miller, 'West Coast Jazz in the 1920s', *Jazz Monthly*, May 1961; 'Los Angeles', 10 Oct. 1928: 61; John Bentley, 'Sonny Clay: A Veritable Giant—Part 2', *Jazz Research*, Jan./Feb. 1963.
8 'Harlem Steppers', *Atlanta Daily World*, 15 Jun. 1934: 4; 'Sonny Clay Plays', *Atlanta Daily World*, 26 May 1934: 4; 'Advert: Harlem Showboat Café', *California Eagle*, 11 Mar. 1932: 10; Bentley, 'Sonny Clay–Part 2', *Jazz Research*, Jan./Feb. 1963; 'Sonny Clay', Handwritten notes: 3; 'Handwritten notes of John Bentley's 1960 interview', Oral History Collection, Hogan Jazz Archive, Tulane University; Vacher, *Swingin' on Central Avenue*: 194.
9 Leo McCoy Davis, Tape 76, Frank Driggs Collection, Marr Sound Archive, University of Missouri, Kansas City; R.J. Smith, *The Great Black Way: LA in the 1940s and the Lost African American Renaissance* (New York: PublicAffairs, 2006); Clora Bryant et al. (eds), *Central Avenue Sounds: Jazz in Los Angeles* (Berkeley: University of California Press, 1999): 19, 40; George Simon, *Simon Says: The Sights and Sounds of the Swing Era, 1935–1955* (New Rochelle: Arlington House, 1971): 491.
10 *Billboard*, 23 Aug. 1947: 41.
11 Leo McCoy Davis, Tape 76, Frank Driggs Collection; Buck Clayton, *Buck Clayton's Jazz World* (New York: Oxford University Press, 1987): 69, 79.
12 Leo McCoy Davis, Tape 76, Frank Driggs Collection.
13 Duke Ellington, *Music Is My Mistress* (Garden City, NY: Doubleday, 1973): 94, 124; Bryant et al., *Central Avenue Sounds*: 240; Rex Stewart, *Boy Meets Horn* (Ann Arbor: University of Michigan Press, 1991): 177; US Federal Census 1930, Ancestry.com; Barry Ulanov, *A History of Jazz in America* (New York: Viking Press, 1955): 179–181; 'Crowd Greets Duke Ellington on Arrival', *California Eagle*, 11 Mar. 1932: 10.
14 Vacher, *Swingin' on Central Avenue*: 15.
15 Bentley and Miller, *Jazz Monthly*, May 1961; 'Sonny Clay Tapes 1 and 2', Oral History Collection, Hogan Jazz Archive, Tulane University.

Chapter 41 What Now?

1 'Brevities of the Week', *Everyones*, 25 Apr. 1928: 38; 'Geelong Theatre To-Night "Michael Strogoff" Reaches Screen', *Geelong Advertiser*, 2 Apr. 1928: 10; 'Negroes Leave', Sydney *Sun*, 21 Apr. 1928: 7; 'Gone Coons and Coons Staying', Sydney *Truth*, 22 Apr. 1928: 10.
2 'Hear Australian Bands Last', Melbourne *Truth*, 12 May 1928; 'Lyceum Theatre', *Brisbane Courier*, 1 Jun. 1928: 25; 'Mackay Greets Famous Son', *Daily Mercury*, 21 Jul. 1941: 4.
3 'Bomb Outrages', *Argus*, 7 Dec. 1928: 8.
4 'Fought Like a Man', *West Australian*, 12 Sept. 1925; 'Woman Complains of Police', *Argus*, 4 Jul. 1928; 'Constable Dodges a Bottle', Adelaide *Advertiser* 29 Dec. 1928; Agnes Barnes' name appears on Magistrates City Court Register on 20 December,

1928: Charge: Vagrancy, Decision: Entered in Error; Charge: Vagrancy, Decision: Remand; 29 December, 1928: Convicted: one month. In each instance, Saker is the applicant. VPRS 1665, 193.

5 'Tivoli Circuit', *Everyones*, 12 Dec. 1928: 142.

6 *Everyones*, 12 Dec. 1928: 107.

7 In 1937, Nina Mae McKinney toured the Tivoli circuit.

8 Matthew Wittman, Empire of Culture: U.S. Entertainers and the Making of the Pacific Circuit, 1850–1890, Ph.D. thesis, University of Michigan, 2010; 'Across the Pond', *Philadelphia Tribune*, 15 Jul. 1937: 10; 'What's It Like in Malaya?', *Afro-American*, 24 Feb. 1945: 5; 'Coast Dope', *Chicago Defender*, 21 Mar. 1928: 7; Langston Hughes, *I Wonder as I Wander* (New York: Wang and Hill, 1964): 251–255; 'Touring the World', *Chicago Defender*, 21 Nov. 1925: A10; Irene West, 'India Is Colorful, Sometimes Shocking', *Afro-American*, 21 Oct. 1944: 12; 'Buddy Letter', *Chicago Defender*, 5 Jan. 1929: 7.

9 Roger D. Cunningham, 'The Loving Touch: Walter H. Loving's Five Decades of Military Music', *Army History*, 64 (Summer 2007): 5–10.

10 Ali Rajabally, 'Melody Lingers on', DO170; Ali Rajabally, 'Those Enchanted Evenings', DO173, The Collection of Naresh Fernandes at the Archives and Research Centre for Ethnomusicology, The American Institute of Indian Studies.

11 'London Season', *Sydney Morning Herald*, 20 Oct. 1928: 13; 'Negro Act Due: First Since Sonny Clay', *Everyones*, 12 Jun. 1929: 6; 'Admission of a Negro Troupe', *Age*, 12 Jun. 1929; 'Negro Performers', *Sydney Morning Herald*, 12 Jun. 1929; 'No Objection to Negroes of Good Character', Sydney *Sun*, 12 Jun. 1929; also see 'JC Williamson Ltd, Coloured Theatrical Artists', NAA A1 1929/4892.

12 'Walter Richardson to Sing for Australians', *Chicago Defender*, 24 Aug. 1929: 6.

13 'Immigration Law Offends', *Argus*, 19 Aug. 1937: 5; Negro troupe—'Kentucky Jubilee Singers'—Departure from Sydney per 'Niagara' October 1929, NAA: B13, 1929/18230.

14 'To Keep Australia White', *Daily Telegraph*, 2 Apr. 1928: 7.

15 'Among the Diggers', Adelaide *Advertiser*, 9 Aug. 1929: 17; 'We Want Billy', *Morning Bulletin*, 19 Sept. 1929: 7.

16 'Great Gathering of Diggers', *Sydney Morning Herald*, 9 Aug. 1929: 11; 'People', *Farmer and Settler*, 18 Oct. 1929: 4: 'State-Wide Ballot', *Dungog Chronicle*, 25 Oct. 1929: 6.

17 Perth *Sunday Times*, 6 Jan. 1929: 7; 'Italian Consul Refers to Latest Bomb Outrage', *Barrier Miner*, 20 Oct. 1928: 1; 'Greek Club Bombed', *Western Argus*, 11 Dec. 1928: 26; based on a survey of newspaper articles, bomb attacks targeting Southern Europeans took place in Melbourne (May to December, 1928); Innisfail (September 1928 and May 1932); Sydney (October 1930); Darwin (December 1931); Townsville (July 1933); Tully, Qld (September 1933 and October 1934).

18 Hugh Buggy, *The Real John Wren* (Melbourne: Widescope, 1977): 213; the most notorious anti-labour act by Blamey's police occurred in November 1928 when police fired on waterside workers attempting to maintain a picket on Prince's Pier (*Smith's Weekly*, 10 Nov. 1928: 3).

19 'Bombing of the Greek Club', *Argus*, 23 Dec. 1933: 13; 'Plainclothes-Constable Saker Buried', Melbourne *Herald*, 12 Sept. 1930: 3.

20 *Professional Musician*, September 1929 cited in Kay Dreyfus, *Silences and Secrets: The Australian Experience of the Weintraubs Syncopators* (Melbourne: Monash University Publishing, 2013): 55; Kay Dreyfus, 'The Foreigner, the Musicians' Union and the State in 1920s Australia: A Nexus of Conflict', *Music and Politics*, 3:1 (2009): 1–17.

21 Albrecht Dümling, *The Vanished Musicians: Jewish Refugees in Australia* (Bern: Peter Lang, 2015): 177, 183.
22 NSW District Minute Book 1926–1930, p. 143, MUA NBAC T7/1/8 cited in Dümling, *The Vanished Musicians*: 213.
23 Cited in Dümling, *The Vanished Musicians*: 171.
24 Quoted in the minutes of the New South Wales committee, 5 August 1938. NBAC MUA T7/1/10 cited in Dümling, *The Vanished Musicians*: 193; Dümling, *The Vanished Musicians*: 184, 186, 192; Dreyfus, *Silences and Secrets*: 178.
25 'Doing the Dance With Jim Russell', *Arrow*, 17 Feb. 1933: 27; 'Doing the Dances', *Arrow*, 27 Jan. 1933: 27; 'Try the Money-Verse Contest', *Arrow*, 31 Jul. 1931: 16.
26 'The USA as Seen by Ted Henkel', *Australian Dance Band News*, 1 Jun. 1932: 11; Andrew Bisset, *Black Roots, White Flowers: A History of Jazz in Australia* (Sydney: Golden Press, 1979): 74–87; 'On with the Dance', *Brisbane Telegraph*, 25 Mar. 1936: 17. For examples of reviews see: 'Jim Davidson Band under Review', *Australian Music Maker and Dance Band News*, June 1934: 37; 'Sonny Brooks Season at Sydney Palais Reviewed', *Australian Music Maker and Dance Band News*, Sept. 1935: 19; 'Would Imported Bands Boost Biz', *Australian Music Maker and Dance Band News*, March 1935: 3.
27 'Swing—It's the New Rhythm', *Australian Women's Weekly*, 1 Aug. 1936: 3.
28 'Epoch Making Influences', *Australian Music Maker and Dance Band News*, 1 Jun. 1932: 8; 'Ellington's Methods and Compositions', *Australian Music Maker and Dance Band News*, 1 Dec. 1933: 26.
29 Alister Kershaw, *Heydays: Memories and Glimpses of Melbourne Bohemia 1937–47* (Sydney: Angus & Robertson, 1991): 7.
30 Wolfgang Sievers, *The Life and Works of Wolfgang Sievers* (Canberra: Australian National Gallery, 1991).
31 'Australian Authors', *Smith's Weekly*, 12 Mar. 1932: 3; 'Women's Column', *Labor Call*, 31 Jan. 1935: 3; 'Variety in Films', Melbourne *Herald*, 1 Sept. 1938: 6.
32 'Epoch Making Influences', *Australian Music Maker and Dance Band News*, 1 Jun. 1932: 8.

Chapter 42 Bagging the Cat

1 'How Ban on Overseas Players Affects Music Here', *Sydney Morning Herald*, 17 Jan. 1949: 2.
2 Michelle Arrow, 'Sir Eugene Goossens: Sex, Magic and the Maestro', *Rewind*, ABC Radio National, 5 Sept. 2004, http://hdl.handle.net/1959.14/1235848
3 Kay Dreyfus, *Silences and Secrets: The Australian Experience of the Weintraubs Syncopators* (Melbourne: Monash University Publishing, 2013).
4 NAA ST1233/1 N19220; NAA MP529/2 WEINTRAUB/S; Dreyfus, *Silences and Secrets*: 178, 208–210.
5 'Society Folk Prefer Alien Musicians', Sydney *Truth*, 16 Nov. 1941: 21.
6 Kay Saunders, 'Conflict between the American and Australian Governments over the Introduction of Black Servicemen into Australia during World War Two', *Australian Journal of Politics and History*, 33 (1987); Kay Saunders, 'In a Cloud of Lust: Black GIs and Sex during World War II' in *Gender and War: Australians at War in the Twentieth Century*, eds Marilyn Lake and Joy Damousi (Cambridge, New York: Cambridge University Press, 1995): 178–190; Sean Brawley and Chris Dixon, 'Jim Crow Downunder? African American Encounters with White Australia, 1942–1945', *Pacific Historical Review* 71:4 (2002): 607–632.

7 Booker T. Washington Club, *Hindsight*, ABC Radio National, 1990; Interview with Pansy Hickey, *When the War Came to Australia*, Look Television Productions, 1991, Australian War Memorial F04148; 'Claimed to Be Oldest Aboriginal', Burnie *Advocate*, 22 Mar. 1941: 4.
8 'Wartime Living', *Daily Telegraph*, 27 Sept. 1942: 11.
9 Booker T. Washington Club, *Hindsight*, ABC Radio National, 1990; *When the War Came to Australia*, AWM F04148; Christine Brett Vickers, '"The Mother of the Home", Jennie Parsons Smith' in *Uncommon Ground: White Women in Aboriginal History*, eds Fiona Paisley and Anna Cole (Canberra: Aboriginal Studies Press, 2005): 31; Joanna Penglase and D.M. Horner, *When the War Came to Australia: Memories of the Second World War* (Sydney: Allen & Unwin, 1992): 113; 'Claimed to Be Oldest Aboriginal', Burnie *Advocate*, 22 Mar. 1941: 4.
10 'Shocking to Sydney Siders', *Daily Telegraph*, 10 Nov. 1943: 7.
11 *Sydney Morning Herald*, 24 Sept. 1977: 27; Charlotte Meacham, 'Listen to the Aborigines: A Quaker Report on Aboriginal Affairs' (The Religious Society of Friends, Quakers, in Australia, 1973); 'Indigenous Welcome Kicks Off Australia Day', *ABC*, 26 Jan. 2009, abc.net.au
12 Booker T. Washington Club, *Hindsight*, ABC Radio National, 1990.
13 'The Merv Acheson Story', *Jazz Magazine*, Mar./Apr. 1982 and Summer/Autumn 1986.
14 Clem Gorman, 'Bodgies and African American Influences in Sydney', *Dictionary of Sydney*, 2015, https://dictionaryofsydney.org/entry/bodgies_and_african_american_influences_in_sydney
15 *Daily Telegraph*, 2 May 1943: 18; 'Coloured Men, White Girls in Brawl', Sydney *Truth*, 2 May 1943: 6.
16 Quoting Joe Lane cited in Gorman, 'Bodgies and African American Influences in Sydney'; John McDonald, The Bodgie, BA Honours Thesis, University of Sydney, 1951; 'This Is the Duck-Tail', Melbourne *Herald*, 2 Sept. 1950: 9; Jon Stratton, *The Young Ones* (Perth: Black Swan, 1992); Jon Stratton, 'Bodgies and Widgies in the 1950s', *Journal of Australian Studies*, Nov. 1984.
17 Booker T. Washington Club, *Hindsight*, ABC Radio National, 1990; *Army News*, 27 Apr. 1943: 3.
18 'Hollywood Films Insult the Negro', *Tribune*, 4 Jun. 1946: 5; *Tribune*, 28 Sept. 1944: 8; *Western Star and Roma Advertiser*, 19 Jun. 1942: 5; Sydney *Sun*, 20 Aug. 1944: 4; '12 Million Problems', *Age*, 29 Mar. 1941: 10.
19 'This is How Americans See It Here', *Daily Telegraph*, 6 Aug. 1943: 6; Sean Brawley and Chris Dixon, 'Jim Crow Downunder? African American Encounters with White Australia, 1942–1945': 607–632.
20 For example see *Worker*, 20 Mar. 1944: 10; 1 May 1944: 7; *Daily Telegraph*, 19 Jun. 1944: 5; 4 Jun. 1944: 5.
21 'Crazy', *Daily Telegraph*, 1 Aug. 1944: 8; 'Is He an Aussie', *Sun*, 28 Jan. 1949: 2; 'I'm No Kreisler but I'm an Aussie', *Sydney Morning Herald*, 18 Jan. 1949: 2.
22 *Argus*, 17 Aug. 1949: 7; *Australian Women's Weekly*, 3 Sept. 1949: 20, 21; *Canberra Times*, 21 Sept. 1949: 2.
23 Alan Heffernan, *Big Shows: The Lee Gordon Years* (Clear Island Waters, Qld: A. Heffernan, 2003).

INDEX